Modern Manuscripts

MODERN MANUSCRIPTS

*A Practical Manual
For Their Management,
Care, and Use*

Kenneth W. Duckett

American Association for State and Local History
Nashville, Tennessee

Library of Congress Cataloguing-in-Publication Data

Duckett, Kenneth W
   Modern manuscripts: *a practical manual for their management, care, and use. Nashville, American*

   Bibliography: p.   *Association for State and Local*
   Includes index.
   1. Archives—Handbooks, manuals, etc. I. American *History, 1975.*
Association for State and Local History.   II. Title.
CD950.D8   025.17'1   75-5717
ISBN 0-910050-16-3

375p.
24cm.

CD
950
D8

    Author and publisher make grateful acknowledgment to the following for permission to quote from their published works:
    Houghton Mifflin Company for permission to use as epigraph a quotation from *The Collected Short Prose of James Agee,* edited by Robert Fitzgerald. Copyright © 1968 by Houghton Mifflin Company.
    The Society of American Archivists, for permission to excerpt for the glossary of this book many terms from "A Glossary of Basic Terms for Archivists, Manuscript Curators, and Records Managers," compiled by Frank B. Evans, Donald F. Harrison, and Edwin F. Thompson, and edited by William L. Rofes, published in the *American Archivist* 37 (July 1974). Copyright © 1974, the Society of American Archivists.
    The Society of American Archivists also granted permission to quote from "Conflicts in Collecting" by David C. Duniway, which appeared in the *American Archivist* 24 (1961). Copyright © 1961, the Society of American Archivists.
    Harcourt Brace Jovanovich, Inc., for permission to quote from *One Great Society: Humane Learning in the United States,* by Howard Mumford Jones. Copyright © 1959, Harcourt, Brace and Company.

Dedicated to
Josephine L. Harper
and
William B. Hesseltine

Letters are in every word and phrase immediate to and revealing of, in precision and complex detail, the sender and receiver and the whole world and context each is of: as distinct in their own way, and as valuable, as would be a faultless record of the dreams of many individuals. The two main facts about any letter are: the immediacy, and the flawlessness, of its revelations. In the true sense that any dream is a faultless work of art, so is any letter; and the defended and conscious letter is as revealing as the undefended. Here then is a racial record; and perhaps the best available document of the power and fright of language and miscommunication and of the crippled concepts behind these. The variety to be found in letters is almost as unlimited as literate human experience; their monotony is equally valuable.

—James Agee, *The Collected Short Prose of James Agee*

Contents

Illustrations

Foreword

The idea for this book developed, as do most ideas, out of a chain of events that is difficult to reconstruct as the links recede into history. The very reason for the founding of the American Association for State and Local History in 1940 was to help historical organizations meet their responsibilities in collecting and preserving historical materials. Two decades after our founding, we published Lucile M. Kane's splendid little booklet, *A Guide to the Care and Administration of Manuscripts*, and it quickly became the classic work in its field. In the next fifteen years, Kane's *Guide* became a best seller, as quickened interest in local history and the growth of the manuscripts field accompanied the postsputnik boom in higher education.

Along with the increase in manuscript collecting, there grew a demand for more information to help curators. The time had come, we thought, for a big, detailed book that might serve as a text for archival and library students and as a reference work for curators themselves—something to which working professionals might turn for information that was beyond the scope of Lucile Kane's *Guide*. That time had also come in the view of Fred C. Cole, President of the Council on Library Resources, which has done so much over the years to advance the professionalism of the library and archives field. We discussed the idea with Dr. Cole, prepared a proposal, and soon received from the Council tentative approval, subject to our selection of an author.

At the outset, we were determined to have a person who combined solid expertise in the field with an ability to write clearly and interestingly about a topic that is not inherently exciting. In discussions with leading people in the manuscripts field, the name of Kenneth Duckett came up repeatedly. As the long-time secretary of the Manuscript Society, he had wide contacts with private collectors. He was an active participant in the Society of American Archivists and in the American Association for State and Local History. He had held important curatorial positions with the State Historical Society of Wisconsin and the Oregon and Ohio historical societies before taking his present position at Southern Illinois University. And he had a book and a number of well-written articles to his credit.

Happily, Mr. Duckett responded to the challenge of producing the first comprehensive treatment of the work of the manuscripts curator. There was, to be sure, a brief interlude of discreet arm-twisting.

In the end, however, he sensed our confidence in his ability to do the job. The results are for the reader to judge, but they are offered with confidence that he has made the contribution we had expected of him, producing a work that meets a long-felt need of his profession.

WILLIAM T. ALDERSON

Nashville, Tennessee
March 1975

Preface

THE title of this book is intended to indicate that its scope is limited to manuscripts of the seventeenth century to the present. Examples and techniques are drawn from institutions in the United States with occasional references to practices in Great Britain and Canada. The book is directed toward the novice curator of manuscripts, and, again, as the title indicates, it is intended to serve as a practical guide, not as an exposition of theory.

For the above limitations to be meaningful, the reader must have some definition of manuscripts, but given the current state of confusion regarding the terms *archives* and *manuscripts*, and my lamentable lack of skill as a lexicographer, this will be difficult to do within the reasonable confines of the preface. I could ignore the problem, of course, and be in good company. For example, Theodore Schellenberg in his book *The Management of Archives* defines neither term in his "Explanation of Terms," except indirectly: manuscripts are records held by a manuscript repository, and archives are records held by an archival institution. There was a time when such an explanation might have been useful, but now, if not the cause of much confusion, it certainly compounds it. Today many archives collect manuscripts, an equal number of manuscript repositories accept archives, and the lines of demarcation become more blurred each year. For acceptable working definitions of these terms, I refer the reader to the glossary in the appendix of this volume. The terms there have been excerpted from a larger compilation which is the work of the Committee on Terminology of the Society of American Archivists. I would only add that it might help the reader to know that the directives in this manual were formulated within the framework that, *generally*, archives are public or government records, while manuscripts are public or private papers.

This book is a co-operative effort and in acknowledging the assistance that I have had I can give an idea of how it took form. Co-operative though it was, I should note that, contrary to prevailing practices, the research was completed without resorting to the ubiquitous questionnaire.

William Alderson, Director, American Association for State and Local History, secured the grant from the Council on Library Resources which enabled me to take two three-month leaves to do the writing. The book was not an assignment that I would have sought, but his confidence in my ability encouraged me, I hope, to rise to the occasion. Ralph McCoy, Dean of Library Affairs, Southern Illinois University, Carbondale, urged me to accept the assignment, approved of my leaves, and supported my research with released time to visit other institutions. I am convinced that a book of this nature could not be written without access to a major research library, and the staff of Morris Library, SIU, were unstinting in their efforts, especially Alan Cohn, Humanities Librarian, and Ruby Kerley of the Social Studies division, now retired.

In September 1971, Mr. Alderson appointed an editorial advisory committee to assist me with the manual. Chaired by Lucile Kane, Curator of Manuscripts, Minnesota Historical Society, the committee included Robert Adelsperger, Special Collections Librarian and Curator of Rare Books, University of Illinois at Chicago Circle; H. Bartholomew Cox, Chief, Center for the Documentary Study of the American Revolution, National Archives; H. G. Jones, Director, North Carolina Department of Archives and History; and Robert Warner, Director, Michigan Historical Collections, University of Michigan. Early in the project, when the press of Mr. Warner's newly assumed duties as Secretary of the Society of American Archivists forced him to leave the committee, Douglas Bakken, Archivist, Anheuser-Busch, Inc., accepted the appointment.

I wrote to each member of the committee for suggestions about what the scope and content of the book should be, and each offered invaluable assistance in getting started. In the same vein I wrote to forty individuals, including curators, librarians, and archivists, whom

I respected for their contributions to their professions. Five did not reply (two of the five were later to give a generous assist to the book), three offered excuses, and one offered his congratulations. The thirty-one replies received ranged from the terse comment that manuscripts should be collected, arranged, and kept neat, clean, and dry, through four pages of single-spaced advice, to a thirteen-page draft of a manual. The respondents were: Howard Applegate, H. Richard Archer, Rodney Armstrong, Edmund Berkeley, Richard Berner, Maynard Brichford, Marion Brown, Robert Brubaker, Frank Burke, Arline Custer, Dorothy Eaton, William Ewing, William Filby, Shonnie Finnegan, Elsie Freivogel, Sara Fuller, Gerald Ham, Bruce Harding, Jacqueline Haring, Herman Kahn, David Larson, Robert Lovett, Matt Lowman, Watt Marchman, David Mearns, Robert Metzdorf, Kermit Pike, Mattie Russell, Martin Schmitt, Margaret Scriven, and Fred Shelley.

On the basis of the suggestions I had received, I drafted an outline of the book which was the subject of a full day's discussion by the advisory board in the spring of 1972. Following the meeting, I began the first of several trips to visit the following manuscript repositories: Boston Athenaeum; Boston University; Buff-Erie Public Library; Buffalo and Erie Historical Society; University of California, Berkeley; University of California, Los Angeles; Chicago Historical Society; University of Chicago; Columbia University; Cornell University; Denver Public Library; Detroit Public Library; Duke University; Grolier Club; Hoover Institution on War, Revolution and Peace; Herbert Hoover Presidential Library; Henry E. Huntington Library; University of Illinois; University of Illinois, Chicago Circle; University of Kansas; Church of Jesus Christ of the Latter-day Saints; Library of Congress; University of Michigan; Minnesota Historical Society; National Archives; National Library of Medicine; New York Public Library; State University of New York at Buffalo; Newberry Library; North Carolina Department of Archives and History; University of North Carolina; Northwestern University; Ohio Historical Society; Oregon Historical Society; University of Oregon; University of Rochester; Smithsonian Institution; South Carolina Department of Archives and History; University of South Carolina; Stanford University; Syracuse University; Tennessee State Library and Archives; Toronto Public Library; University of Toronto; Harry S. Truman Library; University of Washington; Wayne State University; State Historical Society of Wisconsin; University of Wisconsin; University of Wyoming; and Yale University.

With one or two exceptions, the colleagues with whom I talked were generally helpful, especially Carole Sue DeLaite, Herbert Finch, Gene Gressley, James Moore, William Murphy, Susan Rosenberg, Colton and Nancy Storm, Saundra Taylor, Robert Warner, and Peter Waters. Four others, Frank Evans, Eleanor McKay, Dave Maslyn, and Alexandra Mason, devoted an unusual amount of time to my project, and have my special thanks.

Supplementing the experiences gained in these visits were notes I took on two two-week trips in the 1960s, one down the Atlantic seaboard from Massachusetts to North Carolina, and the other through the midwest, south, and southwest, visiting, in all, some additional forty collecting agencies. Also I drew upon knowledge of other repositories I had toured while attending the annual meetings of the AASLH, SAA, the Manuscript Society, and the Rare Books and Manuscripts section of ACRL for the past ten years.

The first draft of seven of the nine chapters was written in the summer of 1972. They were typed by Janice Briley, and in the fall I presented them to the advisory committee for another full day's discussion. Several subsequent drafts were typed by Nancy Stout, and in the fall of 1973 a finished draft was submitted to the committee for their final written comments. Lucile Kane, who had been a great stabilizing force throughout the project, was particularly helpful at this time. She and her associates at the Minnesota society, Lydia Lucas, Sue Hobert, James Fogerty, and Deborah Neubeck, made many critical suggestions, which forced me to do some rethinking and rewriting that I feel improved the manuscript.

Four other persons read selected chapters of the manual for subject content, and all saved me from some grievous errors: Virginia Ingram, Charles Lee, Harold Tribolet, and Allen Veaner. Kenneth Rendell, Meyer Fishbein, Curtis Simic, and Norton Webster each read sections of the manuscript for the same purpose.

The flawless typing of the final manuscript was done by Barbara Moreno. Katharine Lockwood read proof and offered numerous invaluable editorial corrections.

Although it seems contrary to all natural laws, my wife did not check footnotes, help with the typing, nor do any of the other tasks that are so often acknowledged in prefaces. Grudgingly, she did proofread a few of the early chapters and was heard later to remark, "No, it wasn't so bad; I learned what he has been doing all these years."

The role of expert ill fits me. In my own work I have never succeeded in writing a manual of operations, and in the preparation of this text I was painfully aware of the old adage, "Don't do as I do, do as I say." But at the same time, once the work was under way, I was pleased with the opportunity to learn more about my profession and to express some very personal views about it that I have developed over the years. Several members of my committee assured me that this is not the type of book that they would have written. Others on the committee have taken exception to the sometimes cynical tone of the text. I appreciate their concern, as I appreciated the help they extended in criticizing the drafts. Almost all of their suggestions I was happy to incorporate into the final copy, and it is a better book for their interest.

It has, however, several flaws, for which I will accept the blame, most notable of which is its unevenness. I have intentionally stressed certain aspects disproportionately because I felt that they have not been sufficiently covered in the literature. A different organization of the material might have avoided some loose ends apparent in the text, but I believe that the breadth of the field makes a completely systematic presentation very difficult. Another flaw of which I am aware is that I was unable to write of the curator except in the male gender, but it would have been artificial and awkward for me to have attempted to do otherwise. I hope this will not be taken to mean that I am blind to the contributions that women have made and are making to the field. Quite the contrary; I sincerely believe that they have supplied more than their proportionate share of leadership.

Another device which some readers may find disconcerting is my depicting of the curator in countless roles from fund-raiser to micro-filmer to conservator. It would be an extraordinary situation even in a one-man shop where a curator would be involved in such a wide range of activities, and obviously in a well-staffed repository, special-ists perform these tasks. Yet, surprisingly, at one time or another most curators are expected to demonstrate some expertise in all the areas touched upon in the text.

I think perhaps my editors feel that I flawed the book by including a great deal of discursive material in the notes which they would have preferred to have seen incorporated into the text. My reasoning was that a reader who wished to go beyond the text and suggested readings could find additional detail in the notes. To facilitate this kind of use, the book has been designed with headings at the top of each page of notes keying it to the appropriate pages of the text.

Writing any book entails occasional frustration and disappoint-ment. As this volume was being prepared, they came—with the failure of what seemed a novel plan to supplement the text with a microfiche appendix containing copies of several in-house manuals and a sampling of assorted forms. Beginning curators often write to established collecting agencies for copies of manuals and forms, and I thought that the appendix would provide the copies cheaply and lessen the reference burden on the agencies. However, repositories which initially supported the concept later developed reservations, and the idea was abandoned.

Another frustration which any author faces is the appearance of new material after it is too late to revise his manuscript. I was very conscious of this in writing on subjects which are changing almost daily. Since the time the manuscript was submitted for editing, I have seen a series of fine papers on access in the *AB Bookman's Weekly* and *College & Research Libraries,* read an excellent manual on microfilming procedures by the Ohio Historical Society, and noted the findings reported in *Paper Conservation News* concerning the use of Tetrahydrofuran (THF) in the removal of pressure-sensitive tapes and their stains. The reader will not find references to these developments in the book since the terminal date of the research was January 1, 1974.

The experienced curator who may have reason to look at this manual should appreciate the following, a second epigraph which was appended by an assistant after having read the manuscript:

NOTICE
The objective of all dedicated curators of manuscripts should be to thoroughly analyze all situations, anticipate all problems prior to their occurrence, have answers for those problems, and move swiftly to solve them when called upon;

HOWEVER
When you are up to your . . . er . . . ah . . . ears in alligators, sometimes it is difficult to remind yourself that your initial objective was to drain the swamp.

KEN DUCKETT

Carbondale, Illinois
September 1974

Modern Manuscripts

I

Introduction:
A Survey of
Manuscript
Collecting

THERE is a story of a nineteenth-century historian writing a history of France who came to Great Britain to do research. The keeper of the royal manuscripts showed him fourteen hundred folios of charters, royal autographs, and personal papers bearing upon his topic. He spent two hours, left, and later wrote the keeper that he could complete his history "without further aid of such *paperasses* or 'paper rubbish.'" [1]

One wonders what the poor Frenchman's reaction would be to the manuscript collections of twentieth-century United States.

It has been estimated that in 1960 the total manuscript holdings of the repositories reporting to the National Historical Publications Commission for inclusion in the Hamer *Guide* was 150 million, with at least 39 libraries each reporting holdings of more than a million manuscripts.[2] Added to this is an estimated 72 million manuscript pages in the presidential libraries system in 1967.[3] Neither figure is intended to reflect the infinitely greater amount of records in federal, state, and local archives; but based on these estimates, the total manuscript holdings in the United States today is probably half a billion pieces.

Again based on the figures submitted for the Hamer *Guide*, of the manuscript repositories reporting in 1960, 30 percent were historical societies, 45 percent colleges and universities, 10 percent public libraries, and 15 percent miscellaneous.⁴ These figures give some idea of proportion, but little of the variety of repositories: state historical societies like those of Minnesota and Wisconsin; private historical societies like those of Massachusetts and New York; city historical societies like those of Cincinnati and Chicago; county historical societies like those of Lancaster (Pa.) and Buffalo and Erie (N.Y.); state universities and colleges like those of Michigan, Kansas, and California; private universities and colleges like Yale, Boston, and Duke; a prep school like Phillips Exeter (perhaps unique); public libraries like those of New York City, Detroit, and Denver; private libraries like Pforzheimer, Newberry, and Huntington; state libraries like those of Connecticut and Indiana; and associations like the American Philosophical Society and The Filson Club. Fine manuscript collections can be found in what, to the uninitiated, seem such highly unlikely locations as Eleutherian Mills-Hagley Foundation, State University of New York at Buffalo, St. John Seminary, and Southern Illinois University.

Collecting at these repositories has sometimes been based on a geographical area such as a state, but more recently also upon a region, as, for example, the Southern Historical Collection at the University of North Carolina, the Southwestern Historical Collection at Texas Tech University, and the Rio Grande Historical Collection at New Mexico State University. Other collections have been built around a subject area: psychology, physics, medicine, art, theater, and labor come readily to mind. History and literature, the two traditional subject areas of collecting, have undergone great changes in the second half of the twentieth century, the period one critic calls the "age of the archive." ⁵

Although facets of the "age of the archive" can be found in most modern collecting, this critic feels that nowhere is it more apparent than in the presidential library. Here he finds all the "records of public relations . . . self-consciously assembled." The cabinet, staff, secretaries, and assistants, all are watching the President, and he is aware that many of them are taking notes. "He is the man who, as never before—more than the fabled kings of old—stands constantly before the mirror of history and of time." But this great bulk of records is, the critic believes, "a very abundance designed deliberately to conceal."

For no man in the public eye but is aware that he must talk in private. There may be more pieces of paper than ever; but where are the telephone calls of yesteryear—and telephone calls on highly private wires? The intimate personal conferences; the "smoke-filled rooms" of tradition, where no minutes are kept and everyone has a different version when the smoke clears away; the hidden history, "the reverse of the tapestry," as Balzac said—is not all this concealed behind the masses of paper? [6]

Obviously this criticism was written pre-Watergate, but the author has a valid query when he asks, "How is the biographer to face such weight and mass and density? How is he to encompass such immense stockpiles?" [7] The mass of manuscripts being collected has forced the historian to use new research techniques. It may be true that in the past he relied too heavily upon the most commonly collected form of manuscripts, the personal correspondence files. Traditionally curators have felt this to be the prime series, but at least one historian feels that by their nature letters are nonsystematic and that history written out of them "is exceptionally restricted in its technical competence." He cites, for example, traditional diplomatic history, which is composed mainly from dispatches. "It may seem odd," he asserts, "that the most personal and individual type of document should produce a specially unreal type of history." [8]

Though the interaction between the scholar, the sources, and the curator can be interpreted in various ways, the results of the interaction are as readily apparent in literature as in history. Of the four forms of literary scholarship—linguistics, textual criticism, literary criticism, and literary history—traditionally it is the latter which has drawn most heavily on manuscripts, since one of its major concerns is the biographies of authors. Students of linguistics and literary criticism have made less use of manuscript collections, but the textual critic, in his effort "to recover the author's final intentions," [9] has changed the thrust of literary scholarship and in the process has urged the curator into new forms of collecting. This type of collecting has forced the poet and the author out of the "age of the private lamplight" and brought to the fore questions of propriety and the right of privacy. It is one critic's contention that in an earlier age the writer's home was blessed with fireplaces where "trivial letters received, old irrelevant things, those pages recording the writer's struggle—all went up in a bright cheerful smokeless flame." Today, with a "pecuniary motivation that is beneficent and irresistible," the man of letters is induced "to create archives larger than life." [10]

A British librarian, noting the affectation of calling an author's papers a "literary archive," suggests that the phenomenon is American in origin and carries with it a connotation of completeness. Such an archive would, he thinks, contain a complete collection of the author's printed works, proofs, fair copies, manuscripts, and rough drafts. It would contain copies of his correspondence, particularly with his publisher. His diaries and reading lists would be there, as well as his library, with copious marginalia.[11]

The American curator's propensity to make contracts with contemporary authors for their working papers as they produce them leads to the danger that "authors will cheat by producing spurious worksheets," but the British librarian does not think it matters. The effect, he feels, is to circulate alternative versions of the work of an author who, if he is cynical, might say, " 'I printed what I thought would sell best, but the real me, distilled for a discerning few, is to be found in Plateglass University Library.' " [12]

But some critics of modern collecting feel that the dangers go beyond spurious worksheets. One young author who had been approached by a well-known university was surprised to learn that his works and his correspondence "had won a place in the archives of posterity even before they had been written," and rather than being pleased, it somehow gave him "an unpleasant feeling of being buried alive." A friend with whom he shared the letter thought the library was meddling with "the judgment of posterity." "As we see it," the friend wrote, "libraries should leave young writers alone, and stop betting on them as though they were horses, even if this means losing a few grocery lists and love letters that the writers have yet to write. They would do better to concern themselves with what has already been written, and let posterity shift for itself." [13]

Another author sees modern collecting as a "kind of paper madness of modern times," this collecting of letters, papers, programs, notes, diaries ("the butt ends of our days and ways"), to which are added the Xerox copies, microfilms, photographs, kinescopes, and oral history, "which multiply the fragments of the images of ourselves and our contemporaries." He feels that few of these documents are really significant, that they are ephemera, "curiosities for the memorabilia hunter and autograph collector; they constitute raw—sometimes very raw—data for the poetaster, gossipmongers, and graduate students of the future who are expected to sharpen their wits on these posthumous fragments of our lives." Doctoral dissertations, which are studded with extensive quotations from the writer's unpublished files, are objects of this author's special ire; "often inimitable prose is set within a turgid narrative—it is like putting real diamonds into a piece of costume jewelry." [14]

While historical novelists, academicians, genealogists, and journalists have traditionally patronized manuscript repositories, it is true that today's graduate students, particularly those in literature and history, have also become inveterate users of manuscripts. Such was not always the case, for two obvious reasons: the great manuscript collections and graduate schools are both modern phenomena in this country. No college in the United States offered courses in American history for more than half a century after the Revolution.[15] History was the province of the antiquarian and the amateur, and it was with them that much of the significant manuscript collecting began, although they represent but one of the four strains of manuscript collecting that can be traced in this country: the historian-collector, the editor-collector, the institutional collector, and the private or autograph collector. Each deserves more attention than can be given in this brief introduction, particularly the private collector who has never been the subject of scholarly study. There is an overlap in time and form of the four strains of manuscript collectors, but in the interest of clarity they will be discussed separately.[16]

America's earliest known collecting of manuscripts and their use are inextricably intertwined. William Bradford, known as the "father of American history," relied largely upon memory when he began writing the *History of Plimoth Plantation* about 1630, but he also drew upon his journal of the first year of settlement and a letter-book of company correspondence. His history was consulted in manuscript form by historians for more than two hundred years before it was printed. To one of these men, Rev. Thomas Prince, South Church, Boston, he lent or gave his Plymouth history and it remained in Prince's library until the time of the Revolution.[17]

Prince, born in 1687 and educated at Harvard, may have been America's first manuscript collector of note. His collecting probably began when he was a freshman, but his interest in history undoubtedly developed earlier, when he was sent to live with his maternal grandfather, Thomas Hinckley, sixth governor of the colony. After graduation, Prince traveled and lived in England for a time. In 1717 he returned to America and the next year accepted the associate pastorate at South Church, where, until his death in 1758, he accumulated books and manuscripts relating to America. Although Prince wrote little history, he enjoyed the reputation of a scholar in the colonies, and because of its research, his *Chronological History of New England,* the first volume of which was printed in 1736, has been called a pioneering work in "scientific historical writing." [18]

Among the manuscript sources Prince assembled at South Church were many financial and legal records of Plymouth Colony and correspondence of its governors which had come to him from his grandfather, Governor Hinckley. Also included in the collection were the Increase Mather Papers; the John Cotton Papers; notebooks of William Brinsmead and John Marshall; the "ancient records" of several churches; and the "Original Journal of a very Intelligent Person deceased, who desires not to be named." While his citations may leave something to be desired, Prince has been called by one historian the "father of American bibliography." [19]

Of the historians to whom Prince allowed access to the South Church manuscripts, none had a more profound effect on collecting in America than Jeremy Belknap, another Harvard-educated divine. In Belknap's career are mingled at least two of the four strains of manuscript collecting, and he epitomizes aggressive collecting, both personal and institutional. He was born in Boston in 1744 and from his youth was interested in history, perhaps urged on by Thomas Prince, who had been one of his teachers. Also from Prince, Belknap may have got a feeling for original sources and a desire to collect. In any event, soon after he accepted his first pastorate, he wrote friends that he was spending his leisure hours gathering facts for his history of New Hampshire from " 'manuscripts, and the information of aged and intelligent persons.' " The first volume was not published until 1784, but in the meantime he lamented to a colleague about "hunting in 'garrets and ratholes of old houses' for private papers when not one paper in a hundred 'would repay him for the trouble.' " [20]

It was Belknap's interest in collecting manuscripts that led to the formation of the Massachusetts Historical Society, the forerunner of the state-and-local-historical-society movement in America. In England, The Society of Antiquaries of London had gone through a revival in 1707, and the Royal Society of Antiquaries of Scotland had been formed in 1780. Similar societies were being formed on the continent to carry forward the ideals of historical scholarship and the practice of collecting manuscripts. In this country, both the American Philosophical Society, which had been organized in Philadelphia before the war, and the Library of Congress, which was founded at the turn of the century, would in time develop fine manuscript collections. But in 1791, when Jeremy Belknap and five of his friends met to organize the Massachusetts Historical Society, they laid a solid foundation for institutional collecting of manuscripts in the United States. Belknap, writing to a friend about a field trip to pick up manuscripts in Connecticut, set the tone for institutional collectors for generations to come. "There is nothing like having a *good repository*, and keeping a *good look-out,* not waiting at home for things to fall into the lap, but prowling about like a wolf for the prey." [21]

Other state and local societies followed Massachusetts' lead, but slowly. More often than not, the founders may have seen the societies as "booster" organizations to promote the growth of their area. Societies flourished, and most died; thirty-five were founded between 1830 and 1850, the most active in New York and New Hampshire. It was in the west, however, that the society movement blossomed and many strong state-supported societies developed. Here, at the Wisconsin State Historical Society, the now legendary Lyman Draper, private collector turned institutional collector extraordinary, gathered the manuscripts of the Revolutionary heroes of the middle border and pioneers of the trans-Allegheny West. Draper's methods and techniques have been emulated (and sometimes improved) by later generations of great institutional collectors: James G. de Roulhac, Edith Fox, Lucile Kane, Philip Mason, Mattie Russell, Don McNeil, Gene Gressley, Howard Gotlieb, and others. [22]

By the mid-1880s there were more than two hundred state, local, and regional societies, but few were as active in manuscript collecting as Wisconsin and Massachusetts. As one manuscript dealer put it succinctly in 1890, "In America, with a few exceptions, credit for preserving the records of the nation's past must go to the private collectors. About the deadest thing in the country is the average Historical Society." [23] But even active societies were coming under fire for concerning themselves largely with "old" records and neglecting contemporary manuscripts. The new breed of academic historian in the von Ranke tradition, fresh from the seminars at Johns Hopkins and Harvard, reflected the emerging nationalism in their criticism of the "local" collecting of most historical societies. One eventual result of the scientific historians' dissatisfaction with historical societies was the growth of great manuscript collections at their universities; graduate seminars at Michigan and Columbia were training professional historians with awakened insights into the need for original sources. A more immediate result of the dissatisfaction was the founding in 1884 of the American Historical Association. [24]

The association's continued interest in documentary sources is evidenced by the appointment of a Historical Manuscripts Commission, its first standing committee, in 1895. The commission's avowed purpose was to locate, calendar, and publish manuscripts in private collections. It did send circulars to several hundred individuals and institutions, and in 1900 published a list of their holdings, but over the years concentrated its efforts in printing manuscripts from institutional collections.[25]

From its inception, the commission had urged repositories to collect the neglected sources of social, economic, and recent history, but the association itself did not systematically pay much attention to historical societies until 1904, the year that it sponsored the formation of the Conference of State and Local Historical Societies. One of the principal aims of the conference was to effect intersociety co-operation. Within a short time, this co-operative enterprise was to center upon the efforts of ten Mississippi Valley institutions to finance a calendar of documents in French archives relating to the history of their area.[26]

The outbreak of war in 1914 halted the co-operative project, and the conference seemed to lose momentum. It continued to compile and to publish digests of the holdings and activities of historical societies, but its meetings were "tacked on usually at the end of the annual meeting of the American Historical Association, its sessions sparsely attended, its papers scarcely ever printed, and its officers and policies constantly changing." Finally, in 1940, after many years of what one critic has called "unreciprocated affection," the conference disbanded to form the American Association for State and Local History.[27]

From the outset, the association evidenced an interest in publication, reflecting a tradition of many of its member historical agencies. Virtually every successful historical society in the United States has supported or is supporting a program to edit and publish documentary sources, and this movement can be traced back to the progenitor historical society, Massachusetts, which, under Jeremy Belknap's direction, published its first volume of *Collections* in 1792. In that same year, one of Belknap's friends, Ebenezer Hazard—who, during the War of Independence, conceived of the first collection of state papers— began to publish the material he had collected. But Hazard was before his time; the project languished, and it was another thirty years before the documentary editor as manuscript collector came to full fruition in the career of Peter Force.[28]

Peter Force, a journalist and printer, began in 1822 to collect state papers, debates, letters and "other notices of Publick Affairs," for a monumental set of six series of volumes. Before his government subsidy ran out in 1853, Force had published a dozen or more volumes under two titles, *American Archives* and *Tracts and other Papers*. Many of the manuscripts remained unpublished and Force continued to add to his collection until 1867, when he sold it to the Library of Congress for $100,000. In addition to substantial numbers of pamphlets, books, and newspapers, the collection contained 429 volumes of original autographs and manuscripts and 360 volumes of manuscript material transcribed for publication in the *American Archives*. The Force manuscripts were dispersed throughout the library's collections and for many years it was impossible to determine the extent of the collection. It was known, however, that he had acquired substantial amounts of material from other collectors, some of the giants like Hazard, Belknap, John Dickinson, Eugene du Simitière, George Chalmers, Henry B. Dawson, and Rev. William B. Sprague. Within the last few years, the Manuscript Division of the Library of Congress has attempted to reassemble the Force manuscripts, and it is now evident as never before that he was a collector among collectors.[29]

The manuscripts collected by a second editor, Jared Sparks, another Harvard-educated minister, repose today in the vaults of his alma mater, the institution where he later taught and of which he was president, 1849–1858. Soon after he finished his divinity studies, Sparks began his first historical project. In doing his research, he had traveled to France and England, and in the process he had become chagrined at the meager library resources of his own country. In an article on "Materials for American History," published in 1826, he numbered but seven libraries in the United States in which all the books about America could not be housed in a single case. In the same article he praised the work of historical societies in preserving the documentary sources of American history, but urged them strongly to undertake wide-scale publication programs.[30]

Suiting his own actions to his words, Sparks embarked on twelve volumes of diplomatic correspondence completed under contract to the federal government in 1830. These were followed in seven years with the multivolume life and writings of George Washington. Sparks's editing continued apace for the next fifteen years; a library of nearly seventy volumes represents his life's work. His rank as collector rests secure, but his frailties as an editor are well known. In his defense, one historian has written that Sparks altered the language of his various Revolutionary heroes "to fit the character created by a worshipful America."[31] Another, in a broader view of historical editing, sees the difference between nineteenth-century editing and that of today as one in which letters have become "documents" to us; the modern editor, "instead of presenting a literary work, is setting up an archive."[32]

When, in 1827, Sparks's precarious negotiations with the Washington family had finally culminated in his being allowed to bring the letters from Mt. Vernon back to Boston for study, "the New England literary capital acclaimed with delight this coup that had brought him and the city so much distinction." [33] In studying the papers, Sparks would have duly noted a goodly number of "fair copies" in place of the originals, evidence of a far greater coup by William B. Sprague, America's first and premier autograph collector. As a young Yale graduate, Sprague had become interested in the emerging European hobby of collecting signatures and single letters of kings and noblemen. He decided that, in lieu of nonexistent American royalty and nobility, he would collect autographs of America's heroes—the signers of the Declaration of Independence and the Constitution of 1787, and the Revolution's military elite. Soon after he decided upon his life's avocation, circumstances placed him in an advantageous position to begin it with éclat. The year after he was graduated from Yale College, he accepted the position of tutor in the family of a nephew of George Washington. The nephew's house was a scant two miles from Mt. Vernon, and it was not unnatural that Sprague should visit and become acquainted with another of the president's nephews, Judge Bushrod Washington. What does seem extraordinary is that Sprague persuaded the judge to let him have original letters for substituted copies. Within the year, when the young man left Virginia to attend Princeton Theological Seminary, he carried with him over 1,500 holograph letters of Washington and his associates! [34]

Having completed his theological training, the persuasive parson took up his first ministry in Massachusetts. Ten years later, when he moved from the area, the librarian of the American Antiquarian Society breathed a sigh of relief. "I'm heartily glad he has gone out of New England," he confided in his diary, "for he is so much esteemed wherever he goes that people let him into their garrets without any difficulty, and, being a Doctor of Divinity, they never think to look under his cloak to see how many precious old papers he bears off with him." Sprague, he thought, had such a "fury about him in collecting autographs that he would carry off everything that had a name attached to it." [35]

One might discount this complaint as the grousing of a bested competitor, but other testimony to Sprague's "larceny" gives witness that the mark of the mania was on him. "Autographomania," it was called. Sometimes collecting has been called a game, a hobby, a fad. Historically, it has been all of these and more. Most scholars, and to a large extent curators, too, have either ignored or been contemptuous of the phenomenon, seemingly unaware that much of the richest of the past's documentation is available to them because of the mania of the autograph collector. This attitude was typified by the keeper of manuscripts of the British Museum, who confided to his journal that he felt "great contempt" for the " 'quackery of autograph collectors, who only value the documents as *writing,* and who, when they have stuck in a portrait or two, think that the value is greatly increased instead of being diminished.' " [36] But this curator was only seeing part of the picture. The librarian at Kings College, Cambridge, puts his country's autograph collecting in better perspective:

At its lowest the *autographomania* resulted in a wearisome series of signatures of Members of Parliament cut from letters or from franked covers, about as significant as a collection of match-box labels; at its highest it led to the preservation and logical arrangement of research material of great value and importance.[37]

Measured by numbers of devotees, autograph collecting in its varied phases reached its zenith in England and the United States during the last decade of the nineteenth century. As with other aspects of Victorian culture, Americans looked to the British for models and guidance in collecting. There was an exchange of ideas, and of autographs themselves. However, to understand collecting in this country, one must look, not only to its English roots, but to its earliest origins, as well.

Any survey of manuscripts must perforce deal with man's first textual records—stone carvings, cuneiforms, wooden and wax tablets, leather scrolls, and papyri—but they probably have little meaning in a discussion of autograph collecting. They are, to a great degree, records of people which have been saved for history originally by chance rather than by design, although at some point they did become collectable objects. One historian theorizes that ancient people of the western world did not conceive of time in the same way as modern man, who thinks of a flow from past to present to future. The ancients, he believes, were less aware of the past because their records were scant. Rome, to illustrate, had no official archives until the time of Cicero (first century, B.C.).[38]

While it is true that Lutatius Catullus built the Tabularium, the state archives of Rome, sometime between 121 and 60 B.C., nonetheless record-keeping was a common practice of this and earlier times. The magistrates kept *commentarii* which they took with them when they retired from office. Roman businessmen kept daybooks *(adversaria)* in which they recorded daily business transactions. Many private citizens kept their own papers in their "house archives," or *tablinum.* For example, the papers of the Flavius family of this period contain records of its own prisons, postal service, racing stable, public baths, hospitals, counting houses, Nile boats, and monasteries—an early conglomerate.[39]

Private record-keeping dates to a much earlier time than Republican Rome. For example, in Babylon the Egibi family recorded on clay tablets several generations of trade in slaves and real estate in the period 690 to 480 B.C. From Elephantine, a Persian military post on the Nubian-Egyptian frontier manned by Jewish mercenaries, have survived records written in Aramaic on papyrus. These papers, probably those of a Jewish family, the members of which included both soldiers and merchants, consist of official records, documents of the Jewish community, bills, letters, and private memoranda.[40]

Just as it is impossible to know when persons began writing manuscripts, so is it impossible to determine who was history's first collector. However, we have evidence of some of the famous ones. For example, Cicero had a collection, as did Pliny—who complained that, though Julius Caesar had lived but a century earlier, even then his letters were scarce. Caesar had established his own personal files called *sacrarium* apart from the Tabularium, and his successors followed this custom. The fate of these papers is not known. If they were shipped to Constantinople when Constantine established a new capital there in A.D. 300, they could have been destroyed in the fire that swept the *sacrarium* during the reign of Emperor Justinian.[41]

Among the earliest manuscripts ever offered on the American market was a group of parchment documents—three of Pepin le Bref, King of the Franks, three of Charlemagne, and two of Arnulf, the last Carolingian emperor, all dated between 753 and 896. The survival of these documents is proof to one dealer in manuscripts that "shortly after people commenced to write they also began to preserve autographs." [42]

These documents may be evidence of early collecting, but it could not have been extensive. Throughout the medieval period, manuscripts were seldom collected and preserved except by religious groups. Increasingly, from the fifteenth century, city and new national governments established archives and libraries. The Vatican library was formed in the fifteenth century, the Bibliothèque Nationale is nearly as old, and the first modern archives was established at Simancas in Spain in 1543. At about the same time, families engaged in business began keeping records, and men who saved their own letters cautioned their sons to do likewise, thus giving rise to the great family business archives. There was increased letter writing between individuals; and because letters were rare, they were saved to pass on their welcome news.[43]

Modern autograph collecting, characterized by one author as "third party" collecting—the setting out to acquire letters and papers not addressed to or concerned with oneself—was begun about this time, but the authorities are in dispute as to when and where. One theorizes that it had become general in Europe, especially in Germany, by the sixteenth century; another states that it grew up in England in the early seventeenth century. Our earliest concrete evidence of this new collecting comes in a letter dated April 1638, written by Elizabeth of Bohemia to Sir Simonds D'Ewes, obviously a British autograph collector:

I send you as you desire a letter of the King my housbands which he did write to the late Lord of Dorchester and one of my eldest sonnes to me. I thought also you would be glade to see my cozen the Duke of Brunswicks hand which I also send you.[44]

In England, with a few exceptions like D'Ewes, autograph collecting was not a patrician hobby, but was practiced instead by the middle classes, especially members of mercantile families who rose to affluence in the nineteenth century. One writer describes collecting of the period as on two levels. At the simplest level it could be pursued with very little expense. Want lists were drawn up and sent to friends, acquaintances, and fellow collectors. Trades were arranged and names were ticked off the list as specimens were acquired. This kind of collector more resembled the philatelist than the bibliophile. More intellect was required for the higher level of collecting; to seek letters which "really illuminated and typified the careers and characters of their writers needed an element of sentiment and sensitivity not necessarily present in collectors of books and manuscripts." [45]

William Upcott, an assistant librarian at the London Institute, typified the higher level of collecting. More than any other person, Upcott was responsible for the growth of autograph collecting in England. Around 1808, when he began accumulating autographs, he was one of a dozen or so collectors; twenty years later autograph collecting had become a fashionable pursuit, and his competitors numbered in the hundreds. He became known as the "Emperor of autographs," and beginning collectors wrote to him frequently for advice. With his infectious enthusiasm, he contributed substantially to this increased interest. "The very mention of the word 'Autographs,' " he wrote to another collector, "is as great a cordial to my heart as is a glass of full proof Geneva to a Billingsgate fishwoman." [46]

Upcott's enthusiasm had not come upon him full-blown. Like many another collector, he had moved from engravings, to extra-illustrating, to autographs, to what he referred to as his "Manuscript Collection," which contained, for example, several volumes of David Garrick's correspondence, Samuel Johnson's corrected proofsheets of *The Lives of the Poets,* and William Hogarth's original ledger of subscribers to his works.[47]

With his retirement, Upcott followed a not uncommon pattern: his avocation became his vocation. While at the London Institute, he had bought and sold enormous quantities of autographs, many of them perhaps under the since time-honored guise of "upgrading" his collection. When he left the institute, he looked to his collection to provide his current income and a legacy for his old age. He christened his home Autograph Cottage and there carried on his business while attempting various schemes to sell his collection *en bloc* to an institutional library. Over the years he negotiated with, among others, the British Museum, the Bodleian Library, and the Library of Congress. None of the negotiations were successful, and he was reduced to selling bits and pieces from the collection. The collection was further dispersed at auction after his death.[48]

Upcott's sales in his waning years and the public auction at the time of his death reflect the commercial aspect of collecting about which we know even less than about the collectors themselves. It is known that the early booksellers, many of whom were also stationers, printers, and publishers, did not issue catalogs of their stock until after 1595. It is also known that the first book auction in England was held in 1676. The catalogs listed many manuscripts, but most of them were the holograph texts on vellum of religious and secular books which had been sold from the earliest times. Occasionally historical manuscripts would be sold, too, as for example, at the sale of one peer's library in November 1687. Included in the more than two hundred manuscript volumes (the largest collection to be auctioned in this era) were charters, voyages, histories, and unpublished treatises from the time of Henry VIII and Queen Elizabeth.[49]

There had been a sporadic trade, then, in manuscripts for centuries, most of it by auction, before the autograph mania of the Victorian age. As early as 1819, British dealers responded to collector demand by issuing the first auction catalogs devoted exclusively to collections of autographs. Every year thereafter, the number of such catalogs increased until the 1890s, when the fashion of collecting autographs reached its peak. At the same time, more importantly, some booksellers began to stock autographs and to advertise them for sale, first in their book catalogs and then in separate catalogs. For example, Thomas Thorpe, Picadilly bookseller, issued regular periodic catalogs advertising his stock of 25,000 items.[50]

A curator in competition with Thorpe might call him a "monopolizing bugbear," but his fame and his catalogs were known far and wide, even in the United States. For example, *Graham's Magazine* for May 1848 reviewed a catalog received from Thorpe which contained five thousand autographs priced from a shilling to ten pounds. The book-review editor speculated that there would be comparatively few American collectors willing to pay "such exorbitant prices." Americans, he continued, built their collections largely by exchanges with others at home and abroad.[51]

The commercial trade in autographs and manuscripts in the United States arose many years after it had been thriving in Great Britain. The first American book auctions to include manuscripts and autographs respectively were in 1844 and 1851. Six years later saw the first sale devoted exclusively to autographs, and by the time of the Civil War the hobby was so widespread that autographs were frequently auctioned to raise money at the Sanitary Fairs. However, it was not until 1867 that the first sale of a major autograph collection occurred. Offered by the estate of the late Israel Tefft of Savannah, Georgia, it comprised 2,630 auction lots and required a catalog of 264 pages.[52]

To a great extent collections sold at auction would have been dispersed, but some were channeled to libraries. That of Mellen H. Chamberlain (1821–1900), for example, went to the Boston Public Library, where it now forms the bulk of the library's Revolutionary War manuscript holdings. Another Chamberlain, Jacob C. (1860–1905), who was curious about the authors of the books he had collected, spent the last five years of his life searching out literary manuscripts. He visited the friends and relatives of authors, he went to the old homes, and the end result was startling: included in his collection were Hawthorne's school books, Washington Irving's manuscript diaries and notebooks, and the Longfellow-Greene correspondence consisting of hundreds of letters which the poet had written to a college classmate.

Fig. 1. A manuscript and book auction at Bangs Brothers and Co., Park Place, New York, as drawn by an artist for *Frank Leslie's Illustrated Newspaper*, April 5, 1856. (Courtesy Southern Illinois University)

Charles Goodspeed, Boston bookseller, bought the Longfellow correspondence at the Chamberlain sale in 1909 for the Craigie House Library in Cambridge.[53]

While bookdealers like Goodspeed, his predecessors and successors, have sold autographs, the post-Civil War period saw the emergence of the exclusive autograph dealer. The first of these was Charles DeForest Burns, New York publisher of the *American Antiquarian*, a combination newssheet, historical journal, and sales catalog. Burns did not have the field to himself long. In 1887 Walter R. Benjamin established a firm to deal in autographs and began publication of *The Collector*, which remains an important trade journal to this day.[54]

The fashion of autograph collecting began later in the United States than England, peaked earlier and with less commercialism here, and gradually diminished. Today, most private collectors think of themselves as manuscript collectors; they are interested in letters of content rather than signatures. Some institutions still seek single letters, but their principal emphasis is on large bodies of papers. One English writer commenting on the change in collecting observed, "Instead of single album-pieces the emphasis has shifted to blocks of manuscript research material, and public opinion has become rightly critical of the raiding of an archive for a few choice plums." [55] That the raiding still goes on and that bodies of papers are dispersed (always the chief criticism of autograph collecting) can be seen by perusing the catalog of any present-day dealer or auction house. But the economic facts of the market place may help determine this. Mary Benjamin, successor to her father, Walter R. Benjamin, likes to speak of the added appraised value that a collection has above and beyond the sum of the values of the individual manuscripts. But she is also quick to relate that when her father acquired the papers of William Lloyd Garrison, the abolitionist editor of *The Liberator*, two carloads in all, he was unable to find a buyer and was obliged to sell the items individually.[56] To some, trading in the documentary heritage of the country is indecent. But in the larger view, perhaps as the commercial value of manuscripts grows, more may be preserved and, ultimately, history and humanity will be better served.

Contrary to the scholars' opinions set forth at the beginning of this chapter, the cultural and academic value of manuscripts is generally accepted. Few curators of manuscripts, either at the historical society or the university, are asked to justify collecting manuscripts. Few would deny that manuscripts are one of the roots of humanist learning, and fewer still could describe their worth as well as Howard Mumford Jones:

Although the tooth of time constantly gnaws at everything man makes and keeps, it is upon the more nearly permanent monuments of culture that the humanities depend for their existence. These monuments humanists labor to preserve, understand, and interpret to their fellow men.

Jones defines these monuments as works, sayings, deeds, and creations worthy of enduring through some long space of time, and he divides them into two classes, artifacts and documents. The latter he further defines as:

discourse, written, carved, or otherwise recorded (as on a tape). A document carries with it some intention of permanence. Documents may be the latest novel, the text of a political treaty, the Rosetta stone, a Buddhist prayer, stenographic writing (as in the case of Pepys's diary), the morning

newspaper (already become history), a cancelled check, and the like. . . .
[If the documents] are to yield their full values to successive generations of
men and in varying cultures, it is evident they must be exposed to at least
five processes:

(1) The artifacts and documents must be discovered.
(2) They must be identified.
(3) They must be preserved and, if possible, duplicated both as a
    precaution against loss and as a means of widening their study.
(4) They must be studied until they are understood by specialists versed
    in the knowledge of the time, place, and conditions that produced
    them. . . .
(5) They must be ever and again rescanned for new understanding, new
    meanings, and new relevances or applications to present culture.[57]

It is toward an explanation (partial and imperfect though it is)
of how the curator of manuscripts attempts to fulfill his obligations
within the humanist framework that the remainder of this book is
devoted.

SELECTED READINGS

Almost nothing has been written about the history of manuscript collecting; most
references are found in writings on book collecting. The best single source on the subject
is A.N.L. Munby, *The Cult of the Autograph Letter in England,* but it, too, is limited
geographically and to one phase of collecting. The nearest comparable coverage for
the United States first appeared in the *Wisconsin Historical Society Collections* (Vol.
10), was reprinted, and now is out of print: Lyman C. Draper, *An Essay on the Autograph
Collections of the Signers of the Declaration of Independence and of the Constitution.*
Three excellent essays supplementing that of Draper are: Lyman H. Butterfield, "Draper's
Predecessors and Contemporaries," Roy P. Basler, "The Modern Collector," and Lucile
M. Kane, "Manuscript Collecting." See also two chapters, "The Origin of Manuscript
Collecting in America," and "Private Manuscript Collections and Collectors," in the
book by Lawrence O. Burnette, Jr., *Beneath the Footnote: A Guide to the Use and
Preservation of American Historical Sources.* A fine article by Robert L. Brubaker,
"Archives and Manuscript Collections," surveys modern American institutional collecting.
The few books written by dealers contain very little about the dealers' pivotal role in
collecting, but by far the best is Mary A. Benjamin, *Autographs: A Key to Collecting.*
See also Lester J. Cappon, "Walter R. Benjamin and the Autograph Trade at the Turn
of the Century."

II

Administration

THE elements of administration include organization, planning, staffing, directing, co-ordinating, reporting, and budgeting.[1] Each of these elements will be discussed here, but in this limited space the coverage can be neither systematic nor inclusive because of the diverse nature of manuscript repositories.

This diversity is compounded by the unique character of each repository, which is reflected in its external organization, and, to a lesser extent, internally. The reasons for the variety of organizations are many. The history of the repository, the structure of the building, the governmental relationships, the existing personnel, the financial support given by the administration, the objective or goal of the institution, the type and nature of the collection—any or all of these factors can account for the varying organizational structure of manuscript repositories.

External Administrative Structures

In historical societies, which often are concerned with museum and historic-site operation, educational programs, publications, and other functions, the administration of the manuscript collection frequently falls under the library's jurisdiction. In some cases, the manuscript collection will be small and static; in others, it dominates the division so that the printed material is more or less a reference adjunct; in yet others, the two are equal partners in a research collection. In some societies, the library and manuscripts share space, but both the curator and the librarian answer to the director. The combination of archives and manuscripts into an administrative unit is another frequent type of organization. The Wisconsin and Minnesota societies operate area depository systems where manuscript collections held by a local college are jointly administered by the college and by the society through the manuscript division. Another historical society (Ohio) and a state library (Texas) have adopted similar networks.[2]

Relative advantages or disadvantages of any of these organizational configurations may depend as much upon the personnel involved as upon the lines of authority, but generally curators seem to feel that archivists have a better understanding and orientation toward manuscripts than do librarians. Apart from personalities, which could alter any situation, the affinity of the curator to either the librarian or the archivist may be colored by the type of manuscripts being collected. To illustrate, the archivist will understand the need for the curator to acquire the voluminous files of the local congressman, but he may feel it is wasteful to spend $300 for a letter of a literary figure.

In some instances, college and university collections of manuscripts are administered similarly to historical society collections, but in others quite differently. Here, too, archives and manuscripts often are linked in a single organizational unit. Once archives are established on campuses where the library previously exercised the archival function, the archives-manuscript section tends to remain in the library administration. In several instances, however, the curator and the collection are both housed in the library while the curator answers administratively to a vice-president for research and development. With the constant competition for space, this type of organization makes for confrontation and conflict, if nothing else. On other campuses, the archives have been established as an agency of the president's office, and on still others it is part of the registrar's or business affairs office. An archives in the latter instance is likely also to be involved in records management and may be linked administratively to the systems and data processing unit on campus.

Another common combination is for the manuscripts and rare books to be administered jointly out of the library. Archivists have been critical of this combination, but if anyone has any doubts about some librarians' support of manuscript collecting they need only to look at the superb collections at Princeton, University of California, Los Angeles, Texas, and other schools. In other institutions the archives, manuscripts, and rare books form library special collections, which may also administer photographs, pamphlets, microforms, and other nonbook materials. On some campuses—Cornell, for example—manuscripts, rare books, archives, and the graduate library have been housed in a separate research library. The Widner at Harvard, the Lilly at Indiana, and the Beinecke at Yale are all separate libraries built to house rare books and manuscripts, largely literary manuscripts. The Spencer Library at the University of Kansas administers rare books, manuscripts, regional history and archives. Separate facilities to house archives and historical manuscript collections have been built recently at the University of Michigan, and are nearing completion on the Wayne State campus. The curators of these two collections hold joint appointments in the history departments on their respective campuses. Teaching appointments are not uncommon for curators in their subject area specialties. Finally, the various academic departments have been fertile ground for manuscript collecting, and it is not unusual for the department libraries, particularly history, medicine and law, to administer manuscripts.

In some states, notably North Carolina, archives and manuscripts are jointly administered as the Department of Archives and History, which shares a building with the State Library. In Indiana, major collections of manuscripts are held by the state library and administered as one of its divisions, and by the historical society. Both are

Fig. 2. Elevation drawing of the Bentley Historical Library, University of Michigan. (Courtesy Michigan Historical Collections)

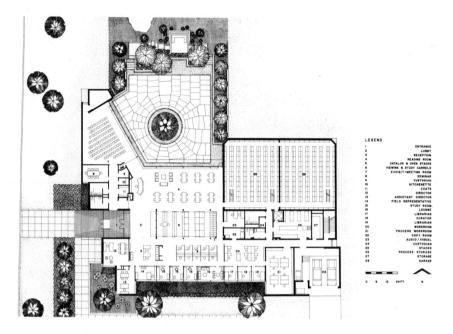

LEGEND

1 ENTRANCE
2 LOBBY
3 RECEPTION
4 READING ROOM
5 CATALOG & OPEN STACKS
6 VIEWING & STUDY CARRELS
7 EXHIBIT/MEETING ROOM
8 SEMINAR
9 CUSTODIAN
10 KITCHENETTE
11 COATS
12 DIRECTOR
13 ASSISTANT DIRECTOR
14 FIELD REPRESENTATIVE
15 STUDY ROOM
16 LOUNGE
17 LIBRARIAN
18 CURATOR
19 LIBRARIAN
20 WORKROOM
21 PROCESS WORKROOM
22 COPY ROOM
23 AUDIO/VISUAL
24 CUSTODIAN
25 STACKS
26 PROCESS STORAGE
27 STORAGE
28 GARAGE

Fig. 3. Main floor plan of the Bentley Historical Library, University of Michigan. (Courtesy Michigan Historical Collections)

housed in the same building, and they sometimes compete for the same material. Private libraries will vary from situation to situation. At the Huntington, manuscripts is one of four library departments. The librarian answers to the director who also administers the art gallery and the botanical garden.

Relatively few public libraries collect manuscripts but those in the major cities, which have committed themselves to collecting programs, have done a good job. At the Denver Public Library, manuscripts are administered by the Western History Department. History is the focus at Detroit also, where the Burton Historical Collection is endowed to collect manuscripts. The Berg Collection (literary) and the Manuscript Division (historical), are two of six divisions of the Special Collections at the New York Public Library.[3]

The holdings of six presidential libraries, although administered by the National Archives and Records Service through the Office of the Presidential Libraries, are largely manuscripts, rather than archives. With the exception of the Kennedy Library, which is not yet housed in its own building, the libraries combine museum, and, in some cases, site administration, with research facilities. Each library is administered by a director, and under him the archives and manuscripts are in charge of the research archivist. The presidential libraries may have set a pattern for the establishing of other personal memorial libraries for political figures, as with the Everett Dirksen papers, housed in a new wing of the Pekin Public Library, and the Sam Rayburn Foundation Library in Bonham, Texas.

Other national collections would include those of the Smithsonian Institution. Manuscripts there are administered by the Smithsonian Archives and two distinct depositories, the Archives of American Art and the National Anthropological Archives, as well as numerous research collections which are under the individual care of various curators. And last but by no means least, the nation's major manuscript collection, the Library of Congress, where the Manuscript Department is administered as a part of the Reference Division.

From this review, it should be apparent that manuscript repositories are parts of a great variety of administrative structures, but that none exists as an administrative unit unto itself. And while there is notable diversity in the external administration of manuscript collections, internally there is great similarity, despite staff size that can range from the single curator to the large staff complement at the Library of Congress.

Internal Administrative Organization

An actively growing collection will soon expand beyond the capacities of a single curator to administer. In the early stages of growth, expanded one-person operations tend to retain their old character, with each assistant following a collection from accessioning through arranging to description. In time, the curator may either consciously or unconsciously develop specialists on his staff. They may specialize in a chronological period, but more likely in a subject area. As long as a staff is small, it is natural (and usually beneficial) that everyone take his turn at reference or processing; but with growth, the curator concentrates his efforts on acquisition and development. He may, out of pride (or habit), continue to try to guide the visiting researcher, when in reality the reference specialist, who is thoroughly familiar with the finding aids, or the processor, who may have become an area specialist—or is at least the specialist in the collections he has arranged—could better advise the researcher. Some curators remain well-informed about their collections long after the press of administrative work has kept them from first-hand contact with the manuscripts in their care, but for many the general overview supplants the specific and concise.

As a manuscripts collection grows, the administrative tasks increase, and the chief administrator (curator, director, head, librarian, or archivist) may acquire one or more administrative assistants. But sometimes this does not seem to decrease the curator's load. He is supposed to be devoting more of his time to planning, but he finds routine tasks smothering all creative planning. Subordinates, as one administrator has observed, often tend to "push up the tough ones," because they do not want to take responsibility or bear the consequences for decisions.[4]

There may be at least two other factors at work which the administrator does not recognize. His staff and program may have grown to the point where he needs to devote increasing amounts of time to evaluation, budgeting, personnel, and other administrative tasks, although his institution lacks the resources to allow him to spend full time on administration. When this split focus exists in a manuscript collection, the curator may not develop good administrative techniques. He may, for example, urge his assistants to take more responsibility, but by his demands for a constant flow of information, which he uses to "second guess" their decision, nullify his delegation and indicate to them that he still feels he must be responsible for decisions.

Part of the routine that bogs down the curator is the reporting process which is inherent in manuscript collections, most of which grew like Topsy. When the collection is small and the staff numbers two or three, reporting is informal. Later, with collection growth, the curator will want to be kept advised, but it then becomes a matter of finding a way to do this in a more orderly fashion.

The staff meeting is one of the reporting methods most often used. Some curators call staff meetings when they feel the need arises, and others regularly schedule meetings. The entire staff can report, or one person or section can report comprehensively on a project. A less formal approach is the weekly coffee-hour or "tea," where discussion can be free-ranging.

Another device, the newsletter, gives the curator an opportunity to report both up and down the administrative chain, but it is little used because it takes time to prepare. Memoranda can serve the same purpose as a newsletter, and the bulletin board also has a place in the reporting process.

In reporting to his administrative superiors, the curator will probably be involved in processes similar to those used within his own division. If it is his responsibility to attend staff meetings of division or department heads, occasionally he should allow one of his assistants to go as his alternate. This is good for staff morale and makes for a better-informed assistant who must act for the curator when he is in the field or at another meeting.

Written weekly or monthly reports may be part of the reporting process. One curator thinks that manuscript departments, because they tend to be "self-contained" and often not interrelated to the other work of the institution, may leave those up the administrative ladder "frustrated, puzzled, and sometimes, antagonistic." He sees brief and factual written progress reports as a mitigating force in this situation.[5] The summation or distillation of the weekly or monthly reports or the annual report serves other purposes than the curator's report to his supervisor. The balance in all reporting is to keep the administrator informed without giving him a sense of being badgered, lest the result be, as one administrator put it, the feeling that manuscripts are "messy, expensive and a nuisance." [6]

Instead of the vertical hierarchy of administration described here, the one-time curator of the regional history collection at Cornell proposes a manuscript collection staff organized along functional lines: processing, reference, administration, development, research, instruction, and publication; and it might involve oral, audio, and machine techniques. Staff members would operate in and contribute to a chosen area according to their abilities and interests and would advance through the ranks of assistant archivist, senior assistant archivist, associate archivist, and archivist upon the evaluation of their peers. The staff would meet regularly to determine priorities and to assign clerical and support staff. Rank and salary would be determined according to professional contribution rather than administrative advancement. "The person responsible for administrative duties need not be the senior member of the department nor the one most capable of professional contribution nor, for that matter, the one most able in promoting his own career." Instead, the administrator would be elected by the staff in line with his interest and ability. Not just the staff-elected administrator, but all professional staff, would report programs to the higher administrative level.[7]

To some, peer evaluation, an elected administrator, and the reporting of all staff, may seem fraught with peril, not the least of which might be an unmanageable degree of backbiting and infighting among the staff. In submitting his innovative proposal, the curator may have had this in mind when he said the proposal contained "flaws and weaknesses." He asked his colleagues "to develop objections to it or to describe more effective schemes," [8] but none have appeared in professional journals. In fact, archival literature, to which most curators look for guidance in administration, is of very little practical use. It bears a strong resemblance to most of the writings on management which appears in library journals—the curator's other principal source of instruction—which have been described in this manner:

There is a regrettable lack of first-hand acquaintance with management literature, and of orientation in the management field, on the part of library administrators and those who write on library management. Much of librarians' writings on this subject is more descriptive than analytical and, often, more naïve than sophisticated. There is a real lack of "bridging" literature; that is, articles that relate the concepts and practices of "professional" management literature to library situations. [9]

Management Techniques

On the whole, curators evidence a singular lack of interest in or understanding of management techniques. Perhaps the literature reflects this indifference, or it may be, in part, a cause. Again, this may be an outgrowth of the conditions mentioned above—the one-person operation which gains staff and programs without the curator being allowed time and resources to develop administrative skills. Another cause may be that the majority of curators are humanities-trained and -oriented. Administration, especially quantitative management, may, as one writer intimates, be "repugnant" to curators who feel "unsuited" to this field. Yet the curator, if he is to fulfill his duties adequately in planning and development, badly needs the tools that management can provide. [10]

Cost analysis, for example, is virtually unknown by curators, and very few have studied their procedures to see if they could be streamlined; yet work analysis techniques could provide valuable administrative data in both areas. It is granted, however, that time-and-motion studies, which have been most effective in examining repetitive tasks, would be less effective in providing meaningful performance standards for professional work.

The three methods used in work analysis are: direct observation, self-recording or diary technique, and activity sampling. The observer with the stopwatch would find little favor with a manuscript collection staff, who, like most professionals, do not like being rated, but the other two methods might work, especially the self-recording or diary technique. Here the difficulty probably would be in allowing time—or remembering—to record work and time for the curator to identify tasks and work units.[11]

Very possibly, one reason work analysis is difficult to administer in many manuscript depositories is that staff members rarely work long at any task without interruption. This in itself should tell the curator something about his operation. It may indicate nothing more than that the collection is under-staffed, but it could indicate, too, that work-flow patterns are faulty, that space is poorly designed or utilized, or any one of a number of other reasons.

The obvious objection to work analysis of manuscript processing and description is that the unique character of each collection makes it next to impossible to arrive at meaningful statistics. Of course, this is a valid objection, but only to a point. Despite the variables which all curators recognize—size, complexity, physical condition, organization, subject matter, etc.—nonetheless, there are certain similarities between collections which would allow for at least approximate measurement and comparison. It is most likely that resistance of the staff (not excluding the curator) to measuring professional tasks, rather than the difficulty of obtaining statistics, accounts for the lack of work analysis in manuscript administration.

Even if imperfectly executed, a work-study project would be almost certain to produce some worthwhile results, one of which might be to discover the difference between doing a task efficiently or effectively. One management specialist defines the former as doing anything (right or wrong) in a less wasteful manner, and the latter as doing the correct thing to achieve the institution's objective.[12] Many systems which have grown more or less spontaneously without much planning will be discovered to contain duplicate or unnecessary processes. One midwestern historical society, for example, changed its accessioning process ten years ago, but, through inertia, retains part of the old system duplicated in another form. Even if the work-study program fails to uncover any anachronistic appendages, it will inevitably produce some statistics which the curator has not had before and which will be of inestimable value in his planning.

In development and planning, the curator will be concerned primarily with three major areas: personnel and training for the profession; funding and the budget; and the building or physical plant. Each of these areas, beginning with personnel, estimated to account for 50 to 75 percent of operation costs,[13] will be treated in the remainder of this chapter.

Personnel

Depending on the curator's situation, he may have the complete obligation of screening and hiring his personnel, or he may be dependent upon a personnel department for preliminary selection. In the latter instance, the curator can serve his own cause by working with the personnel office to formulate adequate job descriptions for his staff positions. Civil service * forms rarely have the space needed to describe positions in manuscripts. To offset this lack, one historical society, for example, submitted a five-page memorandum entitled "The Nature of Manuscripts and the Special Occupational Descriptions for Employees of a Manuscripts Center" to the state civil service to help its classifiers establish more realistic job grades.[14]

If the curator screens and hires his own personnel, what criteria should he use in his selection? Traditionally, persons who had majored in history were thought to be the best qualified for positions in manuscript repositories. Allied fields in the social studies were given second preference. This tradition is rooted in the theory that history students, who have had a course in historical methods, will better recognize the relative importance of research materials. It is rooted, too, in the profession's desire to achieve status. In practice, an administrator may find that the academic background of an employee is at best only an indication of his potential, and that ingelligence, logic, common sense, and most of all, intuition, are the qualities most needed. One curator phrases her quest in slightly different terms. She says she looks for a person who has "wide familiarity with many phases of American history and culture and a knack for empathy—above all, the latter. This ability to perceive in any collection of papers the uses to which they may be put distinguishes the competent manuscript cataloger from the incompetent." [15]

Whether empathy and intuition manifest themselves more often in history majors than in those from other disciplines may be open to question. Again, in practice, the curator may find that a fine-arts major who has some understanding of people may very well do a much better job than a history student in recognizing the importance of a diary or a group of letters revealing the human side of history. There may be some question, too, about the minimum of four years of college which curators have insisted was necessary background for

---

* *Civil service* should not be read in the text to mean *clerical,* since the majority of archivists and curators in state and federal service hold civil service appointments.

professional assistants. The truth is that a college degree was thought desirable because it was hoped that the recipient would have read widely and would generally be brighter and more alert than a non-college graduate. If this was once true, it is changing today. Enthusiasm, a feeling for research materials, and an ability to separate the mundane from the pivotal are characteristics rarely learned in a history class and often not found in a college course.

Many manuscript repositories will have a ready-made pool of talented and skilled labor, the volunteers. Most volunteers are women. Some may be Junior Leaguers, others retired faculty wives or church-women, but in most instances they are volunteers because of their enthusiasm; and, if the curator has the time and patience to channel this enthusiasm, it will benefit the collection. Perhaps the chief factor to remember in utilizing volunteers is that their work should be meaningful. "Make-work" kills the initative of any worker, professional or otherwise, but it is especially restrictive for volunteers. If an important project can be assigned to volunteers and if their work can be overseen by a professional, the end result may be most productive for the institution, particularly if the project is one that lends itself to a flexible schedule.

One important factor often overlooked by administrators is that volunteer labor is not "free." To be properly utilized, the volunteers must be trained and supervised like any other staff member. Work plans should be made and rules drawn up that both the administrator and volunteer understand in advance.

The objections to using volunteers usually center on the thought that they are a threat to the professionalism of the staff, and there is a general uneasiness that in using them the institution's administration is being allowed to avoid its rightful obligation to provide adequate funding for the collection.[16]

Curators who are on or near a college or university campus and can draw on a ready supply of student workers are twice blessed. Students can be the most talented and cheapest form of labor available to the curator. The principal disadvantage of student labor is that its turnover is rapid and continual retraining is necessary. If this can be adapted to, student aid is invaluable.

This mobility recalls a session at an SAA meeting in recent years, the topic of which was "The Nonprofessional: Buttress of the Profession." During the course of the session, several panelists alluded to the rapid turnover in nonprofessional assistants and one wit in the audience asked if perhaps the session was not really dealing with the "flying buttress of the profession." The question does remain, however, whether it is better to hire undergraduates or graduates. This is best resolved by the curator's needs: if he wishes to arrange and describe quantities of material with minimum inventories and cataloging, a bright undergraduate can do the job perhaps better than the graduate, and certainly at a lower cost in salary. Some curators have gone so far as to advocate hiring persons who know nothing about the subject area in which they are to catalog, the theory being that if a check-list of certain information to look for in the collection is provided, any person of average intelligence can follow through. As one curator has noted, "Our very limited experience suggests that it is wasteful to use individuals for indexing who have a relatively high degree of education." [17]

If, on the other hand, a more detailed analysis and inventory of the collection is wanted, a graduate student who is specializing in the subject area covered by the collection may provide the best results. However, the more detailed the inventory is expected to be, and the more specialized the knowledge of the student, the more important the time factor becomes. Graduate students tend to read more than is necessary in processing. Their goal, conscious or unconscious, is to educate themselves; the curator's goal is to get the collection arranged, described, and on the shelf. This means a constant conflict which requires compromise: the curator urges the graduate processor on to complete the work as rapidly as possible, and the graduate student often bogs down in the details and nuances that only he can appreciate. The tendency of the subject-matter specialist, as one curator expressed it, is "to interpret rather than to expose content." [18]

Yet this unevenness in the quality of work need not result from graduate training, but may be rooted in the worker's personality. As one curator observed, one assistant who insists upon minutely detailed descriptions is seeking "to satisfy his own inner needs for perfect order in an imperfect world." Balanced against this may be another worker who tries to produce controls for a collection without doing the hard exacting work that is necessary. Blending these contradictory forces takes "shrewdness and sagacity" on the part of the curator. [19]

Any discussion of the personnel manning manuscript collections must deal with the professional-versus-nonprofessional concept. Attending the manuscript and archival meetings and reading the organizations' journals convinces one that curators and archivists are very conscious of the difference in status between the professional and nonprofessional. Personal observation of on-the-job activities do not seem to bear this out. Although there has been no systematic survey, it would appear that curators and the professionals on their staff are a lot like professional librarians characterized in a recent study; they spend a great deal of time doing nonprofessional work, and many persons performing highly professional tasks are often not paid significantly more than the nonprofessional.[20] In part, this situation results from small and inadequately staffed collections, but it also may reflect an uncertainty as to what constitutes professional training.

Professional Training

In any discussion of professional training, it must be noted at the outset that there are no courses of study accrediting curators of manuscripts per se, but rather courses combining administration of rare books and manuscripts, or courses combining archives and manuscripts. Of the latter, a recent world survey concludes that, in relation to the size of the profession, there are a large number and a great variety of archival training courses. There are even independent schools, such as the École des Chartes in Paris or the Moscow Institute, which devote the entire curriculum to archives administration, but in Great Britain, Canada, and the United States, most archival training courses are taught in colleges and universities.[21]

The most comprehensive listing of courses in archival education in the United States and Canada is issued by the Society of American Archivists. It describes courses offered at American University, Bates College, University of California, Los Angeles, Case Western Reserve University, University of Denver, Emory University, University of Illinois at Urbana-Champaign, McGill University, University of Maryland, University of New Brunswick, University of North Carolina, North Carolina State University, University of Oregon, Sacramento State College, University of Texas at Arlington, Texas Christian University, Washington University (St. Louis), Wayne State University, and the University of Wisconsin—in all, nineteen colleges and universities and two institutes, one sponsored by the National Archives, the Library of Congress, and the Maryland Hall of Records, the other by the Ohio Historical Society. Most of the courses are offered out of the history department; one is cross-listed as a library science course; and some are offered by the library school. In some cases, only a single course is offered, in others a sequence toward a minor at the master's and Ph.D. levels.[22]

There are courses that are not listed in the SAA directory but which would prove useful training for curators, especially those who will work with literary manuscripts. Schools which offer courses in rare book librarianship include Drexel, McGill, the University of Missouri, the State University of New York at Albany, the University of Pittsburgh, the University of Texas at Austin, and the University of Toronto. Manuscripts are covered to some extent in the courses at any of these schools, but the University of Toronto offers a specific course, Rare Books and Literary Manuscripts. Two other graduate library schools, the University of California, Los Angeles, and the University of British Columbia, offer sixth-year courses, the first toward certification as a specialist in rare books and manuscripts, and the second as a special collections librarian with specialization either in rare books and special collections or in archives and manuscripts.[23]

Numerous other courses, institutes, and conferences relating to several specialized fields with which the curator is associated are offered periodically. The University of Illinois, Chicago Circle Campus, in conjunction with the Newberry Library; the New England Document Conservation Center; the New York State Historical Association at Cooperstown; and other organizations have offered courses in paper conservation. Columbia University, School of Library Service and Department of History, inaugurated a three-credit course in the summer of 1973 in oral history. The National Archives conference on the Use of Audiovisual Archives as Original Source Materials, held in the fall of 1972 at the University of Delaware, was but one of a great many similar conferences held throughout the year.

Ideally, the curator might wish to hire personnel trained in manuscript management, or to take advantage of the courses offered to train persons already on his staff. In a great many cases, neither ideal can be attained. There remains, then, the alternative of on-the-job training. There is much to be said for this method; after all, the senior members of the profession who teach the academic courses were themselves self-taught and served apprenticeships for their training. The weakness of on-the-job training is that the apprentices are limited in their exposure to alternatives. If, at some point in their training, they can attend an institute at another manuscript repository, they will gain a healthier, broader perspective.

From the curator's point of view, the prime difficulty of apprenticeship is the great amount of time he must spend in supervising the trainee. In the training period, especially the early weeks, the curator's burden will be lightened considerably if he is able to refer the employee to an in-house manual of operations.

Most major collections have developed their own manual of operations, but few have been planned or organized as formal publications.[24] These manuals are usually the outgrowth of descriptions of routines which have been written for staff guidance. Gradually, as a sheaf of these segments accumulates, the curator, if he can find the time, will bring them together into a formal manual. No matter what form the manual takes, it is a signal administrative tool. Once the curator has thought through a problem and arrived at a decision, the decision should be recorded for his guidance and that of his staff. The manual becomes a great time-saver in training new personnel and in carrying on the day-to-day operation. Without it, cataloging and processing will lack uniformity.

As a supplement to the manual, the trainee should be guided to bibliographies in the field and helped to select articles and books that will give him a broad general knowledge of manuscript practices. From time to time, the curator will need to supplement the reading with specialized directions applicable to the institution's particular problems.[25]

As the apprentice gains expertise, it would be helpful if he could test his knowledge in practical application at another repository. To this end, two manuscript-collecting agencies with similar programs

Fig. 4. A typical scene at a professional meeting—waiting for the session to begin.

might agree to exchange trainees for a short period. A variation of this would be for an agency to develop a program of sabbatical leaves, or perhaps minisabbaticals, for employees. Opportunities of this nature would benefit not just apprentices, but most staff, and would help combat institutional myopia. Travel to several institutions over a period of a couple of months would be the best kind of educational experience. To see a program in operation is far different from reading about it in a professional journal.

The professional meeting may seem at first a doubtful training tool. Too often, those staff members who could most benefit from the exchange and interchange of ideas are those who must mind the shop while the administrator attends the sessions. The numerous regional archival associations around the country, all creatures of the 1970s and some not yet with their feet firmly planted, offer great promise in this regard. Curators and other staff members who have been unable to attend national meetings because they lacked "enough seniority to command an expense allowance," are now participating in workshops and how-to-do-it sessions.[26]

The greatest benefit from the national meetings comes usually to the curator who runs a one-person operation and whose previous experience had been on-the-job training as an assistant to a better-established curator. Although the manuscript profession may not be an innovative one, the new ideas that do bubble up seem to come from this group of curators who are anxious to establish a place for themselves as leaders in their field. Still, the benefits are not confined to the emerging leadership alone. Other curators who see value in the meetings include newcomers to the profession, whatever their level, who know something about their field and are alert to expand their knowledge. Even the well-established administrators can find the meetings useful because they offer them the occasional opportunity to shake free of their intellectual rigor mortis by being exposed to new technology and techniques. Meetings can be good seedbeds of ideas, but perhaps their greatest utility is to make the average curator aware that his problems are not unique. The mutual sharing of problems may be a tonic of sorts, even when, as is often the case, the curator discovers that solutions arrived at for *his* problems were no more unique than the problems.

Personnel-management literature, which in the past dwelled at length on motivating the employee, today speaks of "self-fulfillment," and "commitment" through participation in decision-making.[27] These are terms which have never had great urgency to the staff members of most manuscript repositories. In the past, people who have worked with manuscripts—or those who have done so over any period of time—have not seemed to need a great deal of external motivation. They were often inner-directed. For them to have a genuine sense of self-fulfillment in their work, it seemed less essential that they have a strong sense of commitment to the goals of the institution or to participate in the decisions of its administration. They had what some management experts called a "desired internalized state," i.e., they were self-motivated and recognized their own good performances. This came in a large part from the nature of their work. It was self-directed; it offered large degrees of both freedom and responsibility; it allowed for imagination, ingenuity, and creativity; and it afforded great opportunities for decision-making—in short, it was "good work." [28]

Today self-fulfillment is more difficult for staff members working in repositories where jobs have become stratified and where a preponderance of massive collections has made partial processing, eschewing final analysis, a rule of life. What was once naturally satisfying work has been fractionalized and the staff members lose their sense of achievement when they can no longer see the beginning or the end of their tasks. The intellectual content of work is diminished, while tasks that are repetitive increase. The absence of time off for research contributes to the lock-in and may help drive out of the profession some of its most imaginative young people.[29]

Funding

Obviously, everything relating to the administration of a manuscript collection pivots upon funding and budgeting. The majority of the collecting institutions in the country are operated on public funds, supplemented by some private money. Despite this, few curators will be involved in legislative budget hearings and those who are usually will be only indirectly involved. For them, however, the major administrative responsibility may be formulating the budget request that goes to the institutional administrator, who sees it through the legislative process.

Aside from appropriations, however, the funding for a manuscript collection can come from Friends groups, foundations, federal granting agencies, corporations and business firms, and private donors. Private donations, either as endowments, unrestricted capital gifts, or gifts in kind have played a major role in building most of the great manuscript collections in this country. Traditionally, the endowed collections were those in private libraries and the private colleges and universities, particularly the Ivy League schools, but state schools are seeking endowed funds also. For example, in a survey made in 1956, twenty-two university libraries (evenly divided between state and privately supported) received $1,175,631 in cash and $773,195 worth of books and manuscripts in that year. In the same period, the schools spent from endowed funds $906,842 for books, manuscripts, and other materials. This represented 18.5 percent of the libraries' total expenditures for the private schools and 2.5 percent for the state schools; but, as another authority has pointed out, the figure for private schools cannot be accepted as a national average, since seven out of eleven surveyed were Ivy League institutions. The proportion of the total $2,855,668 received by cash or gift allotted to manuscripts would be estimated at a third to half.[30]

Gifts can be a mixed blessing, especially gifts in kind, but occasionally this is true even of cash gifts. Donated manuscripts will be treated extensively in the chapter on acquisitions, but here might be the place to note one librarian's summary of the negative aspects of these transactions, a point of view rarely seen in print: "For all their interest and generosity, library donors can be something of a problem. Not infrequently they attach great value to gifts which have very little value or which are not appropriate to the library's needs, and they frequently feel their benefactions deserve separate and distinctive treatment." He goes on to say that college presidents and faculty can be the library's "worst enemies." Often they accept gifts outright or indicate their worth and the university's desire to have the gift without consulting the library staff in either situation, when in reality the gift may be valueless or the conditions of the gift impossible to administer.[31]

It is the impossibility of administering conditions that occasionally forces an institution to refuse a gift of money. A donor of manuscripts might become quite interested in a repository during the acquisition process. He offers to finance the preparation of a finding aid, if he can approve its content, and if the papers can be processed out of priority order. Or a patron might offer to endow a collection provided he or someone he names is appointed honorary curator. For a variety of reasons, such arrangements would be acceptable to some institutions and not to others. Although it must happen with less frequency, even multimillion-dollar gifts are refused; one institution turned down a proposed gift to build a research library because the donor wished to control the finance committee of the board.

A building campaign or a major endowment drive would of necessity involve many others besides the curator. The part that he plays in soliciting gifts will depend, among other things, upon the place he holds in the institution's administrative structure, his personality, and what he feels are his professional responsibilities. Some curators are eager to acquire gifts of manuscripts but feel that the responsibility for raising money belongs to others—the development office, the president, the board of trustees, the director, or the librarian. To some, asking for money is demeaning, and they look at their fellow curators who are aggressively trying to raise money as having got out of their field. These curators say they have opted for manuscripts because they were scholarly oriented and not by temperament suited for a career as a salesman. Other curators realize that selling the collection to potential donors is often necessary, but essentially this comes through first-hand knowledge of the needs and goals of the collection, and imparting this knowledge need not smack of huckstering.

The curator may or may not actively solicit funds, but in either case he can provide the facts to help match potential donors with the collection's needs. The planning and imagination which goes into displaying and expressing those needs in a project that can be grasped by the donor is crucial to all giving, private, foundation, or corporate. Seeking gifts for general operating expenses is rarely successful; corporate donors particularly seem to prefer to finance a well-defined, discrete project or program.

Tax-supported institutions may have some initial resistance to overcome in seeking corporate support. Corporation officers are quite conscious of the taxes their companies pay, yet they are usually on the alert to find ways to improve the firm's public image. For these and other less obvious reasons, corporations budget monies for gifts which can be tapped by the curator, but it should be remembered that foundation reports show that three-fourths of that money will be channeled through a company foundation. Part of the secret of tapping these funds is for the project to have special appeal to the corporation (perhaps through product association), and that it lend itself to widespread but prestigious publicity. A good example of a corporation's being involved in a manuscript project is that of Shaker Savings Association, which was solicited by the Western Reserve

Historical Society for funds to arrange, microfilm, and publish a guide to the institution's unexcelled collection of Shaker manuscripts.[32]

Corporate gifts can come directly through a well-presented program, and they can come indirectly through corporate officers being involved in a Friends group. The first Friends group was organized in 1913 to support the Bibliothèque Nationale. The concept came to this country first in public libraries and then at Harvard, where the first Friends of an academic library was established in 1925.[33] Today, Friends of the Library is a common phenomenon on most campuses and in other places throughout the country. Museums and other institutions have followed suit. Even the National Archives has set up a membership organization called Associates of the National Archives. "Friends of the Archives" is still in the future, and for the moment the curator must look to library literature for guidance in this as in all other areas of fund raising.

The objectives of Friends "are to promote understanding of the library—its problems, its resources, and its needs. They aim to foster a favorable climate for support of the library—its services, its physical facilities, and its resources. More specifically, they may and frequently do promote and encourage gifts to the library, either materials or money." [34]

The genesis for organizing a group of friends into a Friends of the Library generally comes from the librarian, but in a campus situation faculty and alumni have taken the lead occasionally. The librarian usually serves as secretary to the group, or as advisor, but in some instances the group's constitution expressly denies him the privilege of being an officer or board member. This provision is made to keep the administration of the two organizations separate. Although there must be close co-operation between the two organizations, strict separation of their affairs is necessary, particularly financial affairs. Membership may be limited (again excluding library staff, board members, etc.), but it is likely to be open, and dues vary depending on the purpose of the group. Some libraries wish to make an exclusive appeal to persons of wealth; others rely on a broadly diversified base of membership. Two groups of people that the curator will be most anxious to see included in the membership, and perhaps represented on the board, will be collectors or dealers of manuscripts.[35]

Very specific literature exists telling how to organize and work with Friends. If the curator is interested in helping form such a group, he should read the literature carefully, especially with the view to recognizing his and his institution's obligation to the Friends. The institution must be willing to invest money and time for what are not always immediately tangible results.[36]

The successful operation of a Friends organization requires the combined efforts of many persons, but the curator, largely through his own efforts, may be able to secure a grant for his collection. It is, however, important that, in this, as in all other solicitation of funds, he have full support of his institution's administrative and financial officers. Grants probably are discussed more and applied for less than any other area of fund support. Of the two types of grants, foundation and government agency, the latter are least utilized by curators. Two major grant programs have drawn most of their attention: the National Historical Publications Commission grants to underwrite the micro-filming of selected manuscript collections and the Federal Work Study Program, through which archives and libraries hire disadvantaged persons whose salaries are largely subsidized by the federal government. A scattering of manuscript repositories have received grants from the National Endowment for the Humanities, most of which have related to letterpress editions of manuscript collections, oral history projects, and film archives. These were well-publicized programs, and curators would have been irresponsible not to have taken advantage of them. But money is available from less-publicized sources if the curator uses his imagination. For example, the archivist of a midwestern university received a grant from his state department of mental health to prepare and publish an inventory of the research projects and resources on his campus relating to mental health and work with the disadvantaged. The same archivist has received two grants from the Council on Library Resources, one on documentation in science and technology and the other on archival education in the United States and Europe.

Grants by the Council on Library Resources are the foundation grants with which curators are likely to be most familiar. The CLR, which itself operates on funds granted by the Ford Foundation, has supported, among other things, the National Union Catalog of Manuscript Collections, the extensive research of the William Barrow laboratory on conservation of paper; the establishment of a preservation office at the Library of Congress; SPINDEX II, the computer indexing system for manuscripts/archives materials; and the report of Society of American Archivists, Committee on the Seventies.[37]

Competition for CLR grants is keen, and for the curator to get a grant from the Ford, Rockefeller, or Carnegie Foundations would not be impossible, though it would be unlikely. However, there were

5,454 foundations in 1971 big enough to be listed in the Foundation Center's *The Foundation Directory,* and there are hundreds of local and family foundations too small to list. A local foundation too small to list could still have very healthy assets and would be a prime prospect for a curator's program. The Tax Reform Act of 1969 requires that by 1975 all foundations must pay out annually an amount equal to six percent of the market value of their assets. Since, soon after the act's passage, fewer than half the foundations were meeting this requirement, foundation giving should soon reach a peak. This means, the authorities agree, that the small family foundation is now a very promising source of funds. There also seems to be a pattern of giving; many small foundations make their grants in November or December at the end of the tax year, often on the basis of requests in hand at that time.[38]

Where can one get information on grant-making governmental agencies and private foundations? Most colleges and universities have research administration or development offices that can help. For the curator who has to seek out his own possible sources, there are many services available—some free, some at considerable cost. A couple of small investments may be in order: in the latest edition of *The Foundation Directory,* noted above, and in the annual edition of *Catalog of Federal Domestic Assistance,* available from the U.S. Government Printing Office. Information on the programs, regulations, guidelines, and application deadlines of government agencies can be acquired through diligent letter-writing and telephoning. If absolutely stymied, one can call on his congressman for help in getting information from federal agencies or on his state representative for help with state agencies.

The Foundation Center offers much valuable assistance, either free or at low cost. With major offices in New York and Washington, D.C., and a series of about fifty regional offices being established across the country, information will be readily available to most curators. Among the resources at the center's offices are primary public records, reference works, annual reports of those foundations that issue them, reports, guides, and other background information. The public records are the most recent tax returns of the approximately 26,000 grant-making foundations in the U.S. These records are important, for they give the foundations' purposes, officers, assets, disbursements, and lists of grants made. By using the returns, the researcher can see the range in size of grants given by a foundation, subjects in which it is interested, and types of organizations to which it gives. The regional offices usually hold IRS returns only for the state in which the office is located. The center sells microfiche copies of IRS returns and foundation annual reports, periodicals that include grants indexes, and a data-bank service that will provide a computer-printout list of grants made, selected by subject (black history, drug abuse, etc.), foundation name, amount of grant, or geographic location of recipient.

Complete sets of returns of private foundations by state may be ordered from the IRS. Sets range in cost from $2 for Alaska's to $787 for New York's. The sets come on microfiche aperture cards, which can be read in a hand-held viewer or with a microfiche reader.[39]

How does the curator prepare and present his request? The author of a recent technical leaflet issued by the American Association for State and Local History, Securing Grant Support, says there is no magic in the process, but that it still remains a mystery to most administrators. In attempting to clear up the mystery, William Alderson, director of AASLH and a practiced professional in "grantsmanship," offers the following suggestions, many of which are applicable in applying for grants from federal agencies as well as from private foundations. This leaflet is must reading for the novice proposal-writer.[40]

Assuming that the curator has had his "moment of intuitive brilliance," the ideas for the project must be patiently cast and recast into a program acceptable to a foundation. This means studying the potential foundation, as suggested above, and selecting the one whose stated purposes encompass the program. If possible, study the foundation's tax returns, annual reports, and proposal guidelines, if it issues them. Honor its restrictions regarding subject areas in which it will make grants, geographic area served, or maximum grants made. In developing a project and writing a proposal, use the good advice offered in publications such as the AASLH leaflet. A good grant proposal has on its first two pages the information essential to the foundation board in reaching its decision. Costs in salaries, travel, office supplies, etc., must be carefully estimated and a budget of indirect and direct expenses submitted. The leaflet gives a sample budget and a step-by-step procedure to follow right through to the preparation of a final report for a completed grant project.[41]

Budgeting

Obtaining a grant or other outside funding is not easy. Spending it is easier, but spending it wisely is not, and a good budget is prepared every bit as carefully as a grant proposal. However, before turning to some of the elements of proper budgeting, there is a need to make some general observations about financial support of manuscript collecting.

A recurring theme throughout this book is the considerable expense involved in the proper management of a manuscript collection. Specially trained personnel, storage atmospherically controlled with extraordinary safety and security factors, costly equipment—these and many other conditions make manuscripts expensive to collect and care for, and the institution that is not willing to accept this financial burden ought not embark upon such a program. In a word, the acquisition of rare and unique material implies responsibility for proper housing and service.

In a similar vein, the administration must view manuscripts as a necessary research collection, which implies certain budgetary obligations. As one curator explains very aptly, if manuscript collecting

is to be treated as a luxury, to be indulged in when appropriations are plentiful but cut off when times are stringent, then it is better not to adopt this stepchild. If an administrator cannot make a case for his collecting in hard times (when bargains may be available) as well as in flush times, he should confine himself to the obviously "useful" materials.[42]

If the administration accepts this tenet, the curator should be able to have a definite sum or percentage of the institution's appropriation earmarked for the acquisition of manuscripts, travel, etc. This is necessary because requests to purchase current and popular materials often take precedence. Even with earmarked funds, often there will be pressure to spend these reserves if they have not been drawn upon for a time.

Although it may seem so obvious to the curator that it hardly need be stated, accountants, purchasing officers and other administrators have difficulty grasping that the manuscript curator "cannot budget his money so as to spend so much each month, because he is not buying an article that is being manufactured."[43] He must buy when something is offered for sale and take when donors are ready to give. Similarly, his expenses for travel, shipping, and other things may fluctuate greatly, depending upon circumstances over which the curator may have slight control. This, of course, poses particular problems when his institution is government-funded and appropriated funds must be spent within a fiscal year or returned, usually to the detriment of the budget for the next year.

Budget preparation is, for some curators, what has been referred to as an "add a little on, take a little off" process. A curator of this predilection comes to an intuitive decision about what additional costs will be for the coming year and he may add a certain percentage to each budget line. From past experience, he expects that the administration will pare his budget, so he perhaps pads a little. In times of expanding economy, this kind of budgeting may work, but when stringency is demanded and budget cuts must be made, the curator who has not planned his budgets in previous years will be hard pressed to know where to effect the needed economies.

The key to budgeting is planning, but one management authority contends that most people do not believe in planning. It is hard work, and it is costly, but less so, he claims, than *ad hoc* cost reduction schemes devised in tight times. Planning experts claim that, without short- and long-range plans (there is nothing in the literature about medium-range planning!), the natural inclination is to spend money to take care of an immediate need which may not mesh with a long-term objective.[44]

Systems and management authorities have devised a method of budgeting for libraries which can be easily applied to a manuscript collection. Called PPBS (Planning-Programing-Budgeting Systems), it is "not concerned with items, or objects of expenditures, or aggregations of cost categories (e.g., salaries, travels, communications) but with activities that can be measured (e.g., reference services, study space, microforms) for long-term involvement." [45] The components of such a system are identified as (1) the determination of objectives for the organization; (2) the preparation of plans for achieving the objectives, including the development of compatible cost and time schedules based on plans; (3) the authorization of the required work; (4) the monitoring and evaluation of progress toward objectives; (5) the identification of alternative corrective action as problems develop.[46]

This budgeting program has two phases, a planning and an action phase. The formula for establishing a plan includes preparing a written document which defines the *mission* of the collection, sets forth its *goals* and *continuing objectives*, and spells out the *activities* and *operations*.[47] In preparing this document, the curator must be cognizant of the relativity of his unit to the overall financial goal structure and objectives of his institution. To illustrate, the university libraries at Cornell define their mission as follows: "To provide bibliographical, physical, and intellectual access to recorded knowledge and information consistent with present and anticipated teaching and research responsibilities and social concerns of Cornell University." [48] Cornell's curator and archivist, Collection of Regional History and University Archives, who was quoted earlier in this chapter, notes that his staff "is task-oriented and therefore ancillary to the basic university purpose." His proposed realignment of administrative relationships in the unit would allow for better realization of the collection's most important functions, which he sees as "(1) educating nascent scholars in the significance of primary source material for the investigation of problems and (2) helping investigators study their problems through intellectual mastery of our resources and the intelligent presentation of that information using the techniques and concepts of modern scholarship." [49]

If properly prepared, the planning phase portion of the budget will be adequately detailed. For example, the manuscript division of the Minnesota Historical Society needed a full page—nine paragraphs of concise terms—to describe its functions. [50]

The action phase of a PPBS budget involves defining costs and tasks, assigning responsibilities, establishing timetables, and making periodic reviews. Much of this will hinge on the analysis of statistics. The weakness of this budgeting system will be the curator's dilemma, as has been mentioned earlier in this chapter. He lacks accepted standards of measurement, and where he can measure, it is quantity rather than quality that is measured.

In summing up, no matter what form the curator's budget takes, it should serve these purposes: it will allow him to make a regular periodic reconsideration of his collection's and his institution's purposes and objectives; it will facilitate his comparative evaluation of his programs and other programs of the institution; and it will provide a periodic link between working units within and outside the collection. [51]

Any discussion of funding and budgeting must conclude with reference to the curator's fiscal authority, his power to spend money. Ideally, he should have an independent budget. If he has the fiscal responsibility for the collection, if he hires the personnel, signs the payroll, and buys the manuscripts which are purchased, it is he who largely determines the character of the collection. Truly "the hand that controls the purse" applies to manuscript collections, and it is only offset in those situations where the collection's growth comes largely through gifts. Here, if the curator does the collecting and has the final authority for accepting gifts, again he guides the growth of the collection.

In some instances, the curator shares this responsibility with or is subservient to a committee on manuscripts. A typical situation might be a curator of special collections at a medium-sized eastern university. The librarian, for a variety of reasons including public relations, asks a dozen collectors, business leaders, wealthy philanthropists, etc., to serve on a manuscript committee. The committee will serve several purposes: it will act as final authority in accepting gifts; it will approve purchases and, it may be hoped, help raise funds to pay for them; it will provide leads and contacts and may even collect. Such a committee may also be a screening committee, acting on researchers' requests to use material or to have photocopies prepared.

The rewards and the hazards of a committee are about equal for the curator, and they would not be substantially different if the committee is composed, for example, only of faculty. In some instances, it will provide him a welcome means of refusing an unwanted gift. A committee's restrictions on use or photocopying seem more acceptable to the researcher than those of an individual curator. But a committee that is other than advisory may be difficult to channel, and individual members may expect special privileges. Committees can also be a real block to the fast, decisive action that is sometimes necessary to acquire a collection.

Ideally, the curator should seek a committee relationship that will allow him to call on the committee when needed as a buffer, but otherwise leave him free to use his authority. Still, while many curators would find it demoralizing if their judgments had to be approved by a committee, others adjust to the situation and find other ways of exercising their professional prerogatives.[52]

Physical Plant

Although concern with the physical plant is a phase of development and planning, for most curators it is not a day-to-day function of administration and may seem out of place discussed here. Some, too, may feel that within the section on planning of buildings, fire protection systems have been given disproportionate space. Adequate quarters and their protection from fire are stressed here because they are areas of administration which are neglected in many institutions.

As an administrator, the average curator is a very adaptive animal, and this is most apparent perhaps in his response to his immediate environment, his physical plant. A tour of the country's manuscript collections, even an abbreviated one, will amply demonstrate this. A prime example of this adaptiveness is the many times the curator must "make do" with cast-off library shelving which is often less than adequate and somewhat dangerous.

Many curators have learned also to adapt to some of the least desirable space assignments in institutional buildings. The general philosophy of locating services with high frequency use as close as possible to ground floors has resulted in many manuscript collections being housed in basement areas or in the upper reaches of a building. As one writer has observed, ideal space is difficult to obtain in a central building where "there is strong competition from other library functions." [53]

Attempting to cope with his quarters can be one of the curator's most frustrating problems, for in most cases he will be powerless to make significant changes. Few curators will be involved in a major building renovation and fewer still will be participants in the planning or construction of a new facility. Those who are will find disappointingly little in the literature to guide them. For example, the definitive work in the library field, Keyes Metcalf's *Planning Academic and Research Library Buildings,* devotes but two short paragraphs to manuscripts and a bare half-page to archives and manuscripts combined. Metcalf does hint at what is perhaps one of the major planning problems: estimating the growth of archives and manuscript collections. As he notes, the bulk of this kind of material is "frightening"; during his eighteen years at Harvard as librarian, the accumulated archives occupied space which could have housed 350,000 average-sized books.[54] Another study of special collections in university libraries offers only general hints about growth planning. The Lilly Library was built to allow it to double its size and the Beinecke Library allows for three-fold growth. Planning to accommodate a ten-year growth seems about average for the libraries surveyed. The University of Chicago estimated that its special collections division of the Regenstein Library, which opened in 1970, had space for twenty-five years' growth when it opened, but this seems optimistic when it is remembered that the Houghton added space to double its holdings seven years after the original library building was completed.[55]

The literature offers only general assistance in planning the allocation and arrangement of space. In general, curators are advised to separate reading rooms from staff and exhibit space to insure optimum study conditions. Stack areas are to be designed for easy access by the staff and the exclusion of the public. For special collections reading rooms, which would accommodate manuscript researchers, thirty-five to forty square feet per reader is considered adequate, and the Lilly Library, for example, provides space for twenty-eight readers. A survey of European archives in the late 1960s indicates that the average search room accommodates twenty persons and encompasses 1,200 to 2,000 square feet of space. Exhibit space seems to be assigned in about equal proportion to reading-room area. Incredibly, *not a sentence, not a phrase, not a single word* appears in the special or research library literature about processing or work space, and only occasional passing reference is made in archival works. One work devoted to college libraries estimates that cataloging and order departments need a minimum of 100 square feet of space per staff member, above and beyond closet, toilet, and utility accommodations.[56] Authorities on archives buildings estimate that the space ratio in a library is likely to be 80/20, stacks to administrative facilities, and 60/40 for an archives, but this differential still may not be sufficient.[57] These statistics are not so useful as they might be, since the curator is offered little guidance about how administrative space is allotted. The one overriding fact that becomes apparent in any general examination of manuscript collections is the very inadequate space provisions which have been made for the processing. In nooks and crannies in the stacks, in hallways and aisles, behind a stack of empty Hollinger cartons, in a corner of the reading room—staff members can be found almost anywhere

Fig. 5. A view of a student carrel in the manuscript processing section, State Historical Society of Wisconsin. (Courtesy State Historical Society of Wisconsin)

Fig. 6. A view of two staff carrels in the manuscript processing section, State Historical Society of Wisconsin. (Courtesy State Historical Society of Wisconsin)

trying to arrange and describe manuscripts. Most of these areas lack sufficient work-shelf or table space, the light is often bad, and they are generally inaccessible to reference collections. It is a credit to the people who work under these conditions that so much has been accomplished, but it would be difficult to describe a more wasteful and inefficient utilization of space and personnel.

Ideally, all processing should be centralized so that processors have easy access to the inventories, shelf list, card catalog, and other bibliographic controls. If possible, the processing section ought to have its own reference works shelved in the immediate area. If this is not feasible, thought should be given to making the trips to such reference works as the *Dictionary of American Biography* and *Who's Who* as short as possible. The workroom can be subdivided by temporary shelving, tables, and perhaps occasional free-standing partitions, into individual working areas for each staff member. In one type of arrangement a work "room" can be created by butting two sorting tables together to form an **L** and doing the same with two sections of shelving in an upside-down **⅂** to close the rectangular space. There are many ways of arranging space for processing, but two of the best examples can be seen in the manuscripts and archives divisions of either the Wisconsin State Historical Society or Yale University.

In planning a renovation or a new building, an architect advised curators at a recent meeting to provide their architect with work-flow information and function descriptions to assist him in the preparation of their sketch plans. He should be told what duties are performed in an area, how much space is needed, and the relationship between work spaces. If the architect understands the unique nature of manuscripts and their arrangement and care, he has a better chance of translating the special needs of a repository into a good set of sketch plans. These plans, which are tentative and precede the working or construction drawings, should be studied carefully by the curator for possible modification. The more work he can do with the function descriptions and sketch plans, the less trouble he will have with the structure when it is completed. As one authority puts it, "paper is patient." [58]

The arrangement of space will affect the curator's day-to-day administration of the collection materially, and its consideration deserves his concentrated study in the planning and blueprint stage of a new or renovated building. But while space management is crucial, it palls beside the obligation of the curator to plan for proper safety for his staff and the collection. Of the disasters that can strike, the most common and the most destructive is fire. Fearsome though fire is, because it is a common danger, a great body of knowledge has developed about its prevention and protection.

The National Fire Protection Association sells a long list of publications which are of great value to the curator in his planning. Obviously, to achieve a fire-safe building in any new construction or renovation, the curator must rely ultimately on the knowledge of his architect, but the NFPA does offer some simple guidelines. In general, the building ought to comply with requirements for three-hour fire-resistive construction, and records-storage areas in excess of 40,000 square feet should be separated by fire walls. The air-handling system should be designed so that it can be manually converted to outside air and used for smoke removal. All electrical control boxes and light switches should be in the building entranceway and no transformer should be allowed in the stack area. Light fixtures, of all-metal construction, ought not to be more than nine inches wide and should have thermally protected ballasts. Records should not be stored closer to any light fixture than twelve inches. Stacks running perpendicular to the wall should not deadend but should be at least eighteen inches from the wall, and the minimum safe aisle width is thirty inches (average width in most repositories is twenty-eight to thirty inches). Stairwells should be enclosed, with concrete floors between levels, and stacks should be free-standing shelves. Compact or mobile shelving, which is used in 17 percent of the archives in Europe, is perhaps less of a necessary expense in this country, except in those institutions where space is at a premium or expansion impossible.[59]

The fire-detection and extinguishing system the curator needs depends upon the manuscript collection being protected and the physical structure in which it is housed. Detection devices include some that respond to the heat generated by a fire and are of two general types: those that activate the extinguishing system at a fixed temperature and others that react to the "rate of rise" in temperature. In recent years, other detection equipment, known as "early-warning detectors," have been marketed. They respond either to visible smoke or to the invisible products of combustion. Either type can detect a fire within seconds, whereas the heat-activated systems allow the fire to reach more substantial proportions before activating.[60]

Automatic sprinkler extinguishing systems incorporate heat-detection devices in the individual sprinkler heads. In the "pre-action" systems, the pipes are dry until a control valve opens when the heat detectors sense a fire. Experts contend these systems can be adjusted to confine sprinkling to the immediate area of the fire and that it is the cheapest and most reliable method of fire protection. If manuscripts are housed in stapled, die-cut cartons (as opposed to glued containers) the experts claim there will be little water damage and that sprinklers will control or extinguish most fires before they reach major size.[61]

Many curators, archivists, and librarians continue to fear the effects of water in some ways more than fire. At the Lilly Library, all vertical water lines are of copper and are enclosed in concrete viaducts, which, in the event of a leak, carry the water to a basement drain; and at the Houghton, troughs were constructed under each pipe. At Hofstra University, after leaks occurred in the special collections reading room from the open patio on the floor above, the librarian recommended that all areas housing rare materials ought to be at least one floor level below any roof level.[62]

The curator of the large twentieth-century collection might do well to look beyond his profession's long-standing fear of water damage. With newly developed techniques, most water-damaged manuscripts can be restored; a burned record is irretrievable, and we have

Fig. 7. The Military Personnel Records Center, St. Louis, showing collapsed shelves and debris after the fire, July 12, 1973. (Courtesy National Archives and Records Service)

no effective treatment for charred paper. Still, for those curators to whom the thought of even limited water damage is anathema, the answer to fire protection may be in one of the more recently developed extinguishing systems which flood an area with either carbon dioxide, high-expansion foam, or a halogenated agent. Each system has its strengths and weaknesses; all would be much more expensive than a sprinkler system.

Carbon dioxide extinguishes a fire by denying it oxygen, and its use in protecting a manuscript collection from fire, obviously, could be very dangerous to personnel. The system installed in England at the newly constructed Essex Record Office, for example, when activated by a smoke-detection device, floods "the strong room with carbon dioxide gas within two minutes." In a small area, there might be no problem of staff members being trapped by the gas; but in some institutions, as, for example, the Beinecke Library, the system is activated manually from a control board only after warning has been given.[63]

High-expansion foam systems, in which each tiny bubble carries a small amount of water, are very effective at smothering fires and the degree of water damage is much less than from a sprinkler system. However, because the foam expands at such a rapid rate, large vents are needed for escaping air, which makes the use of the systems very difficult in windowless structures or basements where so many manuscript collections are housed.[64]

Halon 1301 (bromotrifluoromethone), a liquified gas under pressure which vaporizes when released in the air, is a very effective fire-extinguishing agent. Scientists are uncertain about how it works, but they theorize that it breaks the chain reaction of the fire. It is particularly effective in putting out gas explosions, flammable liquids, and electrical fires, but is less so against burning wood and paper. It stops the oxidation reaction immediately, but unless the inert atmosphere is retained around the charred area until it can cool, the fire will rekindle. Using Halon 1301 as an extinguishing agent therefore requires several minutes' "soaking time," depending upon the concentration released in the fire area. In some situations, maintaining this concentration might be difficult.[65]

One of the disadvantages of Halon 1301 is that it is expensive. For example, in late 1972 the Harvard Medical School was attempting to raise $400,000 to install the system in the Countway Library. Its principal advantages are that, in concentrations strong enough to extinguish a fire, it is only mildly toxic. It is, of course, dry, and preliminary tests indicate that it is not harmful to paper, leather, or book cloth.[66]

As has been noted early in this chapter, planning and development of the physical plant, especially a fire-control system, is not one of the everyday administrative duties of the average curator, some of which have been discussed here: organization, training, personnel management, soliciting funds, and budgeting. It was also noted above that the curator's fiscal authority, which is central to any discussion of administration, is often intertwined with the authority to collect. Collecting manuscripts, of course, is what gives meaning to administration, and it is to the process of collecting, the ethics and mechanics of acquisitions, to which we now turn.

SELECTED READINGS

In their short chapter "Administering the Library," Ruth B. Bordin and Robert M. Warner in *The Modern Manuscript Library,* give a concise overview of manuscript-collection administration. Frank B. Evans, compiler, *The Administration of Modern Archives: A Select Bibliographic Guide,* is very comprehensive but still reveals the lack of professional literature in most phases of administration, particularly the areas of funding and budgeting.

William T. Alderson's leaflet "Securing Grant Support: Effective Planning and Preparation" is a good presentation of a complex field. The Herbert Finch article "Administrative Relationships in a Large Manuscript Repository" is the most provocative article available on structure and personnel use. Writings on training are largely confined to descriptions of programs available (the Society of American Archivists directory is the best guide here).

This chapter will provide only scattered hints helpful to the curator faced with a building or renovation project, but he will find little additional help in the two best sources available: Keyes D. Metcalf, *Planning Academic and Research Library Buildings,* and Victor Gondos, Jr., editor, *Reader for Archives and Records Center Buildings.*

III

Acquisitions: The Mechanics and Ethics

Authority to Collect

THE authority to collect manuscripts does not rest always with the curator. In some colleges and universities, manuscript collections are sought out and accepted by faculty. In historical agencies, the directors often accept or reject collections without consulting the curators. In other institutions, as has been previously noted, the final authority rests with a committee or, more often, with a board of directors. Each of these situations has its strengths and weaknesses; but where they exist, the curator lacks control over his collection. Each deserves to be studied.

Traditionally, the manuscript-collecting agency on college and university campuses was the library and, in more recent years, the university archives. However, on some campuses, strong and/or aggressive academic departments have begun collecting manuscripts. In some instances, this practice appears to have grown out of a need for research materials which was not being met by the library. One professor, for example, speaks of " 'the refusal of a perverse librarian to provide an adequate flow of manuscript accessions to support a respectable program of conventional graduate research.' "[1] In other instances, department collecting may reflect something as simple as the empire-building of one faculty member. On some campuses, the academic departments collect the manuscripts, but the library provides the housing and administration of the material. In other instances,

56

academic departments have developed and administered research collections.

The theory behind collecting by academic specialists seems a most valid one; who, for example, is more competent than a chemist to judge the importance of the contribution that another chemist has made to his field? Thus, on one campus, a scientific collection springs up under the aegis of the department of chemistry; on another, the English department has brought forth a literary collection; and on yet a third, the department of history has assembled a collection of local history manuscripts. However, if the logic behind this kind of collecting is followed to its end, there will be several unrelated and often competitive research centers on a campus, with unnecessary duplication in facilities and staff. And while no curator can be an expert in all academic disciplines, by the same token he is best suited to make judgments relating to appraisal, processing, preservation, bibliographic control, and other phases of manuscript administration. When the need arises he can, and often does, consult with the faculty for their subject expertise.

Unsupervised collecting almost inevitably involves the curator in administrative difficulties. For example, the faculty member or other collector often makes promises to the donor which are impossible for the curator to fulfill—a promise to provide a microfilm copy to the donor when (1) there are no funds budgeted for microfilm, (2) the camera is scheduled for the next eight months, (3) the material cannot be prepared for filming without intensive and expensive preparation—the research value of the collection may be far less than the cost of microfilming—and (4) the donor has no means of using or interest in a microfilm copy.

Another common fault of faculty collecting is that all too often unnecessary donor restrictions, difficult or impossible to administer honestly, are agreed upon, and, in some cases, suggested by the faculty collector. One form of this is the restriction of the material to the exclusive use of the professor, who may even be assigned the literary rights to the papers. Such restrictions may be ethically dubious and most certainly are a nightmare for the curator to administer.

Realistically, the curator may be faced with a collecting situation he cannot control and cannot change, but, if possible, he should insist upon sharing the collecting responsibility and upon the right to veto individual acquisitions and the conditions or restrictions under which they are acquired. This would be desirable even if the manuscript collection is administered by the library rather than an academic department, because librarians—those in administration as well as those who are subject-area specialists—may pose exactly the same problems for the curator as the faculty collector.

One problem area not usually faced by the campus curator, but often encountered by his counterpart at the historical society, is the board of trustees which establishes itself as the final authority for collecting. In some instances, this may be a procedure as routine as approving the accessions report of the curator at the annual meeting, or, upon recommendation of the director, accepting individual collections by a perfunctory vote. The system operates because the board, composed as it is of public-spirited persons, usually professionals in their own field, recognizes the competence of the curator, a professional in his own right, and accepts his judgments. On the other hand, a board may be political in its composition, and its acceptance of a manuscript collection may be based upon expediency rather than upon historical or literary value.

A good example of the kind of situation the curator could find himself involved in has been noted by an authority who tells of an unidentified institution which made a single copy of letters in the possession of a person who did not hold the literary copyright. When the heirs of the letter-writer ("a famous, deceased person") heard of the copies, they served notice on the institution that showing the letters to researchers would constitute publication in violation of the common law, and they threatened to sue. On advice of counsel, the institution refused to give or sell the manuscript copies to the heirs. "At the later date, however, the President of the Board of Trustees of the institution ordered that the copies be turned over to the complainants, reversing the decision of the library's legal adviser, thus removing important historical material from possible use by scholars." [2]

Expediency can rear its head in any collecting agency, and the curator must learn to accept it or do battle, whichever is his nature. The president of the state university sends a note to the curator suggesting that a certain legislator's papers be accepted. A wealthy donor offers the papers of an author who is not in the institution's field of collecting. Does the curator's commitment end with following instructions of his superiors or the contractual obligations with his donors, or does he have an obligation to scholarship and his profession? These are some of the imponderables of the curator's existence, and his responses may well be shaped by his own nature or by the extent of his authority within his institution.

As can be seen, questions about the authority to collect can involve ethical considerations. These and similar considerations, which color many of the activities connected with acquisitions, will be discussed at the conclusion of this chapter; but to understand what is involved, one needs background knowledge of the kinds of manuscripts which have been collected.

Types of Collecting

An axiom of history is that the victors write the history (and collect the manuscripts). Perhaps this is not as true today as it was twenty years ago; manuscripts relating to the disinherited and the vanquished are now beginning to be collected. There are those who would say that this is not a new trend—that, for example, the Confederate South has always had its fair share of documentation, or that the right- and left-wing extremists (certainly more of the latter than the former) have been avidly collected. Splinter or minority political party papers have been collected for years, and avante-garde literature of any period seems to find its way to repositories.

While all this is true, until the last decade it was a rare midwestern state historical society collection that did not hold a preponderance of the papers of Republican politicians. Historical societies, like other groups in society, reflect the dominant forces in the community at large, and especially the economic and political backgrounds of their boards of trustees. Today it would be difficult to name an art, profession, calling, or trade that is not documented in some institution; but still the papers of politicians and the military, even though both are held in disfavor by many, continue to hold favored positions in the collectors' stakes.

A corollary of this kind of collecting is the "prestige collecting" still much in vogue today. The " 'big name' or 'important personage' syndrome," as one curator called it, seems to permeate all areas of collecting. The papers of the successful scientist, the enterprising entrepreneur, and the accepted artist are all in demand. Perhaps repositories specializing in literature have been particularly prone to this type of collecting.

There are some questions being asked today about prestige collecting. The time, money, and effort spent to acquire the "working papers" of the literary lion's latest novel may provide research material for a textual scholar or two and perhaps a critic and a biographer. A similar or probably smaller amount of the curator's resources expended in acquiring the complete correspondence files of five involved citizens in any profession might provide the raw material for numerous dissertations in history. Some curators are questioning whether collecting decisions should be geared to the needs and uses of academia exclusively. Other queries are being made about how to preserve an awareness of people who do not leave written records. What will be the documentation of family history and guerrilla history or of the street people and the man-in-the-street? [3]

The New Left could become the latest fad in collecting. Fads, which are generally thought to be aberrations of the private collector, manifest themselves in institutional collecting, too. Labor history and business history are two fields that went through the faddist stage in the last three decades, although the roots of each go back much earlier. For example, after the turn of the twentieth century, European business, starting in Germany, began to develop an appreciation of its records. In 1906, the Rhenish Westfälische Wirtschaftsarchiv was established to serve as a depository for the archives of several large German firms. The German approach to business history was transmitted to the United States by such pioneers of economic history as Richard Ely, Edwin F. Gay, and N. S. B. Gras. In 1916, Gras became the first occupant of the Straus Professorship of Business History in the Graduate School of Business Administration at Harvard. That same year saw the business school library begin a systematic collecting program which was restricted largely to the bulky business records of defunct manufacturing companies of New England. The Baker Library was built a decade later to house the collection, and in time the movement to acquire business records swept the country's repositories. However, one authority has suggested that the most potent force contributing to the preservation of contemporary corporate records was not the organized pressure of the archivists and historians, not inertia nor managerial enlightenment, but the authority and omnipresent threat of the Internal Revenue Service. [4]

Most labor and business history being collected today is solidly based, but other fads have taken their place. At the present time, conservation and ecology are "in" collecting areas, and black history, in the forefront for the past decade, probably has been replaced in favor by Indian history, Chicano history, or women's lib. This is not to say that these subjects are not legitimate fields of collecting. Of course they are, but they were equally legitimate fifty years ago; yet it is only in recent years that collecting in these fields has become popular.

There are those who feel that the hallmark of a good curator is to be able to forecast the fads or at least to be in the forefront of each new collecting movement. Certainly the curator's annual report to the administration is much more impressive if the manuscripts he is collecting are fashionable or reflect the interests of new history. This type of collecting is equally impressive if the curator is seeking foundation support or a government grant. In recent years, outside funding of this nature has been responsible for the growth of a number of "instant" research centers.

A good curator should be able to envision his collection in terms other than popular trends. There are generally accepted procedures for accomplishing this, as, for example, collecting within predetermined fields and building to strengths in the collection. These and other sensible solutions will be discussed forthwith, but there is something to be said, too, for suggesting that a curator can best serve his institution by collecting what he knows best and likes. If he can do this within the guidelines already established, so much the better; the quality of the manuscripts will be superior to those collected by the uninformed and disinterested. A collection assembled by a partisan will be uneven, but neither the administration nor the curator should be overly concerned so long as they both recognize the curator's bias. It helps, too, if a collection can be recognized for what it is, a long-lived organism. Successive curators will have other biases, other collecting fads will appear, and in time the result will be a balanced collection. The current curator's mistakes may be the next generation's treasures, and the coveted collecting plums of today may be forgotten fruit of tomorrow.

Collecting Fields

How the majority of curators envision their collections may be more or less academic; they may be employed by institutions with very well-defined collecting fields. But, occasionally, established institutions launch into new programs, and new collecting agencies are constantly entering the field. Thus, curators need to give some thought to collecting areas, how they come into being, and what purpose they serve.

The concept of a collecting field in manuscripts is a relatively modern one. It is based upon the intellectual concept that a scholar can best study like or related materials together and upon the economic premise that a curator who is a specialist rather than a generalist can best conserve the instituion's resources of talent and money. A curator of a university manuscript collection explains: "The value of one collection is greatly enhanced by the addition of a related collection. A valid piece of research is rarely based on a single collection, no matter how voluminous, so that the ability of a library to support research of quality depends on the acquisition of related collections in as many areas as possible." [5]

The curator's view of the purpose of a collecting field may reflect his institution's or his own philosophical bent. One curator may see defining a collecting field as "staking a claim" to a geographical, chronological, or topical area; another may view it as focusing or sharpening the institution's resources for acquisitions; and a third may look upon the policy as setting boundaries and limiting his efforts.

As noted in an earlier chapter, historical societies were the country's principal repositories of manuscripts through the early twentieth century. Each was identified with an easily defined political subdivision—a city, county, or state. The boundaries of their political subdivision were the boundaries of their collecting fields. In a sense, however, this definition is a misnomer, because it denotes planned activity, whereas the majority of the historical societies were passive recipients of historical materials. The passive nature of manuscript collecting changed with the end of World War II and the emergence of two new types of collecting agencies: colleges and universities, where collecting usually centered in the university archives or special collections; and the presidential libraries system of the National Archives. The presidential libraries were new collecting agencies. In a strict sense, the colleges and universities were not, but their increase in numbers, scope, and activity made them a fresh force in the field. What occurred on the campuses was epitomized in the Harvard experience. As late as 1929, the official university library policy was stated as one which "steadily avoided becoming an archival institution," and the curator of manuscripts reported in 1952 that until recent times modern papers, personal correspondence, and other similar manuscripts were turned away.[6]

In the 1950s, conflicting and overlapping collecting fields produced a burst of competitive collecting. State historical societies no longer confined themselves to their state boundaries, regional collections sought manuscripts far beyond their regional boundaries, and colleges intent upon becoming universities, and universities in name which hoped to become universities in fact began to build manuscript and other research collections.

Approaches to Collecting

This post-World War II activity was planned in advance by some institutions, with the curators and the administration, through a series of conferences, determining a field of scholarship where original source material was needed for research and then setting about systematically to collect the manuscripts in that field. But in general, annual reports to the contrary, few collecting programs start by what could be called the "book" approach, and those that do, unless they are exceptionally well managed, are frequently stalled or sidetracked. More often, collecting fields develop out of the acquisition of one key collection which comes to the institution as a fortuitous accident. Of course, this is where the imagination and the skill of the curator come to the fore. If he sees the potential of the key collection, if he can publicize it and can utilize it properly, he can begin to apply the "like-attracts-like" and "snowball" theories of collecting.

As an example of the place of the fortuitous accident in collecting, the curator of a historical agency might discover that the wife of a prominent attorney on the agency's board of directors is the daughter of an internationally known ballet choreographer, Dancelotsky, and that she wants her deceased father's papers to come to the historical society. This is the fortuitous accident. The curator is now faced with three alternatives: (1) he can advise the daughter that her father's papers more logically fit with an established theater collection at an eastern university; (2) he can accept the Dancelotsky papers and wait for the next fortuitous accident (many respectable collections are built in just

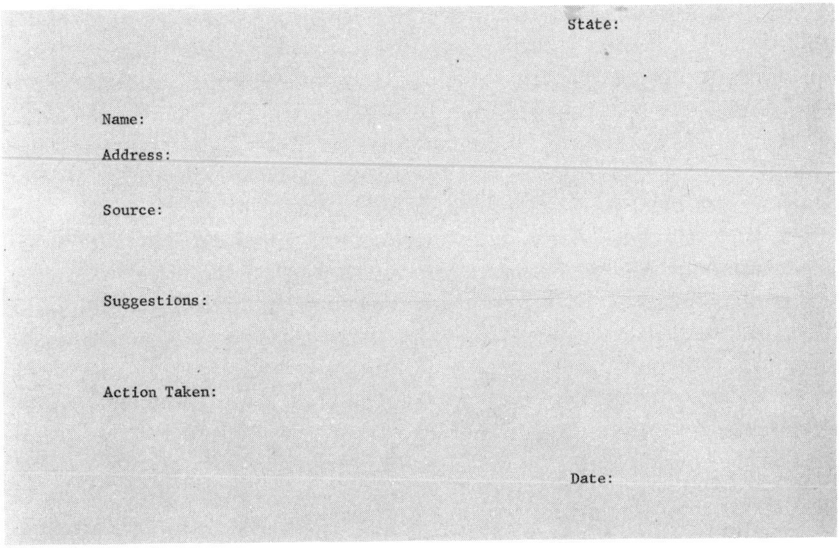

State:

Name:

Address:

Source:

Suggestions:

Action Taken:

Date:

Fig. 8. A common form for a lead card.

this random, "shot-gun," type of collecting); (3) he can launch the Transylvania Historical Society's Collection of Choreography.

All are valid courses of action, but if the curator opts for the last, the next step is building what is known as the "lead file." It is at this point that collecting, which may have been accidental and haphazard, becomes systematic.

First, of course, the curator must settle upon the form for his lead file (see figure 8 for one example), and then, since this is a collecting field new to him, he begins to read the literature. As he discovers the names of other choreographers, he checks the standard biographical guides to determine whether the subjects are living and, if they are not, he tries to trace descendants.

The second source of leads is the donor; Dancelotsky's daughter probably knows the whereabouts of some of her father's co-workers and contemporaries. Leads come, as one curator suggests, by "patient planning and plodding routine." [7] Telephone calls, field trips, and correspondence are all sources. If, by this time, the processing has begun on the choreographer's papers, the curator also alerts the processor to watch for possible leads. If all goes according to form, internal evidence revealed in the papers should produce the most good leads.

The Dancelotsky correspondence will probably provide the obvious leads to other choreographers, dancers, and producers, but the bonuses are the unexpected: the letters from a college chum, or from a dance aficionado, or from a businessman-investor who became a friend—all of these are potential sources of fine collections of Dancelotsky letters. Finally, once the choreographer's papers are processed, researchers who use the papers will often be fertile sources of leads.

Dancelotsky's reputation as a choreographer will determine the curator's stance toward the college chum and the businessman. If the curator thinks Dancelotsky is important enough, he may ask the two men to give him the letters from their friend. In doing so, the curator violates one of his profession's cardinal rules—that is, that a man's papers have unity and integrity which should not be destroyed—but he justifies it on the grounds that the papers of the two men are not collectable entities.

In this instance, the curator reasons that the papers of neither the college chum nor the businessman warrant preservation and that only Dancelotsky's letters will be of interest to researchers. If, on the other hand, he knows that the businessman's papers would be welcomed by a neighboring university, he then has an ethical problem, the best solution to which probably would be to alert the university curator to the collection and hope that he will return the professional courtesy by providing Transylvania copies of the Dancelotsky letters.

The other potential sources pose slightly different problems for the curator. Obviously, he will seek the papers of the other choreographers whose names appear in his lead file. Those who look up to Dancelotsky professionally, as well as some colleagues of comparable status, might feel honored to have their papers housed in the same institution as his. This is an example of like-attracts-like collecting in operation. Others might feel that their work overshadows that of Dancelotsky, or that they represent an opposing system of dance. With them, the curator will need to stress the broad character of the choreography collection and the need for papers of individuals representing varying points of view. In either instance, the curator will find that the Dancelotsky papers give him an entrée to other choreographers, and once he acquires a second set of papers in the subject area, successive acquisitions become noticeably easier. The curator is practicing the "snowball" theory of collecting.

Probably the curator will seek the papers of the dancers and producers also; he will not have much difficulty justifying their relevance in a collecting field of choreography. The papers of the dance aficionado, however, represent the curator's most troublesome quandary. They should be judged peripheral; the man had an equal interest in music, which is reflected in his papers, and of the portion of the papers relating to dance, only a segment touches upon choreography. The curator cannot in good conscience ask for this segment, because he recognizes that the collection as a unit would be a desirable acquisition by any agency collecting in the arts area generally. He can be idealistic and refer the papers to such a collection, but more often he is caught in what can be called "spiral collecting." These papers are borderline, but the next group may be even less germane. Once he has embarked on the spiral syndrome, it is easier and easier to see relationships between collections. For a time he fights the dizzying spiral, but eventually he resolves the problem by reorienting the collecting policies. The Transylvania Historical Society Collection of Choreography becomes first the Dance Collection, then the Fine Arts Collection!

Mechanics of Collecting

As the curator begins to follow up on the leads he has created, he will need another type of file, the collection file. Here, arranged by collection title, he will keep copies of his correspondence and memorandums of his telephone conversations with donors, a copy of the field reports—anything relating to the negotiations for a group of papers. If the papers are purchased, copies of purchase orders or invoices might be filed here. Here, too, might be included a copy of the gift agreement and a list of any restrictions upon access or other special conditions of the gift.

In a small operation, the curator will have to do his own field work, but if he does have a field man or field staff, the key to the growth of the collection rests on their negotiations with possible donors. The field man who does not know at the outset will soon realize that many potential donors have very little understanding of the needs of scholarship. The tendency, he will find all too often, is to keep the worthless and to discard the gems. ("Oh, the letters? I burned them. I thought you'd be interested in these old deeds and newspaper clippings.") Not only must the field man build a bridge of understanding, but often he must overcome some very natural suspicions on the part of people who, he hopes, will become donors— that is, the family that fears a scandal and wants to protect its ancestors; lawyers, doctors, and social workers who do not want to release their files if it means risking an invasion-of-privacy lawsuit; businessmen who want to protect their trade secrets; and union officials who are sensitive about newsmen snooping in the pension-fund accounts.[8]

A guide to good field-work practices might read like a Dale Carnegie self-improvement tract, with about equal added portions of medical text describing the correct bedside manner and a social worker's manual for case work. In some senses, a successful field man cannot be trained; a list of his desirable personal characteristics would include the diligence necessary to do careful background research and the ability to listen with patience and intelligence. But while every good field man does his "homework," he cannot be expected to be knowledgeable in all fields, and if necessary it is far better for him to admit ignorance than to try to bluff, or worse, lie. Most donors appreciate having the opportunity to share their knowledge of a set of papers and the events they represent.

One writer says that a person cannot succeed in field work unless he "can be urbane and reasonably sophisticated when he is dealing with urbane and sophisticated owners of manuscripts, and simple and respectful when he is dealing with old ladies; unless he can work up an instant enthusiasm about a retired colonel's experiences at Gallipoli, or a middle-aged businessman's hatred of bureaucratic government. . . . He must be all things to all kinds of people—and he never knows what kind he will have to deal with next." [9] (The scholar who collects manuscripts for his own research is referred to here; it remains for the curator or archivist with training in psychology to write a professional paper on the role-playing aspects of field work.)

There are curators who find the "all things to all men" approach to field work "a ploy to the sophisticated and an insult to the naive." Lucile Kane, for example, stresses that it is important that the curator have an "empathetic relationship to donors as people and recognize their critical role in building the institution's collection." She feels that the curator needs to have respect for the problems that giving manuscripts may pose for a donor, but while empathetic and respectful, a curator should maintain a reserve, not only from the donor's prejudices, but from his family quarrels (which often intrude into negotiations), and from chitchat or gossip about one's contemporaries. [10]

Some curators like to take a portable tape recorder with them on field trips. The tapes will help assure that gift conditions or access restrictions are understood by both parties and will enable the curator to secure information from the donor which will be of great use in preparing the accession record and in processing the papers. Other curators find the use of the tape recorder awkward and unnecessary. In any event, they should prepare a report on the negotiations for the collection file. They should take an object lesson from their mentor, Peter Force, the nation's first great manuscript collector. As a historian once noted, because Force failed to write "a few timely words, a mere reference, or a jotting or two of explanation . . . the great collection upon which his energy was bestowed must stand to-day too often questionable and uncertain." [11]

All negotiations point toward two conditions: transfer of the papers (that is, the physical property) and transfer of the rights of ownership to the collecting agency. Although the transactions may be nearly concurrent, each is a separate and distinct operation and must be described individually.

If feasible, a representative of the collecting agency should be present when any collection larger than a single file drawer is prepared for shipping. Ideally, whenever possible, he should box, load, and deliver the collection to the agency. This may not always be expedient, but however the packing and shipping is handled, cartons should be numbered (in more than one place) and as detailed a packing list as is practical should be prepared. Careless packing, besides exposing the material to damage en route, can destroy inherent order in files, which, if not impossible to restore, is, at the very least, time-consuming and expensive.

Methods of shipping vary according to personal preference and experience. With a heavy cardboard insert, a handful of letters can be sent in a manila envelope by certified or registered mail. In most sections of the country, the private parcel services are dependable and fast for small shipments. One to five packing boxes, weighing under approximately 500 pounds, can usually best be sent by railway express. For any medium or small shipment which needs special handling and a high rate of insurance, air express is the best but most expensive means of transportation.

Larger collections are shipped either by freight handlers or moving companies. Moving companies ship papers at furniture rates, which are expensive; but insurance above and beyond the usual fifty cents per pound offered by movers on a standard shipment can be obtained at about five dollars per thousand dollars of insured value. Freight shipments are much cheaper, but insurance may be a problem unless the collecting agency carries a floater policy on all shipments. Depending upon the distance, a freight shipment may be handled more en route than a moving-company shipment. It may be loaded and unloaded from truck to truck as it is transshipped from one freight depot to another. Boxes loaded on a moving van usually will be delivered by the same truck. It is difficult to load the van in reverse order, however, and when there is more than one shipment in a large van, some shipments have to be unloaded en route. Moving companies demand cash or a certified check upon delivery (they will not unload without it), and this can pose problems for an agency whose bills are paid from a distant central accounting office.

Although much of what he ships will not be affected, the curator should bear in mind, in preparing shipments, that temperatures in the cargo hold of a high-flying aircraft get as low as minus 40° F. and that the interior of a motor van left in the sun may rise to 120° F.[12]

Although arranging for the shipment of a large collection is no simple task, it pales compared to the transfer of the rights of ownership. There is a great variety of practice among collecting institutions regarding the gift agreement, the standard means employed in conveying the property rights in a set of papers. Some institutions take the stance that the less said about the matter, the better. They do not inquire whether the donor possesses the legal right to make a gift (often the donor does not), and a simple letter of acknowledgement of receipt from the curator serves in lieu of a gift agreement. The reasoning of the curators representing these institutions is that any discussion about property right, common-law literary copyrights, and so-called "legal title" confuses most donors (see chapter 8). These same curators say that a formal legal gift agreement is likely to have one of two effects on the potential donor: scare him off completely, or make him feel that he must have an attorney approve the agreement. Other curators have standard gift-agreement forms, while still others prefer to have their agency's legal counsel draw up a contract to fit each individual gift. The critics of either of the more formal systems claim that it is difficult, if not next to impossible, to draw an "airtight" deed of gift for a set of papers—one that would stand in court. Their contention is that an exchange of letters defining the terms of the gift, or even proof that the donor made a tax deduction for his gift, would probably carry as much weight in court as an agreement. The question is largely academic; rather than risk the attendant bad publicity that might accompany a lawsuit, most institutions would prefer to relinquish possession of a collection. When they have chosen to resist, the issue has hinged on the "intent to give."

Most of the discussion above is based on experiences of institutions whose collections were built through gifts. Today, more and more "donor" relations involve purchase agreements or combination gift-purchase arrangements. Many possessors of manuscripts are becoming aware of their market value, and if they cannot sell to institutions, they seek out manuscript dealers.

Many people deplore the merchandising of manuscripts. For several years, now, some curators have acted as if the trade would die out if they ignored it. They have taken great solace in telling stories like the one about the heirs who gave their papers to an institution rather than sell them to a private collector because "they believed freedom of access to the manuscripts by scholars was really important." [13] They have assured one another of the unmercenary character of people who have traditionally donated family papers to their collections and have claimed that the donors would be "incensed with the idea of 'selling granddaddy.' " But times have changed. As one curator has reported, when his "well-heeled competition in the same city offered fifteen thousand dollars for granddaddy's papers . . . that was a different matter." [14]

The "well-heeled" institutions were blamed by many for "inflating the market" by bidding against one another, while the repositories that depended upon donated manuscripts were "sorely disadvantaged." [15] Selling manuscripts to institutions, as indicated earlier in this book, has a long history in this country. It is true that many institutions will continue, by assiduous field work, to receive donated manuscripts. They must, however, accept the fact that unless they budget money for manuscript purchases, they will lose certain material important to their collections.

Manuscripts will continue to be traded in the marketplace. Therefore it behooves the curator, who once needed to know only the research values of manuscripts, to become well informed about prices. He can acquire this knowledge by studying *American Book Prices Current,* which, although it is never up to date, does contain a section on prices realized at auctions for manuscripts during a given year. The Canadians publish a similar volume, but both must be used with caution. Condition and content of the item, always important factors in price, are not given, nor is there mention of the intangible psychological factors which may influence prices at any given sale. Furthermore, it should be remembered that, although auction prices cannot be thought of as wholesale prices, generally they will be less than what a dealer would list in a catalog. There are always a good number of private buyers or collectors at an auction, but the majority of purchasers are dealers. Although it is recognized that the dealer frequently is bidding as agent for an individual or institutional collector, the many items he buys for his own stock will be marked up before they are quoted by letter or telephone to a potential buyer. Traditionally, a markup of between 40 and 60 percent has been common on manuscripts that dealers bought for their stock. In recent years, the exception has been those items purchased at auction, particularly manuscripts for which there was a strong market, as, for example, Washington and Lincoln letters, whose auction prices have nearly equalled catalog values.

Catalogs are another source of price information on manuscripts. Because they note content and condition, catalogs are much more reliable guides. But here, too, caution must be used. Is the catalog one from a seasoned dealer, or one new to the field—naive, anxious, prone to error? Is the dealer a specialist or a general dealer? Is the manuscript offered for sale in his area of specialty or completely out of his field? [16]

The curator must remember, too, that prices quoted to him or appearing in catalogs are on merchandise offered for sale. The assumption that the manuscript is sold for the asking price is not always true. This is not to imply that dealers will haggle over their published prices or offer discounts. Quite to the contrary, most reputable dealers consider attempts to get them to lower prices very amateurish conduct by curators. But not all the items in a catalog sell. If the curator keeps a record, he will soon discover that items offered by one dealer often appear in a subsequent catalog of a rival dealer and rarely at the same or a lower price. Dealers are probably not their own best customers (one dealer estimates that less than 20 percent of his business is with other dealers), but they offer each other business discounts and trade among themselves to an extent.[17]

A comprehensive collection of priced auction catalogs, to which the institution can subscribe, and well-organized runs of dealers' catalogs are invaluable tools for the curator. He must date the dealers' catalogs for full effectiveness and, if he has time, preparing an index is most helpful. At the Spencer Library, University of Kansas, the guard indexes in his spare time.[18]

A word about buying from catalogs. Most dealers are willing to extend credit to an institution and to send a limited number of items from their stock "on approval." What the curator does not want can be returned, provided it is returned within a reasonable period and without damage. The curator should not hold a manuscript more than twenty-four hours without the approval of the dealer. Manuscripts to be returned must be shipped in envelopes comparable in strength to that used by the dealer in the original shipment. New cardboard should be used (not the used board from the dealer's package, which may be dog-eared), and the package should be returned by the same method employed by the dealer—that is, if it came by air mail, certified, it should be returned the same way. Never send manuscripts in the commercial book bags used by some libraries for interlibrary loans.

Despite what to curators may seem an excessive markup, dealers offer many services, not the least of which is acting as intermediary between a collector and an institution. Over the years, private collectors have been great benefactors of institutions, and many fine gifts were suggested and arranged by dealers. Some dealers have played an active role in building collections, seeking out manuscripts and buying them with one institution in mind. Cynics say that the curators pay dearly for the assistance, and they may, but the truth is that they are buying expertise not available to them elsewhere.

The same is true of the curator who asks a dealer to place his bid at a manuscript auction. The dealer charges 10 percent of the purchase price for this service, which, to the uninitiated, may seem high, but the curator is buying the dealer's guarantee of authenticity. A curator often cannot attend the auctions, most of which are held in London and New York, and he must rely on the dealer to examine the lots he is interested in prior to the auction to be sure that they are authentic and have been described correctly in the catalog. Also, the auction house wants its money at the close of the sale, and the dealer is willing to wait the one to four weeks that it takes most institutions to pay their bills.

Appraisals

For appraisals, the curator often must rely most heavily upon the dealer. (Not all appraisers are dealers, but almost all of them are.) [19] Again, the curator pays dearly for the dealer's expertise; minimum charges are often $250 per day plus travel expense, and double that fee is not uncommon.[20]

Prior to January 1970, when the tax law was changed, most appraisals were made to determine the "fair market value" of a collection, so that the donor giving the papers to an institution could claim this amount as a charitable gift on his income tax return. This is but one type of appraisal. Other types of appraisals include: (1) those for insurance, usually purchased by the private collector of autographs or manuscripts; (2) those for an estate when it includes either an autograph collection or papers recognized to have property value; (3) those for a potential seller of manuscripts to establish an asking price.

Using the Dancelotsky papers as an example, the three types of appraisals can be illustrated in this way. If the papers were a declared part of the estate, as they should have been under the law, since they are real property, they should have been appraised. If the appraisal is done by a regular appraiser (the men listed as appraisers in the yellow pages of the telephone book), who is accustomed to appraising real estate or perhaps household furnishings, the value placed on the Dancelotsky papers would probably be minimal. (An estate containing a collection of autographs or clipped signatures of famous people is likely to be overvalued by the same appraiser.) The choreographer's papers, which could conceivably be valued at $200 by the appraiser, might be appraised by the dealer at $13,000.

Assume another set of circumstances to illustrate another type of appraisal: Dancelotsky's daughter has inherited her father's papers under the residuary clause in his will [21] but did not pay inheritance tax upon the papers. Upon examining them, she decides that they have some monetary value and that they should be insured as part of her home owner's policy. Under these circumstances, if the same dealer appraised the papers, he might set their value at $17,500.

To illustrate the third type of appraisal, shift the scene and assume that, soon after inheriting her father's papers, the daughter reads a newspaper feature story upon the "gold-in-your-attic" theme or sees a television news broadcast about the prices paid by a dealer at a recent auction and decides to find out if some of the letters in her father's papers have a market value. She gathers a folio of letters written by famous people to her father and takes them to the dealer. Will he tell her how much they are worth? Yes, but for a price. In this instance, the dealer would charge the daughter 10 percent of the appraised value as his fee. If he went to her home and appraised the entire collection, his fee would be based on the daily charge plus travel, as mentioned previously, and in this instance his appraisal might be $8,000.

Finally, shift the scene once again and set the time prior to January 1970. The daughter, after her father's death, is approached by the curator to give her father's papers to his institution. If he is a knowledgeable curator, he has a fair idea of the figure at which the collection might be appraised. Depending upon the income of the daughter and her husband for the year, the gift may be made over a two- or three-year period, or the deduction may be taken in a single year. In any event, the same dealer might, in this situation, appraise the papers at $20,700.

In these hypothetical cases, how could the same dealer appraise the same set of papers at $8,000, $13,000, $17,500, and $20,700? The $8,000 appraisal represents the wholesale value of the collection, or what the dealer would pay for the collection, or what he feels other dealers would pay. This is not to say that a dealer would *offer* to buy the collection; most dealers will refuse to make offers on single manuscripts or collections, because in a sense this is a free estimate of value, a free appraisal to the seller. Instead, the seller is expected to name his selling price, which the dealer accepts or rejects. On the occasion when a dealer does make an offer, he is likely to say, "This manuscript (or collection) is worth X amount *to me*," being very careful to establish the manuscript's value only in terms of his needs as a dealer.

The $13,000 evaluation for estate purposes can be explained in several ways. First, as a general rule, all property is undervalued in estate appraisals, and manuscripts more than most, because probate courts are accustomed to accepting modest appraisals from ordinary

Fig. 9. One of the several cartoons drawn during the controversy over the appraised value of President Richard Nixon's papers. (Courtesy King Features)

appraisers. This type of evaluation is known by appraisers as a "forced-sale value." The figure arrived at by the appraiser is the value of the manuscript at the time of the owner's death, and there may not have been much demand for that type of material at that period.[22] It is also possible that dealers take into account the fact that their clients must pay a tax on their inheritance; but whatever the reason, appraisals for estates may be low.

The $17,500 appraisal for insurance may fairly accurately reflect market or near market value, since the purpose of insurance is to pay the insured the money it would take to replace the lost article.

On the surface, this is a contradiction when applied to manuscripts; each item is unique and cannot be replaced. However, market value of like or similar manuscripts, either singly or in collections, can be established. As mentioned previously, insurance appraisals are usually sought on single items or collections of manuscripts for which catalog listings or auction sale prices exist, and in the case of the papers of the choreographer, the insurance appraisal would probably be based largely on the value of the marketable letters in the papers.[23]

Why, then, would the same set of papers have been appraised for a tax deduction at $20,700? The figure is supposed to be arrived at by determining what would be an acceptable price agreed upon by a "willing buyer and a willing seller." But no money is involved and, in actual fact, few dealers could or would buy collections for prices at which they were appraised for tax purposes. Of course, the appraisal does not imply a purchase offer, but represents only the dealer's expert opinion of value. If the taxpayer is questioned by the Internal Revenue Service and the dealer is pressed to defend his appraisal, he might claim that, had he owned the collection, he would have reasonably expected to sell it to the institution at a price equal to the appraised value. This, too, is somewhat specious, in that, of the institutions which benefited most from tax deductable gifts, only a few purchased collections regularly.

Despite these weaknesses in the system, the Internal Revenue Service was generally willing to accept reasonable appraisals for research collections, even those which appeared slightly inflated. The interpretation of their own guidelines seemed to vary from district to district; but when considering a research collection, the IRS generally applied what could be called the "the-whole-is-greater-than-the-sum-of-its-parts" rule. This means that the appraiser first established the value of the individual items in the papers which have a known market value if sold as separate. For example, if the papers contained a series of twenty letters from a well-known author, the dealer might remember that, in his last catalog he had sold a single letter, of similar length and content, for $150. A value of $3,000 could be assigned to the letters; more than likely, however, the appraiser would figure them at $3,500, because, studied together, they reveal details about the stage production of one of the author's books. Taken singly, the letters are mementos, but together they are documentation and have an added research potential.[24]

The same principle would be applied in appraising the entire set of the choreographer's papers. The papers probably would contain several series similar to the letters from the author which the dealer would recognize and to which he could assign a value, but there would be a great bulk which might not fall into this category. Yet these lesser documents, studied in relationship to the other documents that make up the mass of the Dancelotsky papers, tell the researcher much about the man, the development of his art, and the times in which he lived.

A dealer might, then, give four different dollar values to the choreographer's papers, depending upon the purpose for which the appraisal was being made. Somewhat similarly, if four different dealers appraised the same set of papers, they might make four quite different appraisals. No curator and few donors would have the funds at their disposal to make such an experiment; but over the years, if the curator does have several different dealers do appraisals, he will learn that their methods differ, and the appraisals take different forms.

Some appraisers do their homework conscientiously, attempting to place the subject in his proper place. An appraiser of this nature wants to know whether similar papers have been given or sold to the curator's institution or other institutions. How have these papers been used by scholars? Where did the subject stand in his profession? What is unique about the papers? These and other questions the appraiser asks are not unlike the type of information that a good manuscripts processor will seek out before he begins to work with a collection. The appraisal done by this dealer then takes on some of the aspects of a good manuscript collection inventory, and it might run to twenty or thirty pages for a large group of papers.

In the middle ground are the dealers who are perhaps less re-search-oriented but have a solid foundation of practical sales experi-ence. They are most at home appraising the papers of politicians, soldiers, authors, etc., the standard fare in their autograph and manu-script catalogs. Their appraisals tend to be lists of "highlights" with assigned values found in a set of papers. Of this group, a dealer once said that, given knowledge of values, "all appraising means is being able to count and multiply"—that is, twenty letters of Famous Author B, 43 pp., $4,300.[25]

Finally, there are the dealers whose appraisals follow a standard form. After the dealer has completed his examination of the papers and has done whatever computation is necessary, he presents an ap-praisal which may consist of nothing more than two short, signed paragraphs, the first of which identifies and sets out the qualifications of the dealer (years of experience) and the second of which gives the title of the papers appraised, the date of the appraisal, and the evaluation placed on the papers.

Obviously, the curator will have little control over appraisals made of collections still in the donor's possession, but often papers will come to the institution before the dealer can make his appraisal. Since, in a very real sense, "time is money" in appraising, when this happens the curator can do certain things in advance which will assist in the appraisal. The dealer should be provided with a well-lighted work table not unlike that used by a manuscripts processor. The papers should be in as good order as possible and the order explained to the dealer. He should be provided with whatever background information the curator has been able to accumulate, and if the papers contain distinctive letters or series of records, they should be pointed out to the dealer. In essence it may seem that the curator is doing the appraiser's work for him. The alternative is to let the dealer do all of his own research, but, of course, this means that the appraisal takes longer and costs more money.

One final note. When the curator has provided whatever aid and assistance he can, he should then leave the appraiser in peace and quiet to proceed with his work. At his hourly rate, he is very expensive to engage as a casual conversationalist, and, like most of us, he works best without someone looking over his shoulder. The dealers, who do most of the appraising, are very jealous of their trade secrets and they are anxious to keep intact the sense of mystery that seems to shroud the process of appraising. This may be a result of the very competitive nature of dealing in manuscripts. There are no in-training or internship programs for dealers. The field is a limited one, and the only avenue open to becoming a dealer seems to be to risk capital buying and selling.

For years, some curators have contended that they are competent to appraise their own acquisitions. Dealers are willing to concede that curators can be most knowledgeable about their collections and in areas of specialization cannot be excelled by the scholar or the dealer. Certainly the curator could be more aware than the dealer of the research potential of a set of papers and, in purchasing manuscripts for his institution and in studying the dealers' catalogs, he may have developed a fair sense of market values. But the crux of the matter, argue the dealers, is in being engaged daily in the marketplace, buying and selling manuscripts. A curator's mistakes are cataloged and forgotten; there is little cost-accounting in manuscript collecting. The manuscript dealer, who in a sense is one of the country's few examples of free enterprise, must buy and sell with only his wits and his sense of value to guide him.

On the other side of the coin, it can be argued that dealers in manuscripts cannot be disinterested parties in appraising—that, in part, the incredible rise in manuscript prices in the past decades can be laid to the fact that dealers have a vested interest in keeping prices up.

Irrespective of the arguments, some curators are doing their own appraisals, particularly for collections which appraise at a modest figure. Curators suspect that the IRS has an unwritten directive to accept appraisals below a certain dollar amount. Some hazard a guess that the figure is $500, the bolder ones think up to $1,000.[26]

At least one institution does all its own appraising. Since 1958, the Southwestern Collection at Texas Technological University as a routine matter has sent two copies of a "Certificate of Appraisal" to every donor. The amount of the appraisal is figured by a simple formula based upon what it would cost to make a suitable copy of the gift collection. In some instances, this amount would be the estimated costs of photostating or Xeroxing, but more often it would be microfilming. Another institution appraises its own collections for insurance purposes at $100 or $200 per records center carton. Neither system seems to involve much subjective judgment by the curator, and both would result in a minimal appraisal.[27]

Ethical Considerations

Probably no aspect of the curator's profession posed more ethical problems than those of "gifts in kind" which arose in the approximately twenty-year period before 1970. Early that year, Congress passed what was known as the Tax Reform Act of 1969 (H. R. 13270), the net effect of which was that, retroactive to July 25, 1969, taxpayers who made gifts of "self-generated" manuscripts to a library could no longer take the "fair market value" of the manuscripts as a tax-deductible gift to charity.

While it might seem that the problems the tax-appraised gift posed are past history, the specter still haunts the curator. In times past, accepting manuscripts on deposit was considered undesirable and unprofessional. Now, with the Library of Congress leading the way, many prestigious institutions are urging potential donors to deposit manuscripts in their collections until such time as Congress changes the tax law. A concerted lobbying campaign has been mounted by numerous institutions and several professional organizations to change the law to allow for at least a 50 percent deduction. It seems probable that this change, or some other modification in the present law, will be adopted by Congress.[28] For this reason, and because, under the 1969 law, donors can continue to claim deductions for manuscripts they acquired and then gave to institutions, some of the ethical considerations the curator faces with an appraised gift will be discussed here.

Appraisers have claimed that it is dangerous for a curator to do an appraisal because he would set too low a figure for fear that the donor would want to sell the manuscript or want it back if he knew its true value. Also, there may be suspicion of collusion between the donor and the institution when the curator does the appraisal. Appraisers have also claimed that the curator, not content to manipulate his own appraisals, has attempted to influence the appraiser when he was asked to do the job. One appraiser said it was common practice for curators to try to tie the appraisal to future purchases or to offer the dealer first refusal on duplicate and discarded printed material.[29]

There has always been a question, too, about whether the donor or the recipient institution should pay the appraiser's fee. The guidelines issued by the Internal Revenue Service, which have been incorporated into the standards adopted by library and archival groups, state that it is the responsibility of the donor to pay for tax appraisals. The public policies of most collecting agencies have followed the IRS guidelines;[30] many of these institutions have given lip service to the standards of the profession, but nonetheless have paid the appraisal costs. Of nineteen research libraries surveyed in 1968, five paid for all their appraisals and four paid when the circumstances warranted. But the dichotomy between the ideal and practical position may be breaking down. Recently, one librarian wrote in a professional journal that his institution provided "free appraisals" to authors who "did not stand to benefit much from an appraisal for tax purposes." [31]

When institutions pay appraisal fees, they must recognize that some potential donors will "shop" among their ranks to see where they can get the largest tax write-off. Thus, curators will be under pressure to guide the donor to the appraiser who can be influenced to tailor the evaluation to fit the needs of the donor and the institution.

The donor-dealer-curator relationship poses an endless array of ethical questions. What is the curator's obligation as a citizen if he is aware that a donor and a dealer have conspired to rig a gift for his institution? One practice is for a collector who owns, for example, a Civil War collection, to have it appraised by a friendly dealer. After the appraisal—which describes the papers only in a very general way—the collector keeps the letters from Grant, Sherman, and Custer and presents the remainder of the collection to an institution. He takes his full deduction at appraised value and has a very handsome dividend in the three letters which are worth several hundred dollars.

In a similar instance, what is the curator's responsibility when he knows either through collusion or accident that the donor has been given an inflated appraisal? One curator admitted that, for many years, his institution passed on "over-generous appraisals" without a thought that it was "in effect aiding and abetting a tax dodge." [32]

A surprising number of curators are also collectors—of books, stamps, manuscripts, broadsides, prints, a variety of materials—but few seem to sense a conflict of interest. Yet the unwritten history of collecting is filled with examples of curators who were unable to keep their private collecting separate from the institutional. The acquisitive instinct may tempt the most honest of curators. Probably no other profession is so open to manipulation. Because there are so few checks, so great an opportunity for deception and fraud, a curator must be continuously on guard. It seems foolish to put strong temptation in one's way.

Some of the most bitter criticism leveled against the curator's ethical standards has come from dealers. One dealer, for example, says that a curator can become so anxious to secure manuscripts for his institution and to preserve them for future generations of scholars that he is "blinded to the present very real obligation of treating the owners with common justice." Foremost among these obligations, the dealer believes, is the curator's responsibility to tell a potential donor when a manuscript has monetary value as well as research value. To accept a gift without informing the donor about its value, this dealer believes, is "strictly unethical." [33]

Among the kinds of gifts that the dealer is critical of the curator for accepting are photocopies of original manuscripts. She contends that, when manuscripts are copied, their monetary value is substantially decreased. Therefore, she reasons, when a curator asks for permission to copy a manuscript, he is obligated to make the owner aware that he is "handing out" a portion of the manuscript's value. Curators are in honest disagreement about whether copies decrease the value of an original manuscript, but at least one of them agrees with the dealer about the dishonesty of some of his fellow curators, who he claims have solicited manuscripts worth thousands of dollars from unknowing persons in great financial need.[34]

One of the oldest questions of ethics in acquisitions is how the curator deals with estrayed archival material. In the introductory chapter of this book, it was noted that many of the prized documents in the sixteenth-century British collections were estrayed archives, and the practice carried over to the colonies. For example, the earliest documentation of settlement in this country, the manuscript records of the Virginia Company of London and the Council of Virginia, now in the manuscript collections of the Library of Congress, passed from official custody through several collectors' hands before the government purchased them from Thomas Jefferson.[35]

Cases of replevin—legal action to reclaim strayed records—are scattered throughout the nation's history. In one instance, Alden Bradford, secretary of the commonwealth of Massachusetts, separated what he thought were private papers from Governor Thomas Hutchinson's files and with the governor's permission presented them to the Massachusetts Historical Society. Twenty-five years later, Bradford's successor demanded their return and, after another twenty-five years of disputation, the state won its claim.[36]

In another instance, in 1863 the manuscript collection of John Allan of New York City was sold at auction. Included in the sale was a letter of George Washington, dated May 1785, and addressed to the mayor and aldermen of New York City. The city brought suit against the purchaser, won a decision in the state supreme court, and recovered the letter.[37]

More recently, the Lewis and Clark case, probably the most famous replevin action of the twentieth century, and the Sender case, were unsuccessful attempts of the federal government to reclaim alienated documents from a private owner and a dealer respectively. In recent times, the State of Maryland, which for thirty-five years negotiated with the Library of Congress for the return of records and began similar negotiations with the Maryland Historical Society in 1971, decided the "harsh method" of replevin "might be preferable" to extended arbitration. That same year, the archivist, with a writ of replevin from the Frederick County Court, stopped the sale of a large collection of eighteenth-century court records by a Baltimore dealer, and in his annual report called for a consideration of "the whole question of the dispersal of Maryland archives." [38]

The Maryland state archivist, who for years has looked to the courts to resolve the question of estrays, as early as 1963 called for a clear decision in a precedent-setting court so that the thousands of state and federal manuscripts now at large and destined to be fought over one by one may come home quietly. In order to get such a decision the issue should be joined in a friendly fashion and with agreement as to the governmental origin of the record or records in contest. What a great day it would be to see all those estrays now representing Maryland in "Autograph collections up and down the East Coast" come marching home! [39]

The federal government, marching to a different drummer from Maryland's, apparently decided in the latter 1960s to eschew the courts—where in recent years they had lost two replevin cases and gained only some adverse publicity—and instead to try to win approval for a change in the Federal Records Act of 1950. National Archives officials, meeting with a committee from The Manuscript Society, a collectors' organization, worked on a proposed amendment to the records act which would require that all federal archival material, whether held by collectors, dealers, or institutions, be registered. Registration would be accomplished by submitting photocopies of the material to the National Archives. Letters and documents written before a "cut-off" date, provided they were registered, would be free from the threat of replevin, and disputes would be decided by a panel rather than a court. As might be expected, the discussions centered around the "cut-off" date; the collectors argued for 1934, the date of the establishment of the National Archives, and the archivists held for a much earlier unspecified date. There were other areas of disagreement, the principal one being a definition of what constituted "archival material," and to date the matter has not been settled. [40]

A draft of a model law on archives commissioned recently by UNESCO proposes the following resolution of the problem of the "control over private archives":

Any person or private body, not being a dealer, who has in his possession documents more than 40 years old must notify the director of the national or local archives. Within 60 days these must be examined by an archivist and may be declared to be of major historical interest. Once so declared, the state has a power of surveillance and the records automatically become open for research purposes. The owner must preserve the records in a suitable manner, catalogue, and repair them, notify the national archives before transferring ownership or custody, and apply for permission to export. Deposit is to be encouraged by the award of a diploma of merit to the owner, the award of scholarships bearing his name, and the promotion of research on his documents.

Dealers must notify the national archives of all documents in their possession, give 30 days' notice of intention to sell, and register the results of all sales, the register to be inspected by the archives service. The final provision of the Draft allows for the expropriation of any documents in the hands of anyone who breaks the requirements of the articles relating to private archives.[41]

It would seem that the UNESCO draft is not likely to serve as a model for legislation in the United States, but it does indicate the thinking of some archivists and may be a portent of the future.

Conflicts in collecting, some of which are apparent in attempts to recover estrayed records, underlie a great many of the ethical questions in acquisitions. The competitive drive—the force that is so strong in some institutions that they pile up mountains of manuscripts which go for years without being processed—at times seems so pervasive that it is easy to assume that all conflicts in collecting are its result. A writer of a thoughtful article, the only one of its kind in a professional journal to try to analyze the conflicts in collecting, makes the valid observation that many of the conflicts are based upon "(1) the nature of family papers or manuscripts and (2) the motives or philosophies of historical or archival agencies as controlled by their legal framework within geographical or subject areas." The second part of this observation is concerned primarily with the idea that universities and colleges *will* what they want to collect, while historical societies often are restricted to a collecting field by statute or ordinance, and the archives of a government are created by the law of that government to collect its records. The first part of the observation deals with the fractured and compartmentalized nature of modern man whose papers may be legitimately sought by a historical society within whose geographical collecting area he lives or was born; the archives of his alma mater; the archives of his business or profession; the archives of a government he might serve; and any college or university within whose subject area his activities fall.[42]

The author demonstrates that not all conflicts between historical and archival agencies are based upon competition; he also proves that given the character of life today and the number of collecting agencies, the competition is inevitable. Still, the ethical principles he suggests are worth considering:

1. That all archival agencies confine collecting to records of their own government, business, or organization, except insofar as they obtain copies of related records through microfilm and other duplicating processes.

2. That all archival agencies transfer or offer to the appropriate history-collecting agencies records that for no legal reason are in the custody of their government, business, or organization. This does not mean that exhibits should be torn from court or other records.

3. That all history-collecting agencies should confine their active collecting to records that are not the responsibility of existing archival agencies.

4. That all history-collecting agencies should deliver to the proper archival agency any papers they receive that have been removed from office or archival custody and that are easily identifiable as official records. There would be no reason why, in making such a transfer, the records could not be recorded on microfilm and the microfilm retained for use by the history-collecting agency.

5. That all archival agencies and historical agencies refer individuals to the correct collecting agency when offered materials that should belong to another agency.

6. That historical and archival agencies, where there are more than one of a kind, should attempt to delimit their fields of activity so that they will not conflict. In the case of two competing historical agencies this delimitation may not be possible, and each should agree to withdraw if it finds that the other agency is preferred by a potential donor. At the same time, each should agree to furnish microfilm copies of the records at cost to the other interested agency upon request.

7. That for purposes of encouraging the formation of government, business, organizational archives, all historical and archival agencies should transfer to such archives, when established, materials that originally belonged to those governments, businesses, or organizations.

8. That historical agencies accept the responsibility of custodianship of organizational or family records as archival collections. No charge should be made for the service if the records are open to the public and if the historical agency aids in the selection of the materials to comprise the collection. The organization or family would retain ownership of their materials, but the deposit would be considered permanent. Charges for storage and service would be warranted if the use of materials were restricted to the organization or family.

9. That historical agencies agree to accept the responsibility for the direction of business archives, provided that the business pays for the extra staff and space.

10. That historical and archival agencies are not justified in attempting to profit by arrangements suggested involving microfilm or storage.[43]

Although the conflicting areas of collecting probably make it impossible to devise a universal rule of reason, striving to adhere to a set of principles like these might help keep competition within reasonable bounds. That there is a continued and growing need for rationality in acquisitions was stressed at a recent professional session on the ethics and realities of collecting by speakers who described present-day acquisition practices which bordered on the criminal or psychopathic. As a countermeasure, one participant suggested establishing a registry system to define the territorial or content limits within which an agency might collect, and an arbitration board to adjudicate disputes between institutions. He noted that Canada had made some progress along these lines: public agencies have evolved a "systematic national acquisition program" to advise donors which repository should receive what collections, and after the gift of the papers is made, a government body appraises them.[44]

In this chapter an attempt has been made to identify the procedures through which manuscripts are acquired by an institution and some of the ethical questions that must be faced by the curator in the acquisitions process. Once the manuscripts are in hand, the curator must (1) provide for their care and conservation and (2) arrange and describe them. Either process may be attended to first, but most often they will be done more or less simultaneously. Because each process is quite complicated in itself, each will be discussed separately in this book, beginning with Physical Care and Conservation.

SELECTED READINGS

An interesting article that sets forth the British rationale of acquisitions is A. D. Burnett's "Considerations on the Support of Antiquarian and Other Special Collections in University Libraries." Also from the British point of view, the mechanics of acquisitions is the topic of the chapter entitled "Bringing in the Archives" in J. D. Hodson's *The Administration of Archives.* Perhaps the best concise treatment of the American scene is also chapters in a book, "Who Should Collect and What Should be Collected," and "How to Collect," in *The Modern Manuscript Library,* by Ruth B. Bordin and Robert M. Warner.

Descriptions of four representative programs can be read in William Matheson, "An Approach to Special Collections," Donald R. McNeil, "The Wisconsin Experiments," T. J. Easterwood, "The Collecting and Care of Modern Manuscripts," and Lewis E. Atherton, "Western Historical Manuscripts Collections—A Case Study of a Collecting Program." A good over-all view of historical society and university acquisitions programs can be found in Robert L. Brubaker, "Manuscript Collections."

The ethical problems of acquisition have been ignored in print, but a session at the SAA annual meeting—"Collecting Personal Papers: Ethics and Realities"—may stimulate some writing. The best article available is "Conflicts in Collecting," by David C. Duniway. Appraisals are the topic of four fine papers, all by experts in their own fields. Two of these which appeared as American Association for State and Local History Technical Leaflets 31 and 41 respectively, are Ralph G. Newman's "Appraisals and 'Revenooers'; Tax Problems of the Collector," and Seymour V. Connor's "A System of Manuscript Appraisal." The remaining two are by Robert F. Metzdorf, "Appraisal of Literary Properties," and Andreas L. Brown, "Valuation and Appraisal."

IV

Physical Care
and Conservation

AT a recent meeting a young curator described the destroyers of documents as "Rats, mold, people, and things like that." She had the order reversed; as noted in a conservator's more prosaic list, people are the worst enemy of paper, followed by "the air we breathe, light and darkness, heat, moisture, vermin, fungi and acid." [1] Taken on the surface, this list may seem contradictory and frustrating. The ideal advanced by the professional conservators, those who are trained and skilled in the means of conservation * and restoration, is frustrating to the average curator faced with inadequacies of building and budget, but there are practical if not ideal measures he may be able to adopt.

Boxes and Folders

Providing proper storage for manuscripts is the curator's first responsibility in care and conservation. Boxes and folders are the most

---

* Throughout this chapter, the term *conservation* has been used rather than *preservation*, which has been the more generally accepted usage by many curators. One dictionary's first definition of conservation is "Deliberate, planned or thoughtful preserving, guarding or protecting, a keeping in a safe or entire state," but a subsequent definition amplifies the term as "wise utilization."

Fig. 10. This 1840 lithograph by Charles Joseph Travies de Villers probably was intended to portray literary critics at work, but it might well remind the curator of the way in which some patrons handle manuscripts. (Reprinted with permission of R. R. Bowker)

inexpensive way of protecting manuscripts against dust, light, and, to a considerable extent, atmospheric gases. Boxes also insulate against fluctuations in temperature and relative humidity, a particularly important consideration in the storage of bonded materials such as maps mounted on cloth and some photographs and films.[2] Filing cabinets, designed for easy access to current records, are not acceptable for manuscript storage. Folders tend to get jammed when the drawer is closed and searches for material place undue wear upon the document edges exposed at the top of the folders. And, unless the drawer is full, or the folders are snug against a firm backstop, there is a tendency for folders and individual documents to curl.

This tendency of documents to curl when filed on edge has encouraged many curators to provide flat storage. Traditionally, manuscript boxes for flat storage were approximately 15 by 10 by 3 inches, made of library board and cloth-covered. Many repositories had their boxes made to order by a local manufacturer; some used boxes made by the staff. Today, at least one company manufactures this type of box in several styles.

Rising costs of the cloth-covered flat box have caused curators to look for alternatives. With the establishment of the National Archives, a sufficient demand was created and a firm was formed in a nearby Virginia suburb to manufacture a box designed to house records. Today the "Hollinger carton," the grey fiberboard box measuring 15 by 10 by 5 or 12 by 10 by 5 with metal-fastened corners, has become almost synonymous with archival storage, and the impact of this kind of storage has been so great that many manuscript curators

Fig. 11. The "Hollinger carton" (*left*) and a records center carton for which the pattern appears in the appendix. (Courtesy Southern Illinois University)

Fig. 12. Fiberboard boxes designed to store prints and photographs can be used for flat storage of manuscripts. (Courtesy Southern Illinois University)

have overcome their aversion to on-edge filing and ordered their share of the Hollinger cartons.[3]

With the great success of the Hollinger carton, the company has expanded its line to include flat storage boxes designed to store prints and photographs, which can be adapted for manuscripts by the curator who still wishes to file that way. One disadvantage of the box is that the fiberboard from which it is made is so smooth that the boxes are slippery and very difficult to stack or carry. The regional history collection at Cornell uses a flat-storage manuscript box of its own design made out of corrugated cardboard, and hand-stapled at the corners, which any curator could have made by his local box company from plans included in the appendix.

Another common form of manuscript storage is the corrugated box, measuring 15 by 10 by 12, with a fitted telescope lid, generally known as a records center carton. The carton, as originally designed for the federal records center, is the cheapest possible container for manuscripts and archives. Made to store the two standard-size office folders on edge, the records center carton turned lengthwise accommodates legal files; letter-size files fit across the short side. One full carton will house a cubic foot of records. Several modifications of the original design exist (see appendix for the pattern of one variation); and, ordered in quantity from a local box manufacturer to save on freight, the economy is substantial. Ready-made boxes of the records center type can also be purchased from the Paige and Hollinger companies. (Oversize manuscripts—anything larger than legal size—will require flat filing. See the section on map storage for suggestions.)

Acid-free manuscript folders in standard sizes are available from several firms, or the curator can purchase acid-free manila hemp or permanent/durable paper and cut his own folders at some savings. In some cases, good grade, standard office file folders will provide adequate storage.

The concept of acid-free storage is an intriguing one.[4] The commercial possibilities have not been overlooked. Pohlig manuscript boxes are lined with Permalife paper, a permanent/durable paper, and Hollinger records center cartons are manufactured of acid-free corrugated cardboard. Hollinger, like several firms, is selling the acid-free folders mentioned above. But the curator might do well to look behind the fetish to the practicalities of his own situation. What protection do acid-free boxes and folders give to twentieth-century manuscript collections of sulfite pulp paper, particularly those housed in stacks that are not air-conditioned?

Environmental Controls

If the curator is fortunate, his stacks, as well as the work area and search room, are temperature- and humidity-controlled. Laboratory tests have shown that, if good paper could be stored in a near-freezing, dry atmosphere, it would last almost indefinitely, but conservators have agreed that the acceptable compromise, where people must work with the documents, is 68° to 70° F. temperature and 50 percent relative humidity. Storage areas could safely be five or ten degrees cooler, but documents kept at temperatures lower than this would probably need to be brought to the search-room temperature gradually to avoid having condensation form.[5]

Air conditioning works to mitigate against two other destructive agents: fungi and acid. If the curator is fortunate enough to have a new building, it probably has a central air-conditioning system which filters and washes the air, removing sulphur dioxide and other impurities. It also keeps the air in motion; the growth of mold spores is retarded in well-ventilated rooms. Such a system may incorporate expensive thermometers and hygrometers which record temperatures and humidity readings on a continuous roll of paper.

If the repository is not centrally air-conditioned, the curator can, if he has the money in his equipment budget, buy room air conditioners, humidifiers or dehumidifiers (depending on the season and his local climate), or even fans, any or all of which would help control temperature and humidity. Under these conditions, a simple mercury thermometer and a dial-type hygrometer will give him a relatively accurate measure of his success.[6]

Since the ultraviolet rays present in both natural and artificial light fade ink and destroy paper, the curator should keep direct sunlight out of processing, reading, and exhibit areas, and buy protective sleeves for his fluorescent light fixtures. He should remember, however, that the screening properties of the sleeves are relatively short-lived, and they probably should be replaced approximately every five years. Some firms (see appendix) manufacture fluorescent tubes in which the ultraviolet screens are built into the tube. Incandescent is the least harmful light; it gives off far fewer ultraviolet rays than other types.

The curator, having controlled the environment within his building as much as economic conditions will allow, must guard against bringing in vermin and fungi with newly acquired collections. If he has a fumigation tank and follows the directions of its manufacturer, the problems are easily resolved. The tanks are expensive (see appendix) and must be vented to the outside of the building where the poisonous fumes can be discharged.

If he does not have access to a fumigation tank, the curator has few alternatives. Chemicals which are effective against insects and other vermin are poisonous to man, and most conservators do not recommend any do-it-yourself fumigation, except in the control of mold.[7] If papers have gotten damp, if they show evidence of mildew, or if the repository, because it lacks temperature and humidity controls, provides a favorable climate for the growth of mold spores, incoming collections should be treated with thymol vapor.

The first step in the thymol treatment is to dry the papers. In times past, conservators recommended against using artificial heat to dry papers, but emergency experiments after the Florence flood in 1966 indicate that temperatures up to 140° F. are not harmful.[8] When the papers are dry, brush them lightly in the open air to remove the mildew. If the treatment is to be used infrequently, the curator might enclose a section of unpainted wooden shelves with a plastic sheet (polyethylene) and stack the manuscripts as loosely as possible on the shelves. Next he would place a small dish of thymol crystals inside the plastic tent over a lighted seventy-five-watt bulb. The heat from the bulb will cause the thymol to vaporize in an hour or two. Leave the manuscripts in the plastic tent; and, if the treatment is repeated for three successive days, the manuscripts should be free of mold spores.[9]

Another alternative to a fumigation chamber would be for the curator to contract with a professional exterminator to service his building. The stack area should be sprayed at least quarterly, and if a small receiving room could be stacked with recent accessions and sealed, the company might come on call to fumigate the entire room. If such a space is not available, it is also possible that the firm might fumigate incoming manuscript collections on the company's premises before the curator brings the papers into his building, although care should be exercised in these circumstances. Some commercial firms may use fumigants which could be harmful to paper. Those that have been tested as safe by the National Bureau of Standards include: (1) hydrocyanic acid gas; (2) ethylene chloride-carbon tetrachloride; (3) carbon disulphide; (4) ethylene oxide-carbon dioxide; and (5) methyl formate-carbon dioxide.[10]

Cleaning and Flattening

Once the curator has done the fumigation that is within his means, the next major step is to clean the incoming manuscripts. Ideally, papers should be unpacked in a cleaning area equipped with forced-air nozzle and intake air ducts to carry off the surface dirt which is hosed from the papers.[11] Less ideal, but the more likely substitute for most curators, is a tank or hand vacuum cleaner which will pick up most of the loose dirt. (The vacuum will be useful, too, in keeping the stacks dusted.) If a vacuum cleaner is beyond the curator's means, treated dust rags called One Wipe can be used, or Endust can be sprayed on a soft cloth and used for cleaning. Neither leaves harmful residue. The dust cloths can be washed several times and retain their effectiveness. A soft bristle brush, similar to a large camel's hair brush used by artists, also can be employed in cleaning.[12]

Air hoses or vacuums will remove only loose dirt, and other necessary surface cleaning probably will be done during sorting, or at some other point in the processing. The curator has a variety of inexpensive, well-tested, and effective products to assist him. Experimentation will show him which one will be the most useful. Wallpaper cleaner, a dough-like substance sold in cans, can be purchased from any paint store. Absorene is a brand recommended by conservator Carolyn Horton. She suggests that if the cleaner is sticky, it should be allowed to dry for several days. If it has a crust, it should be kneaded, and if it is too dry to work, it should be moistened with a few drops of water and put back in the can for a day or two. The curator holds a ball of the cleaner in his hand and works the dirt from the paper with strokes from the center to the edge. The surface adhesion of the cleaner is considerable and care must be taken not to pull or tear away on the edge. Crumbs from the cleaner should be kept swept up or they will stick pages together, although a drop of water will loosen them. The cleaner leaves no harmful residue on the paper.[13]

If the manuscript is too fragile to be worked with wallpaper cleaner or if the ink is likely to be affected, a mild cleaner, Opaline, a bag containing absorbent powder and other ingredients, is safe, but it will leave crumbs which should be dusted from the manuscript and the work table.

Several kinds of erasers will loosen stubborn ingrained dirt. Any art gum is safe, and two others, Pink Pearl and Magic Rub, have been recommended. As with other cleaners, the curator should work from the center to the edge of the manuscript and should brush off all crumbs when he is finished. Dirt or stains which cannot be removed with the above cleaners are probably not on the surface and should be left for professional restoration.[14]

Often, in unpacking a newly acquired collection, the curator will find bundles of manuscripts rolled or folded tightly, occasional sheets that have been wadded, or papers that are too dry and brittle to unfold and flatten. Exposing folded manuscripts to 90 to 95 percent relative humidity in a pettifogger or humidification chamber will relax the fibers in the paper enough to allow them to be unfolded. An inexpensive substitute for a commercial humidifier has been in use for at least a quarter of a century. When first described in The American Archivist, the container recommended was a lard can, which even then was a scarce item and now would be an antique.[15] Today's homemade humidifier would more likely be a plastic twenty-gallon garbage can with a self-sealing lid. Inside the can the curator places a dinner plate holding a cellulose sponge saturated with water. He then suspends a piece of aluminum or plastic screening over the plate, in an arch so that it does not touch the sponge. A small dish-drying rack turned upside down would work here, too. Into the can, as loosely as possible, he places the manuscripts to be humidified, and closes the lid. If the manuscripts are left in the can overnight, or at the most twenty-four hours, they will have absorbed enough moisture to allow the curator to unfold them, flatten them with his hands, put them between blotters and into a press.

One southern library, which some years ago issued a small pamphlet on the care and repair of manuscripts, uses a method which it calls "damp press" to flatten creased papers. A manuscript is pressed between two sheets of unprinted newsprint, which have been brushed or sponged with water. The damp manuscript is left in the press several days to dry. Although the curator says that he has not had a mildew problem, conservators state that this is a very dangerous method of flattening papers.

Curators of historical society collections will have an advantage over many of their colleagues in that a variety of presses may be available to them in the society's museum collection. Most useful is one which the British call a nipping press, but which is more commonly called a letterpress in this country, since it was used to prepare the letterpress copies of letters prior to the use of carbon paper.

If no press is available, documents can be flattened under weights. Too, in the past, curators have recommended using an iron or a mangle to flatten documents between blotters, but some conservators say the heat is damaging. Many of the creases in manuscripts will not need attention, since they will be flattened by their own weight in the storage boxes on the shelves. During processing, the curator will find some manuscripts with turned-down corners. These he should flatten by gently reversing the fold and, when the turned corner is flat, by turning the manuscript over and rubbing the crease line with a bone folder. If the sheet is not fragile or brittle, other folds can be removed in this manner, but it is very time-consuming (see figure 13; see also equipment list in appendix).

Alternative Restoration Procedures

During the sorting process, the curator will find other manuscripts in need of restoration. Most common of these will be letters in which the weakened paper has broken at the fold. Another will be the volume (or any other sheet of paper handled carelessly) with a torn edge.

Fig. 13. Removing a crease with a bone folder. (Courtesy Southern Illinois University)

Faced with these and other manuscripts needing restoration, the curator must decide whether to seek the help of a professional conservator or to attempt to care for the manuscripts himself. Depending upon his budget, his time, and his inclinations, there are a variety of options open to him. He can (1) do nothing; (2) send all manuscripts in need of restoration to a professional conservator; (3) attempt to do simple "mending" or repairs himself and send more complicated restoration to a professional; or (4) set up a conservation laboratory and do all restoration in the shop.[16]

For the curator working on his own, the first option above is not as negative as it sounds. In fact, conservators consider it good advice. Their contention (a valid one) is that more harm is done by well-meaning but misguided persons bent on "preserving" documents in their care than by any of the forces of nature except fire and flood. The impoverished curator who can do no more than provide adequate storage for his collection can take some consolation in his "do-nothing" conservation program.[17]

And what of the second option? Assuming that a fairy tale came true and that the curator secured a foundation grant to restore his collection, would he be able to find a conservator to do all the work? The answer is, probably not. Conservators, because there are so few of them, tend to accept work which will best utilize their special skills. This is not to say that a conservator will not accept minor repair work, but his prices might be prohibitive.

A curator faced for the first time with the prices charged by restorers may feel that there is much merit in the fourth option, setting up his own conservation laboratory. However, Paul Banks, conservator at the Newberry Library, feels that this is very difficult because there are so few trained conservators in this country.[18] Banks, who is fond of medical analogies in referring to restoration, may have a point when he says that in some ways it is easier to become a doctor than a conservator. There are no courses being taught in the restoration of manuscripts, as such, and the three institutions offering courses in conservation of paper are concerned with art. None of the recognized conservators (see appendix) offer apprenticeships or in-house training. From time to time there have been individuals who offered short courses (anywhere from three days to a week) in restoration, but the emphasis has been on books and only coincidentally on paper.

A solution to the dilemma might be for the Library of Congress and the Newberry Library, two institutions well equipped to do so, to offer training courses, but until one or both does, the alternative seems to be for the curator to train himself.[19] However, the path is a frustrating one because so little has been written about conservation, and what has been written deals almost exclusively with art or books. Furthermore, the writing seems to be either very simple or extremely technical, with little middle ground. But the curator should read everything that is available and then seek practical experience. With time, through trial and error, he will gain the knowledge to care for his collection.

Simple Repairs

Some simple repairs, "mending," the curator can do with a minimum of supplies or equipment, and much of the work can be done at the processing table. Later, after he has developed some skills and if he wishes to expand the operation, he can find lists of supplies and equipment, even suggestions about space and work arrangements in a laboratory. It is understood, however, that the procedures outlined in the text that follows are not intended to be used on really rare manuscripts. Whatever the curator attempts in conservation, he needs to be guided by the principle of reversibility: that is, to do nothing to the manuscript that cannot be undone without physical harm to it.[20]

To begin a repair, the curator, holding a torn document in his hands, must examine the tear for a right and wrong side. This is so basic that most conservators do not bother to state it, but when paper is torn, each edge of the tear is beveled in the opposite direction. If the bevels are not matched, the repaired tear will not be even. Once the curator has examined the tear and matched the two edges of the paper, he is ready to make the repair.

The easiest and fastest way to mend the letter broken at the folds or a torn page in a volume is to use Dennison's Transparent Mending Tape. This is not one of the pressure-sensitive sticky plastic tapes (see below). It is made of glassine paper backed with a water-soluble adhesive. It has been in use for at least fifty years and is perfectly safe to use. In time it may also tend to stiffen and curl, a problem with very fragile paper, and eventually it will yellow with age and may drop off. However, it will not leave a penetrating stain, as all the pressure-sensitive plastic tapes do![21]

Another simple but slightly more complex repair is described by Nancy Storm, paper restorer who, with her husband, operates the Storm Bindery in Sedona, Arizona:

The tear area should first be cleaned with cleaning fluid (I use Energine), followed with Magic Rub eraser, erasing towards the tear. Cleaning is done on both sides of the leaf. Paper fibers are hollow tubes, and if not cleaned before mending, chances are there will be a dark line showing along the original break.

I use acid-free reversible PVA (polyvinyl acetate emulsion), about the consistency of medium cream, which is quite dry. Dip into the adhesive with a needle and run along the ENDS of the fibers on both edges of the tear. In a few seconds some PVA has worked into the hollow tubes, and all the PVA left on the ends of the fibers is pulled off between thumb and first finger. Push the tear together immediately. Additional fussing is not necessary unless there is a ridge which can be erased, pushed down with a dull knife or scraped off with a sharp one. A temporary fold of wax paper over the mend protects the rest of the volume.[22]

Another simple mend can be made with paste and tissue, but it may not be as simple to decide on what kind of paste or tissue to use. In times past, conservators would use only pure wheat- or rice-flour paste, which had to be cooked in the shop. Today the curator can buy pre-cooked flour which can be made with cold water into an approved paste. Japanese tissue paper made of Kozo, a shrub fiber, long has been popular with restorers. Fine tissues known as "alpha cellulose" are made in the western countries, and the thinnest and most transparent of these is lens tissue.

Having chosen a paste and tissue, the curator cuts or tears a piece of the tissue to approximately the shape of the tear, then applies paste with the flat end of a toothpick about ⅛ inch wide along each edge of the tear. He presses the strip of tissue onto the pasted area, waits for a moment, and then gently pulls off any tissue projecting beyond the pasted area. This will leave a piece of tissue with ragged fiber edges imbedded in the paste over the tear. Blot off excess paste, and set aside to dry.[23]

The flood that struck Florence in November 1966 brought conservators from all over the world to help restore the damaged books and manuscripts. Out of the experience there, the restorer of the Lambert Palace Library in London developed a method of dry repair which he describes as follows:

For mending tears a lens tissue coated with acrylic emulsion is used and is applied to both sides of the affected leaf. The leaf to be mended is placed on silicone paper over a light box incorporated within the workbench. Necessary tools include a small flat bristled brush of approximately ½ inch width, scissors or small shears and a tracing or narrow tipped ruling pen. To effect the mend, a piece of compatible Jap paper is selected and placed over the area to be repaired. The light box reflects clearly the damaged edge. The tracing pen is dipped in a 1% solution of Methylcellulose and the damaged edge is then traced onto the Jap paper producing a narrow rivulet approximately ⅛th inch wide. The inclusion of Methylcellulose in the water renders it slightly viscose and by controlling the traced line, prevents it from spreading. The paper is then pulled apart along the line and the web fibres coaxed out by gently pulling between thumb and forefinger. This action produces long fibrous strands which are clearly visible and are then attached to the affected edge. The adhesive, either Methylcellulose at approximately 6% or paste, is brushed onto the fibrillated edges. The repair paper is then placed on to the leaf and light pressure is exerted through silicone paper or terylene to ensure good contact. This mend will dry rapidly. It is the only wet process involved and affects not more than ⅛th inch of both the damaged leaf and mending paper. Occasionally the mend is supplemented by the addition of a second piece of Jap paper where the leaves are of exceptional thickness or weight. In addition, reinforcement to mending paper and damaged edge is given by covering both with a piece of acrylic coated lens tissue, which covers the area of mending paper and extends usually ½ inch to ¾ inch onto the damaged leaf, giving body and support with resilience and flexibility. This has good "see through" and does not seriously impair legibility.[24]

Another kind of simple repair utilizes tissue also, in this instance combining it with cellulose acetate foil. In this type of repair—which is used most often on twentieth-century material—the tissue and acetate are cut together to match the tear. Place the document on a piece of glass, align the tear, and place first acetate foil and then tissue over it. Make a pad by wrapping a piece of fine cotton cloth around a wad of cotton wool. Wet the pad with acetone and swab the tissue gently, and smooth with a bone folder, swab and smooth again and then put in a press until dry. In this repair, the liquid acetone softens the foil to a gelatin and acts as an adhesive between the tissue and the manuscript. Another variation using the same materials is to apply the acetone directly to the document, then press the acetate and tissue into place. After a moment, swab the tissue and smooth again with the bone folder.[25] Whichever method is used in mending a marginal tear, the curator should leave an extra half inch or so of tape, tissue, or acetate at the edge and lap it over onto the reverse side of the sheet.

The curator using either of these variations should remember that acetone is a solvent and will dissolve some inks, particularly the images of the purple hectograph typewriter ribbons used from the 1880s into the 1930s. The same is true of some of the impressions of modern typewriters (the carbon ribbon kind), rubber stamps, ball point pens, and indelible pencils. The curator would do well to test the reaction of the acetone on a comma or a period before beginning the repair.

Another product used for mending tears is called Mipofolie, a clear plastic with an orange backing, which was perfected in Germany during World War II to cover maps used at the front. With the backing removed, a strip of Mipofolie is tacky, but the curator can easily put it in place, shifting it to proper alignment and adhering it by rubbing firmly either with his fingernail or with a bone folder. Conservators do not approve of the use of Mipofolie because the adhesive is not stable, but it is quick and easy to use and will not leave a stain as the pressure-sensitive tapes do. It should not, however, be used on anything of lasting value.[26]

Techniques of Conservation

It is an irony of our times that pressure-sensitive tapes, products advertised to help preserve paper, have instead permanently stained some of our most precious documents. Many years ago, the leading manufacturer of plastic tape, the 3M Company, suggested privately that its tape was designed for use in the home, office, and industry, but was "not recommended for repairing manuscripts." Unfortunately, the message never seemed to have reached their advertising department or the American public. These tapes, which have humorously but fittingly been characterized as "botch tapes," [27] continue to cause untold damage to manuscripts each year. Because the curator will encounter pressure-sensitive tapes often, he must know how to deal with them. In the original stages of deterioration, the adhesive oozes at the edge and if several successive pages have been "repaired," the curator will be faced with a stack of paper stuck together. The tape can be removed with a mixture of toluene and hexane. By carefully lifting a corner and working the solvent under the tape, one can gradually soften the adhesive, allowing the tape to be lifted slowly. Acetone can be used also, but since it tends to dissolve the plastic of the tape as well as the adhesive, it works best when applied through the paper from the back of the document. (Both solvents are *toxic* and *inflammable* and should be used with care, either with a fume hood or in a well-ventilated room.) In some cases, especially where the tape has been in place for years, it will have dried and can be peeled off easily. Either way, once the tape has been dislodged, the surface traces of adhesive can be swabbed off with the solvent, but the penetrating stain, oily, dirty brown, probably can never be removed. [28]

It is possible that the restoration office of the Library of Congress will in time perfect a technique now under experimentation for the removal of tape stain. Technicians there have devised a vacuum pump to apply suction under the stain while the worker dabs the stain with a small quantity of solvent, a wide variety of which are now being tested. However, even after the testing is completed, the curator may not have the specialized equipment necessary to use the technique, and he may wish to do some experimenting on his own. The conservation specialist at the Ohio Historical Society says she has had some success in stain removal with a Dow solvent called Chlorothene Nu (Registered trademark), which is inhibited 1,1,1-trichloroethane. [29]

Also encouraging are indications that pressure-sensitive tapes which will not stain paper now are being produced. In recent artificial aging tests conducted by the *Paper Conservation News* on nine brands of tape, two were judged satisfactory in ease of removal and only slight discoloration of the tapes (no stain was left on the four paper samples).[30] Dennison's gummed tape was tested at the same time and found to be reversible and nonstaining.

Another conservation technique, lamination, has been much mis-understood and misused. Lamination, which in the modern archival sense of the term means sealing a document between two sheets of plastic, was begun at the National Archives in the 1930s. Acting upon the advice of the National Bureau of Standards, the National Archives perfected a flat-bed hydraulic press, which under heat and pressure would fuse two thin sheets of cellulose acetate foil to the face and back of a document. Shortly thereafter, William J. Barrow developed a process whereby the pieces of acetate were preheated, placed on either side of the document, and covered with two sheets of long-fiber tissue. This sandwich was then run through a heated roller press. Barrow felt that the tissue materially strengthened the lamination and that because the document was subjected to less heat it was less damaging than the flat-bed-press method.

Not content with these modifications, Barrow continued his experiments with paper and finally decided that, for lamination to be a successful conservation technique, the chemical nature of the manuscript being laminated, if it contained injurious acids, must be altered. It was not enough to seal out atmospheric pollutants. Under identical storage conditions, he found rag papers from the colonial period that were still fresh and white, while the nineteenth- and twentieth-century papers, made of wood pulp and sized with alum rosin, were yellowed and crumbly. His tests led him to believe that chemical residue, left in the paper in the pulping process, combined with moisture and sulphur dioxide in the atmosphere and with the alum in the sizing to form sulphuric acid. Any acid attacks the cellulose fibers in pulp paper, making it brittle and fragile. The merest trace of acid will cause extensive damage to paper; it acts as a catalyst in hydrolysis; and Barrow learned to measure the degree of acidity in paper in terms of the level of hydrogen ion concentration, what is called pH factor. After much experimentation, he demonstrated that, by soaking a manuscript first in lime water (calcium hydroxide) and then in soda water (calcium bicarbonate), he could neutralize the acid content of the paper and leave a slightly alkaline residue (a fine deposit of chalk) in the fiber of the paper.[31] Acidity is measured on the pH scale from 1 through 14, with 1 to 7 acid (6 to 7 is acceptable); 7, neutral; and

7 to 14, alkaline. In the early days of lamination, a curator did not have to be a chemist to run a pH test on a piece of paper, but it helped. To get an accurate reading, it is still necessary to conduct the same tests, although specially designed kits now speed that process, too. However, the curator today can also use a device called the archivist's pen to get rapid and acceptable pH readings, *within a range.* The felt-tipped pens contain brom cresol green dye, and when the curator touches the pen to the paper, it makes a blue-green dot. The dot does not change color on a paper with alkaline residue; it turns blue on neutral paper, and yellow to orange on acid paper (see appendix for source of pens).

The Barrow process—deacidifying the document and laminating with tissue—has slowly won adherents. Gradually, restorers at the National Archives began using tissue with acetate foil, and they bought Barrow's patented laminating presses to handle the usual letter- or legal-sized file series, while retaining their own flat-bed press to accommodate maps, prints, and other larger documents.

Following the lead of the National Archives, the country's archivists made lamination a catchword, but manuscript curators were much more cautious. Oddly enough, in Great Britain, the opposite seemed to have occurred: the British Museum, the great manuscript depository, has accepted and is using the Barrow method of laminating, while the Public Record Office, which accepts deacidification as a conservation technique, still prefers to restore documents with flour paste and silk gauze, a process hundreds of years old, called "silking." The restorers at the Record Office contend that, despite Barrow's accelerated aging tests, lamination with acetate has not stood the test of time.[32]

The Bodleian Library at Oxford takes something of a middle road between the British Museum and the Public Record Office. In 1972, the library purchased an Ademco laminating press which now enables the repairers "to take advantage of new techniques of paper-repair developed after the Florence disaster." The library now has largely abandoned its traditional "wet" method of manuscript repair—flour-and-water paste and silk gauze—for what it calls a "dry" method. "Now almost all manuscripts coming in for repair are washed in cold and hot water, deacidified with magnesium bicarbonate, which removes the acid and deposits a buffer to protect the manuscript from further acid attack, sized with CMC (carboxymethyl cellulose), repaired with japanese handmade long-fibre papers and lens tissue coated with an acrylic emulsion, and pressed for a few seconds in the heated press."[33]

Much of the controversy among restorers over lamination centers around aqueous deacidification. The major objections of the National

Archives, which was initially reluctant to accept the process, have been that it slows lamination considerably, makes it far more expensive, and that, obviously, it cannot be used on volumes without removing them from their bindings. Barrow and others, principally Richard D. Smith, have worked on a nonaqueous method of deacidification. Smith, while a graduate student at the University of Chicago Library School, developed a process which he later patented, whereby paper was exposed to a solution containing an alkaline earth alkoxide dissolved in a solvent. A document can be bathed or painted with the solution (assuming the ink or color is not affected by the solvent), and Smith is also marketing his product in an aerosol can.

Smith's patent notes also that plasticizing and resin strengthening agents can be added to the nonaqueous solution, which, under pressure, can impregnate bound volumes. Some conservators feel that Smith's process—known as the "Chicago Process"[34]—holds great promise, but that it has not had sufficient large-scale testing. Others, notably the Graphic Conservation Department, R. R. Donnelley & Sons, which adopted the method in June 1968, have publicly praised the process.[35]

W. H. Langwell of Great Britain has developed what is called "vapour phase deacidification." In this process—VPD—packets containing cyclohexylamine carbonate are placed in the manuscript boxes, or sheets impregnated with the chemical are interleaved between the pages of a volume to be treated. Langwell's most recently publicized technique involves placing a page of manuscript on a piece of glass and covering the page for five minutes with a sheet of the impregnated material. He claims that the same sheet may be re-used up to thirty times without losing its effectiveness.[36]

The Langwell process neutralizes the acid in the paper but leaves no alkaline residue. Some British conservators have accepted the process, provided that the documents being treated are kept in the plastic bags and the supply stock of sachets and impregnated sheets is stored in polythene bags or tin boxes. But American conservators say that these precautions are not enough and that the system exposes curators and researchers to a dangerous chemical and poses an extreme health hazard.[37]

The latest entry into what promises to be the very lucrative deacidification sweepstakes is the morpholine vapor process developed by the W. J. Barrow laboratory under the sponsorship of the Council on Library Resources. The process consists of impregnating the paper being treated with morpholine gas, under moderately elevated temperatures, in a vacuum chamber. The commercialization of the process is being handled by a not-for-profit foundation; but as of the winter of 1973, no scientific details or test data had been released about the process.[38]

A British company called Ademco Ltd. entered the lamination market late in 1972 to challenge what had been a United States-dominated monopoly. Originally, Ademco produced dry-mount tissue and presses for mounting photographs, but then the company perfected a product called "Lamatec," a laminating tissue available in three grades (glazed, unglazed, and coated on both sides), and four sizes of laminating presses. According to Ademco's promotional literature, the tissue has a surface pH reading of 6.7, and tests, after artificial aging, for tear strength, folding, and tension "have been satisfactory." A document is laminated by being placed between two sheets of Lamatec. To keep the tissue from sticking to the press, a sheet of silicone release paper is placed top and bottom, and the sandwich is placed in the pre-heated laminator for fifteen to thirty seconds at 80° C. If necessary, the tissue can be removed by immersing the document in a shallow bath of cold water for approximately five minutes.

Ademco suggests what sounds like a most simple solution for deacidification. For documents with inks not fugitive in water, the firm recommends spraying lightly with a hand-held garden sprayer containing a "5% w/v solution of magnesium acetate." If the ink is water soluble, the magnesium acetate can be dissolved in industrial methylated spirits. If a garden-spray can would work, an empty Windex spray bottle should be ideal; but whichever device is used, the curator should remember that only a light, fine spray is necessary.[39]

Any way that the curator approaches lamination, it represents a major fund investment. For example, if he wishes to set up his own laboratory, a laminator from Barrow would cost approximately $12,000 to $15,000; from the Arbee Company, $3,000 to $8,000; and from Ademco, £185 to £850. (Ademco says that "with carriage, freight, and insurance, this price can be halved as much again, or even doubled by the time the laminator reaches its destination.") In addition to this expense, the curator must be prepared to buy or have made other equipment for washing, deacidifying, and drying paper, which will cost him a sum at least equal to that of the laminator. Added to this will be his daily labor and supply costs—no mean amount—for a total beyond the budget (or expectations) of many curators.

Although lamination is the least expensive type of restoration yet devised, it is nonetheless a process that requires a high degree of technical skill and one which does not lend itself to mechanized mass production. Few companies offer the service commercially; and where it is available, prices begin at approximately sixty cents per letter-sized sheet and may range up to $200 for a large map that requires special care.[40]

Lamination, whatever its weaknesses, has caught the public's fancy and various products have been marketed to do home laminating. The curator could wish that neither they nor the pressure-sensitive tapes had ever been invented, because their use has injured manuscripts rather than preserved them. Some of the home laminators consist of plastic sheets backed with adhesive (a big piece of pressure-sensitive tape), and others can be sprayed from an aerosol can; but in time, all of these products will cause the manuscript to turn brown.

Another commercial application of lamination has been office machines, which under heat and pressure seal a document in plastic, usually Mylar. The machines are continuously fed and are not efficiently operated except on long runs of uniform-sized documents. The curator might see the office laminator as one means of caring for the newspaper clippings which clutter up many of his collections, but they would have to be cut to size and spot mounted on any inexpensive uniform-size paper before laminating. In time, the clippings and the mounting paper will disintegrate, but the ink image will remain on the surface inside the plastic.

A less expensive means of handling clippings might be to utilize another laminating technique now known as the "Kathpalia process." This hand-laminating process (described earlier in this chapter as a means of making repairs with tissue, acetate, and acetone) was developed in the Indian Archives and is now used in the Public Record Office and the National Archives. It, too, has spurred an entry into the consumer market: a company in France now sells a machine called the India, which laminates upon the Kathpalia principle and is said to diffuse the fumes from the acetone that make the use of this type of lamination dangerous.

Another machine, more expensive than the India, the Xerox, is an ideal solution for clippings and other similar materials, if the curator can afford it. Clippings can be copied on permanent/durable paper in far less time than is required for lamination, the paper would take less space in the files, and it would be more permanent. Xerox also is most useful in copying carbons, both the flimsies and the yellow-sheet, wood-pulp type, which are so difficult to preserve. Other machines will copy clippings, but they use coated papers; permanent/durable papers can be used only with Xerox. Although Xerox was designed as a line copier, if the curator uses the half-tone screen supplied by the company, he can get satisfactory copies of clippings containing photographs (and photographs too!). Microfilming is another possible solution for clippings and carbons, provided the curator has a long consecutive run, but scattered pages here and there are better reproduced by Xerox.

Microfilm, more than any other process or invention, holds out the greatest hope to the twentieth-century curator. Although it is sometimes not thought of as such, it is the technique most used for care and conservation, especially in two areas. The first is in preparing a copy to be used in lieu of the original manuscripts, which—either because of their great value or fragile nature—cannot be studied in the original. Once the copy is prepared, the original should be withdrawn from use; there are few scholars who must see the original.

Secondly, curators, or at least those who are responsible for large nineteenth- and twentieth-century collections, look to microfilm as a possible solution to what appears to be an almost insoluble problem. The more conscientious a curator is about care and conservation, the more frustrated he becomes when he realizes that he is powerless to cope with the huge quantity of modern records which are slowly but steadily disintegrating. Realistically, he knows that, unless there is a radical breakthrough with an inexpensive process, money will never be available to deacidify this mass of paper, and, although microfilming is not cheap, there is a better chance of financial support there because microfilm offers what appears to be a drastic saving in space.

In equipment and supply costs, there is very little difference between lamination and microfilming. Studies of labor and material costs in lamination by the Library of Congress and the South Carolina Department of Archives and History which showed 23 cents and 25 cents per page, respectively, also compare closely with Yale's cost of 26.5 cents per frame for microfilm mentioned in another chapter. However, laminating equipment takes more space to operate, and page production is much lower than for microfilm. In 1968, a worker in the Library of Congress laboratory could deacidify, effect normal repairs on, and laminate approximately 200 letter-sized sheets a day. South Carolina's laboratory laminates 120,000 pages a year, which, for a crew of four, averages about 125 pages a day per technician. Even taking into account the 2:1 or 3:1 ratio of preparing manuscripts for camera to filming time, and including time to collate, a camera operator can copy hundreds of pages more than a technician could laminate in a day.[41]

Both lamination and microfilming require considerable expense, either for equipment or in fees for contracted services, and a process which has been called "encapsulation" may offer some advantages over either at less cost. Developed by the restoration office of the Library of Congress, the process involves making a sandwich of two sheets of polyester film (for example, Mylar) on either side of the manuscript. Surface adhesion will keep the manuscript from slipping around between the sheets of plastic. The sheets are sealed at the edges with pressure-type plastic tape with an inert adhesive.[42]

The Library of Congress is laminating more selectively now and encapsulating instead many flat paper items, particularly maps. One of the advantages of encapsulation is that the document within its polyester envelope can be crumpled without causing creases. The library's restoration office sees encapsulation as the first step in conservation for the great quantity of material which it feels cannot feasibly be deacidified. When gaseous deacidification becomes a reality, as the restoration office hopes it will be soon, the vapor can be injected into the polyester envelopes with a hypodermic needle, completing the conservation process. The disadvantages of encapsulation, as they have become apparent in the library's map division, are that the process takes longer than lamination and the finished map is thicker, heavier, and harder to use because of the shiny surface. Where large quantities of documents are stored, the weight and thickness factors could be of great importance.[43]

Encapsulating manuscripts in polyester is but one of several processes under experimentation which may replace or at least supplement lamination. For example, in experiments conducted in England two years ago, solutions of soluble nylon, poly (vinyl alcohol), and an alcohol-soluble copolymer were brushed on papers which then were artificially aged and tested for acidity, strength, and color. The soluble nylon substantially increased the fold strength of the papers, which indicated that it has possible uses in paper conservation, although some conservators do not feel it has yet proven to be sufficiently reversible. The results of the experiments relating to acidity may be equally important. Here the experimenters feel their data "suggest that although the acidity in paper may be an important cause of deterioration, as other investigators have proposed, this property may be altered without substantial strength improvement to the paper on aging." Time and more testing may reveal whether the curator has relied too heavily in the past upon the findings of Barrow.[44]

Conservation Laboratory

Meanwhile, such testing is beyond the capacity of most curators. A laboratory, with or without laminating equipment, is a major investment for any institution. But if, after considering the alternatives, a decision is made to equip one, what should the curator request and how much should he estimate for costs? As has been noted, a laminator could cost upwards of $15,000, with an additional $10,000 to $12,000 needed for deacidification sinks, screens, drying racks, workbenches, screw presses, electrical connections, etc. Other essential equipment would include a fume hood, $2,500 to $4,000; deionizer for water supply, $85 to $100; pH meter to test paper, $200 to $250; stero-microscope, 7-80 magnification, $500 to $600; a hydrothermograph, $165 to $250; and a small vacuum fumigation chamber, $3,500.[45]

The manuscript repair room of the Bodleian Library is described as containing "a permanent working surface with cupboards, drawers, and three working bays with inlet glass panels lit from below, a thermostatically controlled heated double sink, a fumigation cupboard, and (planned but not yet built) a drying cabinet. All surfaces are formica-covered, and in addition to the normal presses and guillotine, the work bench is equipped with tacking irons and a pH meter."[46]

An American conservator describes a workroom in about the same terms, except that she says the tables should be covered with absorbent paper, such as building paper, wrapping paper, or unprinted newsprint, because oil and water spots do not show up on a hard shiny surface. It is also essential that work surfaces be kept clean.[47]

A workbench with a hinged plate-glass top lit by two-foot fluorescent tubes from below, measuring approximately 7 by 3 by 3 feet high, made of white painted plywood with a set of drawers on one side and a cupboard on the other (along with presses, racks, and repair tables, and a four-page list of necessary tools and supplies) is described in a new book by a former craftsman from the document repair section of the Public Record Office. In a recently released manual of archival administration, yet another British authority outlines space needs, electrical circuits, and design features not mentioned elsewhere.[48]

Fire and Water Salvage

Some institutions choose to ignore conservation practices with seeming impunity except when disaster strikes, but if this happens, the curator must have some plan to stem the ravages of fire or flood. If either disaster strikes a manuscript collection, the authorities agree that the curator should make an inspection as soon as it is safe to be in the building and before any clean-up or salvage is begun. All authorities also agree upon the desirability of a plan of action which should be put into operation rapidly, but without haste or panic.

In making his inspection after a fire, the curator will be aided in his assessment if he realizes that some fire damage, at least in a rapidly controlled blaze, sometimes is more apparent than real. He will often find that papers in boxes or cartons which have burned to some degree are still in good condition. The same would be true of water damage, if it is not extensive and can be caught in time. Boxes or cartons sodden enough to collapse may contain papers which are still relatively dry.

While inspecting fire damage, the curator also should keep in mind the potential danger of the fire's restarting from spontaneous combustion. Opening a file drawer of a cabinet that has been subjected to intense heat can cause the paper to ignite spontaneously. This danger can exist for up to three days after the fire has been extinguished.[49]

A fire, unless it is a moderate one which was quickly extinguished, will probably involve a great deal of water damage. Because there is relatively little that the curator can do to salvage fire-damaged manuscripts, what can be done will be mentioned first before turning to water damage.

Some of the salvage techniques mentioned by authorities for fire-charred manuscripts might do as much damage as good. One suggests brushing or spraying burned paper with ricinated collodion or almost any other plasticized transparent film base; another suggests applying sheets of adhesive-coated plastic. But the dangers of using these materials have been noted earlier. Probably the only practical alternatives are microfilming or lamination, and the latter has been most frequently used.

In planning a salvage operation of water-damaged documents from either fire or flood, the curator needs to think in terms of space, supplies, personnel, and a system of priorities. In a warm, humid atmosphere, mold growth may be expected to appear on water-damaged manuscripts within forty-eight hours.[50] Thus, in the winter, heat should be turned off in the building and in the summer, the air conditioning should be turned on if possible. If there is electrical service, fans and dehumidifiers should be used to keep the air moving and reduce the moisture in the air.[51]

One of the most difficult of the curator's tasks will be to control volunteer workers, who, intent upon rescue operations, may do irreparable damage. No one should be allowed to remove manuscripts from the area until the overall plan of salvage has been agreed upon and he has briefed his assistants. If, for example, the catalog or finding aids have been destroyed or partially destroyed, identification of material will be particularly critical, and it may be necessary to chart the location of manuscripts as they are removed from the building.

If, upon removal from the disaster area, still-wet manuscripts can be frozen immediately, significantly more material can be salvaged and restored later. Experience gained over the past fifteen years indicates that manuscripts can be kept in a frozen state up to two years and then dried without permanent damage.

A frozen-food locker or plant, if the curator can locate one, is ideal. If possible, manuscripts should be transported to the freezing facility by refrigerated truck. Bundles of manuscripts should be wrapped in freezer paper and kept cold, awaiting transfer with either ice or dry ice. Temperatures between 10° to 20° F. for both initial freezing and storage are preferred. Frozen-food plants often use up

Fig. 14. Fire-damaged records being freeze-dried in the space simulation chamber at the McDonnell Douglas plant, St. Louis. (Courtesy McDonnell Douglas Corp.)

to −40° F. for quick freezing; temperatures in this range can be harmful to manuscripts and should be accepted by the curator only as a last resort.⁵²

If facilities for freezing are not available, the curator should keep the damaged manuscripts as cool as possible and move forward rapidly with cleaning and drying. If possible, the curator should select an outside site with good drainage for the cleaning area. If not, a garage or large shed with duck boards, several plastic garbage cans, and a hose with running water will do.

Dirt should be gently washed from loose manuscripts or bound volumes, which then should be taken to the drying area. Here the curator should assemble quantities of unprinted newsprint, paper towels, blotters, strong toilet tissue, or other such absorbent materials. Expense may force him to use newspapers, which, if he discards the colored sections, will serve. Work tables should be covered with polyethylene.

Volumes, on end with covers open but pages not fanned, are drained and, after drying to a point where they can be safely handled, are interleaved every five leaves. Absorbent sheets are changed every two or three hours. Thymol-impregnated sheets of paper are inserted between cover and body. Inside covers are the last to dry and most prone to develop mold.

Loose sheets of manuscript, which will be very fragile when wet, should be emptied carefully from boxes. If the curator places a wet sheet of polyester or polyethylene film on a pile of single wet manuscripts, sheets will adhere to the film by capillary attraction and can be gently separated from the pile. If the manuscripts then are covered by a sheet of nonwoven polyester fabric, they will dry without sticking to either top or bottom sheet of plastic.

Microfilm, movies, photographic negatives, and any other film-base documents should be placed in polyethylene bags and immersed in a plastic garbage can full of cold water. They can be left there safely for two or three days while cleaning and drying proceeds. Photographic prints can also be held temporarily in ice cold water until washing and drying are completed. Some microfilm companies provide emergency cleaning services, and most professional photographers would have facilities for cleaning and drying prints. Films and prints can be frozen if salvage operations are going to take more than a few days. Some damage may result, but it will be less than what will develop if either films or prints are left wet too long.

A curator who is foresighted will not wait until disaster comes to make plans. He should have firmly in mind the names of experts to call in an emergency and have some notion of where to get supplies and where to find space for a salvage operation.[53]

If, in his efforts at physical care and conservation, the curator remembers the *sine qua non* of the professional conservator—do nothing that is irreversible—he will be on safe ground. This is not always as simple as the conservators make it seem, and sometimes even the conscientious curator will be hard-pressed to know with certainty if his conservation practices follow this basic principle. Ultimately, however, when he has taken the precautions that he can, he must move on to other concerns, as, for example, turning his attention to arranging and describing the collections of manuscripts in his care.

SELECTED READINGS

George M. Cunha was the first author to write a comprehensive study of conservation. Now in a second edition (co-authored by his wife), *A Manual and Bibliography on the Care, Repair, and Restoration of Library Materials* is must reading for the curator. Because of the book, the classes that he taught while at the Boston Atheneaum (see the papers published from the 1971 seminar, Cunha and Norman P. Tucker, editors, *Library and Archives Conservation*), and his position as director of the New England Document Conservation Center, he is perhaps the country's most influential conservator, but some of his peers suggest that he is too willing to accept techniques before they have been thoroughly proven.

Harold W. Tribolet, now retired as manager of Graphics Conservation Department of the Lakeside Press, wrote too little, but one of his best articles was "Conservation," in the collected papers published under the title *University Archives.* Carolyn Horton, *Cleaning and Preserving Bindings and Related Material,* is excellent and much more helpful for the curator than the title indicates. Margaret Scriven's pamphlet is a down-to-earth guide by a practicing librarian. The English approach is outlined in D. B. Wardle, *Document Repair,* and a fine work dealing with a limited phase of conservation is Peter Waters, *Emergency Procedures for Salvaging Flood or Water-Damaged Library Materials.*

Lamination is best explained in William J. Barrow, *Manuscripts and Documents: Deterioration and Restoration,* and W. H. Langwell, developer of a nonaqueous means of deacidification, writes of his process in "The Vapour Phase Deacidification of Books and Documents."

Richard D. Smith, who patented another system of nonaqueous deacidification which he calls the "Chicago Process," has written a great deal, but explains his findings in technical detail in "New Approaches to Preservation." The entire issue of *Library Quarterly,* January 1970, in which Smith's article appears, is devoted to several phases of conservation. Both *Special Libraries* and *The American Archivist* publish frequent articles on conservation, and another periodical devoted exclusively to the field is *Restaurator.*

V

Establishing Bibliographic Control

THE curator has three primary functions: to acquire manuscripts, to conserve them, and to make them available for research. Everything that he does in some way relates to these functions, and at no time is he more aware of it than when he establishes his system of bibliographic control.[1]

The processes of arrangement and description constitute the major aspects of bibliographic control of manuscripts, but also included is the preparation of ancillary records such as the donor, accession, and collection files. If the curator has the opportunity to set up his own system, he should strive to keep it as simple as possible, and if he is taking over an established system, he should analyze it closely to see if it works and if all the parts are necessary. He should not be afraid to abandon procedures that do not fulfill their purpose; too many curators are knowingly "putting good money after bad," in part because they do not wish to admit that time spent in the past may have been wasted, and in part because of the great cost of conversion and the necessity of operating two separate systems during the conversion. Whatever controls the curator decides are necessary, he should resist the temptation of the temporary. How many final inventories are written to replace the preliminary inventory? How many corrected catalog cards are typed to replace the temporary cards? If the institu-

113

tion's collection is vital and growing, there is always the pressure to move on to new projects, and the curator would be well advised not to establish temporary controls that he is not willing to accept as permanent.

Accessioning

The accessioning of incoming manuscript collections is an almost universally accepted bibliographic control; yet in many institutions it is time wasted. It is wasted in the sense that assigning accession numbers to collections is a library technique developed to answer the question, "Who was the previous owner of this book?" In times past, when the curator penciled accession numbers on individual manuscripts, it was possible to answer this question by referring to the accession book or card file, but as the size of collections grew, accession numbers were placed first on folders, then just boxes, then collections, and finally in many institutions the practice was abandoned entirely as a means of identifying cataloged manuscripts. Today, if the curator wants to know the provenance—"Where did we get the manuscript, what is its history?"—he may consult his accession record, but he may also go to his donor/source file or his collections file, which in a real sense are part of the accession records.

Although the accessions record poses under a misnomer and no longer fulfills its original design, it has been adapted by many curators to serve other purposes: as a stock or inventory control, in a business sense of the term; as a temporary finding or reference aid for uncataloged collections; and as identification for component parts of a collection which might be separated from the manuscripts (see Photographs, in chapter 7, "Nonmanuscripts"). All of these functions are valid and useful. However, it might have been better if curators had developed their own terminology for this record and in turn devised a record form more in keeping with the function. Would not *control record* and *control number* be more descriptive terms? Why could not the form of the control record be designed to incorporate the facts traditionally noted on the accession record plus information from the "overview," the informal appraisal or summary of the papers done by the processor at a later date?

Traditionally, manuscripts have been accessioned in the following manner. When the manuscripts, either gifts or purchases, arrive at the collecting institution, they will have come via a variety of routes: by mail, delivered to the curator's office; by moving van, motor freight, railway express, or air freight, delivered to the receiving room; or by the donor or field staff, delivered to the receiving room or office. An accession/control record must be flexible enough to accommodate these variations. It should include the date of arrival, the name of collection, the name and address of donor (or seller), a description of the collection, and an accession/control number. If the accession was purchased, the purchase price should be entered on the record. At the Lilly Library, Indiana University, the purchase price is listed in code in the accession record.[2]

Some institutions follow a strict numerical sequence for accession/control numbers; others incorporate the year date as part of the number, as for example 67–315. An alternate solution might be to let the date alone serve as the accession/control number, that is, 670605 for June 5, 1967. For institutions accessioning more than one collection a day, a single letter suffix would serve to distinguish them. Each box of a multiple-box collection should be numbered separately in any accession system.

Where the record is prepared and who prepares it will in part dictate its form. The three common forms of the accession/control record are the register or bound book, the card file, and the loose sheet. With each type, if the accessioning is done by more than one person, each entry should be initialled to facilitate clearing up questions that might arise about an accession. Accession/control records kept in the volume and card forms are essentially adapted from library technology. Loose-leaf accession/control records are probably a curator's innovation (with perhaps an assist from the archivist).

An accession/control register, which can be carried to storage, the receiving room, or the curator's office, has the advantage of keeping the accession/control numbers in order and the entries precise and compact. Another advantage of the register is that there is no need for a typewriter to record the information. The card type of accession/control file can be prepared by hand, too, but it is usually typed from the curator's notes, meaning a loss of time and an extra chance for error. An accession/control record on loose sheets offers most of the advantages of the other two systems. Sheets on a clipboard can be carried anywhere to do the accessioning and can be filled out by hand. Use of a ball-point pen and carbons allows two duplicates to be made. The original sheet can be filed numerically by accession/control number and bound or gathered into a spring binder each year. One copy can be filed alphabetically by the donor's name, creating the donor/source file (see below). The last copy can be filed in the collections file.

When the accession/control record has been filled out, the curator will want to mark the accession before putting it into temporary storage. Some institutions type box labels, but this seems an unnecessary refinement if the accession/control numbers are clearly lettered on the boxes with a marking pen. Multiple-box collections can be shelved in storage numerically by accession numbers, and single items or collections smaller than one box can be foldered or wrapped and then boxed by number in an adjacent storage area.

The multiple loose sheets in this type of accession/control system can serve at least a dual purpose. Assuming that the institution allows researchers access to unprocessed manuscripts, temporary author and subject cards referring to the collection by accession/control number can be filed, and the original sheet can be issued to the researcher in lieu of an inventory. The copy which will eventually be filed in the collections folder might go temporarily to the curator to keep in a spring binder and thus form for him a composite record of collections in storage awaiting processing. Also it is sometimes useful to keep a copy of the accession/control record in storage with the accession and to send a copy to the publicity office, where it can be used in writing the press release announcing the acquisition. An original and two carbons cannot serve all these purposes, but if the curator has access to copying machines, making multiples of the original is a simple solution.

If the curator has facilities for copying catalog cards easily and rapidly, he might develop an accession/control system based upon cards. Cards are easy to sort for the donor file, they can be filed directly into the dictionary card catalog as temporary cards, and they can be used as temporary labels for boxes in storage.

The donor/source and collection files are accession records of a type and reflect the curator's need for more and different kinds of information than are found in the traditional accession record. The donor/source file was once called the donor file in most institutions. This was in the uncomplicated days when most manuscripts were received as gifts. Today with purchases, deposits awaiting a change in the tax law, combination purchase and gifts, and delayed gifts and fractional gifts, the expanded donor/source file is a necessity. In most institutions, it usually contains the same information as the accession/control record, but in a different form, to facilitate alphabetical filing.

The curator uses the donor/source file to answer such patrons' questions as "May I please see the manuscript Aunt Nellie gave in 1952?"—or his own query, "What *did* I buy from Goodstat's last year?"

A researcher's frequent question, "How did you acquire the John Dewey Papers and have you been in touch with his widow?", can best be answered by reference to the collection file. Some institutions consider the collection and the donor/source files public records, but this viewpoint is questionable. This is not to say that the curator is not obligated to consult his in-house records to extract pertinent information to assist the researcher, but he must recognize that certain inherent dangers are involved. It will assist some researchers to know how and why a collection was acquired, but the curator must remember that occasionally what passes for scholarship may be only personal curiosity. Too, these files may contain excellent leads to manuscripts, which, for one reason or another the curator has not pursued. Scholars often fancy themselves manuscript collectors, and in fact some are quite proficient. But even if the scholar is not a collector, he may be traveling to a rival institution next week—well, there is more than one way to lose a good manuscript collection.

The collection file will contain a variety of materials, which constitute a source of background information on specific manuscript collections. It may contain a copy of the accession/control record, and it should include copies of all correspondence, memorandums of telephone conversations, field reports, gift agreements including restrictions on use—in short, everything that bears upon the acquisition of the manuscript collection. Here, too, should be a record of special conditions of gift—for example, a statement that duplicate and unwanted material are to be returned to the donor, or that the field representative, rather than split the collection, has agreed to provide a microfilm copy of a series of letters to another institution. In time, the collection file should contain copies of all press releases and stories about a collection, as well as letters from researchers regarding its use. As the collection file grows, it may be necessary to split off some elements into a separate contract or gift agreement file, or a "use" file of materials relating to research—projected, in progress, and completed.

The collection file and the donor/source file are easily enough arranged alphabetically. Copies of letters, etc., are turned lengthwise for filing so that the head of the letter is to the left, and the collection or donor/source name is then written in the upper right-hand corner in colored ink. Both of these files will be permanent records, and copies should be prepared on good quality stock.

Arranging

The collection file for the manuscripts to be arranged should be studied carefully by the curator before he begins processing. If a copy of the accession record is not included in the collection file, he should also have it at his processing table. After he has made whatever biographical notes he can from these files, he should go to the library and begin preliminary research. If, for example, he is preparing to work on the papers of an author with whom he is not familiar, he should read his books. If the papers are those of a research chemist with a drug manufacturing firm, he should attempt to learn something about the company and the products that the chemist might have developed. If he can determine what the chemist's avocation or hobby was, this too might be studied. Biographical and subject research is an ongoing process during the arrangement of a collection, and the time spent is usually productive of a more comprehensive inventory and better catalog cards. The curator must remember, however, that, even under ideal conditions, he can devote only a limited time to background research. He should not attempt to become an expert in the fields covered by the papers at hand. Instead, he must be able to assimilate the highlights, to skim, and not to get bogged down in details. It is always difficult to maintain the proper balance.

Because so much time is invested in background research, some curators with large enough staffs develop specialists, with certain people arranging collections that fall within a given subject area or time period. Although the advantage is obvious, the disadvantage may not be as apparent. There is a tendency for the specialist to impose an order upon a collection, whereas someone arranging a set of papers in a subject area new to him will be more apt to let the inherent form of the materials dictate the arrangement.

Having completed his preliminary background research on the papers, the curator is now ready to begin the arrangement. His first task is to obtain an overview of the collection. In making this appraisal of the papers, he will note the numbers on the shipping cartons which indicate the order in which the papers were packed. If he can determine a packing order, he puts the cartons in that order; if not, he can arrange them in accession-number order.

If the size of the collection will allow and if there is enough processing space available, the curator will want to open all of the cartons at one time, so that he can form an impression of the general order of the collection. If the papers are in file folders, are the folders on edge, packed flat, or are some even upside down? Are the letters folded and tied in packets, or have handfuls of loose papers been crammed into the cartons? Does it appear that someone other than the person or agency creating the papers has handled the files before the curator received them? Frequently, descendants will screen a person's papers and in so doing destroy their coherent quality.

At this stage, the curator will be handling the papers carefully, taking material from the cartons in small handfuls and after examination returning them to their place in the carton. As he examines each carton, he will be making brief notes on the inclusive dates of the material, the type of material, and how it seems to fit together. Sometimes nothing fits together, but more often than not the curator, who realizes that arranging manuscripts is a little like putting together a jigsaw puzzle, will have a tentative plan of arrangement in mind by the time he completes his initial survey of the material, and it will help him to clarify his thinking if he prepares a simple outline showing the major series in the collection.

Occasionally the curator is lucky. For example, by the time he has looked at five out of a total of nine cartons, he discovers that the papers of Gail Wilson, a real estate dealer, are in nearly perfect order. Two simple correspondence series relate to two earlier firms, Haggerty Realty and Jones Associates, which merged to form the Bartok Agency before Wilson bought the firm. A year later, she began the "Property File," a list of properties arranged alphabetically by street name and then by street number. The correspondence file is arranged in two alphabetical sequences, one for real estate and the other for insurance, and there is one small subseries relating to Wilson's activities in the Chamber of Commerce. A four-drawer card file of "Prospects" and eleven miscellaneous volumes relating to finances (accounts receivable, check register, ledger, etc.) make up the rest of the collection. The curator decided to destroy the one half carton of newspaper clippings of the firm's weekly advertisement (a complete file of the newspaper is on file in his institution's library). The file folders for the correspondence of one of the earlier firms merged into Bartok are deteriorating. The curator replaced these, and the collection is now ready to inventory.

In this instance, although he may be unaware of what he has done, the curator has arranged the Gail Wilson Papers according to the two basic principles of archival arrangement. The first, the principle of provenance, which stems from an earlier concept, *respect des fonds,* is that records should be kept according to their source. As one source has said about the "natural body of documentation left by the creating agency," the archivist does not "let documents drift away from it," nor does he "let alien documents get into it." The second principle, *l'ordre primitif*, the sanctity of original order, is that records should be kept in the original order imposed on them. Some curators might have arranged the papers of the Haggerty and Jones agencies as separate collections, and most archivists would have kept the clippings with the Bartok files.[3]

Few collections will be as simple to arrange as the Gail Wilson Papers. More often than not, the papers of organizations, institutions, and businesses, although they are archival in nature, arrive at the collecting agency in far from their original order. If it is a matter of careless packing, sometimes, with some study and a little ingenuity, the curator can restore the papers to their original order. The more likely circumstance, however, is that a set of papers arrives in almost complete disorder. A typical example would be papers that have been packed, moved, repacked, stored, and, years later, come into the curator's care after having suffered the natural attrition of such processes. Sometimes the loss and damage is more systematic—such as when a widow removes "personal" material from her deceased husband's files and they are much shuffled in the process, or when the relative who plans to write a biography selects and rearranges the papers according to his chapter outline and discards "useless" material. But whatever the reason, the curator is constantly confronted with collections, large and small, which retain few if any traces of the original order. It is then his job to bring order out of this chaos.

The simplest method of arranging manuscripts is chronological. This traditionally accepted method has much to recommend it. Unlike the subject arrangement, which tends to fragment a set of papers, a chronological arrangement tends to show the relationship between documents and the events to which they relate. The documentation of a person's life is created in a time sequence, and it could be argued that the chronological order is the original order of the documentation. Materials arranged chronologically are simple for the scholar to cite, and they are easy to locate in the collection.

Another method of arranging manuscripts is alphabetically by writer. Traditionally, this approach has been used most frequently with literary material. It has the advantage of allowing the curator readily to satisfy his mail requests for copies of all letters written by a certain author. Within the alphabetical arrangement, the letters of an author would be arranged chronologically, and some curators use what they feel is the best of the two systems by arranging incoming letters by author and copies of outgoing mail by date. One inherent difficulty of any alphabetical system is determining whether letters should be gathered under personal names or the names of firms, governmental units, and other organizations.

Arranging manuscripts by subject is usually less than successful. Determining the author or the date of a document may be difficult enough, but it is simple compared to assigning multi-subject documents to a single subject. Of course, if the curator receives a person's papers which contain materials which the individual may have collected and arranged in subject areas, he may be wise to retain them in this order.

What, then, are some of the problems common to any system of arrangement and how does the curator resolve them? The most difficult and most persistent problem will be striking the proper balance—to read enough of the documents to identify and describe them but not enough to waste time. Ideally, each piece of paper should be studied carefully, but this is not possible, and the curator must learn to skim and to read almost intuitively.

Of course, what the curator reads will have little meaning if he does not take the proper kind of notes. His notes will generally be of two distinct kinds: the "content" notes, which he will use in preparing the inventory and catalog cards for the papers, and "sorting" notes, which are helpful in arranging the papers. In some institutions, taking content notes has been formalized through the use of data sheets, mimeographed forms which are filled out by the curator as he examines the contents of a file folder. Information is abstracted from the data sheet for the inventory, but the data sheets are kept and used as a secondary finding aid when the researcher wants more details on a collection. Data sheets are most useful in arranging large modern collections that are to be retained in original order. The data sheet, which is usually a full letter-size sheet, may be wasteful and cumbersome in taking content notes on individual manuscripts. Mimeographed paper cut in half to give a 5½-by-8½-inch sheet is a convenient size, as are the cheap note pads which can be bought in 4-by-6 size. The latter is also a convenient size for preparing copy for catalog cards, so a supply would have a double use. The exact size is not important. However, a note sheet of about these dimensions provides enough space for an ample content note and yet does not encourage the taking of unnecessarily long notes. But whatever size the curator chooses, content notes should be taken on uniform sheets so that they are easily sorted and arranged to write the inventory.

Notes should be standard in format as well as in size. If the data sheet is not used, some other formal pattern should be developed,

```
Takes job as lit. ed. Daily Herald

Sassoon to Graves                              13 March [1919]

        [Body of the note goes here.  In this instance, Siegfried

        Sassoon's letter to Robert Graves probably would not need

        further description.  If all the letters in the Robert

        Graves Papers are addressed to Graves, the curator may

        decide it is not necessary to list the recipient in the

        heading of each note.]
```

Fig. 15. A simple form for taking content notes.

lest the curator lose valuable information by not being systematic. The advantage of a form like the data sheet is that there are statements which the curator must complete and questions which he must answer. The same effect can be achieved in a simple manner by ruling three lines or blanks at the top of the note, which the curator must fill out each time. Once he gets into the habit of supplying the same information in the same space on each note, in time there will be no need for the blanks (see figure 15). On the top line, left, goes the headline in which the curator, in a half dozen words at the most, gives the title of his note. The line directly below this is the source of the note, the letter, document, volume, etc., from which the note is being written, and the line across on the right is for the date of the source. It is a good policy for the curator to check to see that these items are full and correct before beginning the body of the content note, which he writes below the heading. In some instances, if the headline is well written, little need be added in the body of the note, and as a general rule the entire note should not be more than three or four sentences.

The process of taking content notes is an attempt by the curator to abstract what he thinks is the important information in the collection so that he can synthesize it for the researcher. No finding aid will answer all the researcher's questions, and at best it can serve only as a guide. With this in mind, the curator should strive for clarity and brevity. He should not write on more than one subject per note sheet, and if he uses abbreviations he should confine them to standard ones from an accepted list.

Sorting notes, because they are of a greater variety and are usually more fragmentary, generally are written on a pad, perhaps the common legal pad. In one sense, the sorting notes are extensions of the curator's memory. Here he will record random and odd bits of information which will take but seconds to jot down but which, weeks later, he will have forgotten if they have not been noted. On the pad, the curator will want to write reminders to himself of things to check concerning the papers—a book to look at, a date or a name to verify. In another sense, the sorting notes will be a running commentary of the curator with himself. Here he asks a multitude of questions, the answers to which he hopes to find later in the papers. Here he records his guesses about how the papers came together, his hunches about the relationship of one section of the papers to another—all sorts of working hypotheses which will aid him in completing the arrangement of the papers and preparing the finding aids.

If a name index is one of the finding aids the curator wishes to prepare, he will need to take a different form of note. Name indexes can be all-inclusive or selective, and they can be designed to list letters by, to, and about an individual; but whatever form they take, they are very time-consuming to produce. They are also very convenient to use in answering reference questions, and the curator may decide that they are worth the effort, particularly for small but potentially rich research collections.

In preparing a name index, the curator should equip himself with a box of catalog cards and an alphabetical card guide. The first time he encounters a letter of each person to be indexed, he notes on the card the writer's name and the date of the letter and files it in alphabetical order in the box. At first, he is making out cards continually, but gradually names will recur, and after he has recorded fifteen or twenty letters from the same person, he will need to start a second card. If the completed index is to be an in-house finding aid, these rough cards will do; but if it is to become part of the inventory, it can be typed on other cards or in sheet form.

Some curators do not follow a formal note-taking procedure but enter their more or less fragmentary content notes one after another on a notepad. This procedure is more than adequate for a small collection which can be processed in a matter of a few days, provided it can be completed before moving to another project. If the arranging is interrupted, the curator may find it difficult to pick up after his notes are "cold."

Note-taking is a highly individualistic process. Much depends on the curator, the size and type of collection, the work load and backlog of unprocessed manuscripts, and the form and intent of the finished product—the finding aid. In spite of the variables, there is one constant: the curator will take more notes than he uses, usually a great many more. This is not wasted time. As a result, he knows the collection much better, and the notes will have great value for subsequent synthesizing and consolidating of material. But as important, he probably has saved time by taking more notes than fewer. If the curator is in doubt, he should take a note. At most, it will take a few minutes to record something that he thinks will be important. If he does not make a note, to go back and try to find the source later will be frustrating and very time-consuming.

Irrespective of what kind of arrangement the curator makes of the manuscripts, he inevitably encounters difficulty in dating documents. Sometimes a combination of external and internal evidence will help him date a letter, but it does take some detective work. If the letters are in envelopes, especially if they are in bundles, his chances are very good. Postmarks will give an approximate date, and the position of an undated letter in a packet between two dated letters will help decide its date. Sometimes ink, stationery, and, on rare occasions, watermarks, can help date a letter. By reading the text the curator may be able to date it upon internal evidence, especially with the use of a perpetual calendar (see appendix) when at least a partial date appears in the letter. Phrases in the letter referring to specific events can often be used to establish a date and even answers to questions or some other clue may tie it to a dated letter.

Although few curators have the time to become thoroughly familiar with one person's handwriting, editors of collected works have, and they are able to date manuscripts by this method in conjunction with the external and internal evidence mentioned above. The editor of the Emily Dickinson papers, for example, had photostats made of Miss Dickinson's dated manuscripts, which he cut and pasted into charts. By comparing ascenders and descenders of g's, f's, p's and so on, as well as linked and unlinked letters, he was able to date most undated letters and poems in the papers.[4]

If no positive evidence can be found to establish a date, the curator's educated guess is better than leaving the item undated, for undated material falling at the end of any chronological series is difficult to use. Supplied dates can take a variety of forms. Most common is the *circa* date, written [*ca. 1865*], filed after December 31, 1865, [*ca. June, 1865*], filed after June 30, 1865, and [*ca. June 18, 1865*], filed after all other letters of that date. A *circa* date is normally placed in the upper right-hand corner of the document, and, like all other information which the curator adds to the document, it is written lightly in soft lead pencil and bracketed.* Because researchers tend to overlook undated materials, some curators file them at the beginning of their proper chronological series, where it is hoped they will be more visible. The argument for filing after the series is that the researcher will be better able to use the undated piece if he has already read the series in which it belongs. If the curator thinks he knows the date of a document but is not positive, it might be dated [*June 18, 1865?*], and if he supplies only a portion of the date, only that portion is bracketed, *June 18* [*1865*]. Occasionally, internal evidence will indicate supplying a [*post 1865*] or an [*ante 1864*] date, but [*Winter, 1864*] would be difficult to file and would more sensibly be dated [*ca. Jan., 1864*]. Some authorities advise the curator that, when he cannot supply the year, he should write a date *June 18*, [*n.y.*], but a document so dated will have to be placed at the end of the chronology before the undated documents. It is better to give the document a *circa* year date.

In the past, the curator penciled the date on consecutive pages of a multipaged letter, but this is rarely necessary unless the chronological series contains many letters in juxtaposition that are written on the same stationery.[5] In any other circumstance, there is little chance that parts of two different letters would be transposed during sorting or be mixed later by the researcher. This is not to say that the curator will not be faced with transposed sheets; papers which have been handled frequently before arrival at the collecting agency may be in a very jumbled state.

Manuscripts that have been jumbled also yield a higher than average rate of fragments—letters with missing pages, usually the first or last page. When the curator finds a fragment during sorting, he should mark it lightly [*fragment*] and set it aside in a separate pile.

---

* Apart from supplying dates, the only other information commonly added to a manuscript by the curator is the correct name in brackets below a partial or illegible signature. For all bracketed material, a soft lead pencil is used—even though it may smear a little—because it can be erased without leaving a visible permanent mark on the manuscript.

Later he will be able to match many fragments together. Those that cannot be matched retain their penciled identification and after the final sorting are assigned their proper place in the series.

It is a very small and homogeneous set of papers that the curator can arrange with one sorting. Any collection of more than two or three boxes, unless it is received in good original order which can be retained, will require at least three sortings to put it in chronological order. During the first sort, the curator will be taking very few content notes and only occasional sorting notes; instead, he will be familiarizing himself with the papers and doing some basic housekeeping. For example, when he opens the first carton of the Caroline Hover Papers, he finds it about half full of loose paper, apparently correspondence, with three tied packages of envelopes, a wrapped bundle marked *Important,* several bound volumes, one or two books, and a framed photograph. The photograph and book he sets aside to await his decision about whether or not they are to be retained with the papers (see chapter on nonmanuscripts). He examines the tied packages, sees that the letters are all addressed to the same person, and begins to remove them from their envelopes. He flattens the letters by pressing or reversing the folds gently, and, if necessary, he cleans them and makes small repairs (see "Care and Conservation"). If they need it, he dates the letters and supplies senders' names from the envelopes. Some curators, especially those of literary collections, feel that the place from which a letter was written is important; this information may be copied from a postmark or return address. The flattened letters are then stacked, and the envelopes are set aside.[6] The envelope that has what appears to be part of a reply drafted on it the curator puts in the stack with the letters, since because of the annotation, it is a document itself. In one envelope he finds a letter with a second letter enclosed. On the first, he writes in brackets [*Enclosed a letter from Seth Smith to Ada James, June 18, 1846*], and on the second he pencils [*Enclosed in Ada James to Caroline Hover, July 2, 1846*]. Letters of a more modern date and of less importance he would staple together, probably, and then file under the date of the covering letter.

When the curator comes to the bound volumes, he reaches for his small note pad and slips a carbon in between the first two pages. After examining the volume, he writes the catalog description and a temporary volume number on the pad. The duplicate he slips between the pages of the volume, and the original he places in a folder to be sorted later. With only a dozen or so volumes in this collection, the curator will not have great difficulty arranging them by series and date, and he may not need to bother making the slips. However, in a collection with many volumes, the duplicate slips can be shuffled and rearranged much easier than the volumes themselves until the curator arrives at a final order. When the order is established, the duplicate slips are convenient to hand to a typist working on the inventory.

Meanwhile, the curator has unwrapped and examined the bundle marked *Important,* but he is puzzled by its contents. It appears to contain correspondence of the same nature as the loose papers in the bottom of the carton. He does not see any unity in the group of papers, nor is there any apparent reason why it was marked important; but because he is uncertain, he sets it aside until later. The curator knows that he must be cautious; he can disperse the bundle at the end of the first sorting, or even later; but if he divides it now, he can seldom reconstitute it.

As the curator reaches the loose papers, he removes them carefully in small handfuls from the carton. Although they appear to be in disarray, he knows from experience that the relationship of one sheet to the next may provide him with clues for dating and identifying. He sees that many of the sheets which are clipped together are letters and the carbon copy replies.[7] The curator removes the paper clips, and where they have spotted rust on a page, he scrapes it off gently with a knife. He knows that now the papers are to be placed in air-conditioned storage, paper clips and other metal file fasteners should not rust, but they do take extra space, and they tend to catch other papers. Mixed with the loose papers is a thirteen-page typewritten article and two carbon copies. The curator removes the rubber bands and spot-checks to ascertain if the carbons are exact copies. The carbon containing several manuscript annotations he keeps; the exact duplicate goes into the box containing other duplicates, the calendar, the baby shoe, a square of plastic, and other bits and pieces to be destroyed or returned to the donor. The curator staples the original and the annotated carbon and places them in a stack separate from the correspondence. Later, in the second and third cartons he examines, he finds many more articles and speeches, enough to form a separate series in the arrangement. But if, at the end of his first sort through the papers, he has placed only a few items in this stack, he probably will then incorporate them into the general correspondence series.

Out of the first carton the curator also sorts grocery lists, assorted bills, cancelled checks, and like material. If the papers he is processing are those of a person of sufficient importance, these materials will be rough-sorted by year, perhaps, and grouped in a *Miscellaneous* or *Financial* series. In other situations, he will choose to destroy or return this material. If pressed to explain why he kept the same type of material in one collection and destroyed it in another, he will explain that the decision may be based on how relevant the material is to the collection, its bulk, its age, or intrinsic value, as, for example, in pictorial billheads. Sorting is epitomized by this continual process of evaluation.

At the bottom of the carton the curator finds several hundred carbons of what is essentially a form letter written over a period of two months. He counts the total, selects a sample letter and notes on it the number of letters sent and the inclusive dates. If he feels it important enough, he might type a list of the recipients of the letter and attach it to the sample.[8]

At the end of the first sorting, the curator revises his organization plan. It now appears that one series he had expected did not materialize, and another did. He found the minutes of only two meetings of the Keystone Club, so he abandons that subject as a series; but he remembers finding speech after speech, so he will arrange those in a separate series as he sorts a second time.

During the second sorting, the curator will concentrate upon correcting errors he made in the first sorting and in preparing the bulk of the content notes. By this time, he will have determined whether the papers will be perfunctorily or intensively cataloged. This decision will not be based upon reading the collection; at this point, he will have read very little. But it will be based upon his judgment on the completeness of the papers and their value as a research unit. As the second sorting progresses, this evaluation, too, may change.

During the first sort, the curator had decided that the collection was not important enough to warrant a name index of any kind, but he did see a group of letters from an author and another smaller set from an inventor. He will want a complete list of all those letters by date, with content notes on at least some of them. He remembers seeing several letters from a relative who had gone to the Colorado gold fields, and there were other letters on blue stationery written in a small hand with interesting sketches of some kind of machine. With these and other thoughts in mind, the curator starts the second sorting.

The second sorting is best accomplished with either a rack of sorting bins or enough table space to allow for a couple of dozen piles. As the curator begins to sort correspondence by year or letter of the alphabet, he scans the letters. The routine ones are passed over quickly; he is looking for the letters with content. He will be looking for both the expected and the extraordinary. For example, if the papers of a politician contain very little about his campaign for office, and if the family letters of a midwestern farmer contain a letter describing a battle in the Russo-Japanese War, the curator should make note. The curator must alert researchers that they may not find what they expect, as well as point out the unexpected which would otherwise be overlooked.

Successive sortings to refine the alphabetical or chronological arrangement can be largely mechanical, but the alert curator can gain insights about the collection even at this point. However, in some institutions, clerical staff are assigned these tasks. In others, the first two sortings as described here are combined; and in yet others, the collection is sorted by clerical help and "read" by the curator after it is in final order. If clerks, interns, or volunteers assist in sorting, it is important that the curator, who has familiarized himself with the papers, give them detailed instructions and supervise and review their work.[9]

In the example above, the curator sorted a modest-sized collection of personal papers. If, on the other hand, he arranges a large collection containing series already organized by subject-matter or file-coding systems (common attributes of the papers of an organization or a business), the curator has other special concerns. When he unpacked the collection, he watched for finding aids, such as indexes, registers, file lists, or file-code manuals, prepared by the file originators. He now studies the finding aids while examining the files to determine whether or not they can be helpful in checking on sequences within the series and the integrity of the series. At this point, he can also determine whether or not the "ready-made" finding aids can be used as supplements to those he will prepare.

The size of discrete units within a series may present problems. For example, one file may occupy several folders or even several boxes, and to insure maintenance of sequence, the curator may decide to number the folders. Conversely, other files may contain only one or two items per title, and he must then decide whether to put each file in a separate folder or to group them. If he decides to save folders and storage space by grouping several small files in one folder, he can provide the necessary file identity by affixing title sheets to the files or by putting each of them in a lightweight interior folder.

Reproducing long file titles on the folder label can be time-consuming and wasteful. For example, the curator might have a file title that reads thus: "File No. 168. Appointment of Agents and Attorneys to Receive and Enter Merchandise at Custom Houses and Power of Attorney Appointing George S. Bush and James W. Allen to Serve at Seattle, 1896–1898." If a complete title list is to form part of the finding aid, savings can be effected by recording only the file number on the folder label. Cumbersome and obscure titles assigned by the file originator can often be shortened and clarified. However, this process, too, can be time-consuming, and if the originator has provided a usable file list that can be adapted to form part of the curator's finding aid, the disadvantages of conversion may outweigh the advantages.[10]

Boxing and Labeling

Once the collection is in order, the boxing and labeling are done. The generally accepted amount of manuscripts assigned to a folder

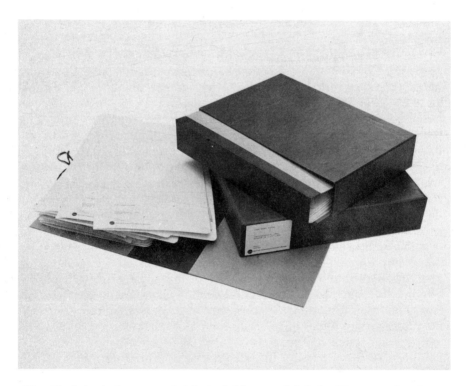

Fig. 16. A typical manuscript box, folders, and labels. (Courtesy Southern Illinois University)

is about ¼ to ½ inch. The quantity in each folder will vary. It depends, in part, upon how the material falls chronologically and upon its fragility. Whenever possible, the manuscripts are divided by folder on a regular calendar basis. For example, if the manuscripts are sparse at the beginning of the collection, the first box might have a folder for each year; and in the concentrated portion, even months might be divided: Jan. 1–10, Jan. 11–20, and Jan. 21–31; or Jan. 1–15 and Jan. 16–31. Wherever possible, the curator should avoid broken or uneven divisions, that is, Jan. 1–26, Jan. 27–Feb. 9, etc. It is also desirable to have similar even division among the boxes. This is more easily done in flat filing than in records center cartons or pressboard boxes, where the container must be full enough to prevent folders from curling, yet loose enough for easy filing.

Ultimately, a regular calendar division of folders is a nicety and the curator can waste a great deal of time shifting manuscripts and folders, especially trying to fill a half-empty box at the end of a series. A simple device to keep folders upright in a less-than-full box is to cut and fold a piece of cardboard as a brace (see figure 17), or to use one of the "half-size" boxes now being manufactured.

Writing copy for folder and box labels is best accomplished with a small note pad and carbon paper. The carbon copies can be paper-clipped to the folders and boxes, and the originals can be given to the typist. Labels should contain the collection or catalog number, the title of the collection, record series, and inclusive dates or alphabetical designation. Folders can be numbered consecutively within the entire record group, but it is probably better to begin a new sequence of numbers with each box. Labels should be uniform in size and design and should be placed consistently in the same location on folders and boxes. It even helps to have all labels typed on the same typewriter. There are so many "ragtag-and-bobtail" things filed on manuscript shelving that whatever uniformity the curator can achieve with boxes and labels is desirable.

To conclude this section on arrangement, note should be made of the unique services offered by Archival Associates, Englewood, Colorado. In 1967, the Western Business History Research Center was formed as an adjunct to the State Historical Society of Colorado. Over the next five years, the staff of the center processed about 200,000 manuscripts, prepared indexes, calendars, and guides (inventories) to many collections, and wrote a comprehensive guide to the society's manuscript holdings. When the center closed in 1972, the staff formed Archival Associates and offered their services as manuscript pro-

Fig. 17. A piece of cardboard cut to hold folders upright in a box less than full.

cessers. They will inventory the total holdings of an institution—"box, label, number boxes, and describe individual collections as to size, inclusive dates and component parts"—at the cost of $4.50 per hour. Finding aids of individual collections are prepared at the following prices: a guide (inventory) ten to twenty cents per item; an index with cross references, fifteen to twenty-five cents per item; and a calendar, $1.00 per entry. Boxes, folders, labels, and the labor to organize the collection are supplied by Archival Associates and are included in the per-item or per-entry price.[11]

Classification

Whether the curator contracts to have a collection arranged, or does it himself, once the boxes are labeled, the collection is ready to shelve. Curators and archivists have been eager to divorce themselves from the library practice of arranging documents within a collection by subject; but strangely enough, many arrange the collections on the shelves in what is essentially a subject classification. In some institutions, material is filed by physical type: bound and unbound and oversize.[12] Other classification systems are listed and summarized as follows in one source: *(1)* Arrangement of collections by accession number, with periodic spacing in the shelves for additions to groups with potential growth. *(2)* Arrangement of collections by chronology. For example, the presidential papers in the Library of Congress are arranged chronologically by term of office. *(3)* Arrangement of collections by type, with subgroupings. There might be, for example, a division between personal papers and records of organizations. Personal papers might be arranged alphabetically by title of collection; the records of organizations might be arranged first by type of organization and then by alphabet. *(4)* Arrangement of collections by geographic unit, with subgroupings. As an example, in the Clements Library the major division is between the Eastern and Western Hemispheres; the subgroupings are by alphabet and chronology.[13]

Most of these systems are wasteful of space and require periodic shifting of entire collections to allow for expansion. There are historical reasons for the development of some of these systems (in others, one curator just copies from another), but there also seems to be a certain mystique about shelving like materials together which the curator cannot defend rationally if he is to make the best use of his space.*

One alternative is to ignore classification and assign stack and shelf position as call numbers, but this can be disastrous if the collection is moved. A similar system and one that is simplest to administer and the least wasteful of space is to assign numbers to collections in numerical sequence as they are arranged and shelved. Single volumes, a box, or two hundred boxes, each is treated as a collection and assigned a sequential number. Collections are shelved up tight and

---

*Subject classification of manuscripts is an irrational carryover from the library practice of grouping like materials together on the shelf to be studied by the patron. Since manuscript stacks are not open to the researcher (or should not be), the concept has no validity in shelving manuscripts.

shelves adjusted to fit, and the only space for expansion is left at the open end of the numerical sequence. Additions to a collection can be assigned a number as received and cataloged as addenda.

Granted, this in time will pose problems for the institution which is relying on yearly increments to build its collections, but it seems no more troublesome than adapting any of the other systems of arrangement to "instant" collecting. Some institutions "save up" the increments over several years and catalog them as a supplement, which would reduce the number of addenda collections, but would require generous storage areas.

The single numerical sequence described above can accommodate everything except collections under a single box in size. These miscellaneous manuscripts can be shelved in a separate numerical sequence by assigning numbers to folders and boxing them in order as received. A single autograph letter or the fifty-piece collection is given a single folder and a collection number. Even collections which are two or three folders in size, anything less than a box, can be shelved here by assigning a block of numbers in sequence, but the curator may decide arbitrarily that any collection over a given number of pieces will be shelved as a one-box collection.

In at least one library, *all* manuscripts are cataloged and shelved in one numerical sequence with the miscellaneous manuscripts grouped in blocks. Each single manuscript or small collection has its own folder and catalog number, and enough are cataloged at one time to fill one or more boxes, which are then labeled with the consecutive collection numbers and shelved next to the larger multibox collections.

For reasons of aesthetics or space, the curator could modify the numerical-sequence system by grouping miscellaneous volumes and oversize and assigning them numbers in separate sequences. Using abbreviations, he would assign call numbers, such as *Coll. 1, Mss. 1 and Vol. 1, Ovsz. 1.* If the numbers are unwieldly after 999, the curator could start a new sequence with a letter prefix.

Aside from its simplicity, the great advantage of this system is the saving in space, but the disadvantage is that space is difficult to hold. Administrators are under continued pressure to utilize high-cost space, but the curator is provided one natural subterfuge to hold space. Many of the containers used to house manuscripts, like the clamshell box or the pressboard carton, are not shipped knocked down. They take a great deal of storage space, but this space in turn can be used for expansion as they are needed.

Finding Aids

Having settled upon a system of arrangement, the curator now must describe the collection in one or more of the commonly used types of finding aids—calendar, name index, register, inventory, or card catalog.

The calendar is little used by modern manuscript curators because the labor involved has priced it out of the market. Occasionally, they are prepared for small, rich collections, especially literary and theatrical collections which may contain a high preponderance of letters of well-known persons. As its name implies, the calendar is a list of descriptions (not unlike content notes), of every document in a collection arranged in chronological or calendar order. Calendars were prepared in the past in lieu of editing and printing documents, but today microfilm editions have largely superseded them.

Name indexes, discussed earlier in this chapter, are only somewhat less time-consuming to prepare than calendars. A curator can justify the cost of preparing a complete index for very few collections, but all collections deserve a selective name index of some degree, and, in fact, that is what the personal-name headings in a dictionary card catalog constitute.

Registers and inventories are today essentially the same thing, each having taken on characteristics of the other. The meld now in use is most often called an inventory, but probably it has more characteristics of the register. Historically, the register was used by the Library of Congress to provide descriptive entries for the *National Union Catalog of Manuscript Collections,* whereas the inventory was developed by the National Archives to describe the vast collection of federal records.

The inventory is the best tool yet devised for maintaining bibliographic control over huge twentieth-century collections; and in a condensed form, it is useful in describing collections of one box and larger. The inventory should contain the following elements in a heading or introduction: the title of the collection; inclusive dates of the material; and a physical description (number of boxes, volumes, linear measure, etc.). Some institutions also include statements on literary rights and provenance in the introduction. Following the heading is a biography or history of the person or organization around which the collection is formed, and then a general statement on the content and scope of the collection. Next comes a container list or, if it is more appropriate, a series description; then, if needed, a folder listing by title. Some inventories contain a list of subject tracings (see below in the section on cataloging); others will have an index to the authors of letters in the collection, and some inventories will contain their own index. If material is removed from the collection, it is usually noted in the inventory (see chapter on nonmanuscript material).

Inventories vary a great deal, depending upon the collection being described and the curator's intent. They can be very mechanical, with a few lines for history and content and the bulk of the pages devoted to a container or folder list. In others, the biography and content sections are woven into a narrative which may even highlight unusual items in the collection. Some inventories supply information on provenance, and the relationship of the collection to others in the institution or to papers in other repositories. An editor gives the reasoning behind this kind of description when he says: "In historical research no body of records is sufficient unto itself. Besides, all these factors have a bearing on the internal evidence not yet revealed. It is the responsibility of the [curator] to make clear these relationships. He is the discoverer, charting the way for the historical writer who follows." [14]

Since some inventories can be very subjective, there is an argument that they should be signed. If the staff is a relatively stable one, with a small turnover in personnel, a signed inventory will indicate the staff member who can best answer the researcher's questions which are not covered in the inventory. Originally, the inventory was meant as an internal tool, but because they are now frequently copied for distant researchers, the standard form should include the name of the institution. Too, curators should consider the merit of dating inventories. [15]

Recently, an archivist has offered a plan for standardizing and upgrading inventories through the technology of computer publishing. He suggested that the Society of American Archivists, the American Association for State and Local History, and the American Historical Association join together to seek a National Endowment for the Humanities subsidy to offer a guide and inventory publishing service. As he envisioned the process, a description of each item in a collection of papers could be "keyboarded and sorted by the computer," and "the magnetic tapes or discs used in the production of individual guides and inventories could be consolidated at will into a national data bank." This is, of course, what SPINDEX II was designed to do at the collection level, but after several years has yet to accomplish (see chapter on information retrieval). The archivist thinks that the computer programs developed to produce the *American Historical Review* bibliography, "Recently Published Articles" (RPA), may be a "ready answer." He notes (but does not identify or locate) that papers of the Revolutionary War era were being arranged and indexed with the RPA program.[16]

Until such time as the computer provides a ready answer, the curator must make better use of the tools already at his command. One tool of librarianship he most neglects is the authority file, or list of subject headings used in the dictionary card catalog. Without it, cataloging will take more time and be less precise, and the researcher will be hampered in his efforts. The authority file can be recorded on loose sheets, but it is more easily revised and kept up to date on cards. If the curator wishes to start an authority file for an already established collection, he will need to list all the subject headings presently used in his manuscript catalog. In the process, he will discover a great many weaknesses: manuscripts cataloged under several similar terms which ought to be consolidated and cross-referenced under a single heading; broad general headings with hundreds of cards which should be arranged under specific subheadings; and confusing or contradictory *see* and *see also* references; and an over-all breakdown in subject-matter representation.

An authority file can be created, or additions can be made to an existing one by selecting subjects from the *Subject Headings Used in the Dictionary Catalog of the Library of Congress.*[17] This expensive volume goes through frequent revisions, and an out-of-date edition, which libraries often discard, will serve the curator's purpose well. Other subject-heading lists have been published, but the Library of Congress headings are familiar and comfortable to most researchers. The index of the *National Union Catalog of Manuscript Collections* is another excellent source of subjects. If the need arises, however, the curator should not be timorous about modifying Library of Congress headings to suit his own situation, nor in creating headings out of whole cloth, as long as they are recorded in the authority file.

In this file, the curator also frequently enters information cards about special cataloging practices. Too, if he wishes to keep a record of some or all of the personal names which appear as authors or secondary headings in his catalog, name cards can be interfiled or be an adjunct to the authority file. The curator should supply birth and death dates for persons whose names appear in his catalog, and frequently getting this information requires considerable research. Also, because of local usage or for some other reason, the curator may use a variant of a name in cataloging. In both instances, he may wish to have a card in the authority file to save looking up dates again or to insure consistency. Finally, an even more elaborate file might contain brief biographical data for persons and historical background for organizations, especially if the information is obscure and hard to find. (Full bibliographical citation is desirable on these entries.) Over the years, an authority file of this type can develop into a most useful cataloging tool.

When the curator is cataloging manuscripts, obviously he will want the authority file at hand. It is also helpful to have a standard one-volume biographical dictionary, a gazetteer, and a note pad on which to write cataloging slips. What the curator puts on the slips will depend upon whether he follows one of the two systems commonly in use, or whether he has developed his own variant system. The curator of manuscripts, neither an archivist nor a librarian, nevertheless has tried to adapt terminology and techniques from both fields, much to the confusion of all. Manuscripts are not public records, nor are they books. Nowhere has the confusion been more apparent than in the attempts to codify and establish procedures for cataloging manuscripts.

Great impetus toward systematized manuscript cataloging came first from the Library of Congress's rules for preparing entries for the *National Union Catalog of Manuscript Collections,* and then in 1967 from the *Anglo-American Cataloging Rules* [18] promulgated by the American Library Assocation, the Library of Congress, The Library Association, and The Canadian Library Association. According to the Anglo-American rules, a catalog card is composed of an entry and description. The first line typed on the initial catalog card is called the main entry, and the main entry will be the name of the person, family, or corporate body around which the collection of manuscripts has been formed. (Corporate body is defined as "an organization or group of persons that is identified by a name and that acts or may act as an entity," and typical examples listed are "associations, institutions, business firms, non-profit enterprises, governments, specific agencies of government, conferences").[19]

Although these rules scrupulously avoid using the term *author* in defining main entry, the first segment of the description (second line on the card) is called *title.* Obviously, few manuscript collections have pre-existing titles, and those most commonly supplied by curators include papers, records, letters, diaries, and correspondence. The title, as defined in the rules, includes the inclusive dates of the manuscripts. Also included in the second line is the physical description—the

number of items or containers. Following on successive lines are the
name of the repository, the form of the manuscripts, and the heart
of the description—the scope and content note. The card concludes
with references to published and unpublished descriptions of the
collection, and statements on access, literary rights, and provenance
(see figures 18 and 19).

```
                                        MS 74-1018
      Stuart, Francis, 1902-
         Papers, 1932-71.   ca. 3 ft.
         In Southern Illinois University Library (Carbon-
      dale)
         Irish author.  Correspondence, mss. of Black
      List, Section H (1971), Victors and Vanquished
      (1959), unpublished novels, and other writings, and
      notebooks.  Correspondents include Maud Gonne,
      Compton Mackenzie, Liam O'Flaherty, and Ezra
      Pound.
         Unpublished inventory and index in the library.
         Information on literary rights available in the
      library.
```

Fig. 18. A recent NUCMC card.

A curator studying the components of this main card will find
some types of information that are desirable in a union list but not
necessary in his institution's own catalog. Other data—for example,
the statement on provenance—the curator might decide would be better
omitted from a public card and kept as part of the donor or collection
file. Nor have curators considered that there is anything sacrosanct
in the arrangement of the elements on the card (see figure 20.) However,
the effect of the Anglo-American rules has been to encourage standardization.

These rules have given legitimacy to one of the two commonly
used systems of manuscript cataloging, which, for purposes of description here, can be called *unit* as opposed to *analytical* cataloging. Under
the unit system of cataloging, exact copies of the main card, herein
called *secondary card,* are given individual headings. These headings

Joy, Verne E   1876–1964.
    Papers, 1905–68. 2 ft.
    In Southern Illinois University Archives (Carbondale)
    Newspaper editor and publisher, of Centralia, Ill. Correspondence, business papers, and promotional material, relating to Joy's years with the Centralia Sentinal and to his philanthropies.
    Inventory in the repository.
    Gift of William Joy, Centralia, Ill., 1969.

Library of Congress   [¹⁄₂]   MS 70–429

Fig. 19. An early NUCMC card.

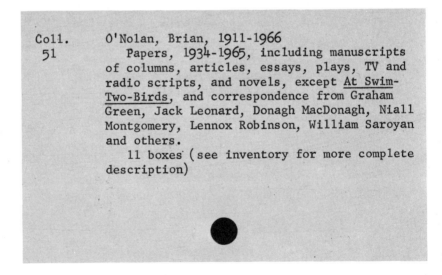

Coll.   O'Nolan, Brian, 1911-1966
  51   Papers, 1934-1965, including manuscripts
          of columns, articles, essays, plays, TV and
          radio scripts, and novels, except <u>At Swim-
          Two-Birds</u>, and correspondence from Graham
          Green, Jack Leonard, Donagh MacDonagh, Niall
          Montgomery, Lennox Robinson, William Saroyan
          and others.
              11 boxes (see inventory for more complete
          description)

Fig. 20. A main card in unit cataloging.

have been called interchangeably *added entries* and *subject headings.* The headings that the curator will give to the secondary cards will include subjects, places, and the names of persons, organizations, or corporate bodies. The headings for the names of persons will be of two kinds: (1) those that refer to persons mentioned in the collection, and (2) those referring to persons who have written documents included in the collection. Traditionally, curators have called the second kind *author entries* [20] and have typed this heading in black to distinguish it from all other headings on secondary cards, which are typed in red.

In either the unit or the analytical system, the curator lists all headings in alphabetical order on the back of the main card. If the *subject tracings,* as this list is called, are too numerous to fit on the card, they are appended to the inventory. Subject tracings allow the curator to remove cards from the catalog for revision.

While the main card is the same in either unit or analytical cataloging, it is in the preparation of the secondary cards that the systems differ. In unit cataloging, the secondary cards are exact duplicates of the main card, with headings added, and in analytical cataloging each secondary card is individually typed. To prepare a secondary card for an analytical catalog, the curator first types the individual heading, which is followed by only the first two items from the main card—the main entry and the title. The remainder of the card, the analytical description, may refer to a single dated letter by or about a person, or perhaps a series of documents about a subject or a place with inclusive year dates.

Because each card must be composed and typed individually, analytical cataloging is time-consuming and costly. If an inventory exists for the collection being cataloged, it is wasteful and repetitious to do analytical cataloging. On the other hand, in a unit system, the inventory and secondary cards can be co-ordinated so that the dictionary card catalog is essentially an index to the inventory.

Even if all cards for a unit catalog are individually typed, they take far less time to prepare and proofread than analytical cards. If the unit cards can be mass produced—for example, on a card mimeograph or Xerox—dozens can be prepared in a fraction of the time needed to type one analytical card. All the typist adds to the secondary card in the unit system is the heading, and if the inventory is a long one, a page reference.

The co-ordinated inventory and unit catalog system has one principal disadvantage: it forces the researchers to use two bibliographical tools. But it more than compensates them for time expended by offering a broader range finding aid.

Unit cataloging also partially resolves the conflict over cataloging collections of a single or very few items. Small collections have tended to be over-cataloged, and often curators could not justify time spent on them. By assigning them numbers in sequence, small collections can be cataloged rapidly and easily with the unit system, although the method for arriving at main entries is different from that for a collection of papers. In cataloging a letter, the name of the writer is the main entry; a literary manuscript would be entered under the author's name; and a volume—for example, an account book—might have as a main entry the name of a person, a corporation, or an association, etc. The title for these small collections is established following the same rules as noted above. In the three examples cited, the titles might read: *a letter; typewritten first draft;* and *accounts receivable ledger.*

Single manuscripts of unknown or anonymous origin are described by what is called *hanging indention.* In this form of cataloging, a short narrative description of the manuscript is used in place of the main entry on the initial card (see figure 21). This type of description takes its name from the indention on the card which is reversed; that is,

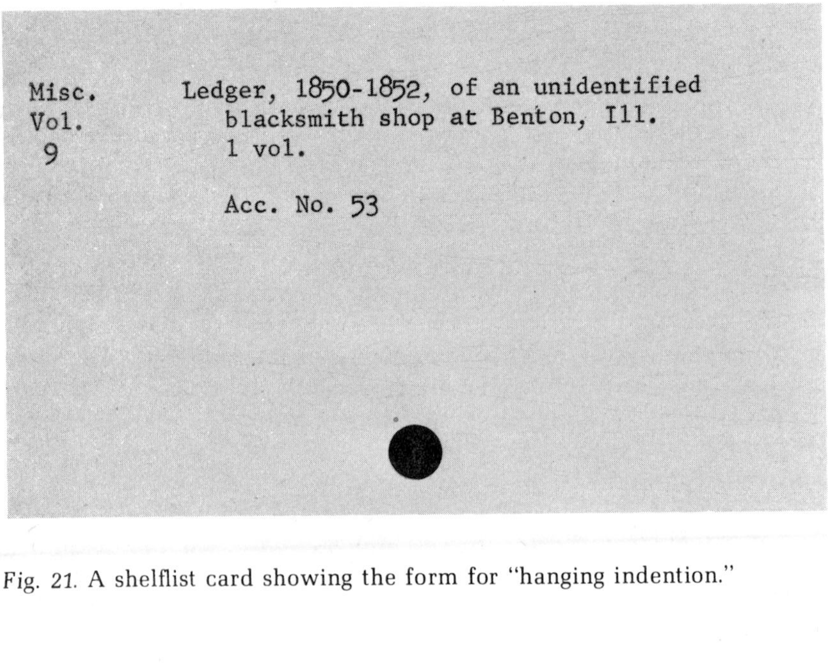

```
Misc.        Ledger, 1850-1852, of an unidentified
Vol.            blacksmith shop at Benton, Ill.
  9             1 vol.

             Acc. No. 53
```

Fig. 21. A shelflist card showing the form for "hanging indention."

the first line is brought out to the margin, and the remainder of the text is indented.[21]

Abbreviations are used to describe single manuscripts or small collections. Those used at Southern Illinois University, Carbondale, which have evolved over a number of years from a variety of sources, include the following:

L	Letter	Designates an unsigned letter in the hand of a clerk or person other than the author
LS	Letter Signed	A letter in the hand of a person other than the author, but signed by the author
ALS	Autograph Letter Signed	A letter in the hand of and signed by the author
TL	Typewritten Letter	*Typewritten* here would include any mechanically reproduced letter, such as mimeographed, offset, ditto, diazo. Printed letters would more logically be cataloged as broadsides. Include here letters signed with rubber stamp, mimeograph, or any other artificial means of reproducing the author's signature.
TLS	Typewritten Letter Signed	A typewritten letter (see TL) signed by the author
D	Document	Any paper of legal or official nature such as an indenture, deed, certificate, receipt, etc. Include here printed documents of the type described above with manuscript additions. Also include documents signed by a clerk or other person in the name of the author.
DS	Document Signed	A document written by another person, but signed by the author
ADS	Autograph Document Signed	A document written and signed by the author
TD	Typewritten Document	Typewritten or otherwise mechanically reproduced (except printed) document. (See also D)
TDS	Typewritten Document Signed	Typewritten document signed by the author. (See also D & TD)
AMs	Autograph Manuscript	Nonlegal or nonofficial papers such as speeches, biographical sketches, sermons, rem-

		iniscences, and such other items of a generally narrative nature, in the hand of the author but unsigned
AMsS	Autograph Manuscript Signed	Manuscript (see AMs) in the hand of and signed by the author
TMs	Typewritten Manuscript	Typewritten manuscript not signed by author. (See AMs)
TMsS	Typewritten Manuscript Signed	Author-signed typewritten manuscript. (See also AMsS)
C	Card	Postcard, picture postcard, or greeting card
ACS	Autograph Card Signed	Any card used in correspondence written, or with a message, by the author and signed
AC	Autograph Card	Unsigned handwritten card or message on a printed greeting card
TCS	Typewritten Card Signed	Entire card, or a message, typewritten and signed by author
TC	Typewritten Card	An unsigned typewritten postcard or printed greeting card
ANS	Autograph Note Signed	A line or two, at most a page, or any fragment which could not be classified as AMsS, such as a signed memorandum
AN	Autograph Note	Any unsigned fragment. (See also ANS) This designation would be rarely used, and then only to classify a manuscript in the hand of a famous person.

Designations, such as *initialed, pencil, Xerox, carbon,* etc., are noted directly following the abbreviation, in brackets and written out in full—that is: TMsS [initialed].

There are several other side benefits derived from unit cataloging. For example, the chronological file, which might not seem worth the investment of individually typewritten cards, is built with the little effort of adding a few extra unit-produced cards. One way of assembling a chronological file is to arrange cards in the drawer by half decades, and alphabetically by collection title within the time period.

The file can be a separate catalog, or it can be made a part of the dictionary catalog by using the word *Chronology* in the heading on the cards, that is, *Chronology, 1835-1839.*[22]

Another system is to prepare a chronology card for either the inclusive dates of a large collection, or for the dates of the period of concentration—when the material bulks most importantly. Cards of this nature, for example, *Chronology: 1824-1856,* are filed by the first date. In small collections, the card might read, *Chronology, 1824, Jan. 3—April 15,* and single items would be entered by date, that is, *Chronology: 1824, June 5.* These two types of cards would be filed following all cards with inclusive dates beginning 1824.

To conclude the list of advantages of the unit system, a duplicate of the unit main card can also be used as the shelflist card. If the inventories include a container and/or folder list, the elaborate shelf list of the past is no longer necessary for bibliographic control. If the curator's stack space is badly scattered and he needs a location file, again, a duplicate of the unit main card will fill the need. Finally, it is easy to keep a separate file of duplicates of main cards for use in producing published guides or bringing them up to date.

Cards for either the unit or analytical system are filed in a dictionary card catalog under library rules, with a few exceptions.[23] Cards are filed for "persons, places, and things" in that order, that is, Washington, George; Washington, D.C.; and the Washington Savings and Loan Company. Those filed under a person's name—for example, Washington—are arranged as follows: (1) main cards: collections formed around Washington containing material written by or to him; (2) secondary cards, black headings: collections formed around another person containing material written by Washington; (3) secondary cards, red headings: collections formed around another person containing material written to or about Washington.

The rules for library filing prescribe that, when there is more than one main card for a person, the cards be arranged alphabetically by title. Since most titles are supplied by the curator in manuscript cataloging, they tend to be uniform, that is, *Papers, Correspondence,* etc. Several cards grouped under titles with the same first word under library rules would be arranged alphabetically by successive letters in the title; but in a manuscript catalog, they are arranged chronologically. The same chronological principle is sometimes applied to cards grouped under a heading such as *Diaries,* where the curator chooses to arrange the cards by the dates of the diary, rather than alphabetically by main entry.

Alternative Systems of Control

The systems of arrangement and description covered in the foregoing portion of this chapter would provide good bibliographic control for most manuscript collections,[24] but there are numerous other systems in operation which have proved equally serviceable. For example, Columbia University, Special Collections, follows a much different method of arrangement. A large collection of papers is inspected and then divided into two categories called *cataloged* and *uncataloged*. In the cataloged section are gathered the letters that the curator judges to be more important. Each is individually described and they are arranged alphabetically. The uncataloged section is arranged chronologically and follows the cataloged section on the shelf and in the calendar (inventory) describing the collection.

At the Newberry Library, manuscripts are arranged and described, depending upon the importance of the material, in one of five ways: (E) "Label and list," roughly equivalent to accessioning; (D) "Rough arrangement by *type* of material"; (C) Arranged but no guides prepared; (B) "Guides (or indexes) and folders are added for *groups* of material"; (A) "Guides (or indexes) and folders are made for *individual* items." [25]

Smaller collections or single manuscripts are arranged differently from the system advocated in this chapter in many institutions. At the Houghton Library, Harvard, miscellaneous manuscripts are arranged alphabetically by author in an Autograph File which is described as "self-indexing," although catalog cards are typed for both author and addressee.[26] The University of California Library, Los Angeles, Special Collections, assigns the series number 100 and a box number to all miscellaneous manuscripts, and they are arranged alphabetically by author within the box.[27]

At the Oregon Historical Society, ephemera and miscellaneous manuscripts are filed under twenty-six subject headings. The Lilly Library, Indiana University, gathers miscellaneous manuscripts in subject collections and calendars each piece. In several institutions miscellaneous volumes are shelved and cataloged by size, although few are as imaginative as one agency which designates size as "Giants, Old Major Giants, and Little Misfits." [28]

The card catalog is still the most used finding aid in manuscript collections, followed by the inventory, although one study seems to indicate that there is little correlation in use between the two.[29] Some institutions rely almost exclusively on the card catalog. For example, at Duke University, Manuscript Department, the sketch, which is a description of the collection in many ways comparable to the inventory, may extend through forty or fifty catalog cards.[30] Other institutions have all but abandoned the card catalog and are relying exclusively on inventories to describe a collection. At Cornell, Regional History and University Archives, for example, no cards have been made now for several months. The University of Washington Libraries, University Archives and Manuscripts, does not have a card catalog. Patrons there consult loose-leaf post binders in which names, subjects, and chronology are cumulatively indexed, which in turn refer them to inventory/guides to the collections. Names are indexed at the file-folder level, and subjects and chronology at the collection level. Fourteen major subject headings are used, followed by one subject subdivision, followed by one geographical place name. When the curator describes a collection, he enters, or "posts," to the proper index the collection title and inclusive dates.[31]

Publication of Finding Aids

The inventory/guide designation used at the University of Washington is but one of many found in the country. Inventories are given other names in various institutions—the Huntington Library calls them summary reports; at Columbia, they are called calendars; and the Southern Historical Collection at the University of North Carolina calls them surveys.[32] Not only is there a lack of uniformity in the name and form of the inventories, there is also a disagreement about their research use. Several institutions, notably Syracuse University and the Ohio Historical Society, began publication of their inventories some years past, but both series have lapsed. The University of Texas at Austin, Humanities Library, has published very elaborate hardcover finding aids for several of its literary * and theater collections.[33] Individual inventories are issued sporadically by various other institutions,

---

* Attention should be directed here to an essential difference in the published descriptions of most literary manuscripts as opposed to historical collections. The descriptions of literary papers usually have been prepared by rare-book librarians trained in bibliography. These descriptions tend to include several details—especially page size measured in millimeters—that are pertinent in describing books which exist in various printings, but that have little or no meaning in describing a manuscript which is unique. Or they may include devices such as reproducing initial lines, which, while useful in identifying variant drafts of a poem, for example, are pedantic in describing correspondence. Curators who have parroted patterns set by rare-book bibliographers ought to look to the archivists in developing their own meaningful and uniform terms of bibliographic control.

but the most concerted effort toward this general kind of publishing in recent years has been the production of guides to the various microfilm editions of manuscript collections published under the aegis of the National Historical Publications Commission. Although inventories are considered an in-house finding aid, most collecting agencies will copy them for researchers. One—the Western History Research Center, University of Wyoming—sends copies of inventories to researchers free of charge.

Publication of finding aids for most institutions has centered upon a guide to the collection. Two institutions which pioneered in this area, the Wisconsin State Historical Society and the Minnesota Historical Society, publish additional volumes to their guides periodically.[34] It would be an unusual issue of The American Archivist which would not contain reviews of several guides. Three of the best-organized and most handsome volumes issued recently describe the manuscript holdings of the University of Oregon, the Ohio Historical Society, and the Western Reserve Historical Society.[35]

One of these guides is a hard-cover publication and two are paper-covered, but still very substantial volumes. However, a guide can be published in a much more modest format. For example, in 1972, the John C. Pace Library, the University of West Florida, issued a guide to the first one hundred manuscript and special collections—the accumulation of its first five years of collecting. This guide is mimeographed and staple-bound and lists collections that range in size and form from the substantial files of a congressman to single letters or a handful of clippings.[36]

Another recent publication, a preliminary guide to the Smithsonian Archives, also is of modest proportion, although it is expensively printed. Some of the ninety-two manuscript collections described in the guide are not processed (in times past, institutions would not list unarranged collections), and another unusual feature is the extended descriptions of the type of arrangement found in each collection.[37]

Another unusual manuscript guide, perhaps unique, is that published by Special Collections, University of Illinois, Chicago Circle Campus. The guide has two sections: a description of the processed collections and a list of collections awaiting arrangement and description. The guide is issued on loose sheets, with each collection described on a separate sheet, and it is intended that it be kept in a binder where it can be periodically brought up to date as new sheets are issued.[38]

Whatever its form, the guide to the collection is essential. It best fulfills the curator's obligation to scholarship, and without it the collection will never reach its full research potential. Unfortunately, in many institutions, given their budgets and staff, it is an undertaking of major proportion. Yet, with proper planning, the curator can produce the entries for a guide as a by-product of the everyday process of arranging and describing the collections.

For those institutions which cannot prepare a guide, the *National Union Catalog of Manuscript Collections* takes on added importance. Now in its tenth volume, NUCMC, first published in 1962, contains descriptions of 29,356 collections in 850 different repositories.[39] Despite the criticism that has been levelled at the project, it is extremely useful to researchers. A curator should not consider any collection completely described until he has filled out a NUCMC data sheet. However, he should not delay cataloging the collection to wait for the NUCMC cards. In the past, the cataloging delay in the descriptive cataloging division of the Library of Congress, which prepares the cards, has been so long that it has discouraged some repositories from submitting entries. At last report, the backlog of entries to be cataloged was down substantially. However, at the same time, financial problems forced NUCMC to start printing cards by offset from typewritten copy, and the cards are now produced with a narrow left margin and no hole drilled at the bottom.[40] The cards are not of a quality acceptable to most institutions and are being used in very few catalogs. The curator should remember, however, that production of catalog cards for the co-operating institutions is not the primary purpose of NUCMC, and it is of prime importance that he assist the project by submitting entries to insure the continued publication of the national finding guide.

As was noted in preceding paragraphs, the card catalog remains the most used finding aid in manuscript collections. It, too, like the inventory, has developed in a variety of forms. The catalogs of some institutions still contain the handwritten cards prepared in an earlier century; in other repositories, cards are being printed by the campus printing shop. In one catalog, main cards, subject cards, and geographical and personal name cards are all filed together. In other places, there is a separate catalog for each category, and perhaps one also for writer and one for addressee of letters. In some repositories, entries for manuscripts are filed in the general book catalog; but in most others, manuscripts have a separate catalog.

A single, unified catalog in the manuscript search room, with information cards for principal collections filed in the institution's general catalog, would seem simplest to use and maintain. Whatever the form, the curator should review the catalog periodically for appearance and consistency. Typists should be encouraged to remember that their work will be on public view probably for at least the next fifty years. Uniform and clean cards give a good impression to the researcher and make his work much easier.

A bibliographer in attempting to cope with the bibliographical description of manuscripts entitled his chapter "Manuscripts and other Awkward Materials." [41] It is hoped that this chapter has provided some assistance in this area, and now the discussion turns to the handling of what, to many curators of manuscripts, are "awkward materials," that is, the products of the computer and microform technology.

SELECTED READINGS

For a historical survey of three attempts at national bibliographic control of manuscripts—*American Literary Manuscripts,* the Hamer *Guide,* and the *National Union Catalog of Manuscript Collections*—see Frank G. Burke, "Manuscripts and Archives." As a guide to the arrangement and description of an individual manuscript collection, Lucile M. Kane, *A Guide to the Care and Administration of Manuscripts,* has no peer, but the following journal articles, the best of the last decade, offer similar, though variant procedures: Ruth B. Bordin, "Cataloging Manuscripts—A Simple Scheme"; Michael Jasenas, "Cataloging Small Manuscript Collections"; Elfrieda Lang, "Arrangement and Cataloging of Manuscripts in the Lilly Library"; and Nathan Reingold, "Subject Analysis and Description of Manuscript Collections." The most persistent critic of the type of cataloging described in these articles is Richard C. Berner, who has written several articles, the best of which, "Description of Manuscript Collections: A Single Network System," describes his practices at the University of Washington. Berner's system has its converts, as can be seen by Jean L. Finch, "Some Fundamentals in Arranging Archives and Manuscript Collections." He was very strongly influenced by his training with the archivist T. R. Schellenberg, whose book, *The Management of Archives,* has had great impact on manuscript processing. In "Archival Principles and the Curator of Manuscripts," Robert L. Brubaker suggests using the inventory in conjunction with the card catalog. The inventory seems to be common ground between archivist and curator, and uniform format and terminology have been sought by the Society of American Archivists, Committee on Techniques for the Control and Description of Archives and Manuscripts, in its "Draft Standards for the Preparation of Registers and Inventories."

VI

Information Retrieval: Automation, the Computer, and Microphotography

IN a recent article, one authority noted the three areas in which the computer can help alleviate the burden thrust upon archives and manuscript repositories by the information explosion: (1) administrative and clerical work, (2) dissemination of information about new acquisitions, and (3) information retrieval.[1] Although each of these areas is examined here and its application to the field of manuscripts is traced, the stress is on information retrieval. When most curators speak of information retrieval generally, what they are referring to specifically is document retrieval. And when the words *automation* and *information retrieval* are linked, the curator who is not a systems specialist is likely to think only in terms of the electronic computer. Other automated retrieval devices are discussed in the pages that follow, but the emphasis is upon the computer and microphotography and their interrelationship.

For centuries, curators have been retrieving documents manually from structured files of papers which were described in a separate index or finding aid. Today's technology offers the curator several machines and techniques to store, retrieve, and disseminate copies of documents and the data they contain. Two of these, the computer and microforms, offer him the greatest promise of automating his information retrieval system. The promise is real, the equipment and know-how exist; but at the outset, it should be understood that any information system involving the computer, and, to a lesser extent, microforms, will be economically feasible for only a few manuscript programs.

In this sense, the promise has been a false one, for many curators have been encouraged to believe that the computer will solve their problems of gaining bibliographic control over the great quantity of material in their care. Still, as with other technological developments, there will be "spin-offs," which the curator must recognize and of which he should take advantage. Some knowledge of how the computer and microforms operate, either separately or joined together in the most sophisticated systems, may enable him to adapt some elements to improve his own system.

In this chapter, there will be no attempt to explain the complex technical processes involved in modern information retrieval. It will be at best a general, nontechnical overview of some of the recent innovations in information storage and retrieval, accompanied by a few examples of manuscript management through automation. Any curator who is seriously considering automation ought to read the books listed at the end of the chapter, which were chosen because they can be comprehended by the nonspecialist. Once he has a basic grounding in the jargon, he should call in a systems analyst to advise him on the program. If the curator has a sense of humor, while he is waiting for the analyst to arrive, he can practice drawing a flow chart and be thinking of an acronym, the two touchstones of a successful system!

Automated Indexing

Fittingly enough, the Manuscript Division of the Library of Congress can be said to have launched the manuscript world into automation with the authorization from Congress in 1957 to microfilm its collection of presidential papers. It was felt that, for the microfilm to be of the greatest research use, each letter should be indexed by date, author, and recipient. However, the prospect of sorting the hundreds of thousands of index items was overwhelming. The solution was to turn to electronic data processing equipment (EDP), and during the first years of the project electronic tabulating machines were used to sort the punched cards which contained the index entries. In 1964, the library shifted the operation to the computer, which has since been used to produce printer's copy for the microfilm indexes.[2]

At about the same time, in the mid-1960s, the Herbert Hoover Institution on War, Revolution and Peace, Stanford University, began a program to computerize the records of the American Relief Administration. The decision was made against item-by-item indexing. Instead, the papers were arranged so that items were "grouped" in a folder containing five to ten pieces. "Invented titles" made up of "keywords" were given to each folder. The folders were given numbers and the pieces within the folders were assigned subscript numbers. The folder titles, which were put into the computer, were run on a KWIC (Key Word in Context) program to produce a printout index. In the index, folder titles appear alphabetically arranged under each term in the title: "Casualties in Madison flood" would printout under "flood," "Madison," and "casualties." [3]

The presidential papers and Hoover KWIC indexes were attempts to use automation to bring manuscripts under intellectual control. Similar programs include that at the Public Archives of Canada, begun in the mid-1960s, where the papers of the prime ministers were coded on cards for an item index. The program differed from the system used for the presidential papers in that each letter was coded for one or more descriptors, which would give the archives a subject index as well as a name index.[4] With foundation support, another similar project is under way at the Center for the Documentary Study of the American Revolution, a special-projects branch in the Office of the National Archives, where the papers of the Continental Congress are being item-indexed. The index, when published, will be in two formats: a chronological listing of documents, and a topical listing, including senders, recipients, place names, and major subjects.[5] One of the small ironies of the project is that, while it is being conducted under the auspices of the National Archives, the country's principal proponent of the use of microfilm in scholarship, and the index is being prepared to facilitate the scholar's use of the microfilm of the papers, the indexers are using the original papers rather than the microfilm in preparing the index. The moral here seems to be merely that curators urge scholars to use microfilm, but avoid using it, themselves, when they can.

The Manuscript Division of the Library of Congress, which had been a leader in achieving intellectual control of manuscripts through automated indexing, took the lead also in using the computer to achieve physical or administrative control over its holdings. Beginning in 1964 and continuing over a six-year period, descriptions of the division's 3,000 collections were coded on cards from "a simple checklist of 'titles.'" At the same time, the user call slip was redesigned for computer input, and when this information was combined and sorted by the computer, the division had its first real idea of the physical characteristics of the collection and how it was being used.[6]

Helpful though these data were administratively, the Manuscript Division still lacked knowledge of the subject content of its voluminous collection. An item index, such as had been prepared for the presidential papers, was out of the question. Instead, the division adopted a system aimed at producing a "Selective Permutation Index" based upon subjects and names coded from container lists. This modified KWIC program, later known as SPINDEX, demonstrated the flawed character expected of any experiment. It was entirely card-oriented, and the

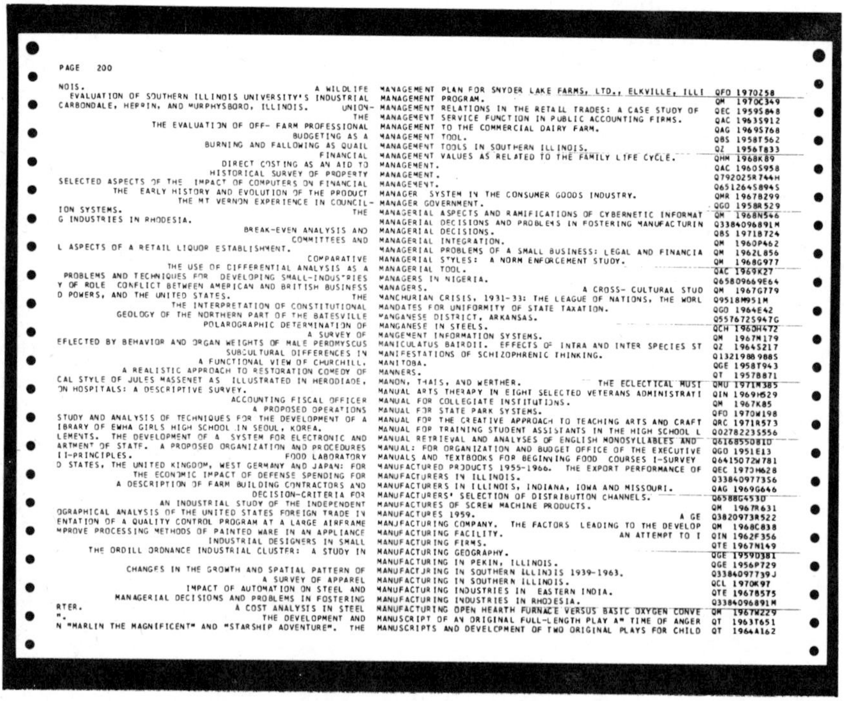

Fig. 22. A typical KWIC printout. This particular example is of the titles of theses and dissertations held by Morris Library, Southern Illinois University. (Courtesy Southern Illinois University)

amount of information that could be coded was not adequate to describe a collection. Printouts were in upper-case type, but more importantly, no effective method of correcting or upgrading the information had been written into the program.[7]

In 1966, the SPINDEX project was suspended at the Library of Congress. That same year saw the inception by the library of the MARC (Machine Readable Cataloging) pilot project, an experiment intended to allow libraries to produce printed catalog cards for books from computer tape coded at the Library of Congress. At the beginning, no attempt was made to include manuscripts in the MARC format, but in the summer of 1973 the library published *Manuscripts: A MARC Format*. The manual was designed for internal use in cataloging single manuscripts and manuscript collections, but also with the view to assisting other institutions "in creating machine-readable records for manuscripts," and to "provide standardization in this area." [8]

No mention is made in the MARC format text, but the sample of a coded description of a manuscript collection used seemed to indicate that entries submitted to the Library of Congress for inclusion in the *National Union Catalog of Manuscript Collections* eventually might be coded following the MARC format into machine-readable magnetic tapes for the computer. Earlier, however, NUCMC had announced that there were "no present plans for implementing the [MARC] system in the NUCMC program." [9]

Meanwhile, SPINDEX, assigned to limbo by the Library of Congress, resurfaced in 1967 with a new program, a new name—SPINDEX II—a new sponsor—the National Archives—and a $40,000, two-year grant from the Council on Library Resources. With what was hoped was the capacity for interinstitutional compatibility, SPINDEX II enlisted the following co-operating manuscript repositories: Library of Congress, Cornell University, the Smithsonian Institution Archives, Wayne State University, the University of Alaska, Ohio Historical Society, Minnesota Historical Society, and the State Historical Society of Wisconsin. Other institutions which showed an interest in the program received periodic progress reports.[10]

The participating institutions and eleven other repositories submitted sample finding aids or inventories to the SPINDEX II staff. The variety in the 125 finding aids was greater than the project staff had anticipated. At first, it seemed as if no real standard existed; but after some study, it became apparent that "many seeming inconsistencies were only variations upon a single descriptive approach." [11]

From the finding aids, the SPINDEX II staff compiled a list of possible data elements and submitted it to the participants, and early in 1968 a conference was called to work out technical problems. After the conference, each institution was asked to punch cards on several collections and from this test data the SPINDEX II staff ran a combined index which formed the matter of discussion for the second participants' conference in the spring of 1969.[12]

On the basis of the second conference, tentative agreements were reached upon testing and evaluating SPINDEX II. Cornell, for example, developed a format to aid the processor in preparing a more informative and standardized inventory as input for SPINDEX II.[13]

But for one reason or another, testing and evaluation bogged down, and the grant expired before the system was implemented. Several of the original co-operating institutions dropped out, but three others, the South Carolina Department of Archives and History, the Hoover Institution Archives, and the International Nickel Company of Canada, Ltd., came into the SPINDEX II project.[14]

At this juncture, NARS "assumed responsibility for SPINDEX II program maintenance," but stated that any further development of the program must await its implementation by many institutions. On the other hand, the participating institutions said that they could not implement SPINDEX II on the basis of the tentative incomplete documentation supplied by NARS. Programmers at NARS were having difficulty getting computer time to experiment and the program was badly afflicted with what one NARS official called " 'Murphy's law'—if something could go wrong, it would." [15]

In the fall of 1972, NARS decided to abandon the "band-aid" method of trying to help SPINDEX II users and committed resources to rewrite the program and convert it from DOS (Disk Operating System) to OS (Operating System, that is, "a set of programs that control the continued operation of the computer over a *long period* of time—in particular, throughout the continuous processing of a large number of individual user jobs.") [16] Tape copies of the programs and photocopies of the draft documentation were sent to Cornell University, International Nickel, and the South Carolina Department of Archives and History for testing.[17]

While the testing was going on, Charles Lee, director of the South Carolina Department of Archives and History, urged NARS to sponsor a meeting of the original co-operating institutions and others which had used SPINDEX programs. At the meeting, in June 1973, NARS, which had been the major user of SPINDEX II, reviewed its application in indexing the papers of the Continental Congress mentioned above. Other applications reviewed were a modified version used to prepare indexes to the guides to captured German documents on microfilm, a guide to maps at the National Archives, and an administrative control program at the presidential libraries to co-ordinate the solicitation of papers of public figures.[18]

NARS representatives noted that the success of these various projects demonstrated the workability of SPINDEX II, but at the same time they announced the administration's decision that such detailed and in-depth control of the total holdings of the National Archives "was not feasible." Participants at the conference were concerned that "NARS had forgotten about, chosen to ignore, or had decided against the concept of a 'national data bank' and the exchange of information among repositories." The conference closed with NARS promising to get SPINDEX II working, to make it available at reasonable cost, and to publish the systems documentation. NARS would serve as a clearing house for information, but would not put any additional funds "into an information retrieval system to be used principally, if not exclusively, by others." [19]

SPINDEX II, as a system to provide interinstitutional indexing, seems dormant, if not dead. Interest remains high among the SPINDEX II alumni, although concrete results are still meager. At the Smithsonian Institution Archives, for example, work has begun on encoding entries to be included in a published guide to the collection. In this program, input into the computer is by punched-paper tape, but as of the spring of 1973, the descriptions of only a dozen or so collections have been punched.[20]

The Hoover Institution, a late comer to SPINDEX II but an early leader in KWIC indexing, suspended work on the KWIC project after a decision was made not to incur the costs of developing a system specifically for the Hoover Institution Archives. With a foundation grant, a management consulting firm was hired to explore SPINDEX II and other available retrieval systems, and when the National Archives made the debugged OS program available in July 1973, the management firm chose SPINDEX II. Testing is under way, and when sufficient financial support is forthcoming—perhaps from another foundation grant—the installation of the system will begin.[21]

The South Carolina Department of Archives and History (referred to in the following paragraphs as the Department) is firmly committed to SPINDEX II. In 1969, the program was obtained from the National Archives and after further study, testing was begun to enable the Department to "break away from the multi-purpose design of the INDEX Listing program and modify this program to produce specialized listings." The listings that the Department's system was designed to supply included a personal-name index, a chronology, a place-name or locality file, a main-topic or subject list, and a list of documents by type. The printout of each of these lists may show the record group, series, volume or box, folder or page, and item number for each entry, but the depth of indexing will depend upon the nature and value of the records and their existing finding aids. Three spaces are reserved in the coding for the Department designation if the entries later are fed into a regional or national data bank.[22]

What the Department system is not designed to do is to perform "co-ordinate searches," or, in the slang of the specialist, "massage the data." The system will not, for example, provide the researcher with a list of all the persons named Pemberton living in Kershaw County in 1830 who were engaged in the growing of hemp. To incorporate the capacity for such searches into the program would be prohibitively expensive, and the Department feels that the individual researcher can shift and assemble the necessary information to answer questions like the hypothetical one posed above from the various printouts provided in the search room.[23]

After some preliminary testing was successfully executed, an extensive test of the entire system was made, using a single volume of eighteenth-century miscellaneous records to provide the data. A printout was obtained of all the different listings given above. With the completion of these tests, the Department has begun work encoding the Judgment Rolls of the Colonial Court of Common Pleas, which previously had been cataloged on 3-by-5-inch cards. Information from the cards is entered on index input sheets, then encoded on magnetic tape for processing. Output from the computer for the Judgment Rolls is in the form of a register and a name index. There are no plans to implement the other types of indexing mentioned previously for the rolls. The printout from the volume of miscellaneous records used in the test was obtained in both the familiar paper form and COM (Computer Output Microfilm—see below). COM will be used in the future. The Department budgeted $8,500 for 1973–1974 and $17,900 for 1974–1975 (exclusive of salaries) for the SPINDEX program and its implementation.[24]

South Carolina has given thought to another area of computer technology also—using the computer to "arrange" dislocated files. This is a concept that has been advanced in the literature by information specialists, but has not been seriously considered generally by archivists and curators. In a paper read at the American Documentation Institute (now the American Society for Information Science), one participant suggested that curators stop organizing collections and devote the time to indexing each item which would be numbered, recorded, analyzed, and filed as it came to hand. When the computer is utilized in retrieval, she reasoned, "the organization of the papers themselves does not matter." [25] Another information scientist recommended a similar approach in an automated system in which he thought that item-indexing made collection arrangement unnecessary. He did recognize that most papers are arranged "as a unit to encourage traditional biographical research methods." To assist this type of researcher in using a collection of randomly filed documents, he suggested filing a set of the indexed document cards (the indexing form from which input was coded into the system) with the papers, which the biographer could arrange in "a desired chronological or subject order" and then retrieve and replace documents by number. [26]

While there has been some theorizing about, and occasional experimentation in, using the computer to service unarranged papers, the archivists of the federal government were forced, in July 1973, to put theory and experimentation to practical test. No attempt was made by NARS to reorder the records salvaged from the fire in the St. Louis military personnel records center (see n. 52, pp. 317-318). File folders were given location numbers, which, along with identifying tags, were encoded to the computer for retrieval. As an assist, the computer printed new labels for each salvaged folder. In the future, all records acquired by the personnel records center will be indexed into the computer system. [27]

Although the survey above is not all-inclusive, it offers some insights into the application of computer technology to the field of manuscripts. In the winter of 1973, after more than a decade of experimentation, it appears as if we are still on the threshold, and there are very few operative programs to offer guidance to what lies ahead. The experience of the institutions involved in the programs noted here, however, points up two areas of concern for curators contemplating a computer program. The first is a matter of economics. That the cost of applying computer technology is very expensive should be apparent from the fact that most of the projects have required a special appropriation or foundation funding.

In analyzing costs, one source notes that, in 1971, the price of computer hardware (the machinery) was about a tenth of what it had been a decade earlier, while the potential performance capacity of the computer had steadily increased during the same period. Thus the potential of a dollar spent for a computer increased relatively a thousandfold in this short time. Unfortunately, the cost of software, such as programming, has not followed a similar pattern. The same source states that a curator should be prepared to pay at least as much for input, typing or key-punching, as for the use of a computer.[28]

Computer time can be very much a cost factor, too, although several of the projects discussed above have had "free time" on a computer. For example, the Stanford Computer Center helped the Hoover Institution in its early automation efforts by "giving free use of machine time," but later made full charges for all services and computer time.[29] Of course, ultimately the concept of free time is fallacious, but in many instances the computer expense was borne by a higher administrative unit to which the manuscript depository was attached or allied.

That the over-all high cost can be a determining factor is demonstrated by the experience of at least two of the institutions participating in SPINDEX II. The Minnesota Historical Society lost much of its original enthusiasm for the project after bearing considerable costs for systems installation and subsequent systems development costs incurred in making the several test runs with all the adjustments. In attempting to estimate and plan for the conversion and bringing up to date of the data from its finding aids, the society found the costs were "staggering to contemplate." Cornell University has expressed reservations about the cost of SPINDEX II also and is concerned about "the whole area of cost/effectiveness in ADP applications to archives and manuscripts in general."[30]

Cornell was critical of SPINDEX II also for not developing a subject-authority file, which points up the second area of concern common to curators working with the computer: the difficulty of developing standard forms for unique materials. Minnesota Historical Society has noted the lack of a thesaurus for the profession as an inhibiting factor in computer project growth. At the South Carolina Department of Archives and History, where SPINDEX II has had its most successful application, there have been several problems in establishing a standard terminology for a subject index. Presently no further work is being done in this area, but future problems are expected.[31]

Some trends appear to be developing on the basis of the decade of experience. It seems to be accepted that item-indexing is too expensive and time-consuming except for collections of very high priority. The cost of item-indexing has been estimated as at least five dollars per document for the intellectual effort involved. At the Public Archives of Canada, for example, even with the substantial savings brought about through the use of COM (see below), item-indexing of the prime minister's papers had to be abandoned in 1970 for a control system based upon file descriptions. Costs have been cut also by using optical character recognition (OCR) for input—a typewriter equipped with a machine-language font which produces copy which a device scans or reads—instead of punching cards. The success of the Canadian program may rest upon the quality of the file descriptors chosen for each file, which are supposed to give the parameters of each file's subject content as a whole, not of individual items in the file.[32]

A broad-based study being conducted at the National Archives seems to indicate that the feeling there is that it is "equally futile" to attempt to analyze its entire holdings either by items, folders, or series. Instead of information retrieval based upon subject indexing, the archives hopes to develop a system of administrative control at the series (collection) level aimed toward producing a number of descriptive, quantitative, and statistical reports.[33]

The University Archives of Illinois at Urbana-Champaign, is attempting a middle approach in PARADIGM (Programmed Annual Report and Digital Information Matrix), a system combining elements of both intellectual and administrative control. For each of the archive's 2,688 processed collections, of which 434 are manuscripts (personal papers of faculty), a card has been punched showing the collection number, inclusive dates, dates of accessioning and processing, quantity, and type of document. Each card also records restrictions, number of pages of finding aids, six subject descriptors, one location descriptor, and three name descriptors. In focusing upon collection rather than item or folder control, the program is less ambitious than some, but it is complete and operative. The primary purpose of the program, as defined in its title, is the publication of an extensive annual report, but the stated secondary goal is the "production of subject indexes and subject searching." [34]

The researcher's use of the computer-stored information is the factor given least attention in the literature relating to information retrieval from manuscripts. As a result many scholars, as well as some curators, have a very hazy concept of the retrieval process. It is possible that this may in part account for the disappointing lack of use by scholars which caused some curators to abandon programs in the late

1960s. In any event, despite predictions to the contrary, the vision of a scholar seated at a typewriter console asking questions of the computer ("on-line" access, as it is known) probably will remain a vision for researchers in manuscripts for years to come.* Although technically possible, individual searches by the computer are prohibitively expensive. They have to be "batched" for access to the computer at nonprime time. The net result of this situation is that the vaunted speed of the computer in retrieving information is at present meaningless to the curator and the researcher. At the Hoover Institution, for example, search requests for information in the American Relief Administration files had to be gathered over a week or two before gaining access to the computer.[35]

In 1971, an authority surveying the application of the computer to the retrieval of information from manuscripts summarized his finding as follows: (1) some computer systems are slower than manual systems and considerably more costly; (2) the cost of a computer is frequently less than the cost of software and usually less than the cost of input; (3) the computer is seldom used in an archives or manuscript repository to search full text of documents; (4) if used as a searching tool, the computer is usually employed for coordinate searches; (5) no information retrieval system presently in use in either an archives or manuscript repository gives the researcher specific answers but refers him instead to documents; (6) the most practical use of the computer in manuscript retrieval is in providing finding aids.[36]

Thus printouts of indexes and subject bibliographies prepared in advance for the scholar, rather than direct access to the computer upon demand, will continue to be the more common research service. But printouts, which are time-consuming for the computer to produce, can be very voluminous, bulky to store, and difficult to use. Fortunately, one of the happy marriages of computer and microfilm technologies, COM (Computer Output Microfilm), now appears to hold the key to the solution of this and other of the curator's information-retrieval problems.

COM is one of four ways microfilm and the computer have been combined to handle information retrieval: (1) the computer input is

---

* At a 1967 conference of archivists, librarians, and computer specialists, one speaker confidently predicted that "remote stations as teletypewriters" would be a "regularly available archive service" within five years (see W. Howard Gammon, "Remotes and Displays," p. 119).

microfilm, (2) the computer memory is microfilm, (3) the computer output is microfilm, and (4) a computer controls the microfilm system.[37]

The first combination makes use of software called OCR (Optical Character Recognition), mentioned above, as it is used in connection with the prime minister's papers project. In this instance, the OCR device scanned typewriter-prepared copy, but some units can scan microfilm by passing a beam of light through the film and measuring the density of the image. Thus visual signals on the CIM (Computer Input Microfilm) are converted to electrical pulses and transmitted as digital input to the computer.[38]

Combination two is perhaps the most logical outgrowth of the strengths of each technology. The computer is the greatest generator of information, while microfilm can store information best. Since digital information can be recorded on microfilm and read back, microfilm can act as the memory of the computer. One of the most sophisticated applications of this technique is the use of a laser beam, which is split into dozens of channels, to burn tiny holes in the film and record the "signal or no signal" type of information found on magnetic tape, the more common form of storage of computer information.[39]

COM, the third combination, was first developed in 1957, but did not demonstrate its great potential until after the advent of the second- and third-generation computers of the mid-1960s. It is the process by which the machine language of the computer is converted onto microfilm in curator-language. COM records are produced in a variety of forms, but most of them are conversions of computer-generated magnetic tapes into 16mm or 35mm nonperforated roll microfilm.

The advantages of COM and its potential applications for the curator may be many. For example, a 2400-foot reel of computer-produced magnetic tape containing approximately twenty million bits equal to a half million words would produce 2500 pages of printout (a six-inch stack). The same magnetic tape can be recorded by COM on a 16mm microfilm cartridge in about six minutes. In volume, film weighs about a fiftieth as much as printout paper and costs about three-fourths less. Because less computer time is needed to generate information, an index of an expanding collection could be brought up to date much more frequently on COM than on computer printout.[40]

COM recorders can be used as a unit in a microfilm information-retrieval system; automatic retrieval coding marks can be programmed to appear on the film during the COM recording process, and indexes can be generated by the computer while it is formating the tapes. Other COM recorders of varying manufacturers can generate microfiche and 16, 35, and 105mm microfilm in rolls and cartridges. These same microforms and others, like aperture cards and film jackets, can be generated manually, and each can be utilized in a variety of microform information storage and retrieval systems. Some are quite complex, computer controlled (combination number four), others are manually controlled and searched. The remainder of this section will discuss sample microform systems, describing first the physical characteristics of the form, and then its applications, with especial emphasis upon microfilm, its production, and uses in a manual system.[41]

Microfiche, a sheet of microfilm containing multiple microimages in a grid pattern, is made in three standard sizes: 75 by 125mm, 105 by 148mm, and tabulating-machine card size. The most common size sheet, 105 by 148mm (nominally 4 by 6 inches), usually shot at one of two reduction ratios, contains either 60 or 98 images. CARD, a desk-top, automated file-and-display unit, is one system which uses 750 coded microfiche, which are retrieved by keyboard operation. Film jackets, which hold strips of microfilm, can be used in the same way as microfiche. Aperture cards, electric accounting machine punch cards with microfiche mounted in a cut-out section of the card, can be keypunched or edge-notched for use in any system designed for EAM cards. Superminiature microforms in the form of ultrafiche can be used in aperture cards and in ultrastrips, 6-inch 35mm filmstrips containing up to 2000 letter-size images. The MINDEX 370 provides image selection via a keyboard from a cartridge of ten ultrastrips.[42]

Microfilm images in rolls, cartridges, or unitized strips, can be locator-coded in several ways for use in information retrieval: photo-optical binary code, bar or code line, image count, film pull-down, and flash cards (see figure 23).[43]

Photo-optical binary coding (a series of dots on the film preceding each document, which give its number or index terms) can be recorded, as noted above, by COM, or by using punched cards and a keypunch coupled to a code camera. Magazines of film coded in this manner and a reader printer with code sensing and logic electronics are the elements of the MIRACODE system. Another similar but more complex system, FILESEARCH IV, includes a recording unit to code 100-foot rolls of 35mm perforated film which are spliced into 1000-foot rolls in the retrieval unit. Output can be either by screen display, paper printout or film-to-film copy of selected pertinent images.[44]

While binary coded films are used in electronic searching, image count and film pull-down indexing—both of which are quite similar— use specially constructed, motorized reader printers for automatic

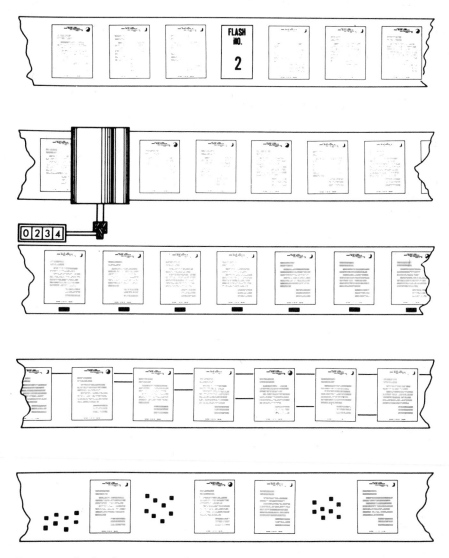

Fig. 23. Methods of retrieving information from microfilm. *From top to bottom:* flash card; film pull-down; image count; bar or code lines; and photo-optical binary code patterns.

mechanical searching. In image-count indexing, marks (blips) on the film are counted by a photoelectric cell in the reader; and in film pull-down, the linear location on the microfilm is measured automatically. Bar-and-code line indexing also uses a motorized reader, but the location on the film is made manually by matching lines on the film with lines on the screen. Finally, flash cards or targets, sometimes used in conjunction with an automatic counter which is filmed in each frame, provide the simplest and cheapest means of indexing microfilm. This is the system most likely to be used by the curator in his in-house projects.[45]

The curator may decide to microfilm manuscripts for information retrieval, but he also may be motivated to save space, as, for example, in filming a series of outsized account books and destroying the original volumes or putting them in dead storage. He may want to film other things to preserve their content: the album of deteriorating newspaper clippings, which then can be returned to the donor, or the much-used fragile letters, which would be placed in the vault and their copies used for research. Also he may use microfilm to fulfill other purposes: providing security for manuscripts especially susceptible to theft; copying selected manuscripts at the researcher's request; and producing microfilm editions of entire collections. The curator should keep in mind, however, that microfilm has a few inherent weaknesses as documentation. Some of the intrinsic value of a manuscript is lost in filming. Paper quality, gatherings, watermarks—except when filmed with specialized techniques—and other important information cannot be "read" from the film by the scholar, nor can he examine two different images (to compare handwriting, for example) at one time.[46]

Whatever microfilming the curator anticipates, he has the choice of contracting to have the work done commercially or having it done by his own institution. He would need to know a commercial firm well to entrust it with doing the filming in its laboratory. The added risks of transporting the manuscripts to and from the firm suggest that this ought to be the curator's course of last resort. Most firms will bring a camera and operator to the institution, but the cost will be considerable, whether the filming is done in the repository or the commercial laboratory. Wherever the work is done, the curator should not rely on an oral explanation to the firm's representative; instead, he should write instructions about how he expects the company to proceed with the microfilming.

Microfilm companies contend that one of the advantages of having a laboratory do the work is that it will usually have better quality control. This is probably true, at least until the curator has developed some skills at filming, and it is easy to lose facility, speed, and familiarity if filming is not done regularly. Cost and depreciation continue when the camera is not working, and an idle camera tends to get out of adjustment and need repair. For infrequent use, the curator might consider leasing a camera on a lease-purchase agreement.[47]

Some institutions have a large enough operation (and budget) to justify an in-house laboratory which takes and develops all their microfilms. Such a laboratory, operated by skilled technicians, is the curator's dream, and if he can instill in the technicians an additional understanding of the unique character of the manuscripts they handle, he should have few problems with microfilm.

If, on the other hand, the agency cannot support its own microfilm laboratory, and for one reason or another commercial service is not feasible, the curator must look for other alternatives. If the decision is made to purchase a camera, the curator will find the choices of models available mind-boggling and expensive. Fortunately, his task is simplified by the National Microfilm Association, which since 1959 has issued a *Guide to Microreproduction Equipment,* with annual supplements. With the *Guide,* the curator can survey the entire gamut of equipment before getting in touch with individual companies.[48]

From the start, the curator's choice will be determined by the kind of material he will be filming. This immediately eliminates one entire type of camera, the rotary, which will not accommodate bound volumes and films single sheets by running them through rollers, a process to which the curator would not wish to subject important or fragile manuscripts. Even if these problems were not present, rotary cameras would still be unacceptable, because the optical quality obtainable is not good enough to prepare preservation copies of manuscripts. Similarly, if the curator wants a camera to do a variety of jobs, he will eliminate from consideration various specialty cameras like the step and repeat models manufactured to produce microfiche, or one of the cameras which codes film for a specifically designed information retrieval system. Only a planetary model offers the optical quality and versatility needed in the general program. There is great diversity in these models. Portable units start at less than $1,000, and standard planetary cameras range from $1,300 to $8,000.[49]

Like cameras, film, the second component in any microfilm program, is bewildering in its diversity, and a rapidly developing technology has now made almost obsolete some terms used for years to describe film. Traditionally, developed microfilm was described as being either positive or negative, and it was a simple matter to tell the difference by sight. Before World War II, when the bulk of the microfilm was made by Eastman in 35mm wide, 100-foot-long reels of silver halide film on a triacetate base, negative microfilm reversed the light image of the original, so that a newspaper which had been filmed appeared to have white type on black paper. In those days, the camera film—the "master," as it was usually called—was negative in polarity and was referred to as *first generation*. A positive microfilm, printed from the negative, reversed the image, so that a positive of the same newspaper would appear to be black ink on white paper. It was called a print, or second-generation copy.

Today, because of its extra sensitivity to light, only silver halide film, in both 35mm and 16mm widths, is regularly used in microfilm cameras to produce master films of manuscripts. In addition to regular microfilm, silver halide is now manufactured in *direct-image film,* so that the first-generation, or camera film (negative) produces a second-generation print which is also negative. Two other kinds of microfilm, *vesicular* and *diazo,* are used for preparing distribution or working copies. At this time neither is thought to produce films of archival quality for permanent preservation; in any case, standards for these films do not yet exist. Vesicular film, which is sold commercially under the names Kalvar or Xidex, is exposed by ultraviolet light and dry-processed by heat. It seems milky or whitish to the eye, and it may appear to be either negative or positive, depending on the angle the light strikes it. Diazo is a dye-image film which is exposed by ultraviolet light and developed by subjecting it to ammonia vapor. The image on diazo film will always be the same polarity as the film from which it was copied.[50]

Unexposed microfilm, raw stock, can be purchased in bulk lots of a thousand feet; but normally, unless his institution has a laboratory, the curator will buy 100-foot rolls of one of the name brands of 35mm silver halide film. A recently developed "thin-base" film (2.7 mils as opposed to 5.4 mils for regular film) will allow 215 feet of usable film per standard-size reel. In either thickness, microfilm which meets the American National Standards Institute requirement for archival permanence (PH1.28-1969) is slow, fine-grained, nonperforated film capable of taking an image with a high degree of sharpness or acuity. Included in the price of a roll of film is the cost of developing, and it is returned to the company laboratory for processing.[51]

Choosing the right camera and microfilm stock will not insure an economically successful program. The curator must realize that the very diversity of manuscripts, plus his not always complementary objectives for instituting a program, will make it expensive. For example, for the curator to prepare a microfilm edition of one of his institution's collections, and at the same time interrupt the project to prepare microfilm research copies of selected manuscripts from other collections for individual scholars, he must be willing to waste great quantities of film and to have either short-footage rolls, or frequently spliced master negatives in his microfilm publications. The only alternative is to accumulate enough orders from scholars to be filmed together on a miscellaneous reel between rolls of the microfilm publication.

Even with the waste of unnecessary footage, film costs represent the smallest fraction of the total microfilming budget. The labor cost of the camera operator will vary with his ability. In filming an ordinary correspondence file in which there is little conformity, with letter to letter varying in color of paper and density of ink, a beginning cameraman will need to take repeated readings with his light meter and adjust his light source up or down in intensity. With experience, he can judge by eye when the amount of needed light changes and calls for a new reading. Also he will learn that the meter cannot always be relied upon (as, for example, in filming a negative photostat). But as he develops skills, he must not become casual; because of the unique nature of manuscripts, microfilming can never become routine. Therefore, labor costs will be difficult to estimate; however, the assumption can be made that they will be high.

But what the curator may not realize is that, for every hour of filming, a comparable amount of time must be allotted for inspecting the film, and approximately three hours must be spent preparing the manuscripts for the camera. This involves, among other things, removing all staples and making a complete sequential check to see that all is in order and nothing is missing. If the curator is not planning to do the filming himself, he must prepare a set of guidelines for the cameraman, directing him how to handle enclosures, blank pages, etc., and he must place written instructions in the series for unusual instances not covered in the guidelines. The manuscripts should be divided in advance, so that the rolls break in a sensible and systematic way—at the end of a year, for example, in a chronological series. These divisions will be not unlike those that the processor makes in arranging a manuscript collection in folders and boxes.[52]

To plan roll breaks in advance, the curator must estimate the number of pages to be filmed, so that, in turn, he can determine the number of exposures needed (see appendix). Each exposure is called a *frame* and the number of frames he can get on a strip of microfilm depends upon the reduction ratio and the position of the camera. In a planetary model the camera head (the box into which the roll of film is threaded to move between two reels above the lens) is mounted on a shaft or column so that it can be raised and lowered to different heights above the bed or table part of the camera where the manuscripts are placed for filming. The higher the head is from the bed, the smaller the page size is reduced on the exposed film. The size of the original page compared to the microfilm image is called the reduction ratio; thus, the image of a piece of paper twelve inches long would measure an inch on a film shot in a twelve-to-one ratio (12:1).[53]

In addition to being movable upward and downward, the head of a planetary camera can be turned or rotated to four different positions, only two of which are normally used in filming. These positions have been given standard labels *A* and *B*. In position *A*, lines of writing on the document are at right angles to the edge of the film; and in *B*, the lines of the image are parallel.* The position of the image on the film is called *placement* and the usual four have a standard designation: in *IA* and *IB*, single pages are filmed a sheet at a time; and in *IIA* and *IIB*, double pages are filmed in a single exposure. In recently developed terminology, placement is synonymous with *image orientation* and modes *A* and *B* are known as *cine* and *comic*, respectively [54] (see figure 24).

The most economical method of filming manuscripts will depend upon the size and nature of the material and whether the images can best be fitted onto the microfilm parallel or at right angles to the edge of the film. The standard guides to microfilming give the curator little solid advice on this point, and it is beyond the scope of this book to offer such detailed instruction. The curator can resolve his own problems best by exposing an extended test strip of microfilm in which he films loose manuscripts and bound volumes at each of the placements and at varying reduction ratios. Each frame on the test strip should be clearly marked, showing placement and ratio, so that the film can be studied later and used as a guide to filming in the future.

The most commonly used reduction ratios in microfilming manuscripts are 12:1 to 15:1. A 12:1 ratio is excellent for ordinary letter sheets; but on some microfilm readers, the image will be magnified too large for the entire page to fit on the screen. Also the field of focus is too small at 12:1 to film some sheets and volumes. Thus a

---

* In using a Recordak camera, for example, in position *A*, the exposed footage counter faces the operator, and in position *B*, the film-loading doors face away from him. Caution should be used *not* to film a volume two pages at a time with the filmloading doors facing the operator. Pages will appear on the film in inverse order, that is, 2–1, 4–3, etc.

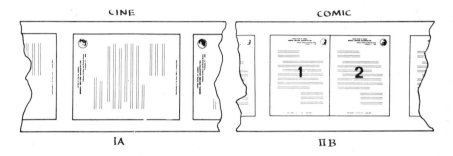

Fig. 24. Standard image placement on microfilm (top figures show two frames).
Left-hand figures are *cine* and right-hand figures, *comic.*

14:1 ratio is most often used for manuscripts. At this ratio, the curator
can estimate between 1000 to 1100 frames per 100-foot roll.[55]

By experimenting with the light meter, reduction ratio, and image
placement, the curator will, in time, master the more technical aspects
of microfilming; but following a few simple rules from the beginning
will help him produce professional-looking, aesthetically pleasing
films. He should settle upon a reduction ratio and an image placement,
particularly the latter, and, if possible, stay with it for an entire project.
Film produced with those two variables being changed frequently is
difficult and annoying to use.

Another mark of the nonprofessional film is improperly aligned
copy on the camera bed. A page which to the eye of the cameraman
may appear to be only slightly off the right-angle axis of the film
will, when magnified on the reader screen, look sloppily aslant. The
curator can avoid this by covering the bed with a sheet of firmly
taped-down paper. Most planetary cameras have a light which will
project on the bed of the camera a square of light which has the exact

dimensions of the field of focus. By marking the corners lightly with a pencil, the curator will then have good visual guides to help him align the manuscript on the bed during the filming. The pencil marks will not show on the finished film, but dirty fingerprints and smudges on the paper will show and it should be changed regularly.[56]

Ghost hands, the image of fingers, can mar a microfilm aesthetically even more than fingerprints. When the camera operator must hold the pages of a volume to keep them from turning, he should use two pointers rather than his hands. Although microfilming volumes is always tricky, particularly tightly bound ones, a book cradle can be improvised by placing a sheet of foam rubber under the book, with wooden wedges to raise up the lower cover and a piece of heavy plate glass to hold the pages open and flat.

But of the several attributes of a professional microfilm, none is more apparent than attractive targets. Targets are of several kinds, and each of them should be large enough to be read on the microfilm with the naked eye. An important target is the trademark, which may be nothing more than the name of the institution, but which may include a symbol or a seal. Since it will appear at the beginning and end of every roll of film, the curator might wish to have it executed by a graphics designer. Next in order on the microfilm comes the title target, which can be a short-form title, since it is followed by the title page, on which are included the name and inclusive dates of the papers, along with the date of the camera work, location of the original manuscripts, and the reduction ratio.[57]

Like the title page it follows, the microfilm introduction is typed; it is, to the film, what the inventory is to a collection. Following this, multiroll microfilm publications should have roll or content notes for each roll. The inclusive dates or letters of the alphabet covered by the material to be filmed on the roll are listed. Also here should be included information about significant omissions, irregularities, and variations in the manuscripts which have not been mentioned in the microfilm introduction. The remainder of the targets are self-explanatory. The most common are: *Start, End, Reel No.* (with a matching set of numerals), *Retake, Original Mutilated, Continue,* and *To Be Continued.*[58]

If, in arranging the collection prior to microfilming, enclosures, fragments, missing pages, and other discrepancies were not marked on the manuscripts themselves (see chapter 5), explanations can be typed to be filmed with the papers. Similar typewritten statements alert the microfilm user to material out of order or not filmed, as, for example, numbered—but otherwise blank—pages in a volume.

With the exception of the film title, title page, and ratio, which will change with each microfilm publication, the targets will be used repeatedly. Thus, the effort to make them look attractive will have long-term benefits. Even someone with a minimum knowledge of type layout can make well-designed targets with a ruler, poster board, and Artype—sheet letters that can be pressed to adhere to the board. Once the targets are made, the curator ought to have them photographed, and when the originals get worn, he can replace them easily with photographic prints.

Even well-designed targets are at best mechanical props to raise the quality of a microfilm publication. The over-all quality depends upon the cameraman. By nature, he should be patient and enjoy attention to detail. For example, he should keep a logbook in which he records the facts of each job: roll number, date photographed, name and dates of manuscripts, number of frames, reduction ratio, voltage-meter reading, optimum light-meter reading, type of film, and image placement.

Cameramen, depending upon their equipment and experience, may develop differing solutions for common technical problems. One of the recurring problems is how to film letterpress volumes. The letterpress process was a means of making retained copies of handwritten letters in the nineteenth century. A sheet of tissue was dampened, placed on the ink side of the letter, and the two sheets put in a screw-down press to dry. If the tissue was evenly dampened, enough of the ink transferred to it for a readable copy. The process was used on letters typed with the hectograph (purple ink) ribbon into the early twentieth century. To film such a volume, one authority recommends interleaving a sheet of white opaque paper between the pages. The sheet screens out the bottom or second page, avoiding bleed-through. At the same time, it heightens the image on the page being microfilmed. Another authority recommends black paper. And a third source suggests that, since the ink image of a letterpress copy was applied to the reverse of the sheet, the back side of the page should be microfilmed and the processed film reversed for reading or printing.[59]

Even with the most meticulous of camera operators, there will be mistakes. Looking for these mistakes is another major labor cost often not properly anticipated. Processed film should be inspected by someone other than the camera operator as soon as possible after being shot. Because most curators must send the exposed film to a distant laboratory for processing, there is always a time lag of at least several days between shooting and inspection. With a continuing operation, this can mean a considerable waste of filming and much reshooting if, for example, the camera is out of adjustment. The reader used for the inspection should be kept spotless and in good adjustment, lest the master film get dirty or scratched. The processing laboratory, if it can catch it in time, can clean a master before printing copies, but scratches cannot be removed and may mar work or sale prints.

The most common things to look for during the film inspection are the following: (1) underexposure, or too little light—film has greyish background in which the transparent letters lose their contrast; (2) overexposure, too much light—film has dense black background and the letters are not transparent, but veiled; (3) overexposed and underexposed areas in the same frame—maladjusted lights or stray light from a window, etc.; (4) blurred image caused by vibration—moving the camera head or the paper during the exposure; (5) fog, usually at either end of the film—improper loading or unloading of roll from camera; (6) "soft" image—camera either slightly out of focus or lens needs adjustment.[60]

The cost of finished microfilm, which would include the price of the microfilm stock, the labor to prepare the manuscripts for the camera, the cameraman's wages, and inspection of the developed film, have been estimated at a low of $60 to a high of $250 per roll.[61] If the cost of equipment (camera, reader-printer, storage cabinets) and equipment maintenance are added to this, it can be seen that the simplest microfilm retrieval system is expensive. Further, the costs of automation through electronics seem almost astronomical to the average curator; for example, a medium-priced COM unit sold for $125,000 in 1970.[62] Obviously, without federal support or foundation funding for a co-operative program, most institutions will continue to retrieve their records manually. But before a co-operative program can be successful, the profession must develop standards for its finding aids and adopt a thesaurus.

Meanwhile, machine-readable records are being created in ever-increasing numbers each year by government agencies, private businesses, and institutions. More and more of this kind of documentation will be found in manuscript collections of the future. How the curator should attempt to conserve, describe and disseminate them, along with other nonmanuscript materials, will be discussed in the pages that follow.

SELECTED READINGS

The most succinct presentation of the over-all theme of this chapter can be read in George H. Harmon, "The Computer-Microfilm Relationship."

SPINDEX II is the program most likely to affect the average curator. When a final report on the project is filed by NARS with the Council on Library Resources, it should be most useful to the profession. There is no up-to-date survey of the state of the art, but two articles by Frank G. Burke, "Application of Automated Techniques in the Management and Control of Source Materials" and "Automation in Bibliographical Control of Archives and Manuscript Collections," give a history of the field to that date.

Three books which should help to make automation intelligible to the curator are: Susan Artandi, *An Introduction to Computers in Information Science;* Basil Doudnikoff, *Information Retrieval;* and Roger Meetham, *Information Retrieval: The Essential Technology.* Two "best buys," both publications of NARS, Office of Records Management, are available at the Government Printing Office: *Managing Information Retrieval: Information Retrieval* (1972) and *Managing Information Retrieval: Microfilm Retrieval Equipment Guide* (1970). Fortunately, both are much more imaginative than their titles. Another equipment guide, indispensable to the curator, is now in its fourth edition with a 1970 supplement: Hubbard W. Ballou, editor, *Guide to Microreproduction Equipment.*

Practical aspects of microfilming are best outlined in Albert H. Leisinger, Jr., *Microphotography for Archives* (with an error on p. 24 in the IIB film-image placement), and Frank B. Evans's pamphlet for the National Archives, *The Selection and Preparation of Records for Publication on Microfilm.* The Allen B. Veaner book, *Evaluation of Micropublications: A Handbook for Librarians,* prepared for the ALA Library Technology Program, has been referred to in the selected readings in another chapter, but deserves top rating here, too.

Despite its title, perhaps the best over-all view of microfilm is Frederic Luther, "The Language of Lilliput: A Thesaurus for Users of Microfilm," which appeared in seven parts in *Library Journal.* A shorter, more up-to-date review can be found in *The Invisible Medium: The State of the Art of Microform and a Guide to the Literature,* an ASIS publication, and another short pamphlet, *Introduction to Micrographics,* a "slick" illustrated publication of the National Microfilm Association.

VII

Nonmanuscript Material

THE manner in which the curator handles nonmanuscript material found in a collection will depend in part upon the facilities and practices of his collecting agency. The agency which has a museum division would have a different policy from one that does not, in regard to the artifacts present in many personal papers. Whether books are kept with an individual's papers or separated from them may depend on whether the papers are being processed in a university special collection or a state historical society manuscript collection. In general, during the last few years, there has been a trend toward leaving more nonmanuscript material with papers. Perhaps the curators have been influenced by the archivists, with their concern for the integrity of a collection.[1]

Artifacts

If the curator is affiliated with an institution which has a museum, the artifacts in a person's papers ought to be sent there. There is little place in a collection of manuscripts for what the manuscript librarian of the Library of Congress once characterized as "hats, guns, and dog houses."[2] If the collecting agency does not have a museum division, it would be well for the curator to set such artifacts aside for return to the donor after the papers have been arranged and described. There are other objects, however, that might be kept with the papers; they could be classed as "badges, buttons, and banners." Ultimately the curator's decision will be based upon the size and quantity of the artifacts, whether they can be easily shelved along with the rest of the collection, and their relationship to the papers.

Printed Material

The curator can be advised at the outset to remove all printed matter from a manuscript collection. Then he can be further advised that there may be certain exceptions. By and large, books would be separated from personal papers and sent to the library. Exceptions can be illustrated by assuming that the curator has received the papers of the author William J. Scribbler. Depending upon how important a place the curator feels Scribbler holds in the American literary scene, the surviving books from his personal library might be kept with his papers.* Certainly, books annotated by him and books dedicated or autographed to him ought not to go into the general library collection. If curators agree, as they seem to, that manuscript notebooks, first and subsequent drafts, galleys, and page proofs of an author's work ought to remain in a collection, then perhaps his books—the final product of these various states—also ought to be left with the papers.

The rules for including or separating pamphlets and periodicals from an author's papers generally follow those for books. The curator must consider whether the separated material can be easily retrieved in the library. Materials which a library would assign to a vertical file perhaps might better be left in the papers. For the papers of nonliterary persons, he ought to be guided by a general question: *Would a researcher expect to find this printed item in this person's papers?* The same principle ought to apply when considering other printed items, such as broadsides and maps. The curator will have little difficulty administering this principle in the obvious cases; there would be little reason for keeping a copy of the *Reader's Digest* with a person's papers unless they are those of the editor or publisher. A modern road map of Massachusetts, unless it is the itinerary of a campaign

---

* The following quotation from a well-known American author might make curators more cautious about personal libraries: "I get loads of books from authors and publishers, but hardly ever read them. Now I am working up a scheme with a friend of mine who has a library of 2,000 volumes he wants to get rid of. We plan to advertise sale in literary magazines, saying they are from my library and contain my ex libris. Will autograph for an added fee. This way we can get a dollar or more above the usual price. I will enjoy signing my name to some stinking books I never even heard of!"

tour, does not belong in a politician's papers, nor does a copy of *National Geographic,* a Montgomery Ward catalog, or a theater poster. Granted, all of these items may have been seen and used by the politician, but they should not be kept with his papers unless they have some closer relationship to his life. For example, a broadside listing livestock and equipment from an estate to be sold at auction might be kept with the politician's papers if the sale was on his parent's farm.

There are other factors that the curator will want to consider before deciding whether or not a particular printed item should be retained in the papers. The decision might rest upon what will be done with the map or broadside if it is separated from the papers. Is there a cataloged and well-cared-for collection of maps in the historical society library, or does the university library have a broadside collection? If so, the curator at either institution would remove the map or broadside, knowing that it would be more accessible to scholars in a specialized collection. If the curator himself is responsible for his institution's collection of maps or broadsides, his decisions about leaving these types of material in a person's papers would be colored by the size and condition of the item. Even if a map or broadside is closely related to the papers, but is fragile or oversize, it might better be stored flat in its own folder. In an instance such as this, the curator would want to place a dated cross-reference sheet in the papers, noting that the broadside or map had been removed and where it can be found.

In sorting a person's papers, the curator will be confronted by a quantity of miscellaneous printed items which do not fit into any of the above categories and which can be classed as ephemera. Here, again, relevance to the collection must be a factor: Does the instruction sheet for assembling a tricycle, the advertising circular for a model home development, or a sheet of chain-store give-away coupons have meaning in the papers? How much space can be saved by disposing of it? Ephemera that can be easily dated—for example, printed letters— probably should be sorted into the general correspondence. Other pieces retained in an individual's papers, assuming they are not enclosures (see chapter 5) would probably be boxed in a miscellaneous printed series.

Other ephemera (pamphlets, brochures, leaflets, programs, invitations, tickets, etc.) which are not relevant to the individual's papers can be cataloged and boxed as a separate collection. Such a collection of ephemera could also include single issues of historically important periodicals and tear sheets of articles from more common ones. One method of caring for such a collection is to file the pieces by subject in folders and in Hollinger cartons and to catalog them with one main entry card. If the author is unknown, the title is used as main entry. The card is clipped to the piece, and after several pieces are gathered, they are classified according to subject. The classification is written in two places: (1) on the card above the hole for the drawer rod, and (2) in the upper corner of the item itself. Cards are then filed in one alphabetical sequence, and the pieces of ephemera are filed by subject in Hollinger cartons. The subject-heading guide on loose-leaf sheets serves as the finding aid. The card catalog provides an additional finding aid, and prevents classifying duplicate materials. This system has been used for years at the Buffalo and Erie County Historical Society. In a similar system developed by the special collections department of the University of California Library, Los Angeles, materials are filed alphabetically by subject in legal folders in file cabinets. They are cataloged by folder and shelflisted alphabetically. The ephemera are divided into three general collections—U.S., California, and Miscellaneous—and four specialized ephemera collections—Literature of Extremist Movements, Film Arts, Theater Arts, and Graphic Arts.[3]

At the time of its creation, ephemera might not be considered to have even secondary research value, but in time it takes on unique documentary value because the curator has conferred a long life on what is essentially short-lived material. So much ephemera is created, however, that an institution must be selective, and the advice of one authority should be heeded when he suggests: "Whenever a research library embarks on the collection of [ephemera] the collection should be kept within bounds by constant review and evaluation by all groups with an interest in the material."[4]

Newspaper clippings, loose or mounted in scrapbooks, form another general category of printed material that tries the curator's patience. The decision on preserving a scrapbook will rest upon its condition, its relevance to the collection, its subject unity, and what newspapers were clipped. Scrapbooks compiled from eighteenth-century, all-rag newspapers pose few problems; they are probably mounted on equally good paper stock with relatively pure paste. The pages in more recent newspaper scrapbooks are often more brittle than the clippings themselves. With even limited use, they will litter the floor with paper scraps, and if the scrapbooks of this type are to be preserved, microfilming is the cheapest and easiest solution.

Some scrapbooks, especially those organized around a person, organization, subject, or event, are fine research tools, particularly if the newspapers clipped are not readily available either in original files or microfilm editions. Also scrapbooks in which the clippings are dated and their newspaper source indicated are more valuable than those which are not. But the best-oriented and best-organized scrapbook of clippings from an indexed newspaper such as the *New York Times* probably does not warrant preservation, unless, of course, it documents the life of the person whose papers are being arranged. The curator can usually with equal assurance dispense with all general scrapbooks, except perhaps those compiled from foreign or special-interest newspapers. Before any scrapbook is disposed of, however, it should be collated carefully, because often it will contain photographs, letters, ephemera, and other valuable research material which can be removed to other specialized collections.

The same criteria used to assess scrapbooks should be applied to loose clippings. If they are kept, the curator usually will sort them roughly by subject, if applicable, or by date, probably by year, perhaps even by decade. A single clipping from a modern paper which is an enclosure, or which is kept with correspondence for some other reason, ought to have its own small folder of acid-free paper or should be enclosed in plastic. Small collections of clippings can be mounted on sheets of stationery: if the clippings are of rag, they should be mounted with a pure paste, but any glue except rubber cement would do well enough for modern newspapers (see chapter on physical care and conservation for suggestions about laminating, Xeroxing, or microfilming clippings).

Once the curator has made the myriad of decisions about retaining or disposing of the variety of printed materials in a manuscript collection, he must then give some guidance to the researcher. He will find it wise, also, to have records to jog his own memory and aid his successor. Cross-referencing, in several different forms, is ideal, but the curator will have to decide if the time spent is worth the effort.

In the past, when collections were smaller and the backlog of unarranged manuscripts less menacing, curators attempted to list all items removed from a collection. Today, this is frequently not done, or if a list is placed in the manuscript collection (or the donor file) it is general in nature, perhaps no more than an item count and brief description.

Another type of cross-referencing is to place a card in the appropriate map, broadside, or book catalog, describing the items left in the manuscript collection. Cards used in this kind of cross-reference would follow the format of the individual catalog into which they were filed, regardless of whether the broadsides, for example, were housed and administered by the manuscript division or by the library.

Fig. 25. A collage of broadsides. (Courtesy Southern Illinois University)

If, on the other hand, no separate collection of broadsides exists but the curator anticipates such a collection will be established at a later date, he can have a subject/secondary heading for broadsides in his manuscript catalog. Cards filed under this heading would indicate manuscript collections containing broadsides; thus, if the curator wished, he could at some time in the future withdraw them and bring them all together in a separate collection.

How does the curator care for nonmanuscript materials that remain in his jurisdiction? It is assumed that in most institutions books separated from a manuscript collection would be assigned to a library and are no longer the curator's responsibility. If, however, books are retained as part of the manuscript collection or as a separate but adjunct collection, they should be cataloged under the Anglo-American cataloging rules. However, they would be handled differently from books in the general library. If, for one reason or another, the books are important enough to be kept in a special collection, they ought to have the minimal care given a rare book. It will greatly assist bibliographers and textual critics if the books' dust jackets are retained and if they are not marked with accession or catalog numbers. Call numbers or other identification can be typed on a flag, a slip of paper interleaved and protruding above the top of the book.

Broadsides and maps each need about the same kind of filing. Their great variation in size and their flexibility and low tear strength in relation to surface area make special handling and equipment necessary for their conservation. Ideally, permanent/durable paper folders in steel blueprint files, or other oversize cases designed for flat filing, should be used to house each. Although there is some disagreement among writers about size, the most practical general map case should have drawers with the inside dimensions of approximately 43 by 32 inches.[5] The drawer should not be much over two inches deep. As many as 300 map sheets can be placed in a drawer of this depth; if the sheets are laminated and heavy folders are used, the drawer will still hold about 250 maps, although retrieval without damaging the maps will be difficult from files filled to capacity. Because of the better production from dust it affords, the type of case with fabric covers that hook at the front of the drawer is preferable to the drawers with metal hoods at the back and hinged compressors at the front.[6]

Horizontal cabinets with suspension filing, sometimes called plan files, are also used for maps and broadsides. They take somewhat less floor space per piece filed than flat storage, but are much more expensive.

Two unacceptable methods of storing either maps or broadsides are cross-folding them to fit letter or legal-sized vertical filing cabinets, or rolling them for storage in tubes or in "roll files," which are wasteful of space and cause paper to curl. The portfolio, a traditional type of storage, does provide excellent protection from dust, but if it is not full, maps or broadsides slide about and curl or tear.[7] Occasionally, the curator will encounter drawings or maps much too large to store flat. If they are not executed in fine detail or minute scale, they can sometimes be sectioned, but more often they must be rolled and stored the best way possible.

Lacking any of the equipment noted above, the curator can purchase inexpensive print boxes to hold the smaller items; and for the larger ones, he can request the cardboard shipping cases for mat board at the local art store. Acid-free kraft paper can be used for folders. If the curator can afford neither boxes nor acid-free paper for folders, maps and broadsides can be stored in brown wrapping-paper folders on double-face open shelves. Cut two pieces of corrugated cardboard so that they overlap the folders a couple of inches on each side and place them at the top and bottom of the stack. This system provides far from ideal storage, but it will keep the prints or maps flat and relatively dust-free.

Both broadsides and maps, frequently overlooked by researchers, are most often used for illustrations or exhibits. Historically, broadsides probably are not as old as manuscripts; since they were posted in public places to be read, they would be rare in times before literacy was common. Manuscripts have been collected for more than 4,000 years, but one authority feels that the making of maps, their dissemination, and their collection have been restricted for centuries by political and military considerations. As he says, "Maps are so closely related to military intelligence and political intrigue that an aura of furtiveness and secrecy surrounds their collection and their study. Maps did not come into vogue as historical documentation until late in the eighteenth century, and they are not as yet as widely used as they might be. Despite all the vital and unique information which they can convey, maps are still relied upon to supplement verbally derived information rather than to serve as substantive sources."[8]

A survey of 360 United States map libraries made in 1953 revealed that 74 percent of the requests for maps were by area, 24 percent by subject, and a few scattered ones by title, publisher, scale, and date.[9] This type of usage has lent widespread support to the area-main-entry concept for cataloging maps, but as one archivist points out, maps often do not show a well-defined, generally recognized place-name area. Maps of the trans-Mississippi West illustrate this difficulty of using a geographical area for a cataloging main entry. The same archivist points out that there appears to be confusion between description and arrangement of maps. There is no reason, he states, why a map cannot be cataloged by author and arranged by area, if that is desirable.[10] Whatever the system of main entry, the authorities agree that the card should include geographical area, subject, date, size or scale, publisher or authority, and notes on edition, series, number of sheets, and classification number.[11]

Several complex classification and cataloging systems for maps have been devised by librarians, the most widely used of which is the Library of Congress "G" Schedule.[12] This schedule provides a detailed breakdown, with each area and potential subdivision being assigned a four-digit number. Such a system is logical, since most research use of maps is by area and date, but in a small collection the curator may find it simpler to assign call numbers in numerical sequence to maps. After studying the storage equipment available to him, the curator may want to divide maps into three general sizes and assign a prefix L, M, or S to his numerical sequence. The collection should have its own shelf list and card catalog with main entry and subject/secondary headings, indicating for example, the cartographer or special physical features of the map.[13] By the time a map collection outgrows such a system, it is probably ready to be administered by a specialist.[14]

Broadsides are usually cataloged and shelved by date, but a numerical sequence, like the one for maps, can be used. Both maps and broadsides can be filed face down with catalog numbers written lightly in a lower corner on the blank side. Again, the standard library practice should be followed in preparing the shelflist, main-entry, and subject/secondary cards. Of course, there will be numerous broadsides with unknown authors, which should be cataloged with a "hanging indention" (see chapter on Establishing Bibliographic Control). Many other broadsides will not have a title, and will have to be cataloged by using the first sentence of the text in its place. A text title, which is often quite long, can be entered in a short form. To facilitate research, the subject/secondary headings should conform to those used in the manuscript catalogs.

Techniques for the repair and preservation of maps and broadsides are similar to those described for manuscripts, except that, because of certain differences in their origin and use, they are more often completely reinforced with fabric or paper backing. Most maps and all broadsides (by definition) are printed on one side. Because of their size, maps are awkward to use and service and are frequently torn; and broadsides, because of their intended ephemeral nature, are often printed on newsprint stock. The traditional method of reinforcing maps was to back them with a good grade of muslin or linen, but as one map librarian notes, "Contrary to popular belief, good-quality paper for backing will outlast fabric whose longevity is limited to between 20 to 30 years." [15] Either wet or dry mounting can best be learned by on-the-spot instruction, but the curator can adapt the detailed instructions available for mounting photographs to maps and broadsides.[16]

For the curator who is anxious to see how maps are cared for and administered, a visit to the Library of Congress, the New York Public Library, and the Clements Library would be worthwhile. Another example of a well-cared-for collection is that of the Newberry Library, where, in November 1972, the Hermon Dunlap Smith Center for the History of Cartography was dedicated. Established in association with the Committee on Institutional Cooperation (the Big Ten universities and the University of Chicago), the center offers an annual course in the history of cartography for collectors and soon will be offering six-week "apprenticeships" to potential map catalogers of the Midwest.[17]

Motion Picture Film

Often enough to be troublesome to the curator, the collections which he is sorting will contain motion picture films, usually of the home variety, but, occasionally, commercially produced reels. Despite the fact that in the United States today there are two motion pictures produced for every book published, few curators have had experience in caring for film.[18] Many might not even recognize some of the home movies made between 1898 and 1923, for, in the first twenty-five years, films were produced in a variety of widths. Then in 1923, the Victor Animatograph Company, followed shortly by Eastman and Bell and Howell, marketed the 16mm home camera. Five years later, Eastman introduced the 8mm for home use.[19]

The 16mm and 8mm home movies are on safety film, but the commercially produced ones, 35mm, are often on nitrate stock, as were some of the early home variety. All film should be examined to see if it is marked "safety film." These words and the brand name usually appear along the edge of 35mm film. If the words do not appear and the curator has reason to believe that the film was made before 1950 (nitrate was still being used in commercial film until this time), he should test it to make sure it is not nitrate-base film. Nitrate is chemically similar to guncotton and under certain conditions can be as dangerous and almost as explosive as that term suggests. Even if it is stored in a container, nitrate can ignite through spontaneous combustion. To test for nitrate film, the curator can cut a half-inch strip of film and fold it the long way. Take this narrow strip of film outdoors, stand it upon end on the sidewalk, and touch a top corner with a match. If it burns slowly, smolders, and goes out when the match is removed, it is safety film, but if it flash-ignites or burns rapidly with a bright yellow flame, it is nitrate.[20]

If the curator still is not sure, he can cut out a circle of film with a paper punch and drop the circle into a test tube or small bottle of trichloroethylene. (Trichloroethylene is nonflammable, but the vapor is toxic. Thus this test should be made outside, too.) Shake the bottle and if, after it is wet, the circle of film floats on the liquid, it is safety film. If it sinks, it is nitrate.[21]

All nitrate film decomposes at room temperature, and when a curator opens a can of it, he may find it in varying stages. If the film is soft, frothy at the edge, or decomposed into a brownish powder, the curator would do well to dig a hole and bury it. If the film is discolored and sticks together at a few spots, he will have to decide if he thinks the film is of sufficient historical importance to spend the time and money needed to preserve it.[22]

The best way of preserving the images on nitrate film is to have it printed on safety stock and then destroy the nitrate film.[23] Most large cities have photographic laboratories which will print the film (see appendix for list of laboratories).* With no complications, the duplicate negative charge would be approximately fifteen to thirty cents per foot, but if the film has shrunk and the perforations will not fit the sprockets of the print machine, it will have to be sent to a special laboratory so that it can be printed frame by frame. Costs in this case would be more than doubled.[24]

If the curator cannot afford to have the nitrate film printed, it is equally unlikely that he can provide the equipment needed for its safe storage. Small quantities of nitrate film can be stored safely in a vented cabinet, but larger amounts should be placed in specially constructed vaults. Temperature in these vaults should be kept at 50° F.

---

* The Code of Federal Regulations, 49 CFR 173.177-79, specifies that, for shipping, nitrate film must be placed in tightly closed metal cans. Cans should be packed adequately braced in the center of a one-piece fiberboard box with a gross weight of not more than sixty-five pounds. Cartons should be clearly marked "Nitrate Film." Nitrate film cannot be shipped by air.

and humidity at 40 to 50 percent for ideal storage. If the curator must keep the film without these precautions, he should store it away from other film and paper. Nitrate will tolerate temperatures up to 70° and 60 percent relative humidity, but there is the ever-present danger of fire, and the fumes from the decomposing nitrate film react chemically on safety film and paper. Sealing a can of nitrate film will only cause the fumes to destroy the film more rapidly.[25]

Color film also poses storage problems for the curator, not for reasons of safety (although some of the early colored commercial movies might be on nitrate stock), but because, in time, the dyes fade. Fading can be retarded by storing films at below zero and at 15 to 25 percent relative humidity, but only for a curator with a large collection would it be economical to buy equipment to condition films from storage to search room and back to storage. While the dyes in color film are not stable, the curator can, with reasonable care, keep film for many years. But if he has a color film which must be preserved, his only alternatives are to have it printed on black-and-white film or to have three-color separation negatives made on black-and-white film from which a new color print could be made at any future date.[26] One authority suggests two other methods of preserving color film archives: either on photosensitive glass exposed to ultraviolet light or on two-inch magnetic video tape. He does not indicate the commercial application of either process, although he does note that, in Great Britain, several firms do color separations of movies, but none did the same kind of work on color still photographs. In the United States, few firms do either stills or movies, but one (see appendix) will make enlarged separations from roll film. This company also offers the service of storing separation negatives in their special vaults and processing color prints on demand. In any form, color separation work is very expensive and could be afforded by the curator in only unusual circumstances.[27]

Another film base, polyester, which presently does not meet standards for permanent record film, may soon be found in manuscript collections. It is being marketed under the trade name "Cronar," and the DuPont scientists who developed it claim it is "eminently suitable for archival purposes." The film is thinner than triacetate (4 mil, rather than 5.5) yet is stronger in fold and tear tests; but because of its thinness, it is more flammable. The manufacturer claims it is resistant to high humidity and many chemicals and that it will not shrink with age.[28]

Standard storage atmosphere for manuscripts, controlled constantly at 70° F. and 50 percent RH, is not optimum, but is acceptable storage for motion-picture film, which is better stored at 40 to 50 percent RH. Paper can stand higher humidity than film; film emulsion gets sticky and mold forms more easily on it than on paper. Removing mold or dirt from a film should be left to a laboratory.[29] If necessary, however, the curator *can* clean film himself with a piece of rayon plush cloth and a commercial film cleaner.

Film should be wound on cores (not reels) and stored flat or shelved in aluminum or stainless steel cans. Motion picture film storage shelving of library dimensions made with 1¼-inch slots to hold reels on edge is designed for audiovisual departments which store current films, and it is not recommended for archival storage. Some authorities suggest sealing cans of safety film with vapor barrier tape (*never* seal nitrate). A common practice for years among private film collectors has been to seal a camphor-saturated blotter in the film can to retard brittleness, but professional film archivists say that they know of no tests that would establish the effects of prolonged exposure of camphor vapor on film.[30]

For the films which have been professionally produced and released, the curator probably should follow a simplified form of the Library of Congress system of cataloging, using the title as a main entry. He can supply titles in brackets for homemade movies or can catalog them by using the hanging indention (see chapter on establishing bibliographic control). A small collection of motion picture films should be shelved in order as received and assigned a call number in sequence.

The most difficult problem a curator holding a few films must face is how he can make them available if needed for research. A historical society or university probably would have 16mm projection equipment, but commercial movie theaters are usually the only place where 35mm projectors can be found today.

The lack of projection equipment may trouble the curator, but he also will need to keep in mind that the first tenet of a film archivist "is that every print must have a back-up or preservation copy before it can be used."[31] If the curator cannot provide the proper service and protection for films in his care, perhaps he should consider other means of making the film available to researchers. For example, he might make it available to one of the major film archives, some of which will provide a print to another institution or to a private owner for the privilege of copying a film for their files.

Despite the existential nature of film as documentation, historians are beginning to make greater use of it in their research, but the greatest use of motion pictures in archives is by producers. The work of these film-makers ranges from independent student production, academic efforts, educational film, and network television to Hollywood feature films.

Reproducing film for researchers' use will tax the ingenuity of the average curator. Should he charge the same for academic and commercial users? What are the copyright regulations? Are other copies of the film available in other repositories? There is no union catalog of films, although the American Film Institute is working toward this goal. The Audiovisual Division of the National Archives recognizes private ownership of film, and thus even though copyright has expired on much of its holdings, it will not reproduce privately owned footage without permission of the owner. Most donors to the archives retain these "ownership rights" through restriction at the time of gift, and they receive royalties from researchers for use of their film.

Although none of the film archives in the United States offer consulting services, most film archivists share in common an appreciation of the moving image and a recognition of the need to preserve film as a historical, cultural, and artistic record of this century. A curator's request for professional assistance to one of the following major repositories of film would surely elicit a helpful response: the Audiovisual Division of the National Archives, the Museum of Modern Art, the Library of Congress, the Academy of Motion Picture Arts and Sciences, and the American Film Institute. The State Historical Society of Wisconsin and the University of California, Los Angeles, both have excellent collections and would offer capable assistance.

Photographs

It will be an extraordinary circumstance for the curator to accession a collection which will not contain some pictorial records, which are listed here in the chronological order in which they appeared on the American scene.[32]

Photography had its introduction to the United States before 1840 with the daguerreotype, a sheet of copper plated with silver on which the image has been "developed" by mercury vapor and "fixed" with hyposulfite of soda.[33] Daguerreotypes are mounted behind glass; and because of a mirrorlike surface, sometimes the image can be seen only if held at a certain angle to the light. The most common sizes are 2¾ by 3¼ inches and 3¼ by 4¼ inches. For years, their hard-rubber-moulded, two-piece cases were sought by collectors for carrying cigarettes, but with fifteen to twenty million made during the period of their popularity, many survived into the twentieth century.[34]

Until a decade ago, historical societies, swamped with unidentified daguerreotypes, threw away hundreds of them. Once, only the libraries of the famous were sought, but today collectors of the history of photography often bid at auction for any daguerreotype.

The first paper photographs—negatives and positives—were called collotypes. They were made on "plain salted paper," a smooth, unglazed paper, in various shades of brown. Photographers learned, years after the first popularity of collotypes in 1853, to give them a gloss with albumen (egg-white).[35]

In 1854, photographers used the collodion process to make a glass negative which they backed with a black surface such as velvet, paper, or metal. These likenesses were called ambrotypes, and they were made in the same sizes as daguerreotypes.[36]

A year later, black japanned metal was sensitized with a collodion surface to produce ferrographs, ferrotypes or melainotypes. Tintypes, as they were popularly called later, made in a variety of sizes, some small enough to be worn as rings, were very popular with the Civil War soldiers. A "chocolate-colored" tintype was introduced in 1870.[37]

Ladies and gentlemen of the nineteenth century carried calling cards when they went visiting; and in 1857, the Duke of Parma decided to have photographs the size of cards made, to leave as calling cards. The Duke's grand gesture was copied first in Paris, then London, and by late 1859 had spread to the United States. In ten years, the fad had more or less run its course, but meanwhile special albums were designed to hold these cartes de visite. Popular actresses, horses, flowers, and even pornographic cartoons were subjects of the popular small brown cards, and during the Civil War, the federal government levied a tax on them.[38]

The picture album was a fixture in the postwar parlor, but no more so than the stereoscope and stereoscopic views. The two prints on a seven-inch-long paper slide, when seen through the viewer, gave an illusion of depth. They were first advertised in 1854, became popular in five years, and could be found in many a home through World War I.[39]

Cabinet photographs, 4 by 5½ inches, a post-Civil War innovation, brought portrait photography to full flower in the United States. With it, in 1867, came the first use of retouching, and the photograph began to lie.[40]

Being able to recognize a photographic process used will help the curator to date the image, at least approximately. For example,

Fig. 26. Some of the more common older forms of photography. *Top left,* daguerreotype, 1/6 plate, in case; *top right,* daguerreotype, full plate; *bottom left,* cartes de visite; *bottom right,* cabinet photographs. (Courtesy Charles Swedlund)

the thin, smooth, brown-sepia-toned prints prepared with albumen would date after 1850 and before the turn of the century. The blue-toned prints, known as cyanotypes, date from 1885 to 1910, and prints on gelatine-based papers, in which the image color varied from yellow to purple, were used from 1888 to 1910. Early glass negatives, the collodion variety known as "wet plates," were made from 1851 to 1880. The glass in these plates was thick and the emulsion often uneven. "Dry plates," thin glass with sharp edges covered with a smooth, even, black coat of gelatin, were used by photographers from 1880 through 1920.[41]

Glass negatives are still used today in scientific or technical photography "where dimensional stability is very significant,"[42] but new or old, these negatives, because of their fragility, pose special problems for the curator. Each plate should have its own acid-free jacket, but if this is not possible, acid-free board or paper should be interfiled between negatives, which should be stored on edge in Hollinger boxes. Because of the weight of glass, the so-called half-box is ideal; but whatever container is used, the negatives must be stored with a snug fit to prevent breakage.

In times past, curators preserved the image on glass plates from loss through breakage by having a quality print made from the glass negative from which a film copy negative was photographed. This was very expensive. Kodak has now developed a direct duplicating film, SO–015, which the company claims can be used in an ordinary contact printer or printing frame to create fine-quality duplicates for "film libraries and archives." [43]

The best preservation technique available to the curator for any of these and other early forms of photography is to have a good copy negative prepared. With modern films and filters, a conscientious photographer often can make a negative that is clearer than the original.[44] Skillful copy work is expensive, but it is the only certain means of preserving the historical data contained in these early forms. The curator should remember, too, that copy costs need not be allocated to conservation alone; any publication or other research use made of a daguerreotype, for example, would necessitate a copy negative. The same would be true of exhibitions, for, because of their sensitivity to light, the curator would not want to exhibit the originals.

Whether he can afford copy negatives or not, naturally, the curator will want to preserve the originals. To do this, he must guard against residual chemicals used in processing the print or negative, industrial atmospheric pollutants, and contamination from materials used in constructing the storage area and materials used in mounting and filing.[45]

Virtually any photograph, from the early collotypes to modern black-and-white prints, will contain varying amounts of residual processing chemicals which, in time, will cause them to fade. There are techniques to fix and wash prints to archival standards, using either standard darkroom equipment or equipment especially designed for the purpose.[46]

Photographs are even more sensitive than manuscripts to airborne pollution: hydrogen sulphide, sulphur dioxide, and ozone are the most harmful. The action of these pollutants is accelerated by high heat and humidity. Photographs are also more susceptible than manuscripts to mold. Therefore, temperature and humidity, especially humidity, in the high but safe range for paper can cause some deterioration of photographs.[47]

Wooden shelving, which at times has been recommended to shelve manuscripts,[48] is dangerous for photographs. Unless the wood is properly sealed, probably with a wax, it gives off peroxide which is harmful to photographs. Paint fumes will damage prints, also. Prints should be stored flat in acid-free folders and acid-free boxes on baked-enamel-coated steel shelves. Ideal temperature is less than 70° and 40 percent relative humidity. Negative storage differs slightly, depending on the type. The albumen paper negatives made about 1848 to 1855 can be treated as prints would be. The collodion glass plate, 1851 to 1880, and the gelatin glass plate, introduced in 1878, should be stored on edge, slightly separated from each other to allow for air circulation. Glass-plate negatives were in use until after the turn of the century; but after 1885, they were gradually replaced with film. Film was on a nitrate base until safety film was introduced, about 1930. Nitrate negatives need air circulation also [49] (see section on nitrate film earlier in this chapter).

Many products sold for storage of negatives can cause deterioration. Glassine envelopes leach out plasticizers, and those made of acetate can serve as moisture traps. The kraft paper and glue used in most negative jackets contain acids. A good negative jacket should be made of acid-free stock sealed at the edge where the lap-over will not touch the image area of the negative. No ink is safe to use on negative, jacket, or photograph.[50] A soft lead pencil can be used, even on the back of prints, if the curator holds the photograph on top of a sheet of glass as he writes.

In addition to these general procedures designed to safeguard any of his photographic media, there are specific conservation measures the curator can take. Daguerreotypes, for example, can be cleaned. Removing them from their case and cleaning the glass will often improve their clarity severalfold; but if oxidation has tarnished the silver image, it can be restored to its original lustre by a bath in a weak cyanide solution.[51] The curator must remember, however, that when the glass is removed, he should not touch the face of the copper plate with his fingers or a cloth. Anything wiped across the silver image is likely to destroy it.

Surface dirt can be removed from collotypes, cartes de visite, stereoscopic views, and cabinet photographs by using any of the methods described herein for cleaning paper (see "Physical Care and

Conservation"). One source says that cartes de visite can be cleaned by swabbing them gently with a soft sponge moistened in cool water and a good liquid cleaner (Fels Naptha liquid). The same process can be used on tintypes and ferrotypes, which also can be cleaned by a cotton swab dipped in mineral oil.[52] The cardboard mounts are a source of trouble; there will be a migration of acid to the print, and in time the board will become brittle. Brittle mounting board will be much more of a problem with larger prints from around the turn of the century. It is not uncommon for a board under a little pressure to snap in the middle. Photographs can be dismounted by soaking them in water, and some surface dirt can be removed with gentle working and rinsing. If the photograph cannot be floated off, a sculptor's tool can be used to cut away the top layer of the mount, and the rest can be steamed off. If necessary, the entire backing can be cut away layer by layer with a scalpel.[53] Fiberglas screening, sold in the hardware store for window screens, makes a good drying rack, and the unmounted photos can be flattened under weights. They can be stored unmounted in acid-free folders. If the curator wants to remount the photographs, he should use a dry-mounting press, dry-mounting tissue, and acid-free mounting board. Extra-large prints can be dry-mounted on unbleached muslin or acid-free paper, using a thermoplastic called Parofilm.[54] (See appendix.)

Modern technology has provided some advanced techniques for the restoration and preservation of photographs. For example, faded early collotypes have been restored by subjecting them to five minutes of radiation. In other experiments at Washington State University, collotypes, tintypes, and glass negatives were activated in a "one-megawatt swimming pool reactor using a stream of slow neutrons," and later exposed to x-ray film from which copy prints were made. Irradiation has been used also in cleaning; a twenty-second bombardment of neutrons followed by seven minutes of autoradiography removed stains from prints and negatives that had failed to respond to solvents.[55]

Advanced techniques such as these are beyond the reach of most curators, many of whom are equally reticent about trying do-it-yourself photographic restoration. For these persons, the service is available commercially at a few laboratories (see appendix). These laboratories will reprocess existing negatives or prints for archival permanence and will mount the prints, if desired, but the service is not inexpensive.[56]

Having roughly identified his pictorial material by type and taken what precautions he can for its preservation, the curator must next decide whether to keep it with the manuscripts or to withdraw it and catalog it separately. This decision will be based upon the same factors listed earlier for other nonmanuscript material; but in addition, it may be based upon the physical attributes of the item; glass negatives and daguerreotypes, for example, probably can be better cared for separately than as part of a manuscript collection. If, however, pictorial material is kept with the manuscripts, it will probably be arranged as a separate series, and it should be listed on the inventory. When the curator catalogs a collection containing pictorial material, he should prepare a single subject/secondary card, probably under the general heading of *Photographs,* for the prints, negatives, etc., in the papers, and file it with the main-entry and other secondary cards in the manuscript catalog.

If he decides to separate the pictorial material, he has made but the first of several decisions. With the possible exception of manuscripts, no other body of historical documentation has had more diversity of arrangement and cataloging than photographs. There are few published guidelines that the curator can follow in establishing his collection; yet, very early, he will need to make decisions which materially affect its growth and use. Primary among these will be whether he will sort, catalog, and store photographs on the item or unit basis. The tendency in the past has been to treat photographs individually, but today, like manuscripts, some photographs are being cataloged as collections.

A recent two-part publication by the bibliographic specialist in the Prints and Photographs Division of the Library of Congress discusses both types of organization and a third method—self-indexing files. In the latter system, prints are filed in one of several alphabetical series, the most common of which is the portrait or personality file. These prints are identified on the reverse side with the file designation (that is, *Portraits*); subject's name; life dates; title, occupation, or identifying phrase; and negative number when applicable. *Geographical files* is another series; *Things, Plants, and Animals* is a third; and the fourth file category is *Events.* Oversize pictures are represented in these files by dummies.[57]

Under the system outlined above, photographs which justify the considerable expense of individual cataloging are those which possess "historical, artistic, documentary or monetary value." The caption on the photograph and the catalog description should contain the photographer's name and dates, a title for the photograph, date of original photograph, place taken, subject, credit line, restrictions, and negative number. This authority suggests that "subject headings for visual material should be inspired by the material at hand," and that it is more desirable and efficient for the curator to create his own expressive subject headings than to base them on nineteenth-century book-cataloging concepts.[58]

Group cataloging, as practiced by the Library of Congress, follows the Anglo-American cataloging system and is used where a group of photographs is a logical entity. The library recommends this type of cataloging also for less valuable pictures with a common theme.[59] While the group concept may have begun at the Library of Congress, it has received its widest use and fullest expression at the Wisconsin State Historical Society. The society's iconographic collection incorporates elements of both item and unit systems of arranging in a way that allows the researcher to do his own searching.

Its item system consists of three easily accessible vertical file series where prints, clippings, post cards, etc., are arranged in a classified subject file, a portrait file, and a place file. Some collections are still dispersed into these three files, but since 1954 most incoming material has simply been assigned a lot number. Each item in the lot, which may range in quantity from a single piece to several hundred pieces, is assigned the same number, but the lot is divided into four standard sizes for storage.

Negatives are handled separately and have their own numerical sequence. One digit in the negative number designates size, another whether it is an original or copy negative, and a third, type (safety, nitrate, glass). A fourth part of the sequence, a Cutter number, identifies the negative series either by collection name or photographer.

The Wisconsin collection numbers more than a half million items, exclusive of negatives, but the curator has published a simplified subject system for arranging a collection of up to 10,000 prints without cataloging and individual print classification. The system is designed to make use of a variety of nonuniform containers to be shelved in a controlled sequence. The curator who is faced with a huge backlog of photographic material to bring under control might study this plan. It can be utilized to bring order to a collection to be shelved awaiting further processing.[60]

A much more complex and time-consuming system, designed to accommodate about 1500 items, including paintings, drawings, and prints, as well as photographs, has been recommended for small museums. With this system, the curator assigns a number to each photograph as received, which keeps accessions together. Letter prefixes designate photograph (P), print (Pr), etc., and each is given an individual folder. If the item does not fit into a legal-size file folder, a note is made of its location. Detailed subject cataloging is done for each item by number.[61]

The Western History Collection at the University of Oklahoma separates photographs from manuscripts but files photographs by the name of the collection from which they were withdrawn. Within the collection, they are arranged by subject, and each photograph is described on a shelflist by collection number and on a main entry and subject/secondary cards in the catalog. Glass plates are separated, but prints and copy negatives are filed with originals up to ten pieces in a single folder. Folders are boxed with a copy of the accession sheet.[62] The University of Oklahoma and the Church of Jesus Christ of the Latter-day Saints are two of a small number of institutions which attempt to arrange photographs according to the archival principle of provenance. One authority explains that, although few repositories follow the principle, this does not mean that "the principle of provenance be laid to rest, but that it be adjusted according to the needs of individual archival institutions and audiovisual records." She sees the need for this adjustment because photographs are "less compatible than textual documents with the rule of provenance." Photograph collections are not crucial to administrative history generally, and because they are "stepchildren" in most agencies, they arrive at the archives poorly arranged. Photographs are exceptionally versatile, which means that they have historical importance quite different from their initial purpose. Finally, because photo researchers are usually interested in subject, source, photographer, and date of photograph, and rarely in the creating agency, arrangement by provenance only creates unnecessary work for the researchers.[63]

The sixty thousand photographs at the Harry S. Truman Library are cared for as part of an audiovisual collection which includes motion pictures and sound recordings. Cataloging is done on an individual-item basis, with each phtograph being assigned an accession number by which it is filed. In the sample number, *SP 73-422-1, SP* refers to "still picture," and the first two numbers are the fiscal year in which the item was accessioned. The next number is the file number, assigned serially as cataloged, and the last figure is a subcategory number used to designate several photographs related to the same subject, or when they are in a series or sequence. Catalog cards (5 by 8 inches) containing the photograph's description are duplicated by Xerox and filed numerically by accession number, chronologically by date of photograph, and alphabetically by subject and person. A print is filed separately from its negative, but each bears the same accession number. Oversize prints are filed separately also, and cross-reference sheets are filed in proper numerical order.[64]

The Herbert Hoover Presidential Library has developed a procedure for cataloging still photographs based upon microfilm prints. As the first step toward gaining control of the collection, the approximately 10,000 prints were arranged roughly by year of origin. Each print was assigned a number, the first four digits of which represent the year the photograph was taken, and the remainder of the number was assigned in serial order. Once the print/negative number was assigned, a scratch catalog sheet was prepared. Persons and subjects were identified and the photograph was dated as exactly as possible. A caption was supplied, but the photograph was not described, because the image would appear as part of the catalog card. The location or scene of the photograph, the photographer's name (or the agency which holds the rights), and the source of the photograph were noted on the scratch sheet.

The photograph and the scratch catalog sheet then went to an editor who checked for accuracy, consistency, and style. When he approved the scratch sheet, it was given to the typist, who prepared the final catalog sheet on the bulletin typewriter.

The catalog sheet and photograph went to the microfilm camera. A black marker was placed on the sheet next to a subject, and the sheet and photograph were filmed (see figure 27). The marker was moved to the next subject and the process was repeated for each subject and the date of the photograph. The film was developed commercially by a firm which supplied 3½-by-5-inch cards of each frame at the cost of twelve cents each. The cards, which needed no tracings, were filed in the catalog according to the marked subject.

The original 10,000 prints were cataloged (a preservation copy negative was made of each print at the same time) in three months with one editor, four catalogers, a typist, and a microfilm operator—all work-study personnel except the editor. The system allows for very rapid retrieval of prints, and it saves great wear on the originals. One of the disadvantages of the system is that a thousand or more photographs must be accumulated at a time for efficient cataloging.[65]

The curator who has his photographs arranged and under bibliographic control must establish a policy for their use. First, he needs to recognize that copyrighted photographs are protected against unauthorized use under the same legal provisions as books. Photographs can be copyrighted for twenty-eight years, and the copyright can be

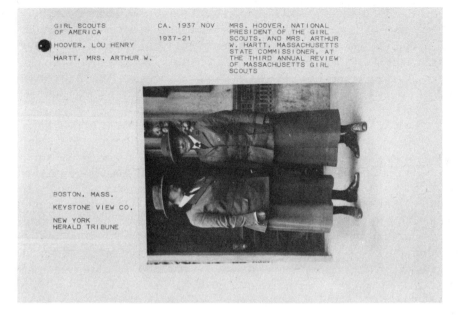

GIRL SCOUTS
OF AMERICA

HOOVER, LOU HENRY

HARTT, MRS. ARTHUR W.

CA. 1937 NOV

1937-21

MRS. HOOVER, NATIONAL
PRESIDENT OF THE GIRL
SCOUTS, AND MRS. ARTHUR
W. HARTT, MASSACHUSETTS
STATE COMMISSIONER, AT
THE THIRD ANNUAL REVIEW
OF MASSACHUSETTS GIRL
SCOUTS

BOSTON, MASS.

KEYSTONE VIEW CO.

NEW YORK
HERALD TRIBUNE

Fig. 27. An example of the cards used in the audiovisual archives at the Herbert Hoover Presidential Library. (Courtesy National Archives and Records Service)

renewed for an additional twenty-eight years. In 1971, the Library of Congress considered "each picture published in the United States before September 1906 in [the] public domain." However, some authorities contend that unpublished photographs are protected by common-law copyright. In any event, the curator must be aware that the copyright in a photograph used to illustrate a book belongs to the book publisher, rather than to the owner or agency which furnished the original picture. Whenever possible, the curator should have permission before reproducing a copyrighted photograph; but if he is unable to locate the copyright owner, he can take solace in the fact that few infringement suits are brought against the users of copyrighted photographs.[66]

When photographs are reproduced, the curator will charge the customer for the copy negative, but will want to retain it for his file, keyed to the original. It is this practice of retaining negatives which one authority says explains why certain photographs are used and re-used. Pictures which have to be copied for the first time are much more expensive, thus putting a premium on the new and fresh.[67] Some institutions scale their charges to cover costs—either a flat fee for any print or the combined cost of print and negative—and both feel that wide use of their photographs with a credit line is their best advertisement. Other institutions are equally aware of the publicity value of a credit line, but feel that they are entitled to something beyond cost if the photograph is to be used commercially. They know that if an advertising firm were to buy a photographic print from a commercial agency like the Bettman Archives, for example, it might pay several hundred dollars for its one-time, nonexclusive use. Consequently, many institutions now have a sliding scale for commercial use, some with a $25 to $50 minimum.

Of course, if the curator charges professional fees, he must give professional service. Prints should be clearly captioned, and there are three ways to do this. The best method is to type the caption, credit line, and collection name, and have the photographer shoot this information with the originals on the copy negative. Any print then would automatically contain the proper identification and caption. Another method is to incorporate this information as part of a printed gummed sticker to be pasted on the back of sale prints. A rubber stamp can be designed for the same purpose. Stickers look more professional, but they take longer to apply than the stamp and will bulk up in a large stack of prints.

This survey has but touched upon some of the problems in administering a photographic collection. The curator who wishes to get professional training to enable himself to work better with this medium will find few educational opportunities. At the present time, only two graduate schools offer courses to help fill this need. The Pratt Institute Graduate Library School offers a course in the "Organization and Use of Pictures as Documents," and the University of Louisville has a graduate program leading to a master's degree in Curatorial Science. Graduates of this program are trained to maintain art history slide collections as well as photographic archives of various kinds.[68]

Sound Recordings

Sounds have been recorded on a variety of media (paper, film, wax, plastic, and metal), and the records take many forms (tape, wire, cylinders, and discs). Few of these have any place in a manuscript collection. The curator will have difficulty in providing storage that will protect their fragility, and most of them will require playback equipment that he is unlikely to have. The accepted norms of temperature and humidity for paper would provide the proper protective environment for some of these esoteric sound recordings,[69] and the curator could rig up a container to store them.[70] If they are to be used for research, however, the possibility of having a sound laboratory dub them to magnetic tape should be explored.

Only magnetic tapes and phonograph discs are common enough to warrant the average curator's concern. The earliest discs were made of wax, then ethyl cellulose, and, after 1930, cellulose nitrate. Shellac discs were introduced before World War II, and more recently they have been made of plastic, either polystyrene or, more commonly, polyvinyl chloride.

Each type is susceptible to dust and fungi, and the physical properties of some are altered by light and heat. Most record jackets contain harmful chemicals, but an interior polyethylene sleeve will protect the record and will allow it to be removed and refiled without scratching. Discs should be stored on edge in an atmosphere of 50 percent RH and 70° F.[71]

Any disc, except a wax one, can be cleaned with a small amount of detergent (Ledtrostat Record Cleaning Kit, Dexter Chemical Corp.) in an applicator of sheared acetate velvet fibers. During playbacks, an ethylene glycol solution applied with a brush and applicator pad (ESL Dust Bag) can be used for routine cleaning. For more drastic cleaning—the removal of gummy film from acetate discs, for example—the discs can be washed in lukewarm water and mild detergent, rinsed in distilled water, and quick-dried with a blower hair-dryer. Ideally, discs should be handled only with gloves; but if gloves are not used, the curator should avoid touching the grooved surface.[72] An authority who says that he cannot "endorse or condemn" washing with mild soap and water (if the labels are not wet) for some shellac discs like Victor's, mentions that Columbia's records were laminated and should not be cleaned with water. He recommends cleaning with a soft cotton cloth or velvet pad sprayed with Micro-Pel.[73]

Discs were designed for playback qualities and low-cost manufacture. Each contains elements which constitute built-in deterioration. Although the curator cannot alter this deterioration chemically, as he does with photographs and paper, he should take heart in the fact that phonograph discs have been manufactured and successfully stored for more than sixty years.

Magnetic tape for recording sound was introduced in the United States shortly after World War II. Early tapes had a kraft-paper base, but this was soon replaced by cellulose acetate and, in more recent years, by mylar.

In protecting magnetic tape sound recordings, the curator must guard against the usual destructive elements. For example, high heat can cause "print-through," the magnetization of one layer of tape altering the magnetic pattern on an adjacent layer, while changes in humidity cause uneven tension and distortion on the reel. The controlled atmosphere of 70° F. and 50 percent RH will resolve these difficulties; but with tapes, the curator faces a different danger: stray external magnetic fields. The electrical circuits in the storage area create magnetic fields; but if they are properly installed, they will balance each other out. Where the curator runs his greatest risk is in inadvertently storing tape close to equipment, machines, or instruments containing magnets.[74]

If the curator finds reels of tape in a manuscript collection, probably the most beneficial thing he can do with them is to rewind them. Rewinding will reduce the danger of print-through and will alleviate curvatures in the reel that develop in storage. Tapes should be inspected and rewound every two years in storage, and care should be taken to rewind at even tension throughout the reel. Probably the curator will not have the means of measuring proper tension (three to four ounces for ¼-inch width of tape), but he can look for too loose a wind—which will cause slippage, called "cinching," resulting in washboard wrinkles in the tape—and too tight a wind, which may cause backing distortion. A scattered wind (alternate tight and loose) allows individual edges to protrude above the edge of the rest of the tape, resulting in signal loss when extruding edges become ragged. A metal reel with an unslotted hub rather than the usual plastic reel is considered ideal storage, and since dust is always a problem, engineers recommend sealed metal cans or polyethylene-coated boxes for reel storage. Boxes or cans should be stacked on edge on either wooden or nonmagnetizable metal shelves. One authority recommends storing magnetic sound-recording tapes in their original cartons in the plastic boxes designed to carry four half-gallon cartons of milk. The cartons allow for circulation of air and have the added advantage that they can be stacked.[75]

The playback equipment used by researchers should be kept clean. Dirty sound heads decrease fidelity, but, more important, they damage and soil tapes. The heads on a recorder should be cleaned periodically with a lint-free pad moistened with Genesolve-D (Allied Chemicals) or Freon TF (DuPont).[76] (See section in this chapter on machine-readable records for additional data on magnetic tape.)

While under normal circumstances a curator's exposure to sound recordings in manuscript collections is likely to be slight, there seem to be few who are not in some way involved in an oral history project. Collecting historical documentation by recording interviews and reminiscences is not new; two of America's great manuscript collectors, H. W. Bancroft and Lyman Draper, used the technique.[77] But in 1948, when Columbia University began recording interviews on magnetic tape and preparing typewritten transcriptions of the interviews for researchers, oral history, in the modern sense, was born. In 1971, in this country, there were 230 reported projects, which ran the gamut from aeronautics to zetatics, including Walt Disney, Dixieland jazz, and JFK. The phenomenon is difficult to explain, but perhaps it has its roots in people's innate desire to talk about themselves, coupled with America's fascination with gadgetry. Perhaps, too, curators who had seen the nature and quality of traditional historical documentation changing under the impact of the technology of communications, grasped eagerly at the opportunity to turn that technology to create new forms of documentation. Whatever the reasons, oral history seems to win more converts every day. It may have begun as an American phenomenon, but its widespread use elsewhere seems to indicate a worldwide acceptance of it as documentation. Curators must be ready to create and/or accept, conserve, and make available for research the fruits of this electronic labor.[78]

For the curator who may be considering an oral history program, several factors should be considered. Over-all, oral history is probably the most expensive means available to the curator for the collecting of historical documentation. One historian, for example, has made what he calls a conservative estimate that, for every hour of interview time, an oral history project must expend forty additional hours of preparation and follow-up. This estimate, he says, does not consider background research, but includes "time for preparation, travel, transcribing, and editing." [79] Costs will vary, of course, depending upon the type of program undertaken, but the experience of some of the leading programs provides a basis for comparison. At the University of California, Berkeley, the total costs seem to divide almost evenly fifty-fifty— that is, researching and interviewing/transcribing and editing. The research time needed for each hour of tape has been estimated at twelve hours by the University of California, Los Angeles, and at twenty hours for each 1½ hours of tape by the Berkeley campus. Columbia, which hires local interviewers to do tapes in other parts of the country, paid one interviewer four dollars per hour for research up to a limit of twenty hours. The same interviewer was paid twenty dollars per tape-hour for the actual interview.[80]

Although these hourly costs may seem high to some curators, especially those conducting oral history programs with regular staff or volunteers, the experience at Cornell indicates that the "annual appointment of interviewers merely encourages poor work." [81] The practice of paying interviewers by the hour varies, but transcribers seem almost universally to be paid in this way. There also seems to be general agreement that it takes six to eight hours to transcribe an hour of tape. At Columbia, transcribers are paid twenty-five to thirty dollars per tape-hour.[82]

Equipment costs will vary depending upon the curator's budget and his concept of the program. A Wollensak 1500 recorder, the sturdy workhorse of many programs, retails for approximately $185, and this same machine, with a foot-pedal attachment, can be used to transcribe tapes. Obviously, planning will be necessary to alternate a single machine between two tasks. At UCLA, the Sony, four-speed Servecontrol TC 800B has been successfully used. To make the best use of a transcriber's time, the curator may want a machine designed specially for this task, and this will cost another $300, approximately.

Cassette recorders are cheaper and much more portable than the reel-to-reel machines. A good model, the CDMI, made by the Crown Corporation of Japan, sells for $150. It can be used for both recording and transcribing and this machine has been the mainstay in the oral history project at the University of Wisconsin, Division of Archives.[83] Cassettes are cheaper than reels, but are prone to stick or jam, particularly the C-90 size which allows forty-five minutes of transcription to a side. The C-60 size (thirty minutes to a side) is more trouble-free; but using this size means that the interview must be interrupted more often to change the cassette. A weakness of most cassette machines is that the interviewer may not notice that the tape has run through the cassette and needs to be turned. At least one company has designed its recorder and its own tapes with an alarm that sounds when the tape is finished. One authority states categorically that a cassette recorder should not be used for oral history unless it has this feature. She also strongly suggests buying a machine with an automatic volume control.[84]

In projects where the transcription is the final and only product, the tapes can be erased and used again; but on those projects where the tape is preserved, tape cost can be substantial.[85] Proponents of keeping the tapes note that the timbre and quality of the voice, the accents, pitch, and phrasing, all make it necessary that the tapes be preserved. Opponents cite the tape costs and point to studies which indicate that scholars use the transcriptions almost exclusively. They say that, if an institution is serious about preserving the tapes, it would have to duplicate tapes for use, and that there is no practical way to edit the tape to conform to changes the narrator made in the type-script. With the equipment to do the dubbing, the curator could prepare duplicate copies of tapes as they are needed for research, but this added cost, plus the cost of the machines needed by the researcher to listen to tapes, could be prohibitive.[86]

Concise over-all costs per hour of tape are difficult to determine, but surveys made in 1966 and 1972 indicate that the figure ranges from about $100 to more than $200. One institution, the Ohio Historical Society, costed one series in 1973 with interviewing and research at $4.68 and transcribing at $3.03 per hour for a total of $122.76 per tape-hour. Since it was a local project, no travel costs were included. A former interviewer for the Kennedy Library, in replying to the 1972 survey, is quoted as saying: "If accurate cost figures were available to administrators at several institutions of which I am aware, I expect that the oral history programs might be considerably cut back. It is a very expensive undertaking." [87]

The curator who has evaluated the costs and decided to begin an oral history program will want to read the extensive literature that has been produced, but he will not want to overlook the methodology of sociology and other disciplines which have used the interview techniques for years.[88] He might also not be too distressed by the fact that he is probably too busy to do the intensive preliminary research most oral history interviewers say is necessary to conduct a good interview.[89] Any moderately intelligent person, if he is interested in people and likes to listen to them talk, can conduct a productive interview, particularly a biographical interview. A beginning interviewer will have more interviews fail by not being able to operate his equipment properly than he will by not asking the right questions or forgetting to write down all the proper names mentioned by the interviewee. The biographically-oriented interview is the most common, according to one authority, because it simplifies problems of organization, tends to encourage respondent initiative, minimizes the consequences of interviewer bias, and can be more easily checked for reliability.[90]

But any beginner can use a few helpful hints, and some of the best not noted in other sources have been offered in a pamphlet published by the American Association for State and Local History. They include two suggestions about equipment and two others about conducting an interview: (1) Separate the mike far enough from the recorder so that the mike does not pick up the noise of the recorder's motor. (2) If the recorder is the type which is ventilated from the bottom, keep it off the rug, because the lack of the circulation of air will cause the machine to overheat. (3) When contemplating a multiple-session interview, tell the narrator that fewer sessions are planned than are expected to be recorded. It is very difficult to lower the number of sessions, but usually easy to expand the number. (4) Do not record the introduction to the tape beforehand or at the beginning of the session, but leave space at the beginning of the tape to record the introduction later. A formal introduction can give the narrator mike-fright.[91]

The attributes of a good oral interviewer are in some ways very similar to those of a good field man.[92] Perhaps this is one reason that most oral history projects have been fruitful sources of manuscript acquisitions. At UCLA, for example, at least a third of the narrators have presented manuscripts to Special Collections, and other projects have had like success.[93] At a recent conference, one oral historian saw an even closer link between the two areas. He felt that if interviewers could process manuscripts and do reference work with them, both the manuscript collection and the oral history project would benefit.[94]

Presumably, the curator will take proper care of manuscripts acquired in the course of an oral history project, but what of the tapes and transcriptions? One authority suggests that, unless repositories "record essential facts about the interviewer's identity, aims, and procedures, and note any restrictions placed on use and photoduplication," there is a danger that oral interviews will be to the future curator what old scrapbooks are to the present-day librarian—"They may be valuable, may even contain original material, but for whom, and how do we know it?" [95]

Institutions are establishing bibliographic control over oral history in several ways. The method used at the Herbert Hoover Presidential Library is an example. The Hoover program was established with private funds in 1966. Five interviewers in different sections of the country had completed a total of 324 interviews in the fall of 1972. The tapes are stored in the project director's office in Washington, and they are scheduled for destruction upon completion of the project. For bibliographic control, oral history transcripts at the Hoover Library are indexed for subjects and names (including the interviewer and narrator), and cards are filed in the oral history composite index. Reading room finding aids include the composite index, individual indexes, an alphabetical list of the transcripts, and a collection of scope and content notes. A list of the approximately 140 oral history transcripts, arranged alphabetically by narrator, which identifies interviewer and notes the number of pages in the transcript, was published in November 1971. Transcripts are filed alphabetically in legal-size folders in manuscript boxes and shelved in the closed stacks.[96]

A tape index, which is described in one of the standard sources on oral history, is used to good effect at the Ohio Historical Society. The index sheets contain the names of the interviewee and interviewer, date and subject of interview, type of recorder, and a short paragraph on the interviewee's background. Index entries are in the form of short, incomplete sentences, each keyed to the number on the digital counter of the tape player. A sample index for one thousand-foot reel is less than three pages, which means that it can be readily duplicated for distant researchers. Of course, the costs of preparing the index are far less than those for transcribing the tape.[97]

Some institutions—for example, UCLA—have published guides to their oral history collections.[98] Others, like the Regional Oral History Office, University of California, Berkeley, have, on occasion, distributed bound copies of the transcripts to other approved manuscript repositories. The library of deposit pays photo-offset and collation charges of about five cents a page, plus fifteen dollars per volume for illustrations, binding, and handling.[99] Columbia has issued a new catalog of its collection and, in conjunction with the New York Times Oral History program, has offered for sale a microfiche edition of two hundred selected transcripts. With Part 2 of the microfiche edition scheduled for release sometime in 1974, a fifth of the collection will be available to readers distant from New York.[100]

In May 1971, the Library of Congress, heeding growing criticism over the years by oral historians, moved to include oral history records in the *National Union Catalog of Manuscript Collections*. The regulations for entry require that "a collection should consist of 10 or more transcripts." They further state that the "interviewing of one person is considered one item regardless of the number of sessions, number of pages of transcript, or the number of hours of interviewing." Curators have been slow to report their holdings, however; to date, fewer than thirty institutions have made reports to NUCMC.[101]

Neither oral history tapes nor transcribed interviews should pose a cataloging problem for the curator. Individual transcripts can be treated and described in the same way as a typewritten manuscript. Tapes can be cataloged as single manuscripts are, with the name of the interviewee as main entry. Cards for tapes should include information about the length of the recording, the recording speed, track, and format.

There is increasing use of oral history as documentation, but still the greatest portion of the transcripts are available only at the institution of origin. One oral historian has suggested devising machinery to review transcripts in scholarly journals and liberalizing use of interlibrary loans of copies. There are, however, certain risks in copying the transcripts. In some instances, the transcripts are copyrighted by the project, but in others the interviewer and narrators both hold common-law copyright in the interview. The courts have not been asked to rule on whether making a copy for scholarly use would violate either statutory or common-law copyright.[102]

The greatest legal pitfalls in oral history concern libel and privacy violations. Because of its spontaneity and current nature, oral history narratives are more prone to libel a person or violate his privacy than more self-consciously created forms of historical evidence, such as addresses and correspondence. Laws concerning libel and invasion of privacy vary from state to state, and the curator should study the laws in his area to make sure that he does not violate them in recording or circulating oral history interviews.[103] Still, he can take encouragement from the opinion of a foremost authority on oral history who notes that, although the curator may face harassment in the lower courts, there is very little danger of damages being awarded against him. "To all intents and purposes," she contends, "slander or libel is a non-existent danger to an oral history project." [104] (See also chapter on use of manuscripts).

Mediagraphics

At a recent professional meeting, the term *mediagraphics* was used in a paper to describe all nonprint materials of an audio and audiovisual nature.[105] Some of these forms have been discussed earlier in this chapter, and the remainder are grouped here for discussion.

Color transparencies and the 35mm or 2-by-2-inch slides, which are appearing with greater frequency each year in manuscript collections, present a special conservation problem. Commercial equipment has been developed for storage and retrieval of large collections,[106] but the quantity encountered by the curator can best be handled, probably, by using the thin plastic envelopes manufactured by Print File specifically for this purpose. Several transparencies or slides can be inserted in each folder, which can then be stored flat or filed in a loose-leaf ring folder made by the company.

Color transparencies and slides should be kept out of the light as much as possible, but even with this care they will fade in time.

Only by having color-separation negatives prepared, a most expensive process, can color photography be permanently preserved.[107]

Audio and video cassettes will be found in manuscript collections in increasingly greater numbers in the next few years. Sound tape cartridges, which measure about 6 by 4 inches, known popularly as 8-track cartridges, will be encountered far less frequently because few home recorders using them are yet available. However, cassette recorders are being sold by the millions annually, and the little 4-by-2½-inch container of ⅛-inch-wide tape will soon become a familiar sight in manuscript collections. Besides being used in amateur home recordings, oral history, and commercially produced information programs, they are finding even wider application in the business world. For example, one major brokerage house sends instructions and situation reports on cassettes to its salesmen every two weeks, and the research manager of another company circulates research notes on cassettes to key people in his firm.[108]

Their size makes them awkward to store, but one sound archives has "found wood library card catalog cases very handy" for shelving cassette tapes. One chemical company with a large collection calls attention to covered boxboard cases manufactured by Gaylord Brothers, Inc., the library supply house, which holds thirty cassettes in cases. A minimum order of three boxes costs less than seven dollars, which would house most beginning collections handily. Steel-drawer storage is available from Gaylord for approximately sixty dollars per drawer with a capacity of about 125 cassettes to a drawer.[109]

They need the same temperature and humidity controls mentioned earlier for magnetic tape, as well as the same safeguards against exposure to magnetic fields. The curator should be especially careful not to subject either cassettes or cartridges to high temperatures. Both are manufactured with splices, which may separate under heat, or the splice adhesive may soften and stick to adjacent tape layers.[110]

The video "cassette" is of several varieties. The most common is the system utilizing ½- or ¾-inch magnetic tape, and although home recorders are still expensive, sooner or later curators will be receiving these tapes to store and conserve.

And, too, already there are straws in the wind, hints of what is to come—the video history project. At Cornell, for example, when the time came in the early 1970s to bring the library orientation program up to date, the decision was made to videotape the half-hour history portion of the program. Included in the presentation were excerpts from two videotaped interviews. The original footage was preserved, "the rationale being the same as for tape recordings of oral history interviews." But if curators have found oral history expensive, video history will be more so. Cornell spent approximately a thousand dollars, exclusive of salaries and equipment, for the videotape history of the library.[111] However, increased production may lower costs, but in any event video history projects with visual interviews are certain to develop. Some oral history programs have experimented already with one form of visual history by taking short movies of their narrators during the oral interview.

Meanwhile, the curator's principle contact with video will be reels rather than cassettes. Because few institutions have playback facilities for research use of the video tape, its image is sometimes transferred to film, but this is expensive. A direct positive costs about seven dollars a minute, with a seventy-dollar minimum charge.[112]

Other video playback systems record on films and on thin 12-inch vinyl discs. In one of the film systems, a tiny laser embosses a hologram on the vinyl film. The forms of the "cassettes" for these systems may be odd-sized for the curator to house, but he is familiar with the proper methods to use in conserving and caring for magnetic tape, vinyl film, and vinyl discs.[113]

The threat of a lawsuit for copyright violation (a much-discussed bugbear in this book) may be present for the curator who makes a copy of a video recording. This was illustrated in December 1973, when the Columbia Broadcasting Company brought suit against Vanderbilt University for the unauthorized copying and distribution of videotapes to which CBS claimed copyright. The company said it was willing for Vanderbilt's television news archive to videotape the evening news broadcasts and to maintain the tapes at the university for the use of scholars, but it asked the court to forbid the archives "to duplicate, edit, rent or sell the tapes." [114]

Microforms

This section deals with the preservation and description of microforms: microcard, microprint, microfiche, and microfilm. A description of each form and its relationship to automation was included in chapter 6 and microfilm editions and scholarly use of microfilm will be discussed in the last chapter.

The shape and size of some microforms may necessitate odd-size storage cartons, but probably, with the exception of microfilm, the curator will not be called upon to care for a large quantity of this medium. Since physical characteristics of all microforms are the same * and since microfilm is the form which most concerns the curator, this discussion will center upon it as a documentary medium.

In the early years of microfilming of manuscripts, from the late 1940s through the early 1950s, there was great concern about stored microfilm becoming dry and brittle. Microfilm storage cabinets came equipped with a special humidifying drawer which the curator had to keep filled with water. Time has seemed to prove that this was an unnecessary precaution and that, if microfilm was going to suffer damage, it was much more likely to be from dampness rather than dryness. Microfilm is more susceptible to the growth of mold and mildew than is paper, and because it is hygroscopic, it is quite sensitive to moisture changes. Every effort should be made to keep microfilm storage at 65° to 70° F. and 40 percent relative humidity. A nonferrous metal can is the best storage container for individual reels of film, but the acid-free cardboard box is a cheaper and adequate substitute. Metal multidrawer microfilm storage cabinets are recommended to house individual cans or boxes, but several companies make cartons to store several individual reel boxes on open shelving.[115] At Yale University, the archives and manuscript division's extensive collection of microfilm is stored in metal stack drawers, which are cheap (approximately ten dollars a drawer) and allow for great flexibility in storage space (see appendix).

Following the best storage practices has not always insured preservation of microfilm. To illustrate, there was a period in the early 1960s when curators and archivists were very much concerned that they had overcommitted themselves to a medium which was not proving to be as stable as they had hoped. It was at this time that the aging blemishes, which were later called microspots, were first discovered, many of them on negative film about twenty years old. Because a considerable percentage of the records of the federal government were stored on microfilm, the National Bureau of Standards undertook an investigation. Fortunately, most of the spots discovered were on the leaders to film, and there was very little image loss. None of the

---

* Care of micro-opaques (microcards and microprint cards) will differ slightly. The curator must watch for residual chemicals left in the processing of the first form, and while this is not a problem with the latter, they are susceptible to abrasion. (See Veaner, *Evaluation of Micropublications*, pp. 6, 19.)

blemishes were found on film processed by NARS, which, along with other factors, led most investigators to believe that the defects were caused by improper processing of the film.[116]

Since the curator usually has little control over the processing of microfilm, his best protection against loss is careful periodic inspection of record films. The experience of many institutions in the early 1970s with a vesicular film produced by one of the country's leading commercial microfilmers underlines the importance of detecting problems early. In this instance, film supplied by the Kalvar Corporation was releasing hydrochloric acid which disintegrated film containers and damaged shelving and storage cabinets.[117]

On the whole, the curator probably has done a better job of preserving the microfilm in his care than he has in making it available for research through proper finding aids. Still, oddly enough, librarians are looking to archivists and curators for guidance in describing microforms. A recent survey sponsored by the Association of Research Libraries states that microforms of archival and manuscript collections are frequently superior to those produced for the library community, and that the bibliographic control of these collections is ahead of that achieved by libraries. The microform bibliography, an outgrowth of the survey, lists about 170 manuscript and archival collections, but the compilers recognized that it is not all-inclusive. By their estimate, archives (with which they include manuscript collections) produce 25 million negative and 150 million positive images annually, and reports from forty countries indicate that the archives of the world expose a half-billion negative frames a year and print a proportionately higher number of positive copies.[118]

While librarians have looked to archivists and curators for leadership in this field, some scholars have been critical of all three professions in their handling of microforms, but especially have they criticized library catalogers who attempt to catalog microforms of manuscripts "just like a book." These historian-critics contend that "to be of maximum assistance, microform catalogers should treat documents as if they were originals. This ideal, unhappily, can rarely be attained because of the expense entailed."[119]

Quite the contrary, this should be standard practice; it is no more expensive to catalog microfilm than to catalog original manuscripts. Microfilm *should* be described as original materials are, except, of course, that note is made on the unit catalog card indicating that the manuscript collection being described is on microfilm. Too, the polarity (negative or positive) should be noted, as well as the width (35mm usually) and either an estimated image count or a footage measurement. If the film is of manuscripts held elsewhere, the curator should make note in his description of the location of the originals. Many collections purchased from other repositories will have their own guides, but if this is not the case, the curator should prepare an inventory—or whatever other controls he uses—for the microfilm in the same manner as he would for an original collection. Microfilms which the curator prepares of his own holdings should be listed in the collection's general guide, or can be noted in a separate publication.[120]

Machine-Readable Records

At a recent conference, one of the participants warned archivists against the tendency to lump machine-readable records together with other nonprint materials for consideration,[121] but, unfortunately, in the context of this book, this is where they fall. Their discussion was left until the last part of this chapter in an attempt to emphasize the importance of these types of records, and although only a small amount of space will be devoted to them (archival or manuscript theory and practice has yet to be developed), it is recognized that they are the wave of the future with which the curator must cope.

The discussion in this section will include the following ADP (Automatic Data Processing) media: punched cards, magnetic tapes, magnetic drums, magnetic disks, printouts, and COM-produced microfilm. The latter two are not usually termed machine-readable records. Printouts, the folded, continuous-flow paper, an individual sheet of which measures 14⅞ by 11 inches, can (after a fashion, for the uninitiated) be read. The common alphanumeric typeface of most strip or line printers looks strange to many curators; words are often abbreviated, and both words and numbers appear on the sheets in forms not familiar to many readers. The curator should care for printouts in the same way that he would any other paper document. COM microfilm is produced in two forms: some are machine-readable records, and others look as if a microfilm had been made of a printout. In either form, it should be stored and serviced following standards established earlier in this chapter for all microforms.

Printouts and COM microfilm are outputs of the computer; punched cards and punched-paper tapes are input for the computer and are forms of ADP media which have already made their appearance in many archival and manuscript collections. In preserving either form, the curator would be guided by the same principles as those relating to other kinds of paper, remembering, of course, that the

GV20-9446

Fig. 28. Magnetic disk pack. (Courtesy IBM Corp.)

information these documents contain is in the arrangement of the holes punched in them and that they must not be torn or mutilated. Stationery stores sell boxes made to store cards (if the demand becomes strong enough, Hollinger will manufacture an acid-free container), and the paper tape, depending upon whether it is a strip or a roll, could be kept in folders or perhaps in microfilm boxes.

Magnetic tapes, drums, and disks are known as *stores.* Information is stored on these media in marks left by the pulse of electrons on a thin surface of magnetic iron oxide. The marks (not visible to the eye, of course) are changes in the magnetization of the surface of the tape, drum, or disk made by the electronic pulse. An early model of the magnetic drum was a cylinder measuring about 9 inches in diameter and 12 inches high. Magnetic disk packs (see figure 28) are like a stack of phonograph records, each separated from the next record on the spindle by a thin film of air over which the head moves to read the data recorded in concentric paths called *tracks* on the surface of the disk. A typical disk measures approximately 14 inches and contains 203 tracks. To preserve either disk packs or drums, the curator should improvise a container that would shield them from dust and immobilize them to keep the magnetized surface from being damaged.[122]

Undoubtedly, computer tapes will be the machine-readable record most often encountered by the curator. A standard reel of tape of a few years ago was ½-inch wide and might contain 20 million bits of information written in seven or nine channels. These tapes, known as 800bpi (bits per inch) tapes, are being replaced with higher density 1600bpi tapes.[123]

Magnetic computer tape is similar to but different from magnetic sound-recording tape. The base of both is either acetate or Mylar, and computer tape is more likely to be the latter. The signal on an acoustic tape is analogue, which means that the information it contains depends on a magnitude or a scale which is stored in a linear continuum of signal strength. Computer tape is a digital store of only two alternative directions of magnetization, with the magnetic impulses recorded in rows across the width of the tape.[124]

Both acoustic and computer tape can best be preserved in an atmosphere of 45° to 55° F. and 45 to 65 percent RH, but temperatures of 68° to 70° are acceptable. Low relative humidity causes static electricity to build up, which attracts dust to the tape, and fungus growth tends to appear on tape when it is exposed to greater than 80 percent RH for more than four hours.[125] Also computer tape, because of the great density of the signals on the tape, is especially susceptible to dust, so much so that in some computer installations the air-conditioning system is engineered to replace the air a minimum number of times a day and thus lessen the movement of air carrying dust particles. As computer tape is used, it builds up clumps of oxide scraped off the surface of the tape by the reading head of the computer. The dust and clumps of oxide must be cleaned from the tape periodically to keep it from causing "drop-outs," or errors, when the tape is run through the computer. Maintaining even wind tension and storing tapes flat are good conservation techniques for either kind of magnetic tape.[126]

Before computer tape is stored, it should be cleaned and rewound to the proper tension. It must be rewound in the same ambience in which it is to be stored; changes in temperature and relative humidity will cause pressure to fluctuate within the tape deck and will result in distortion or "cinching." However, to prepare computer tape for storage properly requires expensive equipment. Basic cleaning and rewinding involves vacuum cleaning, wiping, scraping followed by wiping, and fluid cavitation, ending with tension winding. Thus, the curator needs an ultrasonic wet cleaner, a dry cleaner, and a tension winder, or a piece of equipment capable of performing all three processes.[127]

As discussed earlier, both kinds of tape should be protected from magnetic fields, but the curator who has been cautioned to guard tapes against stray magnetic fields tends to think in terms of motors and machinery, whereas the greatest danger comes from simple, everyday objects he may never suspect. For example, if a magnetic door latch or a magnetic key ring touched a computer tape, the information would be lost from that portion of the tape which came in direct contact with the magnet. The larger the permanent magnet, the greater the loss.[128]

From time to time, rumors circulate about computer tapes being erased by lightning discharges, radio transmissions, static electricity, and high-powered radar beams. Radio transmissions and static electricity are harmless to tapes, but if one is struck by lightning or placed a foot or two in front of a radar antenna, it will be erased. Neither circumstance would seem to need to cause the curator much concern normally, and tape manufacturers say the same is true of x-radiation. Despite the stories of tapes being erased when a package was subjected to x-ray inspection during shipment, tape manufacturers claim that they have exposed tapes to x-radiation far in excess of what would be used to examine packages, and they have not found "any incidence of signal decay or erasure." However, the manufacturers do warn against carrying tapes through antihijacking devices of the "doorway" or "walkway" type now in use in most United States airports. The magnetic field created by some of these devices, while not sufficient to erase a tape totally, would probably reduce the signal appreciably.[129]

Tape, like paper, is very susceptible to fire and water damage, and, like paper, perhaps more susceptible to the first than the latter. At 120° F., acetate tape will curl and shrink; and at that temperature, if the relative humidity reaches 85 percent, severe "blocking" (adhesion of adjacent layers of tape) will occur. At twice this temperature, acetate melts and polyester-base tape suffers some distortion. Water will cause "cupping," or a reverse curvature of the tape, but if the reel is partially dried, rewound loosely, dried again, and rewound, blocking can usually be avoided. Tape manufacturers recommend drying at room temperature, but since fungus grows so rapidly on tape, it would be better to keep the temperature down and to circulate the air with fans.[130]

Proper care for machine-readable records is, of course, only part of the curator's problem. How does he service them, and how can he make the information they contain available to researchers? In 1967, computer scientists were confidently predicting that, within five years, archivists would have "access through remote terminals to service centers" so that they could "input a deck of cards, a reel of punched paper tape, or a reel of magnetic tape and obtain, as required, a print-out of all or selected portions of the material." The dream continues to recede over the horizon, and because computer technology is evolving so rapidly, the problem of compatibility will continue to be a specter haunting the conscientious curator. Obviously, he cannot collect obsolete computers to run programs for researchers. A cooperative museum of computer technology with working models, the ultimate solution often offered at professional meetings, seems very far in the future. Another suggestion which looks to the future is that archivists and curators make a concerted effort to collect the business records of computer companies; if they cannot preserve the machines themselves, perhaps the documentation concerning their creation can be saved. A more realistic approach favored by many is "the conversion of storage media, for which hardware has become obsolete, to tape that is adapted to current drives." [131]

Although a recently completed survey showed that very few institutions in the United States and Canada are accessioning machine-readable records, this will change as archivists and curators become familiar with the complexities of caring for the body of records generated by the computer and as they are given guidance in resolving some of the problems of collecting these records. NARS can take the lead by publishing its standards for appraising machine-readable records and by sponsoring conferences for interested archivists and curators. The SAA Committee on Data Archives and Machine-Readable Records is working on a bibliography and planning to issue a preliminary manual of practices in the near future. The International Council on Archives' publication, *ADPA: Archives & Automation/Informatique,* also offers promise of professional assistance. [132]

Meanwhile, the curator can begin to explore the field on his own. He should get a glossary and try to learn the elementary terms so that he can begin to communicate with programmers, computer scientists, and others in the ADP field. For any machine-readable records he acquires, he should also make a special effort to acquire the external and internal documentation without which the records themselves will be of little use to researchers. External documentation would include, according to one authority, "a data inventory, a data dictionary, a set of directories for variables and codes for the physical storage of data and computer programs, a data item search strategy, a summary of uses made of the data, and copies of the various forms used in collecting the data." Also of great usefulness would be the internal documentation, including a glossary defining terms, schedules of records retention, checks on the accuracy of the data, corrections, and any statements about why the data was collected and which agency was responsible for the collection.[133]

To the average curator with a limited technical background and few physical resources at his command, machine-readable records are an awesome responsibility. However, as with some other aspects of his curatorial tasks, if he swallows his sense of panic and does the best he can, perhaps technology, which bore this troublesome child, will yet help the curator provide the means for its care and coming of age.

Each of the nonmanuscript forms sketchily covered in this chapter is worthy of book-length treatment, but this discussion must turn now to the consideration of the use to which nonmanuscript and manuscript collections are put, with particular emphasis upon questions of security and legal problems arising out of the use of manuscript collections.

SELECTED READINGS

The best single source treating nonmanuscript materials is Jean S. Kujoth, editor, *Readings in Nonbook Librarianship;* but see the Weihs, Lewis, and Macdonald volume for suggestions on an integrated "omnimedia catalogue." For a survey of the way several institutions handle ephemera and a simple cataloging system for it, see Richard C. Berner and M. Gary Bettes, "Disposition of Nonmanuscript Items Found Among Manuscripts," and Walter S. Dunn, Jr., "Cataloging Ephemera: A Procedure for Small Libraries." A fine article by Richard W. Stephenson, "Published Sources of Information about Maps and Atlases," lists dealers, publishers, and journals of cartography. Marie T. Capps, "Preservation and Maintenance of Maps," is much sounder than Clara Le Gear's earlier work.

John M. Calhoun, "The Preservation of Motion Picture Film," adds little new to the classic, Eastman Kodak, *Storage and Preservation of Motion Picture Film.* The best overview of films is Raymond Fielding, "Archives of the Motion Picture: A General View," which can be supplemented with a good article in an obscure source, Patrick Griffin, editor, "The National Archives and The Historian's Use of Film: William Murphy in an Interview with *The History Teacher,*" for insights on research use. Robert Taft, *Photography and the American Scene: A Social History, 1830–1889* is still nonpareil, but the short article by Harvey Zucker, "Old-Time Processes—How to Identify and Date Them," is an excellent survey. Eugene Ostroff, "Preservation of Photographs," is the best concise treatment, but every curator ought to invest fifty cents in the pamphlet published by the East Street Gallery on archival processing of prints and negatives. "Filing Your Photographs: Some Basic Procedures," by Paul Vanderbilt, and the two-part article in *Special Libraries* by Renata V. Shaw will give the most help in organizing a collection.

The study of A. G. Pickett and M. M. Lemcoe on preserving sound recordings is the standard source, but should be read in tandem with Walter L. Welch's article, which disagrees on procedures at some points. David Hall has good practical advice to offer, and the 3M publication *Sound Talk,* available from the company's office in St. Paul, is very useful. The entire issue of *Library Trends* 21:1 (July 1972), deals with archival and reference collections of recorded sound.

The literature of oral history is voluminous, but the curator could get a good grounding in the subject by reading two periodicals devoted to it: *American Archivist* 38:1 (January 1967) and *The Wilson Library Bulletin* 40:7 (1966). The AASLH leaflet by William Tyrrell is a down-to-earth guide on how-to-do-it, and the Willa Baum brochure, the single best source on the subject. The scope of E. Douglas Hamilton's speech, published in the proceedings of the second colloquium on oral history, extends beyond the limits of title and is a good résumé of the legal problems which may be encountered in a program.

A great deal has been written about microforms, but relatively little is written about describing them and caring for them physically. The best two sources are the ALA-sponsored study by Allen Veaner and the Reichman and Tharp book on bibliographic control of microforms. Machine-readable records have been but slightly touched upon by the archivist and curator. Although it is out of date, the best over-all coverage is the obscure publication, *Pioneer Presentation of a National Symposium on the Impact of Automation on Documentation.* Failing to find this, the reader is directed to Meyer Fishbein's article, which, while it is intended to treat appraisal of records, will serve as a good introduction. The literature on the physical care of these forms is confined to tape and it comes from the tape manufacturers: the article by Bruce Shapley of Ampex and the two articles from 3M, "Magnetic Tape Erasure—How Serious is the Threat?" and "Handling & Storage of Computer Tape."

VIII

Use of
Collections

THE curator of one of the country's most respected manuscript collections ended an informative article on the use of manuscripts with the following statement: "In all these problems of use, the curator's first duty is to his manuscripts—to keep and preserve them." [1] Distilled in this short sentence is the essence of the tension always present in the curator's dual responsibility of preserving the manuscripts in his care and yet making them available for use. With various procedures—policy statements, interviews, restrictions, and security measures—he seeks to resolve the conflicts arising out of this dual charge. It is to the delineation of some of these problems and a discussion of possible alternative ways of handling them that this chapter is addressed.

Policy Statements

Most of the older and better established manuscript collecting agencies have a formal policy statement setting forth conditions of use.[2] Policy statements usually attempt to define who can have access to the collection. In times past, most statements contained phrases such as "scholarly research," the implication being that the collections were closed to newspaper feature writers and other "nonscholars."

(It is still the policy at the Huntington, which considers itself a "library of last resort," to exclude the "idly curious and the sensation seeker" from the use of manuscripts.) [3] In some institutions, undergraduates were denied access, and in others those of high school age and below. By and large, access statements followed the practicalities of the agency's existence. State institutions, because of the pressure of tax support, have tended to be less restrictive than those which received their support from the private sector. The public "right-to-know" laws in several states have caused many institutions to rethink their policy statement on use, and the National Archives, especially in the administration of the presidential libraries, seems to have responded to public criticism by making their holdings more promptly and easily accessible. [4]

Many manuscript repositories alert potential users to the agency's dual responsibility, which has been noted above. For example, the recently revised policy statement of the Houghton Library contains the following:

Libraries like the Houghton Library exist for two main purposes: to preserve the heritage of the past and to make it available to scholars. Neither purpose can be allowed to override the other. Our rules are devised not to impede your use but to allow access to our collections as freely as is consonant with conservation and orderly administration. We ask our readers to share our concern for the careful preservation of our books and manuscripts as a permanent resource for world scholarship. [5]

The only restrictions that seem more or less universal in policy statements are the more mechanical ones: forbidding the use of ink or consumption of food, beverages, and tobacco in the search room.

Some policy statements, but by no means all of them, contain sections on the amount of manuscripts that will be given to a researcher at one time and the call procedure, photoduplication instructions, copyright warnings, publication instructions, and forms to be followed in bibliographical citation. Many institutions request that the researcher read, make sure he understands, and then signs the form. The ritual to this point serves to alert the uninitiated and to demonstrate to one and all that the institution cares for its manuscripts and expects its patrons to do likewise. The test, of course, comes after the researcher has his first folder of manuscripts open before him upon the search table. Does he handle the material with care and respect? Does he keep things in order? Does he take notes with the paper on top of the manuscript? The policy statement will strengthen

Fig. 29. A section of the manuscript reading room, William R. Perkins Library, Duke University. (Courtesy Duke University)

the hand of the inexperienced staff member supervising the search room, who must deal with the patron who does not adhere to these rules. It also forms a record of use, and finally, it gives the patron a sense of being treated impartially.[6]

Interview

The policy statement, which can be mailed to potential researchers as well as given to those in the search room, helps to set the tone, but it is in the initial interview that the curator can best establish the manner in which research is to be conducted. Practices surrounding the initial interview have undergone great change in recent years. In times past, a researcher wrote to the institution in advance of his visit; and upon arrival, he might present a letter of introduction from a major professor or a publisher, if a book were involved. The first purpose of the interview, from the curator's point of view, was to ascertain the applicant's qualifications to use certain manuscripts.[7] The researcher, on the other hand, was anxious to utilize the curator's special knowledge of the collections. In more leisurely and polite times, this process benefited both parties, although there was a tendency for the interview to turn into name dropping or one-upmanship contests. Some institutions still attempt to use the initial interview, but as nearly as can be determined, few potential researchers have been denied access to an otherwise unrestricted collection on the basis of the initial interview.

The interview's greatest value, apart from a general introduction for both parties, is that it enables the curator to alert the researcher to others who might be working in either competitive or complementary research. However, the curator must guard against divulging unnecessary details and curb his instinct to gossip. As the head of one presidential library notes, the archivist/curator "should protect the researcher's work to the extent that he does not tell others in detail what documents the researcher is using or the way in which he is developing his theme. The researcher has reason to assume that as a matter of propriety the staffs of repositories will avoid disclosures, in idle conservation or otherwise, that would give away the product of thought and time that the researcher has invested in his own work." [8]

The initial interview is accepted curatorial practice; even those who practice it most cursorily give it lip service. However, no mention is made in the literature of another interview which might be more productive for the curator and his institution. If we follow military terminology, it could be called "debriefing," or, in the language of the personnel office, an "exit interview." Assuming that the researcher is not spending his last half hour writing out Xerox orders and looking for his taxi to the airport, he could spend that time telling the curator what he found wrong with the administration of the collection (there are the inevitable errors in the inventory to be corrected, if nothing else). Better phrased, the curator might ask him what he found helpful. In any event, the researcher can offer much advice available in no other way. Also, if the researcher has had a pleasant and profitable stay, probably he would be disposed to help the curator build his lead file. Almost any researcher worth his salt knows of manuscripts in private hands. It is not uncommon for the researcher himself to have bought or been given manuscripts in the course of his research. Or, if his field of research is modern, his own correspondence files may contain letters which would add depth to the files already under the curator's care. Finally, at the least, the researcher can usually suggest papers in other institutions which might profitably be micro-filmed.

Restrictions

Traditionally, the restrictions placed upon the use of papers are those applied by the donor at the time of gift. Sometimes the conditions are established by a will, but more often by descendants; and, as the collecting of papers of living persons has grown in volume, by the donor, who in this instance is the creator or "author" of the collection. Restrictions, which might more aptly be called controls, most commonly take the following forms: sealed, closed, and restricted access.[9]

An entire collection can be sealed, but more often the practice is limited to sections of the papers selected by the donor. This procedure, most commonly evoked in the case of secret or very controversial matters, is used less today because curators find it difficult to administer. Since only the donor or his assignees have access to a sealed collection, a curator, for his own protection, should insist that a collection so designated be sealed literally as well as figuratively, and that the conditions under which the seal can be broken are clearly defined in the donor file. Manuscripts under seal should be given extra protection to mitigate against accidents and to remove extra temptation from the curious. The time period for which the manuscripts are sealed should be a reasonable one. A person's lifetime plus fifty years would seem to be the maximum acceptable period, but twenty-five years is a more reasonable time. In most instances, a specific period of time—that is, ten years from date of acquisition—is much easier to administer, because the date of death, except of a prominent person, is sometimes difficult to determine.

A closed collection, or a part of a collection, is handled and administered quite similarly to manuscripts under seal, except that the curator and his staff process the closed portions or the entire collection before closing. Closed collections, or portions of collections, should be clearly marked on the inventory, and note should be made on the catalog cards. Special markings, perhaps bands of colored tape, should be applied to the boxes.

The forms taken by limited access are bounded only by the imagination of the donor and their acceptability to the curator. Donors who wish to maintain control, particularly publication or censorship controls, often specify that all requests to use a collection must be approved by them, and, in some instances, that all notes or copies from the collection must be cleared with the donor. Occasionally, the donor will delegate the power to give permission to use and copy to the curator or to an institution's board. Some donors wish to limit access to one person, usually a biographer, giving him first publication rights. This type of agreement can be untenable for a curator unless a time limit is set for publication. Another stratagem which results in limited access occurs when a researcher locates a collection, perhaps arranges for the acquisition, in return for the "finder's rights," again first publication rights. A prime example of the difficulties encountered in making the opening of a set of papers contingent upon the completion of a biography was the Mackenzie King papers administered by the Public Archives of Canada.[10] Other well-known instances include the Robert M. LaFollette papers at the Library of Congress and the Frederick Jackson Turner manuscripts at the State Historical Society of Wisconsin. Most institutions try to avoid limited access in any form, but the Huntington Library, if it holds copyright in a group of manuscripts, will close them to the exclusive use of scholars for up to three years. As a private agency, it probably could adhere to this decision, whereas a public institution would have difficulty justifying the closing.[11]

Not all restrictions then are donor imposed. Many curators are finding it necessary or advantageous to impose the same controls already discussed. In a literal sense, sealing cannot be curator-imposed, since the curator would have looked at the material to have decided it should be sealed. The closing of segments of collections has become quite common in modern collections, especially papers of a person who has held government office. For example, a state historical society acquires the papers of a congressman who sat on a committee, the files of which were classified as secret by the federal government. The curator may close that portion of the congressman's papers pending reclassification by the government.

Perhaps the best-publicized examples of controls imposed by the curator have been the large segments of papers in the presidential libraries which have been closed.[12] Beginning with the Roosevelt Library, some of the restrictions imposed concerned classified documents, as noted above, but a large portion of the material was closed for "reasons of propriety." Government archivists explain these self-imposed restrictions on the grounds that they accepted collections which were not screened, and they felt it was their obligation to protect their donors. Also, the point is made that unless curators and archivists voluntarily restrict modern collections, they must expect donors to censor their own material heavily prior to giving it to an institution.

A respected historian, Arthur Schlesinger, Jr., citing an equally respected archivist, Herman Kahn, was in turn quoted in a recent issue of the *Congressional Record* as saying that too much eagerness on the part of historians for instant access may well defeat their own long-term interests. Substantiating his belief, Schlesinger quoted Mr. Kahn: "My own conviction is that there has been a decline in the qualities of frankness and honesty in our records to a considerable degree because of the great pressure to make everything immediately available to historians and journalists who want to do historical writing about what happened yesterday, last month, or last year." [13]

For at least a decade, remembering a test case in the early 1960s, curators have been secure in the belief that the courts would uphold donor-imposed restrictions. In the New York Public Library case against Peter Kavanagh, Kavanagh was enjoined by the state supreme court from publishing letters of John Quinn, which had been received by the library on the condition that they would not be published until 1988. Today, researchers seem less inclined to accept the "verdict" of the Kavanagh case. [14]

With an increasing number of court cases to test established traditions and a similar trend against secrecy and closed files, curators may be facing the specter of a subpoena to appear in court and show just cause why a group of restricted records should not be opened.

Security and Safety

The idea of receiving a subpoena is too new to impinge upon the consciousness of most curators, who are much more likely to be concerned with establishing safeguards for the collections in their care.

The ever-present catastrophe confronting the curator is fire, and his best margin of safety is a fire-detection and control system built into the building (see chapter on administration). But assuming that the curator must cope with an existing structure without such a system, what can he do to increase his safety and that of the manuscripts in his charge?

The curator's best fire protection is a good program of fire prevention. Many fires result from shorts in electrical equipment, and it is good practice to unplug all office equipment, particularly copying machines, after hours. Keep loose paper at a minimum and do not allow packing paper and boxes from incoming collections to accumulate. See that the janitor empties the waste-paper cans regularly. Strictly enforce a no-smoking rule in the stacks, search room, and processing and office areas.

If the curator must rely on employees during the work day and watchmen after hours to detect a fire, the repository must have an adequate supply of water-type portable fire extinguishers, preferably of the trigger-action, stored-pressure, or charged-cartridge type. Most curators prefer carbon dioxide extinguishers, but safety experts say that this is a "fallacious dependence." A CO_2 extinguisher would not harm the records, but since it is designed to work on flammable liquids, it will not be effective on a deep-seated paper fire.[15]

In attempting to protect against fire, the curator is faced with a dilemma. Although unchecked fire is the greatest natural threat to manuscripts, water—which until recently was the only means of controlling fire—poses almost as much danger to paper, especially manuscripts where the inks are more water-soluble than in printed materials.

Many curators have experienced leaky steam or water pipes or water seepage through less-than-weather-tight roofs, windows and basement walls, and they know the damage from mildew and decomposed paper. Those who know the ravages of fire firsthand are fewer. As a result, some curators prefer to turn off sprinkler systems and take their risks with fire. Safety experts say this is foolhardy: any manuscript repository "has the inherent capability of not only self-destruction of the records holdings but also destruction of the facility itself . . . unless all fires are stopped in their early stages."[16] It should be sobering news that the same experts say the curator has a maximum of between twelve to fifteen minutes—*with an average of five minutes*—to detect and extinguish a stack fire before it is unapproachable and out of control.[17]

At this point, the fire department answering the alarm would have to use its largest-diameter hoses in fighting the blaze. Fires involving great quantities of paper reach such intensity that firemen must attack them from a distance. Great streams of water, each with the force of a hydraulic ram, may control the fire, but they leave a mixed mass of sodden paper.[18]

Even this seemingly hopeless situation may not be the disaster it once would have been. Conservators, drawing upon experiences arising out of several great floods in recent years, have teamed with

Fig. 30. The Military Personnel Records Center, St. Louis, shortly after the July 12, 1973, fire was extinguished. (Courtesy Arteaga Photos, St. Louis)

modern technology to offer new hope for water-soaked records (see last section of the chapter on care and conservation). Water alone, whether from flood or fire control, will not destroy manuscripts unless they are written on coated paper. The mold which grows on damp paper causes the destruction. Once the manuscripts have become damp, the curator has, at most, a week to dry them out before mold will begin to form.

As to the common natural disasters, flood and wind, there is little protection the curator can give his collections except to be sure that, if they are in the basement, nothing is stored directly on the floor. When flood waters back up a basement drain, pallets, four or five inches off the floor, although they may be ungainly and unattractive, can save great quantities of material which cannot be shelved. Of the "unnatural" disasters, the curator shares with the rest of mankind the possibility of reaping the destructive potential of modern military technology. Before World War II, curators were advised on how to construct their storage areas to be bomb-resistant. With the magnitude of bombs today, there seems little any curator can do to protect his collection, unless he works for SAC and has storage space under Cheyenne Mountain in Colorado Springs.

Security in the 1960s took on a new dimension, especially on college and university campuses, when manuscript and archival collections came under attack—metaphorically and literally—as a part of the Establishment. In some institutions, vital records (accession files, card catalogs, etc.), were microfilmed. At others—the University of Kansas, for example—special routines for "firewatch" and "public disorder" were evolved and became part of the permanent manual of operations.[19] For the first time, many curators who had thought of their beautiful "glass houses" only in terms of aesthetics and donor appeal were forced to act like infantry sergeants defending a position.

Although the threat of physical attack on manuscript collections has lessened, the curator faces a growing problem from another quarter in what appears to be an upsurge in theft. Most curators admit that there is almost no defense against a clever thief, yet few will admit manuscript losses. This indicates a reluctance to talk about thievery, but it probably also indicates that many institutions do not know their holdings in enough detail to detect their losses.

In large part, the security the curator is able to establish is keyed to the bibliographic control he has over the collection and the manner in which it is serviced. This, in turn, may be based largely upon the type of collection held by the institution. For example, a large midwestern historical society has extensive twentieth-century holdings which are serviced, a box or two at a time, to a patron and over which the only bibliographic control is a folder title list. What this means is that the exact contents of any specific folder are unknown (there is not even a piece count) and obviously a single letter or group of letters could be stolen and not missed. Although the search room is supposed to be under the surveillance of two staff members, it is a large room and often there is only one staff member at the desk. Briefcases are checked as researchers leave the building, but it is a perfunctory examination.

Another midwestern institution, a university which specializes in collecting literary manuscripts, has much more complete bibliographic control over its collections. Individual pieces within a folder are num-

bered and precise descriptions of individual items exist. Manuscripts
are issued to researchers a folder at a time. With this kind of bibliographic control, surveillance is at a minimum. There is no one on duty
in the search room, although there are windows into offices where
staff members work and occasionally they use the published bibliographic collection shelved in the search room. Faculty members and
visiting researchers on long-term projects are given carrels, closed
separate studies, where they store manuscripts on which they are
working.

On the surface, the university's system of security, even with a
lesser form of surveillance, would seem to be more secure than that
of the historical society. This is not the case. The system breaks down
because the contents of the folders are not checked before they are
issued to a patron and are only occasionally checked upon their return.

It would seem, then, that maximum security can be given to a
manuscript collection only if it is small enough to be counted and
described piece by piece and if it is serviced in small enough units
to be checked in and out of the stack. Obviously, most curators do
not have the time, the staff, and other resources to conduct this kind
of program.

Researchers are irritated by the "practice of parceling out only
five pieces of material at a time," and they accept special arrangements
to allow "mature researchers" into the stacks or to use manuscripts
after hours as manifestation of the close co-operation between the
curator and the researcher. By allowing unsupervised use of manuscripts, the curator may be offering "services consonant with researchers' needs," but also he is being negligent of his responsibilities.[20]

Unfortunately, a system of security built on trust is flimsily constructed. One would think that two priests of the Russian Eastern
Orthodox Church could be trusted, but Yale (and at least seven other
universities) found otherwise, when police discovered that the priests
had stolen "a ton or two" of books, atlases, and manuscripts. This
same year, 1973, saw sixty-five manuscripts, including letters of Washington, Lincoln, and Twain, stolen from the Huntington Library by
a graduate student in political history. The Huntington manuscripts
were recovered, but the personal diaries, memoranda, and letters of
Supreme Court Justice Felix Frankfurter which were stolen from the
Library of Congress have not been. Since the theft was discovered
in September 1972, the library has instituted new security measures,
but the incident probably would not have been widely known except

through the reporting of columnist Jack Anderson.[21] In a recent issue of *Manuscripts* is a notice of another kind of theft, which, though rarely publicized, is quite common: Brown University was alerting dealers and collectors that R. Alain Kersch, known to have solicited Howard Phillips Lovecraft manuscripts in the name of the university, had kept the material for his own use.[22] Similarly on occasion a professor will use the university's name or good office to collect materials for his own private collection, and there are known instances of some field men and curators who have done likewise.

That repositories have usually sought to avoid publicity about thefts was best demonstrated in the famous Murphy case in 1964. Early that year, Robert Murphy and his wife were arrested in Detroit and charged with stealing fifty documents from the National Archives. Within a few days, the FBI confiscated ten cartons of books, manuscripts, and maps evaluated at half a million dollars, which the Murphys had shipped to the Chicago bus station. At the trial, Murphy, whose real name was George Matz, was shown to have used various aliases in his visits to research libraries: R. O. Stanhope, Ashley Adams, Bradford Murphy, Robert McClafferty, and others. He posed as a professor and it was said that his overbearing and bullying manner intimidated repository staffs. Whatever his *modus operandi,* Murphy was for many years an eminently successful thief. In the recovered loot was found material from most of the major collections in the United States, but few stepped forward to claim their treasures and testify against Murphy. *After* the trial, some institutions claimed their property, but even then some preferred to lose manuscripts rather than admit to a successful theft from their holdings.[23]

In recent years, there seem to have been more manuscript thefts, but lest this be laid to the "new morality," it should be remembered that the phenomenon has been in evidence for a long time. Perhaps one of the most celebrated cases was that of Philip McElhone and Lewis Turner, employees of the manuscript section of the Library of Congress. In 1897, these two men were convicted of stealing manuscripts from the Peter Force collection and selling them to New York dealers. One of the dealers, William E. Benjamin, became suspicious and wrote to the library. The library denied missing any documents, but the dealer persisted, asked the senator from his state to investigate, and the theft came to light. The theft, as is often the case, had its positive side. The scandal and subsequent public reaction led to the creation, in September 1897, of the Manuscript Department with a professional head and a small but competent staff to initiate a long-overdue program in arranging and description.[24]

Each of the thefts mentioned here was discovered when manuscripts were sold to a dealer, and in these instances, as is often the case, when the dealer in turn offered to sell the material to the institution from which it had been stolen. Some dealers sustain heavy losses in theft cases, and in England the Antiquarian Booksellers' Association has instituted a central register of stolen books and manuscripts, and, for more important items, a telephone chain to notify all members within forty-eight hours of the discovery of a major theft. In this country, the editor of *AB Bookman's Weekly* urges libraries, curators, and archivists to alert dealers by reporting thefts to his publication. Generally co-operation between dealers and curators has been good. But occasionally curators complain that dealers should be more cautious, and dealers are sometimes quite outspoken about the curator's laxity. For example, one dealer, who had bought an atlas stolen in the Yale theft mentioned earlier, was quoted as saying: "The libraries are as much at fault as the people who take [manuscripts] and sell them." [25]

H. Richard Archer, Librarian, Chapin Library, Williams College, who has made a long-term study of thefts of rare materials, thinks it is about time that institutions face the facts, especially in view of the knowledge that "many thefts occur that we don't hear about." He says it is one of his "serious beliefs that library schools should include pertinent information in courses in rare materials and special collections, warning future professional librarians of the many problems of handling these materials and safe-guarding them from individuals who pose as scholars or serious research people, who are oftentime crooks or petty thieves." [26]

James B. Rhoads, the Archivist of the United States, is one of the few professionals who has attempted to come to grips with the problem. He suggests the following safeguards against theft: (1) around-the-clock surveillance by guards and an alarm system; (2) procedures to deny thieves access to manuscripts—that is, a check-out and charge of a limited number of boxes which are given a pre- and post-use inspection; (3) bar researchers from the stack areas; (4) systematic stamping of manuscripts.[27]

In the matter of surveillance, it is ironic that two of the newest, most modern, special collection libraries in the country should have been publicly criticized for their systems. At Yale's Beinecke, patrons work in a glass-enclosed search room which is supervised from a desk outside the room separated by seventy feet from the most distant researchers. A seating chart is kept of the patrons, but personal supervision of them is at a minimum. The Spencer Library at the University of Kansas has been singled out as having "the ultimate in accommodations" because of the sixty-seven individual studies, yet a librarian studying quarters for special collections noted that there is "no staff supervision of these studies other than visual inspection upon entering and exiting the building." This same survey indicates that there is a trend to supply rooms for typing, microforms, and carrels with the attendant loss of security.[28]

A technological variation of personal supervision is the closed-circuit TV systems to be installed in the reading room of new facilities being constructed at the Minnesota Historical Society and Wayne State University. (Wayne State also may use two-way mirrors.) A system including a self-contained camera, nine-inch monitor, two-way sound intercom, and fifty-foot video-sound cables is available at about $400.[29]

Stamping manuscripts, one of Dr. Rhoads's suggestions, may not be a practical solution for his own institution. With more than 2½ billion pieces, NARS would need an estimated 5,000 man-hours at a cost of 20 million dollars to mark the collection. In 1954, as a result of the theft of eleven documents from the Andrew Elliot Papers, the Library of Congress instituted a systematic stamping program. The ink chosen was easily visible, permanent, semitransparent, chemically inert, and could not be removed with ordinary ink eradicators. Single-page letters were stamped to the right of the salutation, multiple-paged ones, to the left of the signature. In 1962, when the program was still in operation, five to six thousand items a day could be stamped by the one full-time employee assigned to the task, at a cost of about a penny an item.[30]

A few years past, the Maryland Historical Society, "after losing a few Taney letters," started stamping manuscripts, but the ink tended to run when the materials were deacidified prior to lamination, and the program was abandoned. Now "better manuscripts" are Xeroxed and removed from the collections; and with increased security, it is felt "that only a professional could now remove anything *of value*." [31]

Copying selected manuscripts and securing the original is being done in many institutions, as, for example, in the Western History Collection at the University of Wyoming, where sensitive materials removed from a collection are also given the extra protection of a fire-proof file. Other institutions find this solution impractical and take the approach that there is very little to prevent a determined thief from stealing manuscripts. If this is true, it does not follow that the curator should make it easy for the professional thief or put extra temptation in the path of the weak. For example, it seems a simple-minded invitation to leave dealer prices on purchased manuscripts or to list this price information in the public catalog. For years, most dealers have penciled their prices and their purchase codes on the face of each manuscript. In some instances, traces of these marks are very difficult, if not impossible, to remove. Fortunately, most researchers do not know the dollar value of the manuscripts they use, and making it available seems only to invite trouble.

Another invitation to trouble is leaving stamped covers or envelopes in the collection. Stamps seem to attract even the noncollector; perhaps it is because they are bright, they stand out, they even look like money, or at the very least have a symbolic monetary value. By and large, envelopes are removed from a manuscript collection (see chapter on bibliographic control), but those curators who feel that they contain information essential to the collection might be advised to make photocopies of the envelopes and remove the originals. Fewer stamped covers (the lettersheet folded to make its own envelope) will be encountered, but because of the greater relative rarity, a curator would do well to separate the original from the collection and substitute a photocopy. Stampless covers, particularly those with early town cancellations, may be of great value to philatelists, but they pass unnoticed by the usual researcher.

Finally, perhaps the greatest favor the curator can do the researcher in removing temptation is to see that coats and briefcases are checked outside the search area and that a minimum of working materials—only a pencil and note sheets, if possible—are brought to the desk or work table. Some institutions—for example, the South Carolina Department of Archives and History—have installed lockers adjacent to their search rooms for the use of patrons. Not only will this mean less temptation; it will also reduce the possibility of accidents. A curator who has found a manuscript from the collection in a folder of a scholar's research notes, or interfiled in a group of Xerox copies he has ordered, will always wonder if his patron was a thief or an absent-minded professor.

The curator can only assume these are accidents, which points up the final dilemma in patron security. Even if the curator thinks he sees a researcher slip a manuscript into his briefcase, is he going to risk a lawsuit for false arrest? [32] Apart from the personal anguish involved, most institutions try to avoid any publicity surrounding thefts.

If curators are prone to play down patron theft, they are even less willing to admit the dangers of internal theft. Yet, a great many institutions have a skeleton in this particular closet. Considering the opportunities, it is perhaps a tribute to the curator and his staff that more internal thievery does not exist. It cannot be guarded against, and unless there is some method of screening out potential thieves in the personnel selection process, it comes down to mutual trust.

A curator can work toward the establishment of this trust, but what is often discouraging to him is the number of nonstaff personnel who have access to his collection. Depending upon the collecting agency, the curator may find that the janitor, electrician, and perhaps a great many others have keys to his area.

Although it is only an indirect protection against theft, an institution can buy fidelity bonds guaranteeing against loss through the dishonesty of its staff. Originally, bonds were issued individually, but now bonding companies will issue name-scheduled and position-scheduled bonds, as well as bonds on a blanket basis covering all employees.

Two kinds of insurance policies, Fine Arts and Valuable Papers, both include protection against theft. Also these policies are written to cover loss from fire, flood, broken water pipes, and many other hazards, excepting war and insurrection. Some curators have held the view that insurance serves no valid purpose, because manuscripts, by their nature, are irreplaceable. As one authority points out, this may be sound reasoning for the highly specialized collection—a library of Elizabethan drama, for example—but most institutions, although they may possess substantial holdings of rarities, these rarities usually constitute, quantitatively, only a small part of the total resources. A university library, for example, which suffered a fire in its special collections department, might be able to acquire manuscripts in a different field from that of the loss if it recovered funds. The disadvantage of these policies is that the collection has to be well-enough described to satisfy the company. This "accurate and detailed census" of manuscripts will be difficult for the curator to prepare. Also, of course, the collection must be appraised, and to keep the insurance current, reappraisals should be made no less frequently than every five years. To keep premiums within reasonable limits, the institution will want to include a "value level" which would exclude coverage from items valued at less than the set arbitrary figure.[33]

The curator, intent upon security and the protection of the manuscripts in his charge, should always temper his decisions toward the maximum use with safety. A major portion of the use, of course, will come through reference.

Reference

Reference in a manuscript collection will depend on a variety of factors, including the institution's tradition of service, affiliation with a service-oriented library, and the geographical location of the collecting agency. Perhaps only the latter needs any fuller explanation. If the collecting agency is in a remote area poorly served by transportation, the curator must expect to provide more mail and phone reference than if the collection was more readily accessible. Traditionally, the researcher by mail has been given short shrift, perhaps because, when his inquiries are set all down in a letter, the impact upon the harried curator is much greater than if they were asked singly and spread over several days in a visit to the institution. Usually, even the most lenient curators set a limit on the time that they will spend in researching a mail inquiry and on the type of question they will attempt to answer. Researchers accuse curators of being arbitrary, but the curators say that the other side of the coin is that researchers ask them to make interpretive judgments. Or as another administrator explains, "the inquirer surely cannot explain his needs as fully by mail as he can in person." [34]

One general rule of thumb applying to reference in the reading or search room—the curator ought to be cautioned not to do too little or too much! Since most curators like to share their special knowledge of the collection with the researcher, few need to be urged to do more.[35] There seems to be a growing feeling among curators against attempting to do the scholar's research for him. Most of this is directed toward making inventories and other finding aids less detailed, but the same approach can be taken toward reference in the search room. Users of manuscripts should be given every assistance in using the public finding aids, and the curator should be willing to share his knowledge of the collection with the researcher. In the end, however, it must be the researcher's responsibility to seek out and use the manuscripts necessary for his research. This may sound like belaboring the obvious, but one of the outgrowths of the Lowenheim episode seems to have been to shift this responsibility to the curator of a manuscript collection. The Lowenheim matter is extremely complex. In brief, Francis L. Lowenheim accused the staff of the Roosevelt Presidential Library "not only of withholding from him specific letters and concealing from him knowledge of a documentary project but also of doing so deliberately, unethically, and for its own personal advantage." The committee held against Lowenheim, but added: "Although Lowenheim should have been able, on his own, to find at either the Roosevelt Library or the Library of Congress the few Dodd-Roosevelt letters that he lacked, and, in fact, had ample opportunity to do so, *the staff at Hyde Park should have made sure that he did, indeed, see them there"* [36] (emphasis added).

The implications of the Lowenheim matter have not been missed by British archivists, who are speculating that "the cut-throat world of American scholarship may well spread to [English] shores." They are asking, "Is the archivist compelled to produce every document relevant to a particular inquiry?" Archivists in Great Britain, who are being asked increasingly to provide information "which is not for historical purposes and on matters in which expenditure of large sums of money may be involved," have been concerned by a judicial decision in a recent case that nullifies the general disclaimer of liability for information supplied which hitherto has been widely used by archivists. In England, as in the United States, the profession is developing new awareness of the legal implications of its position. [37]

Fortunately, the legalities of the curator's existence have not completely overshadowed the generally good relationship between him and the researchers. One historian has ventured to suggest that, where problems do arise and members of his profession express annoyance at what they feel are obstacles to their research, they do so because they are following an "idealized vocation" which they had chosen because of "deep commitments that transform their labor into intellectual pleasure and excitement." With more contact with the "workaday world," the historian "probably would take ordinary aggravation with less fret." [38]

The aggravation is not one-sided, of course, and despite "strikingly cordial" relationships between historical researchers and curators, the latter have voiced a few complaints often enough to merit discussion here. In the literature, in personal interviews, in workshops at professional meetings, curators comment consistently on two areas where graduate students and many professors demonstrate a lack of preparation for research: lack of familiarity with the facilities of a research library and inadequate training in the use of manuscripts. The curators of some collections, particularly those on college and university campuses, participate in methods courses in literature and history. But since both academic and nonacademic repositories find that approximately half their patrons come from outside the locality, curators will continue to be troubled by this problem. As one curator has said, it becomes "terribly discouraging" to realize that the overwhelming proportion of graduate students are so poorly grounded in the basic amenities of research that "they don't even have the sense to keep their hands clean." [39]

Ignorance can be tolerated, but ignorance combined with arrogance is difficult to abide. One curator, for example, has reconciled himself to the fact that he must give basic instructions in the use of manuscripts to researchers—do not lean on the volumes, keep the papers in order, etc.—but he is still miffed by the occasional researcher who thinks he knows best. He recalls, for example, one professor who wanted to remove a Monroe letter from a collection of Madison materials and put it in the Monroe collection.[40] This sort of thing happens often enough to be familiar to many curators, but few have had a professor so *insistent* upon reordering papers, as happened on an eastern campus recently, that he had to be escorted from the premises by the security guard!

To meet the need of making researchers aware of the resources of the collection, many institutions hold open houses and other similar affairs to give on-the-spot familiarity to the interested. Some repositories notify academic departments of topics that can be developed from their original sources. Professors may not always accept the curator's evaluation, but they are usually pleased to learn of collections. One professor, for example, worked out a system of using honor undergraduates not planning to pursue graduate work as "front runners," to dig into manuscripts in preparation of term papers. On the basis of these papers, he decided what collections warranted further research by his graduate students. He felt it was important not to "run graduate students up blind alleys that might waste a year of their time." [41]

There are professors and curators who feel that exposure to manuscripts, even on the undergraduate level, is much more likely to be beneficial than a waste of time. At Dickinson College, for example, manuscripts are used in an introductory history course as well as in the senior course in historiography. Some students edit letters from the collection and others research biographies of Dickinson alumni, trustees, or faculty members. The curator feels that this exposure not only has academic rewards, but that it benefits the library: "Those who learn about Special Collections through first hand use often become our warmest supporters and collectors in their own right." [42]

Some institutions are encouraging high school students, under the direct supervision of their teachers, to use manuscripts, and if possible, to publish from them. The Western Reserve Historical Society in Cleveland feels that underprivileged and minority-group students, particularly, will benefit from work with manuscripts. The operative theory at this institution is that "education does not begin in college." [43]

However the collections in his custody are used, probably the curator will keep a record. Search-room use statistics can be compiled in many ways,[44] but whatever the form in which the record is kept, it can be useful. A study of who uses the collection and toward what end may provide guides to further collections. Also, a record of each collection used by a patron provides a tool, if it is necessary for tracing a theft. Sometimes such a record is useful in evaluating short-term effects of collecting, trends in historiography, or levels of use. And, of course, the information can be put to very good use in writing annual reports.

Most curators keep reference or use statistics for the search room, but fewer keep similar statistics for reference by mail and by telephone. Assuming that the bulk of telephone reference is for the local area, only minimal effort should be expended by the reference staff. With the decline of radio and television quiz shows, most local calls to the manuscript collection will be in the nature of "How much is this old document I have worth?" If it is General Lee's Order No. 9, the Gettysburg Address, or a federal land patent signed after 1826, the answer is short and to the point: General Lee's order and the Gettysburg Address have been facsimiled many times (see appendix), and federal land-grant patents after 1826 were signed by a secretary in the president's name, so none of the manuscripts mentioned will have great value. Every curator receives a number of these nuisance calls, but he must plow the same ground again and again. Since leads or offers of desirable manuscripts come by telephone, they cannot be disregarded. A telephone log may help keep the repository's reference calls in bounds. Of course, the curator has no control over incoming calls, but a log over a period of time would help him develop some stock answers which could be given by the operator to commonly asked questions.

A similar log for correspondence is even more useful in keeping a record of time and costs. Depending upon the staff load and other duties, the curator may wish to establish a basic maximum time to be spent in mail reference.[45] If the question requires more research than, say, a half to three quarters of an hour, the patron should be directed to private researchers who will assemble the facts for an hourly fee. This is particularly true of genealogical research. Word seems to travel almost with the speed of light about curators who are willing to do genealogical research in the collection. The curator can be swamped with requests, and unless his collection is funded and administered to service this kind of request, it can be a great drain on the rest of the operation.

But where once the genealogist was the bane of the curator's existence, his own colleagues with their eternal surveys have now taken the prize. Close behind come the projects like the *American Literary Manuscripts*, followed by the National Historical Publications Commission's sponsored edited works of prominent Americans (and scores of similar projects variously sponsored), and last, but not least, the "send me Xerox copies of everything you have by, to, or about Mr. X" scholar.

Each of these projects is eminently worthwhile and deserves the full attention and support of the curator; but unfortunately, the average curator is beset by a multitude of tasks. He must decide on his priorities and where he can allot his time. Perhaps the only criterion that can be applied to the surveys is a subjective judgment as to the contribution the data tabulated will make to the profession. The scholarly acceptance of the NHPC-sponsored edited works is almost universal; the curator's questions are of another sort: Does his institution want its hitherto unpublished letters of Jefferson Davis published in the collected works? If he sends the copies of the Davis letters, can he rightfully request that the copies be returned at the time of publication, or at the end of the project? In this, as in any other project requiring large-scale copying, can the curator expect the researcher to pay the true costs of photocopying, which include staff time to locate, select, copy, and refile letters?

Common-Law Literary Copyright

The questions of co-operation with many of the letterpress editions, as well as the checklists and the authorized biographies, often can be academic if the editor or author has been assigned the first publication rights in the manuscripts of his subject. For example, assume that the curator of manuscripts, Transylvania Historical Society, has received a letter from Professor Jones asking that he be sent a copy of the Ernest Scribbler manuscripts held by the society. The professor encloses a copy of a letter from Mrs. Scribbler, widow and sole heir of the respected American author, appointing Jones literary executor of her husband's estate. Although it is not well known, Scribbler, 1890–1970, author of *No More War* (privately printed, 1914) and *The Good Little War* (Renegade and Sons, 1937), was a native Transylvanian. Soon after his death, the society had purchased Scribbler's working papers and notebook drafts after seeing them extensively quoted and described in a dealer's catalog.* Subsequently, the dealer offered a collection of Scribbler correspondence, but THS was unable to raise the funds, and the letters went to Utopian University. The curator's disappointment was eased, in that, soon after the Scribbler Papers came to the society, the institution received a long series of Scribbler letters addressed to his friend Thomas Rewrite, the gift of Mrs. Rewrite.

When the curator acquired both Scribbler collections, he thought he had "legal title," [46] and he considered disregarding Professor Jones's request. What this would have meant, in simple language, was that, if the curator chose not to send the copies, he would incur Professor Jones's certain displeasure. Since, legally, not one word or phrase could be quoted from any Scribbler manuscript or letter without permission of the literary executor, Jones's displeasure would destroy the scholarly usefulness of the Scribbler letters in the curator's collection. The professor might even go to court and secure an injunction enjoining the curator and his institution from exhibiting the Scribbler letters.[47]

The net result of Professor Jones's action seems to the curator to deny his institution the use of its property. In a sense this is true, but the difficulty is that there are two kinds of property in any manuscript. When the curator bought or was given the Ernest Scribbler letters and manuscripts, he acquired the physical property rights, the ink and paper. The common-law literary copyright (also known as

---

* Strangely enough, although scholars have been sued or threatened with suit for the unauthorized publication of letters and manuscripts, dealers, who quote at length in their catalogs, have rarely been bothered. However, there are estates, which dealers know, whose executors sedulously guard against publication. Three of the best examples are Mark Twain, William Dean Howells, and Mary Baker Eddy. The curator should think twice before quoting letters from any of the three in an inventory or catalog.

common-law literary right or the right of first publication), which is also a property right, although an intangible one, remained with Mr. Scribbler during his lifetime and passed to his heirs and assignees at the time of his death.

There is considerable confusion among curators (also researchers and even some attorneys) about common-law literary copyright.[48] The copyright most people are familiar with is the registered or statutory copyright on books and other printed materials. Statutory copyright is a misnomer; it is not a "right," but a franchise granted for a limited time by statute or written law. Several of the colonies had copyright laws and the United States today is regulated under an outmoded federal act of 1909. All of these statutes can be traced to English law.

The origins of what is generally known as "common-law copyright" have been said to be "wrapt in obscurity and uncertainty."[49] Part of the difficulty lies in the inexactness of the term; more properly, it should be either the "right of first publication" or "literary property." Matters are further obscured by the fact that what today is universally considered a natural property right of the author in his writing began as a publisher's right. As if this were not enough, a legal historian tells us that "copyright was not a product of the common law. It was a product of censorship, guild monopoly, trade-regulation statutes, and misunderstanding." As he explains, copyright began in sixteenth-century England

as a device for maintaining order among members of the book trade organized as the Stationers' Company. Supported by laws of press control and censorship, it developed and existed as the private concern of these guild members for a hundred and fifty years. As such, it was the basis of a monopoly in the book trade.
With the demise of censorship, the private copyright of the members of the book trade, no longer supported by governmental sanctions, failed in its purpose of protecting published works. To restore order to the trade, Parliament was finally prevailed upon to enact a copyright statute, modelled on the stationers' copyright, but without its two most objectionable features, its limitation to members of the company, and its perpetual existence. The statutory copyright was available to anyone, and it was limited to two terms of fourteen years each. Instead of an instrument of monopoly, as the stationers' copyright had been, the statutory copyright was intended to be a trade-regulation device.[50]

What happened was that, after William Caxton introduced the printing press to England in 1476, there developed a great demand for and subsequent scarcity of books. By enactment, Richard III encouraged the importation of books and lifted the alien restriction on immigratory "scrivener, alluminor, reader, or printer of such books."

Fig. 31. A color aquatint by Thomas Rowlandson (1797) depicts an author trying to sell his manuscript to a publisher-dealer. (Reprinted with permission of R. R. Bowker)

But over the years, as the supply continued to outstrip demand, and more importantly, as some books appeared to challenge the authority of Church and Crown, Henry VIII halted importation and acted to control the press through licensing.[51]

Meanwhile, the printers, bookbinders, and booksellers (publishers) began to coalesce into a guild to regulate the book trade. The earliest known records of the Stationers' Company, registers dating to 1554, contain "entries of copies," but it is thought that the booksellers' practice of buying "right to copy" from authors might have antedated the record. In 1557, Philip and Mary granted the guild a royal charter. The charter gave the Stationers' Company a monopoly of the book trade and at the same time acted "to prevent the propagation of the Protestant Reformation." [52]

Until the end of the seventeenth century, when the power of the Stationers' Company expired in 1694, copyright had existed for more than a hundred and fifty years as a publisher's right. Not until the Statute of Ann, drafts of which have been said to have been written in part by Joseph Addison and Johnathan Swift, was passed by Parliament in 1710 was there any recognition that the author had any common-law right of property in his writing.

After the Statute of Ann limited their right of copy, the booksellers claimed that the authors had had the right in perpetuity, and that, when they bought the rights to a book from the author, they had acquired a common-law title in property which could not be taken away from them by statute. Some lower courts, the common-law courts, accepted this position and granted injunctions, first in 1735 and again in 1739, to restrain publication of work previously published under the stationers' right of copy. For one reason or another, neither case came to trial, and it was not until thirty years later, in the case of *Millar and Taylor,* that the Court of King's Bench recognized the author's common-law copyright as a natural right. Five years later, in *Donaldson vs. Beckett,* the House of Lords defined this common-law right as the right of first publication.[53]

The dual system of common-law protection for unpublished works and the statutory protection for published works continued in England until the distinction was abolished by an act of Parliament in 1911 which brought copyright under statute.

The distinction still remains in United States law. In this country, today, the chief difference between statutory and the common-law copyright is best illustrated by referring again to the Ernest Scribbler Papers at the Transylvania Historical Society. Included in the papers is the holograph draft of Scribbler's first novel, *No More War,* young Scribbler's pacifist exposé of World War I, for which he could not find a publisher and had to have privately printed. Also included in the papers is the final typescript, heavily emended by Scribbler, of *The Good Little War,* his best-selling novel espousing the Spanish Loyalists' cause.

The THS library, like most libraries in this country with a good American fiction collection, holds copies of the two novels. Their collection also contains a book of criticism and a survey of twentieth-century American literature which have quoted phrases and a sentence or two from the books. Footnotes in these texts cite the novels, but neither the authors nor the publishers asked permission of Scribbler or the Renegade Publishing Company. A third company, Paperback, Inc., which published a chapter from *No More War* and a long excerpt from *The Good Little War,* asked and received permission to quote from the owners of the registered copyright, from Scribbler for the first and from Renegade for the second. Scribbler, anxious to have his early work more widely distributed, charged Paperback, Inc., nothing, but Renegade levied their standard fee for the use of their property.

Thus, three publishers had quoted from Scribbler's war novels, only one had permission, but all had complied with the provisions of statutory or registered copyright under the doctrine of "fair use." The courts have not been consistent in their decisions about what constitutes fair use, but it is generally believed that quotations up to three hundred words can be made from *published* prose works without permission of the copyright holder. The doctrine of fair use *does not* apply to unpublished manuscript material protected under the common-law literary copyright. Some scholars think it does and have speculated that the courts might uphold a test case which applied the fair-use doctrine to quotations from letters and other unpublished manuscripts, but this is purely speculation. Nor does the literary quality of the manuscript have any bearing upon the protection of unpublished writings. The courts have ruled that *any writing*—a letter, an advertisement, a poem, a grocery list, even gibberish—is the exclusive property of the creator, the author. The ideas expressed are in the public domain, but the order and arrangement of the words are a property right that the author can sell or assign as he does any other property.[54]

Another major difference between statutory and common-law copyright is that, while the statutory copyright extends for a limited time (twenty-eight years with provision for renewal for an additional twenty-eight years, or a total of fifty-six years), the common-law literary copyright extends in perpetuity. This means that the right to publish anything from a man's writings—his letters, essays, diary, poetry, any manuscript—rests with the author. During his life, the author can abrogate this right by assigning it to another person or a corporation; and at his death, he can will it specifically as intangible property. If no separate assignment is made in the will, the common-law literary copyright passes to his heirs in the so-called residuary clause—the clause which assigns the residue of the estate not specifically devised or bequeathed.[55] The heirs in turn can assign the rights or pass them to their heirs, either by will or intestate.

It follows, then, that with a very few exceptions all unpublished manuscripts are equally protected.* If the scholar will but contemplate that for a moment, he will recognize the immense task facing him in his research if he is not to violate the law. One writer has characterized the problem in this way: "Permission must be obtained from those who qualify as assignees, executors, administrators, beneficiaries, or descendants. This may mean a search for an innumerable class of people, and raises special difficulties for the historian and biographer." Another scholar sees the problem, in more dramatic terms as "a hand reaching from the grave to stay the advance of knowledge." [56]

Scholars and curators, who had despaired of a court decision which might stay the hand from the grave, had looked to federal legislation to produce the remedy, only to experience more than a decade of frustration.

For several years, now, beginning in 1964, Congress has been considering major revisions in the copyright law, one of which would be to establish a single system of statutory protection for all works, whether published or unpublished. On July 20 of that year, the Librarian of Congress sent to Congress a bill which was the result of nine years' work by the Copyright Office. Copyright law, of course, is

---

* Letters written by public officials in their official capacity are in the public domain. Traditionally the papers of the presidents and the governors of some states have been considered personal papers and therefore not in the public domain, but the public outcry following the publication of Richard Nixon's tax returns may foster legislation to alter this traditional pattern. (See Robert W. Scott, "Governor's Public Records," p. 9, in which a survey of H. G. Jones is quoted as indicating at least a third of the states consider the governor's pages as personal, not public records.) The curator should remember, too, that, since the United States signed the Universal Copyright Convention in 1955, manuscripts of the nationals of the other contracting states are protected in the United States under common law. (See William S. Strauss, "Protection of Unpublished Works," p. 205.

concerned with many other areas than books and manuscripts, but in this sphere the bill limited an author's rights in his works to "life plus fifty years." For anonymous or pseudonymous works, the term of protection would be seventy-five years from publication, or one hundred years from creation for unpublished works.[57]

Hearings were held on copyright revision in 1965. Finally, two years later, the House passed a bill embodying the provisions noted above, but debate got bogged down in discussion over juke boxes and cable television and the Senate referred the measure to the Committee on Judiciary, where it died.[58]

At the next session of Congress, in January 1969, Senator John McClellan introduced an identical bill; but again, it languished in the Committee on Judiciary. The bill was reintroduced on February 8, 1971, again languished and died. Two years later, on March 26, 1973, S1361, another bill to revise the copyright law, was introduced and referred to the Committee on Judiciary. The committee held hearings on the measure from July 31 to August 1, which were occupied largely with the struggle between publishers and libraries over "fair use." An identical bill was introduced in the House on May 29, but there seems little prospect of the passage of either bill. Earlier, in October 1972, a joint resolution passed Congress extending the present copyright regulations through December 31, 1974; so, for the present, the dual system remains and common-law literary copyright continues to plague manuscript repositories.[59]

The knowledgeable curator has been trying to cope with the continuing problem by trying to get an assignment of literary rights by the donor to the institution or the public at the time of gift. However, this in itself is no simple matter and is often only a partial solution. For example, when Mrs. Rewrite gave her husband's papers to the Transylvania Historical Society, the deed of gift included an assignment of all the Rewrite literary rights to THS. This means that the THS can publish the novel in progress at the time of Rewrite's death, but cannot publish, nor give permission to anyone to publish, the letters from Scribbler to Rewrite; she could not give rights she did not possess. But it also means that THS, when it acquired Rewrite's literary rights, received the rights not only to the papers in its collection but, for example, to the Rewrite letters in the Scribbler Collection held by Utopia University.

Literary rights usually are assigned en *toto,* as Mrs. Rewrite did, but, of course, she could have made a specific assignment of the rights to the material in hand when she gave it to the society and retained the remaining rights.

In the above sense, literary rights are divisable, but in another, they are not. Assume that, when Rewrite died, Mrs. Rewrite was not his sole heir and that, either through the residuary clause or through a share-and-share-alike division, the literary rights were equally divided among his widow, a son, and a daughter. If the daughter, assuming she is not a minor, assigns her share of the Rewrite literary rights to a person, a corporation, an institution, or places them in the public domain, the rights of the mother and brother pass at the same time, with or without their consent.

Common-law literary copyright is complex, and unfortunately few cases have been decided by the courts to provide guidance for the curator. In the absence of legal precedent, theories regarding the court's interpretation of common-law copyright are of interest to curators. One of the most commonly held is that, at some future date, the courts will decide that placing manuscripts in a repository constitutes publication.[60] The aftermath of such a decision might be that the curator could be held liable for accepting manuscripts from donors who did not hold and therefore could not assign the literary rights. The ultimate effect would be to put most manuscripts into the public domain because of the indivisible nature of the rights as explained above.

Although it, too, is theory at this stage, probably the curator's more immediate legal risk is in photocopying manuscripts to which his institution does not hold copyright. This question has never been resolved in the courts, but there is some feeling that preparing a photocopy, even for research, constitutes publication. This view is given weight by the NHPC use of the term *microfilm editions* in describing series of papers in various institutions which have been filmed with project funds. If the courts rule on the matter, perhaps the issue will turn upon the number of copies made and whether they were prepared for sale. Meanwhile, although the risks involving violation of the common-law copyright remain for the average curator, the National Archives has been lobbying for specific protection for its staff. While none of the measures have become law, the legislation introduced in recent years to change copyright law has included provisions specifically exempting the National Archives from infringement of copyright in the production of NHPC microfilm editions. In commenting upon a recent piece of legislation, one authority noted that this bill, like its predecessor, contained the following provision: "When letters and other intellectual productions . . . come into the custody or possession of the Administrator of General Services, the United States or its agents are not liable for infringement of copyright or analogous right arising out of use of the material for display, inspection, research, reproduction, or other purposes." The authority concluded that this section of the bill indicated "that the Sovereign has made his freedom from tort liability secure, since he can be sued only when he consents to be, and in this case he does not consent." [61]

Libel and Slander

Another area where the curator may run afoul of the law relates to the laws of libel and slander and their possible violation in the oral history projects. In this instance he, his institution, the interviewer, the interviewee, and the researcher using material all may be liable for damages. Slander and libel are both forms of defamation; oral defamation is slander; and defamation in writing, "or some other permanent form of expression," is libel. Thus, because interviews are taped, an interviewee, even though he is orally expressing himself, commits libel if he defames a person. Libel laws vary from state to state, but generally the following are considered libelous by the courts: attacking a person's reputation; subjecting a person to public ridicule and scorn; charging that one is mentally defective or the victim of a loathsome and contagious disease; and prejudicing an individual in his business or profession. On the other hand, courts have held that a statement is not libelous (1) if the gist or substance of it can be proven with competent legal evidence to be true; (2) if it is a report of an official, judicial, or legislative proceeding; (3) if it is fair comment and criticism, made without malice, upon a matter of public interest and concern. By and large, it is difficult to libel the deceased or persons in public office. [62]

Laws of libel are not fixed rules but standards to guide the courts, which attempt to balance the interest of an individual in protecting his reputation, the interests of a writer in expressing himself, and the interest of the public in having information and news. The curator who is concerned about how these varying interests overlap and conflict in the administration of his oral history project ought to study the libel laws of his state, and he may wish to take measures to try to protect himself and his institution from legal action. At Wayne State and the University of Michigan, for example, oral interview transcripts are made available only to faculty and graduate students of recognized colleges and universities who have been warned that the use of defamatory statements or the invasion of personal privacy is actionable, and who agree to submit the name of their publisher so that the institution can inform the publisher of the possibility of libelous statements in the transcripts. Further, the transcripts are not available for interlibrary loan, nor may they "be microfilmed or reprinted." [63]

These procedures show good faith and provide a measure of security by strengthening the curator's case if he is involved in a lawsuit. It is comforting to know that the plaintiff most likely will not receive the damages he seeks. Indirectly, the institution has diminished but not removed the threat of lawsuit. With libel, as with infringement of common-law copyright, the threat alone may stymie publication. If the threat does not work, suit may still be brought, even if the plaintiff has little hope of gaining damages. Then the curator must retain an attorney and defend himself. Any citizen can end up in court, but the curator's chances have increased materially with the collecting of recent history, and he would do well to understand his risks.

If the "ivory tower" ever existed for curators, it no longer does, and this is even more amply demonstrated in the last chapter of this book, which deals with their services to the public, such as exhibits and publications.

SELECTED READINGS

The academic historian's point of view as a user can be found in two fine books that every curator should read: O. Lawrence Burnette, Jr., *Beneath the Footnote: A Guide to the Uses and Preservation of American Historical Sources,* and Walter Rundell, Jr., *In Pursuit of American History: Research and Training in the United States.* Professor Rundell's article, "Relations between Historical Researchers and Custodians of Source Materials," is helpful, too, but there is a need for studies from other disciplines. Philip C. Brooks, *Research in Archives: The Use of Unpublished Primary Sources,* is intended to be used as a manual in historiography classes. The portions on common-law literary rights should be read with care (see pages in preceding chapter). For two concise scholarly articles on copyright, see H. Bartholomew Cox, "Private Letters and Public Domain," and "The Impact of the Proposed Copyright Law Upon Scholars and Custodians." American Library Association, *Protecting the Library and its Resources: A Guide to Physical Protection and Insurance,* is the best over-all work on security, but the curator should supplement its section on fire protection with the National Fire Protection Association *Manual for Fire Protection for Archives and Record Centers.* The best all-around short study of the curator's responsibilities relating to use is Jean Preston, "Problems in the Use of Manuscripts," although it is somewhat oriented around the privately funded institution.

IX

Public Service

ALTHOUGH occasionally the curator may
lose sight of it, a manuscript collection has great public relations value.[1]
Public relations, however, is but one phase of public service. The
previous chapter touched upon some services of the manuscript collection to the academic segment of the public—the use of manuscripts
in research; this chapter will deal with other aspects of public service—publications and exhibits, which may have more popular appeal.

Exhibits

Before the curator begins preparing an exhibit or series of exhibits,
he should give some thought to the theory behind the particular exhibit
and the general exhibition policy of his institution. Exhibits are
mounted for many reasons. One of the most common exhibits, for
example, explains the mission of the collecting agency and sometimes
develops its relationship to the larger administrative unit. Another
exhibit, an excellent morale builder and orientation device, depicts
the behind-the-scenes operations of the repository and gives credit
to staff members who are not often publicly recognized. These two
types of exhibits are usually semipermanent, but many institutions
also have exhibits which are changed on a more or less regular sched-

ule. Some collecting agencies have annual exhibits, the most common being the exhibit of manuscripts donated or purchased the past year, which is often mounted for the Friends annual meeting. Manuscript curators use exhibits to spotlight a single important accession, too, and prepare the regularly scheduled exhibits to display strengths or themes in the collection. Exhibits sometimes are prepared to coincide with the visit of a speaker or in conjunction with the celebration of a local or national event.

Fig. 32. Looking through the exhibit area toward the reference desk, Kenneth Spencer Research Library, University of Kansas. (Courtesy University of Kansas)

Timeliness, in one form or another, is usually one of the factors which the curator must take into consideration in choosing a subject. He will also be concerned about the potential educational value and popular appeal, as well as the costs in terms of manpower and material.[2]

Some curators have experimented with having commercial firms prepare exhibits, but have found them prohibitive in cost and extremely dangerous for the manuscripts. On the surface, borrowing exhibits appears to be a way to cut costs, but some expenses are involved. Usually, the borrowing institution must pay for packing and shipping and insurance premiums, if it does not have a blanket policy. Still, the expenses are minimal in comparison with preparation costs for a quality product, and the curator should consider traveling exhibits in his schedule. The Library of Congress and the National Archives have offered such exhibits for years; and in 1974, the Smithsonian Institution Traveling Exhibit Service will embark upon a program with a Bicentennial exhibit mounted in co-operation with The Manuscript Society.

Occasionally, a curator will borrow an entire collection (or significant pieces) for exhibit; but more often, he will request the loan of a few items from private collectors or other institutions to fill out an exhibit. In these instances, one curator, who has had considerable experience, suggests that the loan request come from someone in the upper administrative level, the higher the better. The request, he says, should state the inclusive dates that the manuscripts would be needed (which may include considerable time to prepare the exhibit), the terms of insurance, the security during and after hours, and the date that the material will be returned. He notes that curators sometimes get careless after an exhibit has been dismantled. Since a very effective "grapevine" operates between collectors and institutions, he recommends that the curator adhere firmly to the schedule of return and personally supervise the packing and insuring of the borrowed manuscripts.[3]

With borrowed manuscripts, the curator might have to exercise extra security precautions. One of the most famous manuscript thefts happened during the time the piece was on loan. The manuscript of Sir Walter Scott's *Guy Mannering*, which Columbia University had borrowed from the collector, J. P. Morgan, was stolen by a thief who forced the lock on the exhibit case. Losses of manuscripts while on exhibit are rare, however.[4] Some institutions do hire guards, but usually it is thought that the presence of viewers and occasional staff in the exhibit area will serve as a deterrent. Some repositories have installed electronic burglary devices that are sensitive enough to register the slightest sound or movement in the exhibit area when it is closed to the public.

Whether he has borrowed material or not, however, the curator must protect his exhibits. Because the mounting and disassembling of exhibits are the periods of greatest risk of theft, some experts say that they should be put up or taken down only after closing hours. There should be only one or two sets of keys to the cases, and they should not be readily accessible to either the staff or to patrons.[5]

Despite the most careful of handling, manuscripts on exhibit suffer some wear and tear. While many institutions have acceptable temperature and humidity controls in stack and work areas, few have exhibit cases which do not subject manuscripts on display to excessive heat and dryness. To counteract this condition, one authority suggests placing a small dish of water in a badly ventilated case to add moisture to the dry atmosphere. With some ingenuity, the curator should be able to design the exhibit to hide this homemade humidifier.[6] Curators who are aware of the dangers of ultraviolet rays will not exhibit manuscripts in natural light and will insist on having fluorescent tubes with built-in screens or regular tubes with protective sleeves in exhibit cases. Although these precautions can reduce light damage, some still occurs and it is wise to limit the time that manuscripts are on exhibit. Paul Banks, conservator at the Newberry Library, says that there are no hard-and-fast rules, but suggests that important manuscripts should not be displayed more than a month at most and lesser materials not more than six months. He urges that the curator not accept these as "magic numbers," but remember that "the amount of damage is directly proportional to the length of exposure, given the same intensity of lighting." Most important, the curator must keep in mind that "any damage from light is irreversible damage."[7] Finally, apart from whatever deterioration by the elements takes place, some damage is almost certain to occur during mounting or removing an exhibit. If the curator cannot prepare his own exhibits, he should unceasingly remind his exhibit staff of the fragile nature of the material they are handling.

There is no known adhesive which can be used safely in mounting manuscripts for exhibit. Museum wax and Stik, traditionally used, will leave oily residue which stains paper. The manufacturer of Stik claims that the plastic compound contains no wax or grease, but it must be kneaded to activate it for use and it picks up the natural oils and acids from the skin.

The simplest and easiest method of holding manuscripts in place against the back of the exhibit case is to use map pins. The pins can be pushed in slantingly so that the points enter the backboard flush with the edge of the manuscript and the round heads of the pins will press against the paper and hold it. Strips of nylon or fine surgical tubing can be stretched across the face of the manuscript and pinned on either side. (These same strips can be used to hold a manuscript

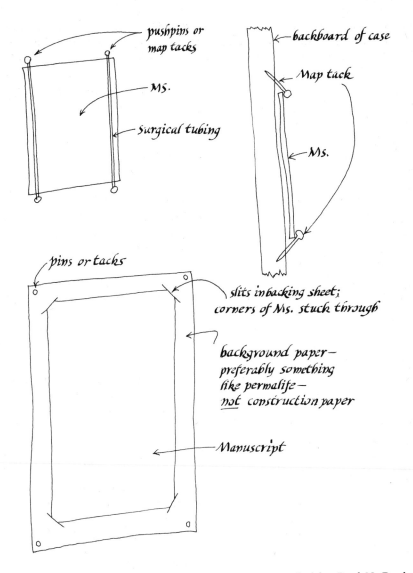

Fig. 33. Methods of displaying manuscripts recommended by Paul N. Banks.

volume open to a given page.)[8] A sheet of clear Plexiglas UF1 can
be attached over the manuscript. This covering, which can be secured
to the exhibit surface of the case, has the added advantage of screening
out harmful rays in natural or artificial light. A step-by-step plan to

assemble a similar mount using two sheets of clear cellulose acetate and a sheet of yellow Kodagraph for protection from light has been described by the director of exhibits at the National Archives. Another means of mounting would be to cut four diagonal slits in a sheet of heavy acid-free paper, slipping the corners of the manuscript into the slits and attaching the sheet to the exhibit case. One expert recommends an even simpler means of mounting with transparent photograph-mounting corners.[9]

The occasional manuscript that the curator will want to frame for exhibit should be matted with all-rag board, but this may pose a dilemma for the conscientious curator if he wants a colored mat, since most acid-free board is a neutral shade. The framed manuscript should be sealed at the back by attaching a piece of moisture-proof material, such as polyethylene, to the frame; framed documents can absorb harmful moisture from a wall, particularly when they are hung on an outside wall.[10]

An exhibit which meets all the requirements for safeguarding the manuscripts on display can still be an artistic failure. It is beyond the scope of this book to set out principles of exhibit technique and case layout, for these are professional skills in themselves. However, if the curator must prepare his own exhibits, there are books he can study to learn museum techniques.[11] He can learn a great deal about layout by studying page design in successful examples of photo-journalism such as *Life* or any one of the many expensive books of photographs published each year. Also, the curator should pay particular heed to one authority on manuscript exhibits, who says that the most basic of all exhibit techniques, upon which everything else turns, is the "selection and development of the subject," which means planning the exhibit with a unified theme or logical story line.[12]

Even without any instructions, there are a few simple things the curator can do to improve any exhibit. Manuscripts are two-dimensional and do not lend themselves readily to exhibition. Therefore, anything which adds depth to an exhibit is useful. Sometimes depth can be created by exhibiting manuscripts on different planes—for example, by constructing platforms under some manuscripts in a flat case. Photographs, which are available in most manuscript collections, add depth by making "windows" in an exhibit. The appearance of most photographs can be greatly improved by matting. The curator can take the photographs to a framing shop where they can be measured and the mats cut later. If necessary, the curator can cut his own mats; even a bevelled edge is not too difficult to master with the proper tools. Finally, the best method of adding depth to an exhibit is very obvious: display three-dimensional objects. Even a few books in a case of manuscripts helps in this regard, but memorabilia and occasional museum objects will add immeasurably to an exhibit, especially if there is a relationship between the object and a manuscript on display.

Line, balance, and emphasis may be too complex for the curator to master without assistance, but he can find a color wheel and use it in his choice of colors in the exhibit. Texture, too, can easily be introduced into an exhibit in a variety of cloth backgrounds. Sound, too, even if nothing more than appropriate "mood music," can be introduced into exhibits fairly easily and inexpensively.

Labels with a concise text and a clean design have a great impact upon the viewer and may be the major factor in producing a successful exhibit. Hand-set type labels are expensive but cannot be excelled in appearance. One way a curator can stretch a modest printing budget is to use an unbound copy of the exhibit catalog, cut up, mounted, and used as case labels, but this requires careful design planning. Typewritten labels, particularly if they can be produced on one of the machines which justifies the right hand margin, are acceptable. Electric typewriters, which smooth out the touch and give a more even density of character, make the best labels. The appearance of a typewritten label can be heightened if it is typed on a printed form, which can be designed to include the name of repository or manuscript collection, with ornamental rules at top and bottom, or any of a variety of printing devices to give the label a more finished professional appearance.

Whether exhibits are designed professionally or mounted by the curator, they involve considerable talent and expense, and any curator who has had the time and patience to watch patrons view an exhibit may be less than sanguine about preparing another. A typical viewer flits from case to case, glancing here, reading a sentence or two of a label, meanwhile talking to a companion. A more conscientious visitor may expend more concentration and time, but this type of visitor may be so infrequent as to be discouraging.

Still, exhibits are special show pieces which can be used in a variety of public-related activities. They can be the subject of press releases, and they can be offered in preview showings, or as special attractions for the institution's Friends group (see below). Featured speakers can complement exhibits and vice versa. Exhibits also can disseminate knowledge of the collection to casual visitors or to those who attend professional meetings. It is impossible to substantiate, but the curator is always hopeful that his exhibit will at least pique the interest of a visitor and perhaps lead to an enrichment of his life and society in general.

Of the benefits derived from exhibits, none have a greater long-range effect than the exhibit catalog. Well-designed and well-printed catalogs will not be inexpensive, but occasionally they can be sold, particularly if the exhibit is an intensive, in-depth treatment of a subject area. Some institutions have prepared mimeographed or other near-print catalogs. No matter how the catalog is produced and used, it will be a major—but justifiable—expense in time, if not always of funds. A catalog, if it is done carefully, can combine elements of an inventory and a published guide, and can, in some ways, serve as both to researchers and curators. Because it describes the finest items of the collection in both pictorial and written form, it is perhaps the best publicity available to the curator. An overrun of catalogs can be used in mailings to Friends groups, to prospective donors, to scholars, and to other institutions.

A supply of catalogs should not be the only evidence kept of an exhibit. Photographs should be taken of each case, and layout diagrams keyed to an exact list of items displayed should be prepared. The text of all labels should be preserved, and if the labels are printed, extra sets should be kept. From these skeletal remains, the exhibit could be reconstituted at a fraction of the original cost; and over the years, a file of past exhibits will prove most useful, especially those for small or rotating exhibits.

As noted above, some institutions sell exhibit catalogs, and some do so with considerable success. The reference librarian of the Peabody Institute, who was in charge of the exhibition of manuscripts, reported that one catalog which the library sold at $6 netted a profit of $8,000 on a printing of 2,000 copies and the edition sold out in two years. He contends that a 25 to 40 percent markup over the cost of printing a good illustrated catalog would insure breaking even.[13]

Before he begins a major publishing venture, however, the curator should consider the theories of common-law literary rights discussed earlier in this book. The courts have ruled that the act of the author exhibiting (showing) his manuscript does not constitute its publication, and the curator can extrapolate from this that the ruling might extend to public exhibit. Although he cannot be sure that he is justified in such a deduction, he *can* be sure that quoting any letter in a catalog is publication. Therefore, if he is exhibiting manuscripts of a living author, it would be wise to notify the author in advance and to give him a chance to object. (Heirs, of course, can institute infringement proceedings also, but may be less likely to do so.) If letters or other manuscripts are quoted in the catalog, the curator should seek permission.

Few institutions have the knowledge and resources to prepare traveling exhibits, either the self-contained mobile units or the study exhibits shipped to banks, schools, and similar places. Both types are expensive, but if the repository can afford this kind of exhibit and can get proper protection for the manuscripts included, there is no doubt that traveling exhibits must be top-rated, if on no other basis than the great increase in total numbers of viewers as compared with an in-house exhibit. If proper security cannot be given, original manuscripts need not be used. Careful photo-duplication will give realistic but inexpensive facsimiles. "Chalk tray" exhibits are two-dimensional poster-type exhibits which cost but a small fraction of mobile or other traveling exhibits and can be exhibited almost anywhere with good results. They usually combine photographic prints, copies of manuscripts, and text which have been dry-mounted on heavy board and are designed to be exhibited by standing them in the tray on the base of the blackboard. Curators have displayed traveling exhibits in some imaginative places, but have abandoned more obvious locations to commercial exhibitors. Examples are the "canned" identical "Heritage of America" plaques on display in many of the nation's airports.

Any exhibition program, even an imaginative one, is somewhat like the theater; because exhibits are largely intangible and transient, it is difficult to assess their effect. Publication, on the other hand, provides a more permanent medium, and it is here that most curators concentrate their public service efforts.

Microfilm Publications

Throughout the 1930s, there had been scattered use of microfilm as a medium for making manuscript sources available to persons unable to consult the originals, but perhaps the first major project was the filming of the Lyman C. Draper Papers begun by the State Historical Society of Wisconsin in 1939, with the actual filming beginning in January 1940.[14] It was the federal government, however, which firmly established the process. Beginning in 1940, the National Archives, in a continuing program, has microfilmed millions of pages of federal records, including papers of the Continental Congress. In 1957, the Library of Congress completed its filming of the papers of the presidents of the United States.[15]

Still, the acceptance of the concept of microfilm publication awaited the efforts of the National Historical Publications Commission. The NHPC, which had been created in the act establishing the National Archives in 1934, had had a "mere statutory existence" until it was reconstituted in the Federal Records Act in 1950. Originally, the commission, housed and administered by the National Archives, had concerned itself with the letter-press publications of the papers of a handful of great Americans. Then, in 1964, at the urging of the commission, Congress voted funds for grants-in-aid and the commission launched its microfilm publication program. Since this time, NHPC has made grants to thirty-three institutions which have arranged, filmed, and prepared published guides to ninety-nine microfilm publications, a total in all of 3,087 reels of microfilm. Under the terms of the grants, the co-operating institutions agree to sell "positive prints at 'reasonable cost' to any person or institution ordering them, or to honor requests for interlibrary loans." [16]

The films financed by NHPC can provide an unequalled body of manuscript source materials for any collecting agency at a fraction of what it would cost to acquire them in any other manner (even by gift), if acquisition and processing costs are included. The films have made an unquestioned contribution to scholarship, and, at the same time, have promoted the good name of the institutions which have participated. What better publicity can a manuscript repository have than to have its collections widely used and cited, and what better way to do this than through the medium of microfilm? And, of course, there is the bonus so easily overlooked: the NHPC editions insure scholarship against the effect of the loss of the original manuscripts and against undue use of the originals.

Microfilm publication has been credited by President Kennedy as a "bloodless revolution" and by Ernst Posner as a "final break with the archivist's proprietary attitude toward his records." [17] The traditional posture of archivists and manuscript curators on microfilming entire collections has been negative. It was thought that, if an institution released a microfilm copy to another institution, it might just as well relinquish the originals, because, to all intents and purposes, it had lost control over the use of the originals. This argument makes sense only if there are restrictions which the institution owning the originals is obligated to enforce. It is true that dissemination of microfilm made a mockery of the traditional picture of the traveling scholar, hat-in-hand, waiting in the curator's office for permission to use manuscripts. More often than not, however, the refusal to microfilm entire collections was based on economics and the competitive nature of manuscript collecting.[18] On the surface, it is perfectly reasonable, for example, for Utopia University, which has paid $45,000 for the Ernest Scribbler Collection and invested another $5,500 in processing and housing the collection, not to be excited about selling a microfilm of the papers to Transylvania Historical Society for about one percent of its total investment.

Reluctance to microfilm is in part rooted in another aspect of the monetary value of manuscripts. The curator today is accustomed to hearing dealers maintain that any copying diminishes the value of a manuscript, but he might be surprised to know how far back this belief has its beginnings. The keeper of manuscripts of the British Museum notes in his diary the proceedings of one of earliest known manuscript auctions at which the price realized on one lot of correspondence was low because, just as the auctioneer opened the bidding, "an agent for Bently, the bookseller, stept forward, and said that a transcript had been made of it for publication." [19] In studying the matter in 1961, one librarian noted that the market value of manuscripts of minor authors decreased with either microfilming or publication in an approved edition, but that neither form of reproduction affected the value of "sought-after" material, such as, for example, letters of Thomas Jefferson, the prices of which had been charted over three decades of sales. Several years later, another scholar surveying a group of dealers, collectors, editors, librarians, and curators came to much the same conclusion, except to modify it by noting that it applied generally only to the single unique letter or document. A collection of a person's letters would almost certainly lose value if it was published.[20]

In part, the continued hesitancy of some institutions to microfilm their collections may rest with the careless scholar who uses microfilm and neglects to cite the location of the original manuscripts. If this negligence can be overcome, if researchers can be prodded into proper citation, does not a widely distributed and used microfilm fulfill the repository's goal of public service? Perhaps the curator should begin to think of microfilm as the final step in processing and to include it in his budgeting. There are even ways to get a bonus for his dollars spent. With a little forethought, he can take advantage of requests for research microfilm to build his institution's collection. Since most institutions retain the negative of these films, it is worthwhile to prepare the materials carefully, to provide the proper targets and roll notes, and to have a duplicate negative and positive printed (see chapter 5 on microfilming). The resultant microfilm edition then can be sold, as well as used internally.

There are drawbacks, however. Despite NHPC's demonstration that, although many repositories do not hold that "control" of their collection is essential, some still might be reluctant to undertake projects simply because the set of papers must be closed to research during the preparation of the microfilm. Furthermore, with increasing pressure to get papers processed more rapidly and with mounting backlogs of unprocessed manuscripts, the curator may not see how it is possible to prepare microfilm for general distribution.

If, on the other hand, he is determined to press for a microfilm copy of a given set of papers and he needs outside funding, how does he proceed? Assuming that the papers are important documentation for a phase of United States history (and their author has been dead for fifty years), the curator should make application to the National Historical Publications Commission for a grant to prepare the microfilm. This can be done by writing to the Director, National Historical Publications Commission, National Archives, Room 100, Washington, D.C. 20408.

Microfilm publication is changing the face of scholarship, but the academic public is less than completely satisfied with the service. Some of the most commonly voiced complaints are that the readers are hard to use and often out of repair. Many persons using microfilm continue to report eyestrain, although the few scientific studies done seem to indicate the strain is psychological and not physical. Of the same nature is the complaint that using microfilm denies the scholar "the feel of the papers or the sense of the run of the material." Also, if the scholar suspects that letters were wrongly attributed or dated in processing, he will have a great deal of difficulty making a final determination from the film. Finally, reader-printers are being improved, but users find that many of the prints, particularly those made from negative microfilm, are very hard to read.[21]

Microfilm, of course, is but one segment of an active publications program which may include a collections guide, inventories series, descriptive leaflets and brochures, exhibit catalogs (discussed earlier in this chapter), and Friends magazines.

Publications

A favorite topic at professional meetings and an accepted corollary of good curatorship is the prime importance of a published guide to the manuscripts held by the collecting agency. Most curators feel that entries to the *National Union Catalog of Manuscript Collections (NUCMC)* are most desirable, second only to the general guide, and in some institutions forms have been devised to allow a single description to serve both ends.

Some curators question the need for the general guide, with the volumes of NUCMC available in most libraries. Although many of the entries are duplicated, advocates of the general guide say its chief attribute is that it contains descriptions of material excluded from NUCMC, primarily the collection of fewer than fifty pieces. It is this inclusion of small collections and single manuscripts, often described in as great detail as multibox collections, which makes for an imbalance in some guides.[22] It almost seems as if the compilers of the guides are padding out. In some instances, this is probably true; institutions have issued guides to collections that might better have been described in a series of inventories. Publishing inventories, particularly those with the fairly detailed narrative introduction, seems to be the pattern of two types of collecting agencies at opposite ends of the spectrum. The new collecting agency, trying very hard to establish a reputation, will invest a good deal of time and capital in producing handsome inventories of their first major accessions. The wealthy well-established collecting agencies have published inventories also, sometimes with funds donated for that purpose. Inventories are expensive to prepare and to publish. Their usefulness to scholars will be limited, but as a promotional device they are excellent.[23]

In 1969, FAUL (Five Associated University Libraries: Binghamton, Buffalo, Cornell, Rochester, and Syracuse) experimented with a regional approach to publishing guides with a listing of selected manuscripts in approximately thirty subject areas. The guide, which contains more than seven hundred descriptive entries, was intended as a reference tool for faculty and students, graduate and undergraduate. It was inexpensively produced from typewritten copy and stapled into a printed cover.[24]

Descriptive brochures or leaflets describing large or important collections are used to help publicize the institution to Friends groups and potential donors. They can be mailed to other libraries, used to answer inquiries by letter, and handed out to visitors. Another type of brochure or leaflet distributed in the same fashion contains a general description of the entire collection, and occasionally an institution will publicize a special program in a similar way. A good example of this is the handsome bibliography of the oral history program at the University of California, Los Angeles, or the catalog of the John Foster Dulles oral history collection at Princeton.[25]

Readers' guides are less common than collection guides. They may be inexpensively printed, as is the one prepared by the Spencer Library at the University of Kansas (eight pages of photo-offset from typewritten copy), or they may be more elaborately produced, as is the illustrated twenty-seven-page pamphlet issued by the Huntington Library. Over the years, many repositories have developed regulations and procedures which may exist in a variety of mimeographed sheets. These could be gathered into a printed booklet at a reasonable expense.[26]

Information circulars are publications which save a great deal of correspondence time. If the same reference questions keep reappearing in the mail, the curator should give thought to developing such a series. At the North Carolina Department of Archives and History, for example, circulars have been written on geneaological research, Civil War records, Revolutionary War pay records, census records, and other topics.[27]

Reprints or offprints of periodical articles, especially those with an added printed cover, often can be acquired at a very reasonable price and are valuable to distribute to Friends and others interested in the collection. Curators may find that they have limited access to publications other than those prepared by their institutions, but those who are in charge of university or college collections have a receptive publisher in their alumni magazine.[28]

One authority says that the annual report usually receives less attention with regard to appearance than any other repository publication. This summary of the year's events, prepared as an official account by the administrator to the governing body can make an attractive printed item, however, as can be seen from the Huntington Library annual report, for example, or that of the Western Reserve Historical Society. Typical contents of annual reports include lists of staff and the governing body, financial reports including a statement of cash receipts and disbursements, lists of donors, and selected acquisitions. Occasionally, repositories issue some of these lists and reports as separate publications, as, for example, the description of selected acquisitions produced by the University of Toronto, Rare Books Department.[29]

Several of the types of publications discussed above may be distributed to Friends groups, but many institutions publish periodicals specifically for their Friends. Among those that have been published for years are the *Princeton University Library Chronicle, Columbia Library Columns,* and *The Library Chronicle of the University of Pennsylvania.* More recently, other institutions, including Yale, Cornell, Duke, the Newberry Library, and the University of Miami have begun regular publication of a Friends periodical.[30]

Opinion about the usefulness and desirability of publishing a periodical for the Friends group seems to vary with experience, but one factor does seem to be agreed upon: It takes a great deal of time to sustain regular publications. In theory, this kind of publication offers the best possible exposure for the collecting agency, since it will contain articles based upon the collection, accessions information, donor lists, and perhaps even staff news. Experience seems to indicate that the most successful Friends publications have been those that have established reputations as scholarly journals, which is in a sense a contradiction. Curators should not expect to achieve this kind of production with part-time effort, and even if articles are available and he or someone on his staff has sufficient editorial and graphic skills to prepare the journal, it will be costly and time-consuming.[31]

Excluding the scholarly articles, everything that can be accomplished with the Friends publication can be done with the annual report. Much depends on the narrative skill of the curator, but even processing statistics and bold lists of users and their topics can be impressive, and a must, of course, is a list (there seems to be no other way to do it) of donors of money and gifts in kind.

Whatever the kind of publication the curator may contemplate, a few practical suggestions should be kept in mind. It is economically wise to size a publication so that it will fit into one of the standard-stock mailing envelopes, or to design it with a self-mailing cover. Two-color printing increases costs, and sometimes similar effects can be achieved by using screens (which shade the ink) and colored paper printing stock.[32]

Every job that goes to the printer must contain a layout (a sheet or pattern of the type and artwork) and specifications, which include directions about typeface, type size, whether type should be caps, small caps, etc.[33] If the curator is fortunate, he will have a designer to whom he can turn for assistance, but he may be forced to learn to prepare layouts and specifications for himself. Many fine books exist which will help the curator to select paper stock and type faces and solve other problems needing this special expertise. Other books will teach him to measure type and space by points and picas, to scale pictures, and to employ a consistent style. Even if he has the services of a designer, the curator will get more for his printing dollar by studying the various handbooks referred to in the notes to this chapter. Some of them, if not available at the library, would be expensive to purchase, but one, *Pocket Pal,* published by the International Paper Company, is sold by the company for only a dollar. It would be a dollar very wisely invested for any manuscript-collection publishing program.

Friends Organizations

Implicit in the remarks on publications is one of the weaknesses of a Friends group: to attract and keep members, the curator must offer something in return for the membership fee; and more often than not, this takes the form of a publication, even if it is but a simple newsletter. Ironically, the institutions which seem to need friends least are those to which Friends seem to flock. But even at the eminent private universities with large endowments, Friends groups do not run themselves. All of them draw upon volunteers from within their ranks, but each needs the direction of a paid officer or staff member. For some institutions, this is time and effort well spent; the return is evident in gifts and goodwill [34] (see chapter on administration for discussion of Friends as benefactors). For others, it seems an exercise in futility. The curator who must spread his and his staff's time thin ought perhaps to look realistically at the return from his institution's Friends. At times, he may find it difficult to remember that the Friends provide him with what are probably his best opportunities to serve the public and in turn be served by it. He is likely to be especially forgetful of these facts when, as one curator notes, a Friends member attempts to "use his position to promote his own prestige, to secure special privileges for himself, or even to serve his own private collecting interests." The curator says that much more common, although not so drastic as any of the above, is Friends' meddlesomeness, which, though it may do little harm, can cause extra work and wasted time by the curator who must listen and "keep them contented." [35]

If Friends' activities are largely social, as sometimes they are, the curator may feel he would be better off devoting his time to individual donors. Guiding Friends' chartered flights to Europe may be a pleasant way to spend the summer, but will it mean any significant growth in the collection? The gala masquerade (Come dressed as your favorite character from fiction) may be loads of fun (and a lot of work for someone), but did anything come of it? It behooves the curator to try, at the very least, to keep the Friends oriented upon manuscripts and their ultimate use—dissemination of knowledge—usually in the form of publications. If the curator cannot get his institution's Friends to view an exhibit unless he lures them with a cocktail party, perhaps their interest is more social than scholarly. This is not to say that the scholarly and social cannot be intermingled—the members' "teas" are an institution among many Friends—and this mixture is perhaps best exemplified at professional meetings.

Professional Meetings

It is one of the sad facts of life that there is no professional organization for curators of manuscripts, *per se,* although several organizations admit or seek curators as members (see appendix; Directory). The Society of American Archivists in recent years has moved to a much more accommodating position, especially since university archivists—who, since World War II, make up the most rapidly growing segment of the organization—are oftentimes also responsible for manuscript collecting on their campuses. As university archivists began to solicit papers of faculty, then alumni, then regional history, the emphasis changed. With these accumulations of personal papers, the archivists know they must look to the curators for guidance. Another factor in the change was the acquisitions policies of the National Archives after the establishment of the presidential libraries. Prior to this time, the official posture of the government archivist was a passive one; he received records created by official agencies of the government. Now, he too, like the university archivist, was actively collecting personal papers. Articles in *The American Archivist,* the SAA committee structure, and the content of annual meetings all reflect this new concern with manuscripts. To all intents and purposes, the SAA is now the professional organization for all curators of manuscripts, keepers of manuscripts, and manuscript librarians who do not mind being called archivists.

Professional meetings as an educational medium have been discussed in chapter two of this book, but these meetings also fulfill a public-service function. Participating in sessions and workshops will enable the curator to alert other members of his profession to his programs and to the distinctive features of the manuscript collection. Few institutions have the facilities to sponsor a national meeting, but serving as host to a regional or area meeting is within the capability of many repositories. Co-sponsorship of smaller meetings of allied professions—librarians or subject area specialists—provides the curator with excellent opportunities to make others familiar with the holdings through programs, exhibits, and tours.

Miscellaneous Public Services

Tours are, of course, a fine means of combining public relations with public service. The curator's difficulty comes in deciding how much time can be given to them. No matter how they are arranged, tours are time-consuming and unsettling to staff routines. One authority has suggested that they not be conducted if they are a great annoyance to regular researchers.[36]

On somewhat the same level with the tour and probably the curator's least-recognized aspect of public relations, is his obligation to "visiting firemen" and their close relation, the ever-present questionnaire. Ordinarily, curators have been over-generous with their time for both, but this may be because they recognize that their profession is largely self-taught. There must be, however, some system of priorities, particularly with questionnaires. Unfortunately, even some of those which the curator recognizes as having great potential impact in his field must be passed over. In looking at a questionnaire, he might see that, if he is conscientious, it will take him several hours to complete the form, and he may be further disheartened by the realization that many of the statistics will be meaningless without considerable explanation of his individual situation.

Some curators are called upon for similar public services. Often they will be asked to serve in counseling or advisory roles. A curator responds to these requests willingly, even at the sacrifice of personal time, provided he sees no ethical conflict. When he is called upon to act in a formal capacity as consultant, the curator is justified in asking for a fee. In these instances, each institution may have its own policy regarding staff members accepting consulting assignments, but whatever the regulations are, ethically the curator cannot accept a fee unless he performs the service on his own and not on the institution's time.

Most of the public-service functions discussed in this chapter are used by the curator in an effort to foster good public relations. Other aspects of dealing with the public are even more consciously directed toward public relations, and preparing press releases is the best example.

Public Relations

It is sometimes difficult to determine whether the press release announcing a manuscript acquisition is intended to serve its nominal function or to enhance the reputation of the curator. The self-serving nature of some releases is difficult to deny, and even the motive behind the lists of acquisitions which appear in *Manuscripts* and *The American Archivist* and other journals could be questioned. The curator's desire to disseminate information and the need for ego reinforcement are often inextricably intertwined.

Yet, apart from this cynical view, press releases do fill a distinct need in the scholarly community by announcing the availability of research resources which might not be noted otherwise until far into the future. For the student whose dissertation is due in six months, they can be crucial news. The curator knows, too, that although the effect of a press release is intangible and difficult to measure, the climate of opinion it can create for potential donors is beneficial. In the conversations between the field man and a donor, it may come to the fore that the donor first considered giving his collection to the Transylvania Historical Society when he read about its acquisition of the Dancelotsky papers. When the potential donor himself is publicity conscious, the press release, dangled by the curator in front of his eyes, may be enough to turn the tide to Transylvania. Finally, though its use has made it almost a cliché, the press release affords the curator the opportunity to keep his administrative fences well mended: "The director of the Transylvania Historical Society today announced. . . ."

Of course, press releases need not be confined to announcing acquisitions. Exhibits, Friends' functions, and interviews with distinguished visiting scholars are all valid subjects for a release. Newspapers usually welcome stories about manuscripts that have a timely flavor. The curator may be hard pressed to find a Lincoln item that the editor will consider newsworthy (what can be added to the Lincoln legend?), but he should remember that national holidays provide him with natural pegs upon which to hang news releases relating to the institution's manuscript collection. He should also be on the watch for manuscripts in the collection that have modern parallels that are faddish or very much in the news. These may seem trivial pursuits and the curator may choose to ignore them all, but he should remember that any collection is a feature story in itself.

The curator must decide how much time he can devote to public relations and how many tangible results he expects. For example, if his personality and talent incline him so, he could spend a great deal of time speaking before various groups. His opportunities to speak on the "banquet circuit" will be numerous. Some manuscript librarians feel that speaking to "school groups, service clubs, women's organizations, and similar gatherings provides an opportunity to enlarge the public's knowledge of the library, to emphasize the importance of the archival profession, and to describe the library's service to society." [37]

Nor will the curator need to confine his speaking to the banquet circuit. The guided tour of the manuscript collection will be attractive alike to the ladies' auxiliary and to youngsters on their spring break, and only rarely is the curator able to discern a connection between a speech he has made and a lead to a fine collection or some other tangible benefit to his institution. Most often he must be content with creating good will and performing a public service.

Whether the curator makes two or twenty speeches a year, he would be wise to plan a carefully thought-out, well-written presentation. He might want to earmark a few manuscripts in the collection that could be taken with him when he makes a speech, but they would have to be dispensable because of the risks. A few rare, beautiful, or in some way especially noteworthy manuscripts ought to be handsomely cased as "showcase" items for presentations in the institutions. A slide show, of course, is equally applicable to speeches at or away from the repository.

Radio and television give the curator the opportunity to reach a much larger audience with the same amount of effort. Almost any station has a local interview or "talk show," especially on cable television, and most of them are constantly searching for persons to interview. Educational and cable television have increased the avenues of exposure available to the curator, but he should recognize that, on these programs, he is pretty much at the mercy of the interviewer and producer. He may have relatively little control over the content of his segment of the program and even less in the choice of his fellow participants. Occasionally, the curator will be fortunate enough to be given something longer than a five- or ten-minute spot to develop a meaningful presentation of his institution's program, and this will be his single best public relations exposure.

The public-service aspects of manuscript curatorship are varied and increasing. The day of the curator as a scholarly hermit is past.

Today's curator must possess businesslike and administrative qualities and yet be able to deal empathetically with people as donors or perhaps oral history interviewees. He must have some technical skills in as diverse fields as the chemistry of paper and electronic computers. He must have an intuitive sense of the research needs of scholars, present and future. A knowledge of some phases of law and a strong sense of personal ethics will stand him in good stead. It is hoped that this book will help him to achieve some of these goals and give the curator and those with whom he interacts a better understanding of the complex field of modern manuscripts.

SELECTED READINGS

Indispensible to any beginning microfilm publication program would be Allen Veaner's small pamphlet, *Evaluation of Micropublications.* The Felix Reichmann and Josephine Tharpe study is useful especially for the appended guide to archival and manuscript collections on microfilm. The best over-all exposition of the program of the National Historical Publications Commission can be found in the report of the hearing on H. R. 15763, which contains Dr. James Rhoads's testimony before a congressional subcommittee.

Very little has been written on the theory or technique of exhibiting manuscripts. The best but limited sources are three papers delivered at a library meeting and later published in *The AB 1968 Bookman's Yearbook:* P. William Filby, "Techniques of Exhibitions"; Dorothy Bowen, "Techniques of Book and Manuscript Display"; and Jean Tuckerman, "Techniques of Exhibition."

The best general survey of a publication program is Hannah French, "Access, Service, and Publication." Edmund Arnold, *Ink on Paper 2: A Handbook of the Graphic Arts,* and Marshall Lee, *Bookmaking: The Illustrated Guide to Design & Production* are excellent and contain many practical suggestions for the beginning publisher. *The Pocket Pal* is a "best buy." Marjorie Skillin and Robert Gay, *Words into Type: A Guide in the Preparation of Manuscripts; For Writers, Editors, Proofreaders and Printers,* and *A Manual of Style . . . Together with Specimens of Type* are indispensable for either author or publisher. In the latter, the eleventh edition of the famed Chicago manual, unlike the subsequent edition, contains a most useful section of about 260 pages of type styles.

The various functions of Friends groups are best described in Frances Brewer, "Friends of the Library," and a more extended treatment can be found in the volume edited by Sara Wallace, *Friends of the Library.* The public-relations aspects of the curator's role are best outlined in Ruth Bordin and Robert Warner in their chapter, "The Library and the General Public" in the book *The Modern Manuscript Library.*

Appendix 1

*Drawings of plans
for records center carton and
flat-storage manuscript box*

The specifications and drawings for these containers may seem unintelligible to the curator, but they should be easily understood by a local box manufacturer. The records center carton is made of corrugated cardboard and is designed not to need staples or paper tape. The flat-storage manuscript box, also of corrugated cardboard, is stapled at the corners.

SPECIFICATIONS, RECORDS CENTER CARTON 15 x 12 x 10 Two-Piece
Body and Cover 200 #

Die-Cut Two-Piece Telescope Case
Body—56½'' - 32¼''
    score across 10 1/16'' - ¼'' - 10'' - 15⅞'' - 10'' - ¼'' - 10 1/16''
    score with 10'' - 12¼'' - 10''
    MAKE SURE FLAPS MEET

Cover—28⅜'' - 18''
    score across 2 13/16'' - ¼'' - 2 13/16'' - 16 ⅝'' - 2 13/16'' - ¼'' - 2 13/16''
    score with 2¾'' - 12½'' - 2¾''
    SLOT FROM ENDS
    SLOT TO OUTSIDE OF SCORES
    DIE-CUT AS SHOWN

Plain

Body Blank Size—57'' x 32¾'' Cuts 1 out
    Corr. 57'' way
Cover Blank Size—28⅞'' - 18½'' Cuts 1 out
    Corr. 28⅞'' way

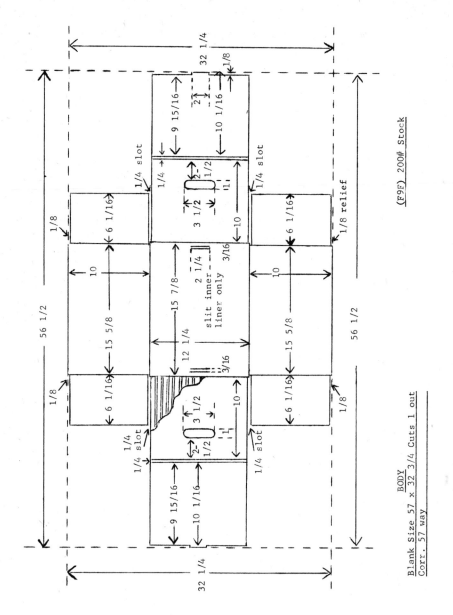

FIG. 1. RECORDS CENTER CARTON
Drawing for making body of records center carton.
Specifications for both body and cover of carton are on preceding page.

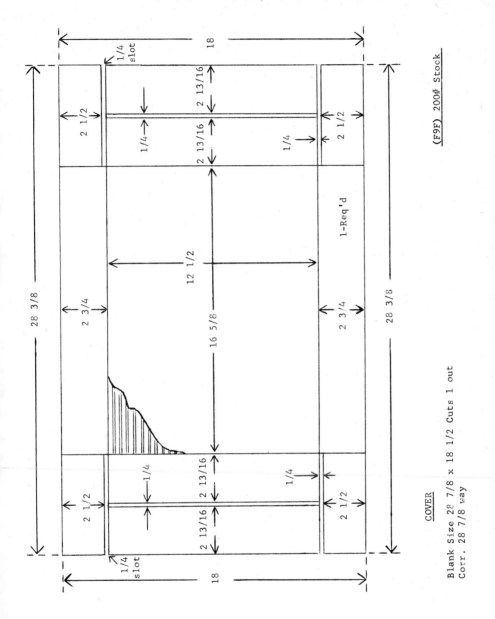

FIG. 2. RECORDS CENTER CARTON
Drawing for making cover of records center carton.

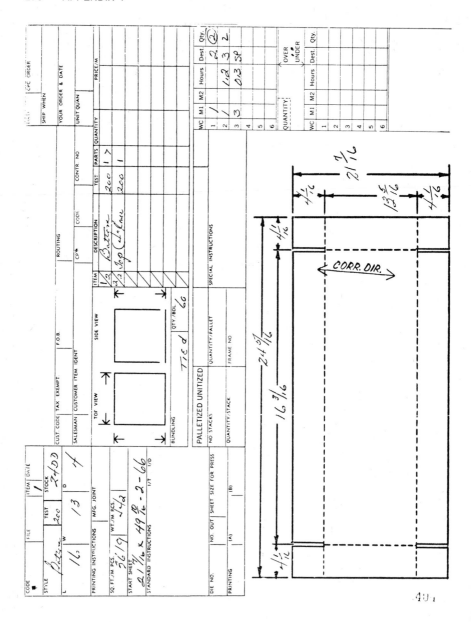

FIG. 1. FLAT-STORAGE MANUSCRIPT BOX

Specifications and drawings for making bottom of flat-storage manuscript box.

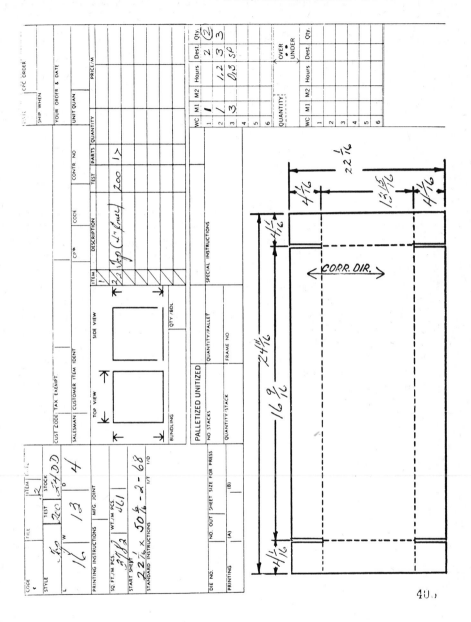

FIG. 2. FLAT-STORAGE MANUSCRIPT BOX

Specifications and drawings for making top of flat-storage manuscript box.

Appendix 2

Table of Equivalents

The idea for this table came from Elsie Freivogel, who suggested that beginning curators, faced for the first time with estimating the contents of a roll of microfilm (or the institution's holdings!) would appreciate some help. The author, having accumulated a few "equivalents" of his own, thought it was a good idea, and assumed he could easily gather others from his colleagues. As it developed, his colleagues offered only the same worn handful he already had in his own bag of tricks. Thus, the counts, weights, and measurements in this table were compiled over the period of one summer in Special Collections, Southern Illinois University. They are offered only as guides, and it is hoped that they will be used with prudence.

All measurements are of interior dimensions. Page counts were made in twentieth-century correspondence files of the university. Weights are based upon similar materials.

Manuscripts

Cubic Volume

Records center carton	15 x 12 x 10	1.0	cubic foot
Hollinger box, letter size	12 x 5 x 10	.35	" "
Hollinger box, legal size	15 x 5 x 10	.45	" "
Manuscript box	15 x 3 x 10	.25	" "
Transfer carton, letter size	24 x 12 x 10	1.6	" feet
File drawer, letter size	26 x 12 x 10	1.8	" "
File drawer, legal size	26 x 15 x 10	2.25	" "

Page Count

Records center carton	2,800 to 3,000 pp.
Hollinger box, letter size	750 pp.
Hollinger box, legal size	750 pp.
Manuscript box	550 pp.
Transfer carton, letter size	4,300 pp.
File drawer, letter size	4,600 pp.
File drawer, legal size	4,600 pp.

Weight

Records center carton	30 lbs.
Hollinger box, letter size	9 to 10 lbs.
Hollinger box, legal size	11 to 13 lbs.
Manuscript box	6 to 7 lbs.
Transfer carton, letter size	50 lbs.
File drawer, letter size	est. 50 to 52 lbs.
File drawer, legal size	est. 65 to 75 lbs.

[One authority estimates records at 40 lbs. per running foot, with a shelf = 1 cwt. (hundred weight). (See Hodson, *Administration of Archives*, p. 115.)]

Tape

Reel, 7 in., 1,200 ft. (1 mil thickness)	Sp. 7½	½ hr. per side
Reel, 7 in., 1,200 ft. (1 mil thickness)	Sp. 3¾	1 hr. per side
Reel, 7 in., 1,200 ft. (1 mil thickness)	Sp. 1⅞	2 hrs. per side
Reel, 5 in., 900 ft. (1 mil thickness)	Sp. 3¾	45 min. per side
Cassette, C-60		30 min. per side
Cassette, C-90		45 min. per side
Cassette, C-120		1 hr. per side

Microfilm

Reduction Ratio	Copy measurements in inches
10:1	17.5 x 12.5
12:1	21 x 15
14:1	24.5 x 17.5
16:1	28 x 20

35 mm nonperforated, 9.3 to 12 frames per ft., 85 ft. of text plus targets on average 100 ft. roll.

Appendix 3

Perpetual Calendar

The calendar begins with 1753, the first full year following the adoption by the British government of the Gregorian calendar, known as New Style.

The number opposite the year in the table of years shows which of the calendar pages is to be used for that year. A dot following the year date denotes a leap year.

TABLE OF YEARS

1753 2	1795 5	1837 1	1879 4	1921 7	1963 3
1754 3	1796.13	1838 2	1880.12	1922 1	1964.11
1755 4	1797 1	1839 3	1881 7	1923 2	1965 6
1756.12	1798 2	1840.11	1882 1	1924.10	1966 7
1757 7	1799 3	1841 6	1883 2	1925 5	1967 1
1758 1	1800 4	1842 7	1884.10	1926 6	1968. 9
1759 2	1801 5	1843 1	1885 5	1927 7	1969 4
1760.10	1802 6	1844. 9	1886 6	1928. 8	1970 5
1761 5	1803 7	1845 4	1887 7	1929 3	1971 6
1762 6	1804. 8	1846 5	1888. 8	1930 4	1972.14
1763 7	1805 3	1847 6	1889 3	1931 5	1973 2
1764. 8	1806 4	1848.14	1890 4	1932.13	1974 3
1765 3	1807 5	1849 2	1891 5	1933 1	1975 4
1766 4	1808.13	1850 3	1892.13	1934 2	1976.12
1767 5	1809 1	1851 4	1893 1	1935 3	1977 7
1768.13	1810 2	1852.12	1894 2	1936.11	1978 1
1769 1	1811 3	1853 7	1895 3	1937 6	1979 2
1770 2	1812.11	1854 1	1896.11	1938 7	1980.10
1771 3	1813 6	1855 2	1897 6	1939 1	1981 5
1772.11	1814 7	1856.10	1898 7	1940. 9	1982 6
1773 6	1815 1	1857 5	1899 1	1941 4	1983 7
1774 7	1816. 9	1858 6	1900. 2	1942 5	1984. 8
1775 1	1817 4	1859 7	1901 3	1943 6	1985 3
1776. 9	1818 5	1860. 8	1902 4	1944.14	1986 4
1777 4	1819 6	1861 3	1903 5	1945 2	1987 5
1778 5	1820.14	1862 4	1904.13	1946 3	1988.13
1779 6	1821 2	1863 5	1905 1	1947 4	1989 1
1780.14	1822 3	1864.13	1906 2	1948.12	1990 2
1781 2	1823 4	1865 1	1907 3	1949 7	1991 3
1782 3	1824.12	1866 2	1908.11	1950 1	1992.11
1783 4	1825 7	1867 3	1909 6	1951 2	1993 6
1784.12	1826 1	1868.11	1910 7	1952.10	1994 7
1785 7	1827 2	1869 6	1911 1	1953 5	1995 1
1786 1	1828.10	1870 7	1912. 9	1954 6	1996. 9
1787 2	1829 5	1871 1	1913 4	1955 7	1997 4
1788.10	1830 6	1872. 9	1914 5	1956. 8	1998 5
1789 5	1831 7	1873 4	1915 6	1957 3	1999 6
1790 6	1832. 8	1874 5	1916.14	1958 4	2000.14
1791 7	1833 3	1875 6	1917 2	1959 5	2001 2
1792. 8	1834 4	1876.14	1918 3	1960.13	2002 3
1793 3	1835 5	1877 2	1919 4	1961 1	
1794 4	1836.13	1878 3	1920.12	1962 2	

CALENDAR NO. 1

	Jan.	Feb.	Mar.	Apr.	May	June	July	Aug.	Sept.	Oct.	Nov.	Dec.
SUN.	1	—	—	—	—	—	—	—	—	1	—	—
MON.	2	—	—	—	1	—	—	—	—	2	—	—
TUES.	3	—	—	—	2	—	—	1	—	3	—	—
WED.	4	1	1	—	3	—	—	2	—	4	1	—
THUR.	5	2	2	—	4	1	—	3	—	5	2	—
FRI.	6	3	3	—	5	2	—	4	1	6	3	1
SAT.	7	4	4	1	6	3	1	5	2	7	4	2
SUN.	8	5	5	2	7	4	2	6	3	8	5	3
MON.	9	6	6	3	8	5	3	7	4	9	6	4
TUES.	10	7	7	4	9	6	4	8	5	10	7	5
WED.	11	8	8	5	10	7	5	9	6	11	8	6
THUR.	12	9	9	6	11	8	6	10	7	12	9	7
FRI.	13	10	10	7	12	9	7	11	8	13	10	8
SAT.	14	11	11	8	13	10	8	12	9	14	11	9
SUN.	15	12	12	9	14	11	9	13	10	15	12	10
MON.	16	13	13	10	15	12	10	14	11	16	13	11
TUES.	17	14	14	11	16	13	11	15	12	17	14	12
WED.	18	15	15	12	17	14	12	16	13	18	15	13
THUR.	19	16	16	13	18	15	13	17	14	19	16	14
FRI.	20	17	17	14	19	16	14	18	15	20	17	15
SAT.	21	18	18	15	20	17	15	19	16	21	18	16
SUN.	22	19	19	16	21	18	16	20	17	22	19	17
MON.	23	20	20	17	22	19	17	21	18	23	20	18
TUES.	24	21	21	18	23	20	18	22	19	24	21	19
WED.	25	22	22	19	24	21	19	23	20	25	22	20
THUR.	26	23	23	20	25	22	20	24	21	26	23	21
FRI.	27	24	24	21	26	23	21	25	22	27	24	22
SAT.	28	25	25	22	27	24	22	26	23	28	25	23
SUN.	29	26	26	23	28	25	23	27	24	29	26	24
MON.	30	27	27	24	29	26	24	28	25	30	27	25
TUES.	31	28	28	25	30	27	25	29	26	31	28	26
WED.	—	—	29	26	31	28	26	30	27	—	29	27
THUR.	—	—	30	27	—	29	27	31	28	—	30	28
FRI.	—	—	31	28	—	30	28	—	29	—	—	29
SAT.	—	—	—	29	—	—	29	—	30	—	—	30
SUN.	—	—	—	30	—	—	30	—	—	—	—	31
MON.	—	—	—	—	—	—	31	—	—	—	—	—

CALENDAR NO. 2

	Jan.	Feb.	Mar.	Apr.	May	June	July	Aug.	Sept.	Oct.	Nov.	Dec.
SUN.	—	—	—	1	—	—	1	—	—	—	—	—
MON.	1	—	—	2	—	—	2	—	—	1	—	—
TUES.	2	—	—	3	1	—	3	—	—	2	—	—
WED.	3	—	—	4	2	—	4	1	—	3	—	—
THUR.	4	1	1	5	3	—	5	2	—	4	1	—
FRI.	5	2	2	6	4	1	6	3	—	5	2	—
SAT.	6	3	3	7	5	2	7	4	1	6	3	1
SUN.	7	4	4	8	6	3	8	5	2	7	4	2
MON.	8	5	5	9	7	4	9	6	3	8	5	3
TUES.	9	6	6	10	8	5	10	7	4	9	6	4
WED.	10	7	7	11	9	6	11	8	5	10	7	5
THUR.	11	8	8	12	10	7	12	9	6	11	8	6
FRI.	12	9	9	13	11	8	13	10	7	12	9	7
SAT.	13	10	10	14	12	9	14	11	8	13	10	8
SUN.	14	11	11	15	13	10	15	12	9	14	11	9
MON.	15	12	12	16	14	11	16	13	10	15	12	10
TUES.	16	13	13	17	15	12	17	14	11	16	13	11
WED.	17	14	14	18	16	13	18	15	12	17	14	12
THUR.	18	15	15	19	17	14	19	16	13	18	15	13
FRI.	19	16	16	20	18	15	20	17	14	19	16	14
SAT.	20	17	17	21	19	16	21	18	15	20	17	15
SUN.	21	18	18	22	20	17	22	19	16	21	18	16
MON.	22	19	19	23	21	18	23	20	17	22	19	17
TUES.	23	20	20	24	22	19	24	21	18	23	20	18
WED.	24	21	21	25	23	20	25	22	19	24	21	19
THUR.	25	22	22	26	24	21	26	23	20	25	22	20
FRI.	26	23	23	27	25	22	27	24	21	26	23	21
SAT.	27	24	24	28	26	23	28	25	22	27	24	22
SUN.	28	25	25	29	27	24	29	26	23	28	25	23
MON.	29	26	26	30	28	25	30	27	24	29	26	24
TUES.	30	27	27	—	29	26	31	28	25	30	27	25
WED.	31	28	28	—	30	27	—	29	26	31	28	26
THUR.	—	—	29	—	31	28	—	30	27	—	29	27
FRI.	—	—	30	—	—	29	—	31	28	—	30	28
SAT.	—	—	31	—	—	30	—	—	29	—	—	29
SUN.	—	—	—	—	—	—	—	—	30	—	—	30
MON.	—	—	—	—	—	—	—	—	—	—	—	31

CALENDAR NO. 3

	Jan.	Feb.	Mar.	Apr.	May	June	July	Aug.	Sept.	Oct.	Nov.	Dec.
SUN.	—	—	—	—	—	—	—	—	1	—	—	1
MON.	—	—	—	1	—	—	1	—	2	—	—	2
TUES.	1	—	—	2	—	—	2	—	3	1	—	3
WED.	2	—	—	3	1	—	3	—	4	2	—	4
THUR.	3	—	—	4	2	—	4	1	5	3	—	5
FRI.	4	1	1	5	3	—	5	2	6	4	1	6
SAT.	5	2	2	6	4	1	6	3	7	5	2	7
SUN.	6	3	3	7	5	2	7	4	8	6	3	8
MON.	7	4	4	8	6	3	8	5	9	7	4	9
TUES.	8	5	5	9	7	4	9	6	10	8	5	10
WED.	9	6	6	10	8	5	10	7	11	9	6	11
THUR.	10	7	7	11	9	6	11	8	12	10	7	12
FRI.	11	8	8	12	10	7	12	9	13	11	8	13
SAT.	12	9	9	13	11	8	13	10	14	12	9	14
SUN.	13	10	10	14	12	9	14	11	15	13	10	15
MON.	14	11	11	15	13	10	15	12	16	14	11	16
TUES.	15	12	12	16	14	11	16	13	17	15	12	17
WED.	16	13	13	17	15	12	17	14	18	16	13	18
THUR.	17	14	14	18	16	13	18	15	19	17	14	19
FRI.	18	15	15	19	17	14	19	16	20	18	15	20
SAT.	19	16	16	20	18	15	20	17	21	19	16	21
SUN.	20	17	17	21	19	16	21	18	22	20	17	22
MON.	21	18	18	22	20	17	22	19	23	21	18	23
TUES.	22	19	19	23	21	18	23	20	24	22	19	24
WED.	23	20	20	24	22	19	24	21	25	23	20	25
THUR.	24	21	21	25	23	20	25	22	26	24	21	26
FRI.	25	22	22	26	24	21	26	23	27	25	22	27
SAT.	26	23	23	27	25	22	27	24	28	26	23	28
SUN.	27	24	24	28	26	23	28	25	29	27	24	29
MON.	28	25	25	29	27	24	29	26	30	28	25	30
TUES.	29	26	26	30	28	25	30	27	—	29	26	31
WED.	30	27	27	—	29	26	31	28	—	30	27	—
THUR.	31	28	28	—	30	27	—	29	—	31	28	—
FRI.	—	—	29	—	31	28	—	30	—	—	29	—
SAT.	—	—	30	—	—	29	—	31	—	—	30	—
SUN.	—	—	31	—	—	30	—	—	—	—	—	—
MON.	—	—	—	—	—	—	—	—	—	—	—	—

CALENDAR NO. 4

	Jan.	Feb.	Mar.	Apr.	May	June	July	Aug.	Sept.	Oct.	Nov.	Dec.
SUN.	—	—	—	—	—	1	—	—	—	—	—	—
MON.	—	—	—	—	—	2	—	—	1	—	—	1
TUES.	—	—	—	1	—	3	1	—	2	—	—	2
WED.	1	—	—	2	—	4	2	—	3	1	—	3
THUR.	2	—	—	3	1	5	3	—	4	2	—	4
FRI.	3	—	—	4	2	6	4	1	5	3	—	5
SAT.	4	1	1	5	3	7	5	2	6	4	1	6
SUN.	5	2	2	6	4	8	6	3	7	5	2	7
MON.	6	3	3	7	5	9	7	4	8	6	3	8
TUES.	7	4	4	8	6	10	8	5	9	7	4	9
WED.	8	5	5	9	7	11	9	6	10	8	5	10
THUR.	9	6	6	10	8	12	10	7	11	9	6	11
FRI.	10	7	7	11	9	13	11	8	12	10	7	12
SAT.	11	8	8	12	10	14	12	9	13	11	8	13
SUN.	12	9	9	13	11	15	13	10	14	12	9	14
MON.	13	10	10	14	12	16	14	11	15	13	10	15
TUES.	14	11	11	15	13	17	15	12	16	14	11	16
WED.	15	12	12	16	14	18	16	13	17	15	12	17
THUR.	16	13	13	17	15	19	17	14	18	16	13	18
FRI.	17	14	14	18	16	20	18	15	19	17	14	19
SAT.	18	15	15	19	17	21	19	16	20	18	15	20
SUN.	19	16	16	20	18	22	20	17	21	19	16	21
MON.	20	17	17	21	19	23	21	18	22	20	17	22
TUES.	21	18	18	22	20	24	22	19	23	21	18	23
WED.	22	19	19	23	21	25	23	20	24	22	19	24
THUR.	23	20	20	24	22	26	24	21	25	23	20	25
FRI.	24	21	21	25	23	27	25	22	26	24	21	26
SAT.	25	22	22	26	24	28	26	23	27	25	22	27
SUN.	26	23	23	27	25	29	27	24	28	26	23	28
MON.	27	24	24	28	26	30	28	25	29	27	24	29
TUES.	28	25	25	29	27	—	29	26	30	28	25	30
WED.	29	26	26	30	28	—	30	27	—	29	26	31
THUR.	30	27	27	—	29	—	31	28	—	30	27	—
FRI.	31	28	28	—	30	—	—	29	—	31	28	—
SAT.	—	—	29	—	31	—	—	30	—	—	29	—
SUN.	—	—	30	—	—	—	—	31	—	—	30	—
MON.	—	—	31	—	—	—	—	—	—	—	—	—

CALENDAR NO. 5

	Jan.	Feb.	Mar.	Apr.	May	June	July	Aug.	Sept.	Oct.	Nov.	Dec.
SUN.	—	1	1	—	—	—	—	—	—	—	1	—
MON.	—	2	2	—	—	1	—	—	—	—	2	—
TUES.	—	3	3	—	—	2	—	—	1	—	3	1
WED.	—	4	4	1	—	3	1	—	2	—	4	2
THUR.	1	5	5	2	—	4	2	—	3	1	5	3
FRI.	2	6	6	3	1	5	3	—	4	2	6	4
SAT.	3	7	7	4	2	6	4	1	5	3	7	5
SUN.	4	8	8	5	3	7	5	2	6	4	8	6
MON.	5	9	9	6	4	8	6	3	7	5	9	7
TUES.	6	10	10	7	5	9	7	4	8	6	10	8
WED.	7	11	11	8	6	10	8	5	9	7	11	9
THUR.	8	12	12	9	7	11	9	6	10	8	12	10
FRI.	9	13	13	10	8	12	10	7	11	9	13	11
SAT.	10	14	14	11	9	13	11	8	12	10	14	12
SUN.	11	15	15	12	10	14	12	9	13	11	15	13
MON.	12	16	16	13	11	15	13	10	14	12	16	14
TUES.	13	17	17	14	12	16	14	11	15	13	17	15
WED.	14	18	18	15	13	17	15	12	16	14	18	16
THUR.	15	19	19	16	14	18	16	13	17	15	19	17
FRI.	16	20	20	17	15	19	17	14	18	16	20	18
SAT.	17	21	21	18	16	20	18	15	19	17	21	19
SUN.	18	22	22	19	17	21	19	16	20	18	22	20
MON.	19	23	23	20	18	22	20	17	21	19	23	21
TUES.	20	24	24	21	19	23	21	18	22	20	24	22
WED.	21	25	25	22	20	24	22	19	23	21	25	23
THUR.	22	26	26	23	21	25	23	20	24	22	26	24
FRI.	23	27	27	24	22	26	24	21	25	23	27	25
SAT.	24	28	28	25	23	27	25	22	26	24	28	26
SUN.	25	—	29	26	24	28	26	23	27	25	29	27
MON.	26	—	30	27	25	29	27	24	28	26	30	28
TUES.	27	—	31	28	26	30	28	25	29	27	—	29
WED.	28	—	—	29	27	—	29	26	30	28	—	30
THUR.	29	—	—	30	28	—	30	27	—	29	—	31
FRI.	30	—	—	—	29	—	31	28	—	30	—	—
SAT.	31	—	—	—	30	—	—	29	—	31	—	—
SUN.	—	—	—	—	31	—	—	30	—	—	—	—
MON.	—	—	—	—	—	—	—	31	—	—	—	—

	Jan.	Feb.	Mar.	Apr.	May	June	July	Aug.	Sept.	Oct.	Nov.	Dec.
SUN.	—	—	—	—	—	—	—	1	—	—	—	—
MON.	—	1	1	—	—	—	—	2	—	—	1	—
TUES.	—	2	2	—	—	1	—	3	—	—	2	—
WED.	—	3	3	—	—	2	—	4	1	—	3	1
THUR.	—	4	4	1	—	3	1	5	2	—	4	2
FRI.	1	5	5	2	—	4	2	6	3	1	5	3
SAT.	2	6	6	3	1	5	3	7	4	2	6	4
SUN.	3	7	7	4	2	6	4	8	5	3	7	5
MON.	4	8	8	5	3	7	5	9	6	4	8	6
TUES.	5	9	9	6	4	8	6	10	7	5	9	7
WED.	6	10	10	7	5	9	7	11	8	6	10	8
THUR.	7	11	11	8	6	10	8	12	9	7	11	9
FRI.	8	12	12	9	7	11	9	13	10	8	12	10
SAT.	9	13	13	10	8	12	10	14	11	9	13	11
SUN.	10	14	14	11	9	13	11	15	12	10	14	12
MON.	11	15	15	12	10	14	12	16	13	11	15	13
TUES.	12	16	16	13	11	15	13	17	14	12	16	14
WED.	13	17	17	14	12	16	14	18	15	13	17	15
THUR.	14	18	18	15	13	17	15	19	16	14	18	16
FRI.	15	19	19	16	14	18	16	20	17	15	19	17
SAT.	16	20	20	17	15	19	17	21	18	16	20	18
SUN.	17	21	21	18	16	20	18	22	19	17	21	19
MON.	18	22	22	19	17	21	19	23	20	18	22	20
TUES.	19	23	23	20	18	22	20	24	21	19	23	21
WED.	20	24	24	21	19	23	21	25	22	20	24	22
THUR.	21	25	25	22	20	24	22	26	23	21	25	23
FRI.	22	26	26	23	21	25	23	27	24	22	26	24
SAT.	23	27	27	24	22	26	24	28	25	23	27	25
SUN.	24	28	28	25	23	27	25	29	26	24	28	26
MON.	25	—	29	26	24	28	26	30	27	25	29	27
TUES.	26	—	30	27	25	29	27	31	28	26	30	28
WED.	27	—	31	28	26	30	28	—	29	27	—	29
THUR.	28	—	—	29	27	—	29	—	30	28	—	30
FRI.	29	—	—	30	28	—	30	—	—	29	—	31
SAT.	30	—	—	—	29	—	31	—	—	30	—	—
SUN.	31	—	—	—	30	—	—	—	—	31	—	—
MON.	—	—	—	—	31	—	—	—	—	—	—	—

CALENDAR NO. 7

	Jan.	Feb.	Mar.	Apr.	May	June	July	Aug.	Sept.	Oct.	Nov.	Dec.
SUN.	—	—	—	—	1	—	—	—	—	—	—	—
MON.	—	—	—	—	2	—	—	1	—	—	—	—
TUES.	—	1	1	—	3	—	—	2	—	—	1	—
WED.	—	2	2	—	4	1	—	3	—	—	2	—
THUR.	—	3	3	—	5	2	—	4	1	—	3	1
FRI.	—	4	4	1	6	3	1	5	2	—	4	2
SAT.	1	5	5	2	7	4	2	6	3	1	5	3
SUN.	2	6	6	3	8	5	3	7	4	2	6	4
MON.	3	7	7	4	9	6	4	8	5	3	7	5
TUES.	4	8	8	5	10	7	5	9	6	4	8	6
WED.	5	9	9	6	11	8	6	10	7	5	9	7
THUR.	6	10	10	7	12	9	7	11	8	6	10	8
FRI.	7	11	11	8	13	10	8	12	9	7	11	9
SAT.	8	12	12	9	14	11	9	13	10	8	12	10
SUN.	9	13	13	10	15	12	10	14	11	9	13	11
MON.	10	14	14	11	16	13	11	15	12	10	14	12
TUES.	11	15	15	12	17	14	12	16	13	11	15	13
WED.	12	16	16	13	18	15	13	17	14	12	16	14
THUR.	13	17	17	14	19	16	14	18	15	13	17	15
FRI.	14	18	18	15	20	17	15	19	16	14	18	16
SAT.	15	19	19	16	21	18	16	20	17	15	19	17
SUN.	16	20	20	17	22	19	17	21	18	16	20	18
MON.	17	21	21	18	23	20	18	22	19	17	21	19
TUES.	18	22	22	19	24	21	19	23	20	18	22	20
WED.	19	23	23	20	25	22	20	24	21	19	23	21
THUR.	20	24	24	21	26	23	21	25	22	20	24	22
FRI.	21	25	25	22	27	24	22	26	23	21	25	23
SAT.	22	26	26	23	28	25	23	27	24	22	26	24
SUN.	23	27	27	24	29	26	24	28	25	23	27	25
MON.	24	28	28	25	30	27	25	29	26	24	28	26
TUES.	25	—	29	26	31	28	26	30	27	25	29	27
WED.	26	—	30	27	—	29	27	31	28	26	30	28
THUR.	27	—	31	28	—	30	28	—	29	27	—	29
FRI.	28	—	—	29	—	—	29	—	30	28	—	30
SAT.	29	—	—	30	—	—	30	—	—	29	—	31
SUN.	30	—	—	—	—	—	31	—	—	30	—	—
MON.	31		—	—	—	—	—	—	—	31	—	—

CALENDAR NO. 8

	Jan.	Feb.	Mar.	Apr.	May	June	July	Aug.	Sept.	Oct.	Nov.	Dec.
SUN.	1	—	—	1	—	—	1	—	—	—	—	—
MON.	2	—	—	2	—	—	2	—	—	1	—	—
TUES.	3	—	—	3	1	—	3	—	—	2	—	—
WED.	4	1	—	4	2	—	4	1	—	3	—	—
THUR.	5	2	1	5	3	—	5	2	—	4	1	—
FRI.	6	3	2	6	4	1	6	3	—	5	2	—
SAT.	7	4	3	7	5	2	7	4	1	6	3	1
SUN.	8	5	4	8	6	3	8	5	2	7	4	2
MON.	9	6	5	9	7	4	9	6	3	8	5	3
TUES.	10	7	6	10	8	5	10	7	4	9	6	4
WED.	11	8	7	11	9	6	11	8	5	10	7	5
THUR.	12	9	8	12	10	7	12	9	6	11	8	6
FRI.	13	10	9	13	11	8	13	10	7	12	9	7
SAT.	14	11	10	14	12	9	14	11	8	13	10	8
SUN.	15	12	11	15	13	10	15	12	9	14	11	9
MON.	16	13	12	16	14	11	16	13	10	15	12	10
TUES.	17	14	13	17	15	12	17	14	11	16	13	11
WED.	18	15	14	18	16	13	18	15	12	17	14	12
THUR.	19	16	15	19	17	14	19	16	13	18	15	13
FRI.	20	17	16	20	18	15	20	17	14	19	16	14
SAT.	21	18	17	21	19	16	21	18	15	20	17	15
SUN.	22	19	18	22	20	17	22	19	16	21	18	16
MON.	23	20	19	23	21	18	23	20	17	22	19	17
TUES.	24	21	20	24	22	19	24	21	18	23	20	18
WED.	25	22	21	25	23	20	25	22	19	24	21	19
THUR.	26	23	22	26	24	21	26	23	20	25	22	20
FRI.	27	24	23	27	25	22	27	24	21	26	23	21
SAT.	28	25	24	28	26	23	28	25	22	27	24	22
SUN.	29	26	25	29	27	24	29	26	23	28	25	23
MON.	30	27	26	30	28	25	30	27	24	29	26	24
TUES.	31	28	27	—	29	26	31	28	25	30	27	25
WED.	—	29	28	—	30	27	—	29	26	31	28	26
THUR.	—	—	29	—	31	28	—	30	27	—	29	27
FRI.	—	—	30	—	—	29	—	31	28	—	30	28
SAT.	—	—	31	—	—	30	—	—	29	—	—	29
SUN.	—	—	—	—	—	—	—	—	30	—	—	30
MON.	—	—	—	—	—	—	—	—	—	—	—	31

CALENDAR NO. 9

	Jan.	Feb.	Mar.	Apr.	May	June	July	Aug.	Sept.	Oct.	Nov.	Dec.
SUN.	—	—	—	—	—	—	—	—	1	—	—	1
MON.	1	—	—	1	—	—	1	—	2	—	—	2
TUES.	2	—	—	2	—	—	2	—	3	1	—	3
WED.	3	—	—	3	1	—	3	—	4	2	—	4
THUR.	4	1	—	4	2	—	4	1	5	3	—	5
FRI.	5	2	1	5	3	—	5	2	6	4	1	6
SAT.	6	3	2	6	4	1	6	3	7	5	2	7
SUN.	7	4	3	7	5	2	7	4	8	6	3	8
MON.	8	5	4	8	6	3	8	5	9	7	4	9
TUES.	9	6	5	9	7	4	9	6	10	8	5	10
WED.	10	7	6	10	8	5	10	7	11	9	6	11
THUR.	11	8	7	11	9	6	11	8	12	10	7	12
FRI.	12	9	8	12	10	7	12	9	13	11	8	13
SAT.	13	10	9	13	11	8	13	10	14	12	9	14
SUN.	14	11	10	14	12	9	14	11	15	13	10	15
MON.	15	12	11	15	13	10	15	12	16	14	11	16
TUES.	16	13	12	16	14	11	16	13	17	15	12	17
WED.	17	14	13	17	15	12	17	14	18	16	13	18
THUR.	18	15	14	18	16	13	18	15	19	17	14	19
FRI.	19	16	15	19	17	14	19	16	20	18	15	20
SAT.	20	17	16	20	18	15	20	17	21	19	16	21
SUN.	21	18	17	21	19	16	21	18	22	20	17	22
MON.	22	19	18	22	20	17	22	19	23	21	18	23
TUES.	23	20	19	23	21	18	23	20	24	22	19	24
WED.	24	21	20	24	22	19	24	21	25	23	20	25
THUR.	25	22	21	25	23	20	25	22	26	24	21	26
FRI.	26	23	22	26	24	21	26	23	27	25	22	27
SAT.	27	24	23	27	25	22	27	24	28	26	23	28
SUN.	28	25	24	28	26	23	28	25	29	27	24	29
MON.	29	26	25	29	27	24	29	26	30	28	25	30
TUES.	30	27	26	30	28	25	30	27	—	29	26	31
WED.	31	28	27	—	29	26	31	28	—	30	27	—
THUR.	—	29	28	—	30	27	—	29	—	31	28	—
FRI.	—	—	29	—	31	28	—	30	—	—	29	—
SAT.	—	—	30	—	—	29	—	31	—	—	30	—
SUN.	—	—	31	—	—	30	—	—	—	—	—	—
MON.	—	—	—	—	—	—	—	—	—	—	—	—

290

CALENDAR NO. 10

	Jan.	Feb.	Mar.	Apr.	May	June	July	Aug.	Sept.	Oct.	Nov.	Dec.
SUN.	—	—	—	—	—	1	—	—	—	—	—	—
MON.	—	—	—	—	—	2	—	—	1	—	—	1
TUES.	1	—	—	1	—	3	1	—	2	—	—	2
WED.	2	—	—	2	—	4	2	—	3	1	—	3
THUR.	3	—	—	3	1	5	3	—	4	2	—	4
FRI.	4	1	—	4	2	6	4	1	5	3	—	5
SAT.	5	2	1	5	3	7	5	2	6	4	1	6
SUN.	6	3	2	6	4	8	6	3	7	5	2	7
MON.	7	4	3	7	5	9	7	4	8	6	3	8
TUES.	8	5	4	8	6	10	8	5	9	7	4	9
WED.	9	6	5	9	7	11	9	6	10	8	5	10
THUR.	10	7	6	10	8	12	10	7	11	9	6	11
FRI.	11	8	7	11	9	13	11	8	12	10	7	12
SAT.	12	9	8	12	10	14	12	9	13	11	8	13
SUN.	13	10	9	13	11	15	13	10	14	12	9	14
MON.	14	11	10	14	12	16	14	11	15	13	10	15
TUES.	15	12	11	15	13	17	15	12	16	14	11	16
WED.	16	13	12	16	14	18	16	13	17	15	12	17
THUR.	17	14	13	17	15	19	17	14	18	16	13	18
FRI.	18	15	14	18	16	20	18	15	19	17	14	19
SAT.	19	16	15	19	17	21	19	16	20	18	15	20
SUN.	20	17	16	20	18	22	20	17	21	19	16	21
MON.	21	18	17	21	19	23	21	18	22	20	17	22
TUES.	22	19	18	22	20	24	22	19	23	21	18	23
WED.	23	20	19	23	21	25	23	20	24	22	19	24
THUR.	24	21	20	24	22	26	24	21	25	23	20	25
FRI.	25	22	21	25	23	27	25	22	26	24	21	26
SAT.	26	23	22	26	24	28	26	23	27	25	22	27
SUN.	27	24	23	27	25	29	27	24	28	26	23	28
MON.	28	25	24	28	26	30	28	25	29	27	24	29
TUES.	29	26	25	29	27	—	29	26	30	28	25	30
WED.	30	27	26	30	28	—	30	27	—	29	26	31
THUR.	31	28	27	—	29	—	31	28	—	30	27	—
FRI.	—	29	28	—	30	—	—	29	—	31	28	—
SAT.	—	—	29	—	31	—	—	30	—	—	29	—
SUN.	—	—	30	—	—	—	—	31	—	—	30	—
MON.	—	—	31	—	—	—	—	—	—	—	—	—

CALENDAR NO. 11

	Jan.	Feb.	Mar.	Apr.	May	June	July	Aug.	Sept.	Oct.	Nov.	Dec.
SUN.	—	—	1	—	—	—	—	—	—	—	1	—
MON.	—	—	2	—	—	1	—	—	—	—	2	—
TUES.	—	—	3	—	—	2	—	—	1	—	3	1
WED.	1	—	4	1	—	3	1	—	2	—	4	2
THUR.	2	—	5	2	—	4	2	—	3	1	5	3
FRI.	3	—	6	3	1	5	3	—	4	2	6	4
SAT.	4	1	7	4	2	6	4	1	5	3	7	5
SUN.	5	2	8	5	3	7	5	2	6	4	8	6
MON.	6	3	9	6	4	8	6	3	7	5	9	7
TUES.	7	4	10	7	5	9	7	4	8	6	10	8
WED.	8	5	11	8	6	10	8	5	9	7	11	9
THUR.	9	6	12	9	7	11	9	6	10	8	12	10
FRI.	10	7	13	10	8	12	10	7	11	9	13	11
SAT.	11	8	14	11	9	13	11	8	12	10	14	12
SUN.	12	9	15	12	10	14	12	9	13	11	15	13
MON.	13	10	16	13	11	15	13	10	14	12	16	14
TUES.	14	11	17	14	12	16	14	11	15	13	17	15
WED.	15	12	18	15	13	17	15	12	16	14	18	16
THUR.	16	13	19	16	14	18	16	13	17	15	19	17
FRI.	17	14	20	17	15	19	17	14	18	16	20	18
SAT.	18	15	21	18	16	20	18	15	19	17	21	19
SUN.	19	16	22	19	17	21	19	16	20	18	22	20
MON.	20	17	23	20	18	22	20	17	21	19	23	21
TUES.	21	18	24	21	19	23	21	18	22	20	24	22
WED.	22	19	25	22	20	24	22	19	23	21	25	23
THUR.	23	20	26	23	21	25	23	20	24	22	26	24
FRI.	24	21	27	24	22	26	24	21	25	23	27	25
SAT.	25	22	28	25	23	27	25	22	26	24	28	26
SUN.	26	23	29	26	24	28	26	23	27	25	29	27
MON.	27	24	30	27	25	29	27	24	28	26	30	28
TUES.	28	25	31	28	26	30	28	25	29	27	—	29
WED.	29	26	—	29	27	—	29	26	30	28	—	30
THUR.	30	27	—	30	28	—	30	27	—	29	—	31
FRI.	31	28	—	—	29	—	31	28	—	30	—	—
SAT.	—	29	—	—	30	—	—	29	—	31	—	—
SUN.	—	—	—	—	31	—	—	30	—	—	—	—
MON.	—	—	—	—	—	—	—	31	—	—	—	—

CALENDAR NO. 12

	Jan.	Feb.	Mar.	Apr.	May	June	July	Aug.	Sept.	Oct.	Nov.	Dec.
SUN.	—	1	—	—	—	—	—	1	—	—	—	—
MON.	—	2	1	—	—	—	—	2	—	—	1	—
TUES.	—	3	2	—	—	1	—	3	—	—	2	—
WED.	—	4	3	—	—	2	—	4	1	—	3	1
THUR.	1	5	4	1	—	3	1	5	2	—	4	2
FRI.	2	6	5	2	—	4	2	6	3	1	5	3
SAT.	3	7	6	3	1	5	3	7	4	2	6	4
SUN.	4	8	7	4	2	6	4	8	5	3	7	5
MON.	5	9	8	5	3	7	5	9	6	4	8	6
TUES.	6	10	9	6	4	8	6	10	7	5	9	7
WED.	7	11	10	7	5	9	7	11	8	6	10	8
THUR.	8	12	11	8	6	10	8	12	9	7	11	9
FRI.	9	13	12	9	7	11	9	13	10	8	12	10
SAT.	10	14	13	10	8	12	10	14	11	9	13	11
SUN.	11	15	14	11	9	13	11	15	12	10	14	12
MON.	12	16	15	12	10	14	12	16	13	11	15	13
TUES.	13	17	16	13	11	15	13	17	14	12	16	14
WED.	14	18	17	14	12	16	14	18	15	13	17	15
THUR.	15	19	18	15	13	17	15	19	16	14	18	16
FRI.	16	20	19	16	14	18	16	20	17	15	19	17
SAT.	17	21	20	17	15	19	17	21	18	16	20	18
SUN.	18	22	21	18	16	20	18	22	19	17	21	19
MON.	19	23	22	19	17	21	19	23	20	18	22	20
TUES.	20	24	23	20	18	22	20	24	21	19	23	21
WED.	21	25	24	21	19	23	21	25	22	20	24	22
THUR.	22	26	25	22	20	24	22	26	23	21	25	23
FRI.	23	27	26	23	21	25	23	27	24	22	26	24
SAT.	24	28	27	24	22	26	24	28	25	23	27	25
SUN.	25	29	28	25	23	27	25	29	26	24	28	26
MON.	26	—	29	26	24	28	26	30	27	25	29	27
TUES.	27	—	30	27	25	29	27	31	28	26	30	28
WED.	28	—	31	28	26	30	28	—	29	27	—	29
THUR.	29	—	—	29	27	—	29	—	30	28	—	30
FRI.	30	—	—	30	28	—	30	—	—	29	—	31
SAT.	31	—	—	—	29	—	31	—	—	30	—	—
SUN.	—	—	—	—	30	—	—	—	—	31	—	—
MON.	—	—	—	—	31	—	—	—	—	—	—	—

CALENDAR NO. 13

	Jan.	Feb.	Mar.	Apr.	May	June	July	Aug.	Sept.	Oct.	Nov.	Dec.
SUN.	—	—	—	—	1	—	—	—	—	—	—	—
MON.	—	1	—	—	2	—	—	1	—	—	—	—
TUES.	—	2	1	—	3	—	—	2	—	—	1	—
WED.	—	3	2	—	4	1	—	3	—	—	2	—
THUR.	—	4	3	—	5	2	—	4	1	—	3	1
FRI.	1	5	4	1	6	3	1	5	2	—	4	2
SAT.	2	6	5	2	7	4	2	6	3	1	5	3
SUN.	3	7	6	3	8	5	3	7	4	2	6	4
MON.	4	8	7	4	9	6	4	8	5	3	7	5
TUES.	5	9	8	5	10	7	5	9	6	4	8	6
WED.	6	10	9	6	11	8	6	10	7	5	9	7
THUR.	7	11	10	7	12	9	7	11	8	6	10	8
FRI.	8	12	11	8	13	10	8	12	9	7	11	9
SAT.	9	13	12	9	14	11	9	13	10	8	12	10
SUN.	10	14	13	10	15	12	10	14	11	9	13	11
MON.	11	15	14	11	16	13	11	15	12	10	14	12
TUES.	12	16	15	12	17	14	12	16	13	11	15	13
WED.	13	17	16	13	18	15	13	17	14	12	16	14
THUR.	14	18	17	14	19	16	14	18	15	13	17	15
FRI.	15	19	18	15	20	17	15	19	16	14	18	16
SAT.	16	20	19	16	21	18	16	20	17	15	19	17
SUN.	17	21	20	17	22	19	17	21	18	16	20	18
MON.	18	22	21	18	23	20	18	22	19	17	21	19
TUES.	19	23	22	19	24	21	19	23	20	18	22	20
WED.	20	24	23	20	25	22	20	24	21	19	23	21
THUR.	21	25	24	21	26	23	21	25	22	20	24	22
FRI.	22	26	25	22	27	24	22	26	23	21	25	23
SAT.	23	27	26	23	28	25	23	27	24	22	26	24
SUN.	24	28	27	24	29	26	24	28	25	23	27	25
MON.	25	29	28	25	30	27	25	29	26	24	28	26
TUES.	26	—	29	26	31	28	26	30	27	25	29	27
WED.	27	—	30	27	—	29	27	31	28	26	30	28
THUR.	28	—	31	28	—	30	28	—	29	27	—	29
FRI.	29	—	—	29	—	—	29	—	30	28	—	30
SAT.	30	—	—	30	—	—	30	—	—	29	—	31
SUN.	31	—	—	—	—	—	31	—	—	30	—	—
MON.	—	—	—	—	—	—	—	—	—	31	—	—

294

CALENDAR NO. 14

	Jan.	Feb.	Mar.	Apr.	May	June	July	Aug.	Sept.	Oct.	Nov.	Dec.
SUN.	—	—	—	—	—	—	—	—	—	1	—	—
MON.	—	—	—	—	1	—	—	—	—	2	—	—
TUES.	—	1	—	—	2	—	—	1	—	3	—	—
WED.	—	2	1	—	3	—	—	2	—	4	1	—
THUR.	—	3	2	—	4	1	—	3	—	5	2	—
FRI.	—	4	3	—	5	2	—	4	1	6	3	1
SAT.	1	5	4	1	6	3	1	5	2	7	4	2
SUN.	2	6	5	2	7	4	2	6	3	8	5	3
MON.	3	7	6	3	8	5	3	7	4	9	6	4
TUES.	4	8	7	4	9	6	4	8	5	10	7	5
WED.	5	9	8	5	10	7	5	9	6	11	8	6
THUR.	6	10	9	6	11	8	6	10	7	12	9	7
FRI.	7	11	10	7	12	9	7	11	8	13	10	8
SAT.	8	12	11	8	13	10	8	12	9	14	11	9
SUN.	9	13	12	9	14	11	9	13	10	15	12	10
MON.	10	14	13	10	15	12	10	14	11	16	13	11
TUES.	11	15	14	11	16	13	11	15	12	17	14	12
WED.	12	16	15	12	17	14	12	16	13	18	15	13
THUR.	13	17	16	13	18	15	13	17	14	19	16	14
FRI.	14	18	17	14	19	16	14	18	15	20	17	15
SAT.	15	19	18	15	20	17	15	19	16	21	18	16
SUN.	16	20	19	16	21	18	16	20	17	22	19	17
MON.	17	21	20	17	22	19	17	21	18	23	20	18
TUES.	18	22	21	18	23	20	18	22	19	24	21	19
WED.	19	23	22	19	24	21	19	23	20	25	22	20
THUR.	20	24	23	20	25	22	20	24	21	26	23	21
FRI.	21	25	24	21	26	23	21	25	22	27	24	22
SAT.	22	26	25	22	27	24	22	26	23	28	25	23
SUN.	23	27	26	23	28	25	23	27	24	29	26	24
MON.	24	28	27	24	29	26	24	28	25	30	27	25
TUES.	25	29	28	25	30	27	25	29	26	31	28	26
WED.	26	—	29	26	31	28	26	30	27	—	29	27
THUR.	27	—	30	27	—	29	27	31	28	—	30	28
FRI.	28	—	31	28	—	30	28	—	29	—	—	29
SAT.	29	—	—	29	—	—	29	—	30	—	—	30
SUN.	30	—	—	30	—	—	30	—	—	—	—	31
MON.	31	—	—	—	—	—	31	—	—	—	—	—

Directory

A guide to associations, publications, equipment, supplies, and services

ASSOCIATIONS AND PUBLICATIONS

This list is highly selective, but it is intended to aid the curator in finding sources of information to assist him with technical problems directly or indirectly related to his profession. With one exception, associations and journals relating to specific subject areas have not been included. More information about the associations, their publications, and about the individual periodicals listed directly below them can be found in two standard guides: *Ulrich's International Periodicals Directory*, 14th ed., 2 vols. (New York: R. R. Bowker Co., 1971), and *Standard Periodical Directory*, 4th ed. (New York: Oxbridge Publishing Co., 1973). In this list, when the title of a journal includes the name of the association, the name has been abbreviated in the title.

American Association for State and Local History. *History News*. Technical Leaflet series
American Film Institute. *AFI Report*
American Library Association. *American Libraries*
American Records Management Association. *Records Management Quarterly*
American Society for Information Science. *ASIS: Journal of ASIS*
Antiquarian Booksellers Association of America. No publication
ASLIB. *Journal of Documentation. ASLIB Proceedings*
Association for Recorded Sound Collections. *ARSC-Journal*
Association of College and Research Libraries (ALA). *College & Research Libraries*
Association of Records Executives and Administrators. *Records Management Journal*
Bibliographical Society of America. *Papers of the BSA*
British Records Association. *Archives: Journal of the BRA*
Computer Micrographic Technology Users Group. *Quarterly Newsletter*
Data Processing Management Association. *Data Management*
International Association of Paper Historians. *Information*

International Council on Archives. *Archivum. ADPA: Archives & Automation/Informatique*

International Federation of Film Archivists. No publication

International Graphoanalysis Society. *Journal of Graphoanalysis*

International Institute for Conservation of Historic and Artistic Works. *Studies in Conservation*

International Micrographic Congress. *IMC Journal*

Library Association of Australia, Archives Section. *Archives and Manuscripts*

The Manuscript Society. *Manuscripts*

National Microfilm Association. *Journal of Micrographics*

Oral History Association. *Newsletter*

Rare Books and Manuscript Section, Association of College and Research Libraries (ALA). No publication

Resources and Technical Services Division (ALA). *Library Resources & Technical Services*

Royal Photographic Society. *Journal of Photographic Science. Photographic Journal*

Society of American Archivists. *American Archivist*

Society of Archivists. *Journal of the SA*

Society of Motion Picture and Television Engineers. *SMPTE Journal*

Special Libraries Association. *Special Libraries*

Special Libraries Association, Geography and Map Division. *Bulletin of the SLAGMD*

Technical Association of Pulp and Paper Industry. *TAPPI: Journal of TAPPI*

AB Bookman's Weekly; American Book Collector; Collector: A Magazine for Autograph and Historical Collectors; Computers and the Humanities; Information and Records Management; Information Retrieval & Library Automation; Journal of Librarianship; Journal of Library History; Library Journal; Library Quarterly; Library Trends; Microform Review; Newspaper Collector's Gazette; Paper Conservation News; Picturescope; Prologue; Resources for American Literary Study; Restaurator

EQUIPMENT

Dry Mount Press

Bogen Photo Corporation, PO Box 448, Englewood, N.J. 07631

Caltura Manufacturing Co., PO Box 613-C, Camarillo, Calif. 93010

Seal, Inc., Derby, Conn. 06418

Laminator

Arbee Company, Inc., 6 Claremont Rd., Bernardsville, N.J. 07924

W. J. Barrow Restoration Shop, Inc., Virginia State Library Bldg., Richmond, Va. 23219

Lisle Industries (North American agent for Ademco, Limited), 209 Forward Ave., Ottawa, Canada K1Y 1L1

Microfilm cabinet (stack unit)

L. E. Muran Co., 60 Old Colony Ave., Boston, Mass. 02127

Recording hydrothermograph

Science Associates, Inc., Box 230, Princeton, N.J. 08540

Ultraviolet filtering, tubes, sheets, and sleeves

ACI Plastics, Inc., 3923 W. Pine Blvd., St. Louis, Mo. 63108
Glass Distributors, Inc., 1741 Johnson Ave., N.W., Washington, D.C. 20009
Verd-A-Ray Corporation, 615 Front St., Toledo, Ohio 43605
Westlake Plastic Co., West Lemni Rd., Lemni Mills, Pa. 19052

Vacuum fumigation chamber

Vacudyne Corporation, 375 E. Joe Orr Rd., Chicago Heights, Ill. 60411

SERVICES

The work of the persons or firms noted in the following lists is known personally to the author. Others, obviously equally qualified, are excluded, and this is in no way meant to deny their ability or competence.

Appraisers, New England

Gordon T. Banks, Goodspeed's, 18 Beacon St., Boston, Mass. 02108
Robert E. Metzdorf, Route 183, North Colebrook, Conn. 06021
Kenneth W. Rendell, Kenneth W. Rendell, Inc., 154 Wells Ave., Newton, Mass. 02159
Paul C. Richards, 101 Monmouth, Brookline, Mass. 02146

Appraisers, Middle Atlantic

Mary A. Benjamin, Walter R. Benjamin Autographs, 790 Madison Ave., New York, N.Y. 10021
Andreas Brown, Gotham Book Mart, 41 W. 47th St., New York, N.Y. 10036
Mrs. Louis H. Cohn, House of Books, 667 Madison Ave., New York, N.Y. 10021
Emily Driscoll, Flatiron Bldg., Rm. 1109, New York, N.Y. 10010
Edward Eberstadt & Sons, 888 Madison Ave., New York, N.Y. 10021
Lew D. Feldman, House of El Dieff, 139 E. 63rd St., New York, N.Y. 10021
John F. Fleming, 322 E. 57th St., New York, N.Y. 10022
Lucien C. Goldschmidt, 1117 Madison Ave., New York, N.Y. 10028

Charles Hamilton, 25 E. 77th St., New York, N.Y. 10021

David Kirschenbaum, Carnegie Book Store, 140 E. 59th St., New York, N.Y. 10022

H. P. Kraus, 16 E. 46th St., New York, N.Y. 10017

Michael Papantonio, Seven Gables Bookshop, 3 W. 46th St., New York, N.Y. 10036

Sotheby Parke Bernet Galleries, 980 Madison Ave., New York, N.Y. 10021

Benjamin Swann, Swann Galleries, 117 E. 24th St., New York, N.Y. 10010

Charles Sessler, Inc., 1308 Walnut St., Philadelphia, Pa. 19107

Appraisers, Midwest

Miss Francis Hamill, Hamill and Barker Books, 230 N. Michigan Ave., Chicago, Ill. 60601

Kenneth Nebenzahl, Kenneth Nebenzahl, Inc., 333 N. Michigan Ave., Chicago, Ill. 60601

Julia Sweet Newman, PO Box 99, Battle Creek, Mich. 49016

Ralph G. Newman, Abraham Lincoln Bookshop, 18 E. Chestnut, Chicago, Ill. 60611

Appraisers, Southwest

Conway Barker, 1231 Sunset, La Marque, Tex. 77568

John H. Jenkins, The Jenkins Co., 1 Pemberton Pkwy., Austin, Tex. 78703

Appraisers, West

Dawson's Book Shop, 535 N. Larchmont Blvd., Los Angeles, Calif. 90004

Franklin Gilliam, Brick Row Book Shop, 251 Post, San Francisco, Calif. 94108

Doris Harris, 6381 Hollywood Blvd., Rm. 422, Los Angeles, Calif. 90028

W. H. Howell, John Howell, Books, 434 Post, San Francisco, Calif. 94102

David McGee, 3108-B Filmore St., San Francisco, Calif. 94123

Charles W. Sachs, The Scriptorium, 427 N. Cañon Dr., Beverly Hills, Calif. 90210

William Wreden, 200 Hamilton Ave., Palo Alto, Calif. 94301

Jacob Zeitlin, Zeitlin & Ver Brugge, 815 N. La Cienega Blvd., Los Angeles, Calif. 90069

Appraisers, Pacific Northwest

Preston McMann, Old Oregon Book Store, 610 S.W. 12th, Portland, Ore. 97204

Shorey Book Store, 815 Third, Seattle, Wash. 98104

Conservators

Paul Banks, Newberry Library, 60 W. Walton St., Chicago, Ill. 60610

Dennis Blunn, 58 Warwick Rd., London S.E. 20

Cuneo Studio, 2242 S. Grove St., Chicago, Ill. 60605

George Cunha, New England Document Conservation Center, PO Box 446, North Andover, Mass. 01845

Carolyn Horton, Carolyn Horton & Associates, Inc., 430 W. 22nd St., New York, N.Y. 10011

Kner and Anthony Bookbinders, 407 S. Dearborn St., Chicago, Ill. 60605

Lakeside Press, Graphics Conservation Department, R. R. Donnelley & Sons Co., 350 E. 22nd St., Chicago, Ill. 60616

Robert Organ, Conservation Analytical Laboratory, Museum of History and Technology, Smithsonian Institution, Washington, D.C. 20560

Ivan J. Ruzicka, 27 Pinewood Rd., Avon, Mass. 02322

Willman Spawn, American Philosophical Society, 105 S. Fifth St., Philadelphia, Pa. 19106

Storm Bindery, Drawer L, Sedona, Arizona 86336

Peter Waters, Restoration Officer, Library of Congress, 110 Second St., S.E., Washington, D.C. 20540

Marilyn Weidner, 612 Spruce St., Philadelphia, Pa. 19106.

Lamination

W. J. Barrow Restoration Shop, Inc., Virginia State Library Bldg., Richmond, Va. 23219

Arbee Company, Inc., 6 Claremont Rd., Bernardsville, N.J. 07924

Archival Restoration Associates, Inc., 84 Bethlehem Pike, Philadelphia, Pa. 19118

Motion picture, nitrate to safety

Bono Film Services, Inc., 1042 Wisconsin, N.W., Washington, D.C. 20007

DeLuxe General, 1000 Nicholas Blvd., Elk Grove, Ill. 60007

Filmack Studio, Inc., 1327 W. Wabash, Chicago, Ill. 60605

Filmservice Laboratories, Inc., 6327 Santa Monica Blvd., Hollywood, Calif. 90038

Foto-Kem Industries, Inc., 3215 Caheunga Blvd. West, Hollywood, Calif. 90068

MGM Laboratories, Inc., 10202 W. Washington Blvd., Culver City, Calif. 90230

Motion picture, cleaning and reconditioning

International Filmtreat, 250 W. 64th St., New York, N.Y. 10023

International Filmtreat, 160 E. Illinois, Chicago, Ill. 60611

International Filmtreat, 829 N. Highland Ave., Hollywood, Calif. 90038

Photographs and negatives, archival processing

Archival Processing Co., 111 E. Burlington, Iowa City, Iowa 52240
East Street Gallery, 723 State St., Grinnell, Iowa 50112

Photographs and negatives, B&W separation of color

Berkey K & L Custom Services, Inc., 222 E. 44th St., New York, N.Y. 10017
East Street Gallery, 723 State St., Grinnell, Iowa 50112

Processing, arrangement and description

Archival Associates, 6284 S. Oneida Way, Englewood, Colo. 80110

SUPPLIES

Two firms which handle a great many of the special supplies required
by the curator are: TALAS Division, Technical Library Service, 104 Fifth Ave.,
New York, N.Y. 10011, and Process Materials Corporation, 329 Veterans Blvd.,
Carlstadt, N.J. 07072.

Conservation, cleaning

Absorene: Paint and wallpaper stores
Endust: Hardware and grocery stores
Magic Rub Erasers: TALAS; art and stationery stores
One-Wipe Dust Cloths: TALAS; hardware and grocery stores
Opaline Cleaner: TALAS; art supply stores
Pink Pearl Erasers No. 101: TALAS; art supply stores

Conservation, repair

Dennison's Gummed Paper: TALAS
Dry Mount Tissue: Seal, Inc., Derby, Conn. 06418; Eastman Kodak Co.,
    Rochester, N.Y. 14650
Filmoplast P: TALAS
Methyl Cellulose (Culminal): TALAS
Methyl Cellulose Paste Powder: Process Materials Corporation
Mipofolie: P-S-F, Inc., Box 392, Pottstown, Pa. 19464
Paste: Samuel Schweitzer, 660 W. Lake St., Chicago, Ill. 60606
Permafilm: Denoyer-Geppert Co., 5325 N. Ravenswood Ave., Chicago, Ill.
    60640
PermaFilm Mend-O-Tape: Transparent Protection Co., 5 Lawrence St.,
    Bloomfield, N.J. 07003
Polyvinyl Acetate Adhesive, DuPont Elvace 1874: TALAS
Polyvinyl Acetate Adhesive No. 436, Schweitzer: TALAS
Polyvinyl Acetate Adhesive No. 5714, Schweitzer: TALAS
Wheat Paste No. 6, Schweitzer: TALAS

Conservation, general

Archivist Pen (acid-indicating pen): TALAS
Deacidification, Morpholine Vapor: Research Corporation, 405 Lexington Ave., New York, N.Y. 10017
Deacidification, Non-aqueous: Wei T'o Associates, Inc., 5830 56th Ave., N.E., Seattle, Wash. 98105
Deacidification, Vapour Phase (paper and sachets): Russell Bookcrafts, Hilchin, Herts, England
pH Test Kit: Applied Science Laboratories, Inc., 218 N. Adams St., Richmond, Va. 23220
Thymol: Chemical supply house

Paper

Acid-free (white, woodpulp): Wilcox-Walter-Furlong Paper Co., 3305 N. 6th, Harrisburg, Pa. 17110; B. W. Wilson Paper Co., 915 E. Cary, Richmond, Va. 23219
Fabriano: Andrews-Nelson-Whitehead, 7 Laight St., New York, N.Y. 10013; TALAS
Japanese: Washi No Mise, 2583 Turk Hill Rd., Victor, N.Y. 14564; Yasutomo & Co., 24 California St., San Francisco, Calif. 94111
Japanese (Sekishu and Skizuoka): Andrews-Nelson-Whitehead, 7 Laight St., New York, N.Y. 10013
Mounting Board (all rag): Andrews-Nelson-Whitehead, 7 Laight St., New York, N.Y. 10013
Acid-free (wrapping): Process Materials Corporation, New York, N.Y. 10013; Andrews-Nelson-Whitehead, 7 Laight St., New York, N.Y. 10013; Bainbridge & Sons, 20 Cumberland St., Brooklyn, N.Y. 11205; Strathmore Paper Co., Front St. West, Springfield, Mass. 01089
Permanent/Durable: Andrews-Nelson-Whitehead, 7 Laight St., New York, N.Y. 10013; S. D. Warren Co., 225 Franklin St., Boston, Mass. 02110
Rope Manila: Paper House of Pennsylvania, 7 Walnut St., Philadelphia, Pa. 19106
Silk Tissue: Aiko's Art Materials Import, 714 N. Wabash Ave., Chicago, Ill. 60611; Andrews-Nelson-Whitehead, 7 Laight St., New York, N.Y. 10013; TALAS

Miscellaneous

Acetate Sheeting: Celutone Plastic, Inc., 276 Park Ave., South, New York, N.Y. 10010; Transilwrap Co., 2615 N. Paulina St., Chicago, Ill. 60614; Transparent Products Corporation, 1729 Pico Blvd., Los Angeles, Calif. 90015
Bone Folders: TALAS

Boxes (clamshell): Pohlig Bros., Inc., 25th and Franklin Sts., Richmond, Va. 23223

Boxes (pressboard): Hollinger Corporation, 3810 S. Four Mile Run Rd., Arlington, Va. 22206

Boxes (record center): Paige Co., Inc., 432 Park Ave., South, New York, N.Y. 10016; Hollinger Corporation, 3810 S. Four Mile Run Rd., Arlington, Va. 22206

Folders (acid-free): Hollinger Corporation, 3810 S. Four Mile Run Rd., Arlington, Va. 22206; Milletex, 3305 N. Sixth St., Harrisburg, Pa. 17110

Negative Files (polyethylene): Print File, Inc., Box 100, Schenectady, N.Y. 12304

Negative Files (acetate): Nega-File Co., Furlong, Pa. 18925

Paper Clips (plastic): Baumgarten's Exclusive Imports, 1190-A N. Highland Ave., N.E., Atlanta, Ga. 30304

Paper Clips (stainless steel): Noestring Pin-Ticket Co., Inc., 728 E. 136th St., Bronx, N.Y. 10454

Polyester Non-woven Web: DuPont, Textile Fiber Dept., Reemay Div., Central Rd. Bldg., Wilmington, Del. 19898

Polyester Film and Fibremat: 3M Co., 3M Center, Bldg. 230, St. Paul, Minn. 55101

Tote Box: Fidelity File Box, Inc., 705 Pennsylvania Ave., Minneapolis, Minn. 55426

Facsimiles

A list of items more commonly reproduced

To the unwary curator, a good facsimile may be as difficult to detect as a forgery; and while only a sixth sense and a sharp eye will help with the latter, it is hoped that a list of some of the manuscripts more commonly reproduced in facsimile will be useful. Some of the items on this list are taken from *Autographs: A Key to Collecting* by Mary A. Benjamin (see her chapter, "Facsimiles, Reproductions and Manuscript Copies," for an informative and interesting account). Other facsimiles were located in the accession lists of the British Museum, in exhibit catalogs, and in the subject files of several institutions. However, it is realized that the list is far from inclusive. For example, no attempt was made to list the individual facsimiles printed in the several volumes which are noted at the close of this list. Finally, because there are few curators who at one time or another are not confronted with a facsimile newspaper, a few of the more notorious ones are listed immediately following the manuscript entries.

MANUSCRIPTS

Albert, Prince of Wales:	To Frederick William Louis, April 8, 1853
Austen, Jane:	To Cassandra Austen, October 15, 1808 and May 29, 1811
Bernardino, S.:	To the Magistrates of Sienna, January 21, 1439

Bismarck, Otto von:	November 20, 1867
———:	Letters acknowledging birthday greetings, various years
Brontë, Charlotte:	To Constantin Heger, 1844–45
Brown, John:	To Luther Humphrey, November 13, 1859
———:	Statement, December 2, 1859
Bunyan, John:	Warrant for his arrest, March 4, 1674
Burns, Robert:	To Clarinda (Mrs. McLehose), March 2, 1788 (signed "Sylvander")
Byron, George Gordon, Lord:	To the editor of *Galignani's Messenger,* April 27, 1819
Charles II:	To William Belasyse, March 18, 1660
———:	Certificate of marriage to Catherine of Braganza, May 22, 1662
Columbus, Christopher:	To Nicolo Oderigo, December 27, 1504
Elbert, Frederick:	February 9, 1923
Fox, Henry:	To William Bunbury, March 9, 1762
Franklin, Benjamin:	To William Strahan, July 5, 1775
Frederick I:	January 26, 1708
Frederick II:	October 13, 1777
Frederick-Wilhelm I:	November 18, 1728
Frederick-Wilhelm III:	October 3, 1820
Frederick-Wilhelm IV:	December 21, 1840
Garrick, David:	To the Duchess of Portland, October 29, 1767
George V:	Address welcoming American troops, April 1918
Guignard, Pierre Louis:	October 29, 1812
Harding, Warren G.:	To Alex Kirkadden (?), April 27, 1900
———:	To "Dear Mac," (Malcolm Jennings), March 12, 1917
Henry, Patrick:	To George Rogers Clark, January 12, 1778

Hindenburg, Paul von: April 16, 1915 (postcard)

Jefferson, Thomas: To Craven Peyton, November 27, 1803

_____: Draft of the Declaration of Independence, 1776

Johnson, Esther: To Captain Dingley, May 25, 1723

Johnson, Samuel: Agreement regarding the publication of *The Rambler*, April 1, 1751

Lee, Robert E.:   General Order No. 9, April 10, 1865

Lincoln, Abraham: To A. H. Stephens, November 30, 1860

_____: To Major Ramsey, October 17, 1861

_____: Gettysburg Address, November 1863

_____: To Mrs. Bixby, November 21, 1864

_____: Thirteenth amendment signed by Lincoln, Hannibal Hamlin, and Schuyler Colfax

London, Jack: To Houghton Mifflin Co., four-page typewritten, ca. 1900

Ludendorff, Erich: October 5, 1903 (postcard)

Luther, Martin: To Johann Lange, July 29, 1520

McLehose, Clarinda: To Robert Burns, January 31, 1788

Poe, Edgar Allen: To William Green, circular letter, November 1845

Sherman, William Tecumseh: To John Burton, September 6, 1847

Stevenson, Robert Louis: To Mrs. Ehrich, n.d.

Tounson, Robert: To John Isham, November 1618

Washington, George: To John Langdon, April 14, 1789

_____: To Jean Baptiste de Ternant, September 24, 1791

_____: Expense account submitted to the government

Wesley, Susanna: To John Wesley, October 25, 1732

White, John: To Queen Mary, 1556

Kaiser Wilhelm II: January 15, 1913

NEWSPAPERS

The Daily Citizen:	July 2, 1863 (The last issue of the famed "wallpaper" newspaper of Vicksburg, Miss., published before the surrender of the city to U.S. Grant).
Desert News:	June 15, 1850 (First issue of the well-known Mormon paper).
London Times:	November 7, 1805 (Account of the Battle of Trafalgar and the death of Admiral Nelson).
New York Herald:	April 15, 1865 (Report of Lincoln's assassination).
Ulster County Gazette:	January 4, 1800 (Obituary of George Washington—more than a million facsimiles are thought to exist and only two originals).

PORTFOLIOS AND BOOKS

The Autograph Miscellany, Executed in Facsimile by F. Netherclift. London: J. R. Smith, 1855.

Autographen-Album in Liedern Moderner Meister mit deren Porträts und Namenzügen. Leipzig: R. Forberg, 1907.

Autographs of Prominent Men of the Southern Confederacy and Historical Documents. Houston: Cumming & Son, 1900.

Brotherhead, William, ed. *The Book of the Signers: Containing Fac-simile Letters of the Signers of the Declaration of Independence . . .* Philadelphia: William Brotherhead, 1861.

Greg, Walter W., ed. *English Literary Autographs, 1550–1650.* London: Oxford University Press, 1932.

Netherclift, Frederick G. *The Hand-book to Autographs, Being a Ready Guide to the Handwriting of Distinguished Men and Women . . .* London: J. R. Smith, 1858.

Netherclift, Joseph. *Characteristic Extracts and Signatures from the Correspondence of Illustrious and Distinguished Women of Great Britain.* London: Netherclift, 1838.

Nichols, John G. *Autographs of Royal, Noble, Learned, and Remarkable Personages Conspicuous in English History . . .* London: J. B. Nichols and Son, 1829.

Sechzehn Handschriften von Dichtern. Chemnitz: Gesellschaft der Bücherfreunde zu Chemnitz, 1936.

Stevens, Benjamin Franklin. *B. F. Stevens's Facsimiles of Manuscripts in European Archives Relating to America, 1773–1783, with Descriptions, Editorial Notes, Collation, References and Translations.* 25 vols. Reprint. Wilmington, Del.: Mellifont Press, Inc., 1970.

Notes

CHAPTER 1

1. Henry C. Shelley, *The British Museum: Its History and Treasures,* p. 156.
2. Robert L. Brubaker, "Archive and Manuscript Collections," 3:249; Philip M. Hamer, editor, *A Guide to Archives and Manuscripts in the United States.*
3. H. G. Jones, *The Records of a Nation: Their Management, Preservation, and Use,* p. 164.
4. Brubaker, "Archive and Manuscript Collections," 3:249.
5. Leon Edel, *The Age of the Archive,* p. 1.
6. *Ibid.,* pp. 2–4.
7. *Ibid.,* p. 9.
8. Geoffrey R. Elton, *Political History: Principles and Practices,* pp. 100–102.
9. Fredson Bowers, "Textual Criticism," p. 31.
10. Edel, *The Age of the Archive,* pp. 5, 8.
11. R. J. Roberts, "Rare Book Collecting—A View from Mid-Atlantic," pp. 14–15.
12. *Ibid.*
13. *The New Yorker,* July 25, 1970, pp. 19–20.
14. American Academy of Arts and Letters and the National Institute of Arts and Letters, "On the Use of Private Papers," pp. 43, 44, 47.
15. Homer C. Hockett, *Critical Method in Historical Research and Writing,* p. 208.
16. To the author's knowledge, only one modern American scholar has written about manuscript collectors and dealers. See Lester J. Cappon, "Walter R. Benjamin and the Autograph Trade at the Turn of the Century," pp. 20–37.
17. Michael Kraus, *A History of American History,* pp. 33, 87.
18. Kraus, *A History of American History,* pp. 85–90; Carl L. Cannon, *American Book Collectors and Collecting,* p. 1.
19. Cannon, *American Book Collectors and Collecting,* pp. 6–7; *Dictionary of American Biography,* 2d ed., s.v. "Prince, Thomas"; Thomas Prince, *The Chronological History of New England,* pp. vi–viii.
20. Kraus, *A History of American History,* pp. 134–135; *Dictionary of American Biography,* 2d ed., s.v. "Belknap, Jeremy."
21. Kraus, *A History of American History,* pp. 135, 139; O. Lawrence Burnette, Jr., *Beneath the Footnote: A Guide to the Use and Preservation of American Historical Sources,* p. 168; Lyman H. Butterfield, "Draper's Predecessors," p. 6. That there was no question about the preeminence of manuscript collecting by the Society can be seen from the plan of organization which read in part: "Each Member on his admission shall engage to use his utmost endeavors to collect and communicate to the Society—Manuscripts, printed books, and pamhlets . . ." See Walter Muir Whitehill, *Independent Historical Societies: An Enquiry into Their Research and Publication Functions and Their Financial Future,* p. 6.

22. David D. Van Tassel and James A. Tinsley, "Historical Organizations as Aids to History," p. 128; Hockett, *Critical Method*, pp. 212, 215; Alice E. Smith, "Draper Manuscripts," pp. 45–61.

23. Mary A. Benjamin, *Autographs: A Key to Collecting*, p. 11.

24. Lucile M. Kane, "Manuscript Collecting," pp. 33–34; Van Tassel and Tinsley, "Historical Organizations," pp. 134–135.

25. Van Tassel and Tinsley, "Historical Organizations," pp. 134–135; David D. Van Tassel, "John Franklin Jameson," pp. 86–87; "Fifth Annual Report of the Historical Manuscripts Commission," pp. 595–607.

26. Kane, "Manuscript Collecting," pp. 33–35; Whitehill, *Independent Historical Societies*, pp. 500, 504–505.

27. Whitehill, *Independent Historical Societies*, pp. 505, 508.

28. Lester J. Cappon, "Historian as Editor," p. 174; Hockett, *Critical Method*, p. 210.

29. Lyman Butterfield, "Draper's Predecessors," pp. 18–21; Fred Shelley, "Manuscripts in the Library of Congress: 1800–1900," p. 7.

30. *North American Review* 23 (1826): 286–287.

31. Kraus, *A History of American History*, pp. 171–172, 200–215.

32. Robert Halsband, "Editing the Letters of Letter-Writers," p. 125.

33. Kraus, *A History of American History*, p. 203.

34. Lyman Butterfield, "Draper's Predecessors," p. 11; *Dictionary of American Biography*, 2d ed., s.v. "Sprague, William Buell."

35. *Dictionary of American Biography*, 2d ed., s.v. "Sprague, William Buell"; Lyman Butterfield, "Draper's Predecessors," p. 14.

36. A. N. L. Munby, *Cult of the Autograph Letter in England*, p. 30.

37. *Ibid.*, pp. 10–11.

38. Boyd C. Shafer et al., *Historical Study in the West*, p. 9.

39. Ernst Posner, *Archives in the Ancient World*, pp. 178, 165, 157.

40. *Ibid.*, pp. 49, 125.

41. Benjamin, *Autographs*, p. 7; Posner, *Archives in the Ancient World*, pp. 192, 198.

42. Benjamin, *Autographs*, p. 7.

43. See Shafer et al., *Historical Study*, pp. 12–13.

44. Colton Storm and Howard Peckham, *Invitation to Book Collecting: Its Pleasures and Practices; With Kindred Discussions of Manuscripts, Maps, and Prints*, p. 117; Benjamin, *Autographs*, p. 10; and Munby, *Cult of the Autograph*, p. 2.

45. Munby, *Cult of the Autograph*, pp. 83–84.

46. *Ibid.*, pp. 31–32; David C. Mearns, "Nineteenth-Century Comments on Autographs and Collectors," pp. 49–50.

47. Munby, *Cult of the Autograph*, pp. 23–24.

48. *Ibid.*, pp. 24–29; Mearns, "Nineteenth-Century Collectors," pp. 49–50; Fred Shelley, "Manuscripts in Library of Congress," p. 7.

49. Marjorie Plant, *The English Book Trade: An Economic History of the Making and Sale of Books*, p. 247; John Lawler, *Book Auctions in England in the Seventeenth Century*, p. xl.

50. Munby, *Cult of the Autograph*, pp. 21, 81, 85; Mearns, "Nineteenth-Century Collectors," pp. 49–50.

51. *Graham's Magazine*, May 1845, p. 238, as quoted under the title "Autograph Prices in 1845," *Manuscripts* 2, no. 1 (1949), 17.

52. George L. McKay, "*American Book Auction Catalogues, 1713–1934; A Union List*," no. 39, pp. 339, 405, 462, 562; Lyman Butterfield, "Draper's Predecessors," p. 13.

53. Boston Public Library, *Manuscripts of the Revolution in the Boston Public Library: A Descriptive Catalog*, p. iii; Cannon, *American Book Collectors*, p. 176.

54. Lyman Butterfield, "Draper's Predecessors," p. 13; Cappon, "Walter R. Benjamin and the Autograph Trade," pp. 24–25.

55. Munby, *Cult of the Autograph*, pp. 79–80.

56. See Benjamin, *Autographs*, p. 14.

57. Howard Mumford Jones, *One Great Society: Humane Learning in the United States*, pp. 103–105.

CHAPTER 2

1. Kenneth E. Beasley, "Library Administration: An Overview," p. 13.

2. Richard A. Erney and F. Gerald Ham, "Wisconsin's Area Research Centers," pp. 135–140.

3. Many public libraries (rivaled only by the average ill-equipped county historical society) hold the worst-administered manuscript collections in this country. Unfortunately, few of these institutions will turn their collections over to the agencies which can care for them properly.

4. Warren Bennis, "The University Leader," pp. 43, 49.

5. Letter of Robert Adelsperger to Kenneth Duckett, December 17, 1973.

6. Amy W. Nyholm, "Modern Manuscripts: A Functional Approach," p. 337.

7. Herbert Finch, "Administrative Relationships in a Large Manuscript Repository," pp. 21–25.

8. *Ibid.*, p. 25.

9. Donald Coney, "Management in College and University Libraries," p. 91.

10. Herbert Finch, "Administrative Relationships," p. 24; Fred J. Heinritz, "Quantitative Management in Libraries," p. 236.

11. Alan Gilchrist, "Work Study in Libraries," p. 129; Richard H. Logsdon, "Time and Motion Studies in Libraries," pp. 405–407.

12. Gilchrist, "Work Study," p. 131.

13. G. C. K. Smith and J. L. Schofield, "Administrative Effectiveness: Times and Costs of Library Operation," p. 247.

14. Minnesota Historical Society, "The Nature of Manuscripts and the Special Occupation Descriptions for Employees of a Manuscripts Center," pp. 1–[5].

15. Ruth B. Bordin, "Cataloging Manuscripts—A Simple Scheme," p. 85.

16. Alice Warner, "Voluntarism and Librarianship," pp. 1241–1245; Harold Jenkins, "Volunteers in the Future of the Library," pp. 1399–1403.

17. Rita R. Campbell, "Machine Retrieval in the Herbert Hoover Archives," p. 302.

18. Lucile Kane to Kenneth Duckett in comments on this chapter, November 19, 1972.

19. Nyholm, "Modern Manuscripts," p. 338.

20. Leslie B. Rothenberg et al., "A Job-Task Index for Evaluating Professional Utilization in Libraries," pp. 320–328.

21. Lionell Bell, "The Professional Training of Archivists," pp. 191, 196.

22. Society of American Archivists, *Archival Education Directory*, pp. 1–6. The SAA Council denied a request to reprint the 1974 edition of the directory as an appendix to this volume, and the author was unable to obtain the information necessary to bring this text up to date. Copies of the directory, which contains information on twelve programs, twenty courses, and six institutes, are available for free distribution from

the office of the secretary. (Letters to Kenneth Duckett from Maynard Brichford, October 24, 1973, and from Judith Koucky, January 18, 1974.)

23. Ann Bowden, "Training for Rare Book Librarianship," pp. 226–230.

24. Cornell has published a useful loose-leaf manual which is for sale: see Richard Strassberg, compiler, *Cornell University Libraries Manual of Manuscript Processing Procedures.*

25. Frank B. Evans, *Administration of Modern Archives: A Select Bibliographic Guide.* The two most important sources for the curator will be Lucile M. Kane, *A Guide to the Care and Administration of Manuscripts,* and Ruth B. Bordin and Robert M. Warner, *The Modern Manuscript Library.*

26. Robert M. Warner, "Secretary's Notes," p. 34.

27. Charles Martell, "Administration: Which Way—Traditional Practice or Modern Theory?," p. 107.

28. Douglas McGregor, *The Human Side of Enterprise,* pp. 47–48; Robert N. Ford, *Motivation Through the Work Itself,* pp. 29, 148–149.

29. *Ibid.,* pp. 116, 119.

30. Benjamin E. Powell, "Sources of Support for Libraries in American Universities," pp. 180–184; Andrew J. Eaton, "Fund Raising for University Libraries," p. 352.

31. Guy R. Lyle, *The Administration of the College Library,* p. 323.

32. Kermit J. Pike, "Private Sources of Special Funds for Archives and Manuscript Repositories," p. 7.

33. Mabel L. Conat, "History of the Friends of the Library," pp. 2–4.

34. Errett W. McDiarmid, "Role of the Friends in the Library Organization," p. 12.

35. *Ibid.,* pp. 12–16; Mary A. Benjamin, "Columbia Wakes Up!" pp. 10–11.

36. Eugenie M. Suter, Elinor N. Brink, and Dorothea O. Christian, "How to Organize a Friends of the Library," pp. 20–29; Lawrence V. Mott, "Activities of the Friends of the Library," pp. 30–34.

37. Council on Library Resources, *Sixteenth Annual Report,* pp. 31–35.

38. Eaton, "Fund Raising for University Libraries," pp. 356–357; William T. Alderson, Jr., "Securing Grant Support."

39. The text of the three preceding paragraphs was supplied by Sue Holbert, assistant curator of manuscripts, Minnesota Historical Society, formerly grants officer for Macalester College.

40. Alderson, "Securing Grant Support."

41. *Ibid.*

42. Howard Peckham, "Acquisition of Rare Materials," pp. 26–27. Peckham is speaking here specifically of rare books, but it is certain he would apply the principle with equal force to manuscripts.

43. *Ibid.,* p. 33.

44. David Y. Sellers, "Basic Planning and Budgeting Concepts for Special Libraries," pp. 70–71.

45. Dean Tutor, "The Special Library Budget," pp. 518–519.

46. Fred L. Bellomy, "Management Planning for Library Systems Development," p. 188.

47. Tutor, "Special Library Budget," pp. 518–519; Sellers, "Basic Planning and Budgeting," p. 73.

48. Sellers, "Basic Planning and Budgeting," p. 72.

49. Herbert Finch, "Administrative Relationships," pp. 21, 22.

50. Minnesota Historical Society, "Functions of the Manuscripts Division."

51. Tutor, "Special Library Budget," p. 517.

52. H. Richard Archer, "Special Collections," pp. 356–357.

53. Cecil K. Byrd, "Quarters For Special Collections in University Libraries," p. 228.

54. Keyes D. Metcalf, *Planning Academic and Research Library Buildings*, pp. 110–111.

55. Byrd, "Quarters for Special Collections," pp. 225–226.

56. Lyle, *Administration of the College Library*, p. 384.

57. Victor J. Gondos, Jr., "Archival Buildings—Programing and Planning," p. 479.

58. Philip M. Chu, remarks made at the session entitled "What To Do Before the Architect Comes," annual meeting of the Society of American Archivists, September 26, 1973; Lyle, *Administration of the College Library*, p. 382.

59. American Library Association, *Protecting the Library and Its Resources: A Guide to Physical Protection and Insurance*, pp. 98–118; J. O. Kellerman, "Observations on Archival Depositories in Overseas Countries," p. 56; and National Fire Protection Association, *Manual for Fire Protection for Archives and Records Centers*, pp. 22–25.

60. National Fire Protection Association, *Fire Protection for Archives*, pp. 10–11.

61. *Ibid.*, p. 17

62. See Byrd, "Quarters For Special Collections," pp. 232–233.

63. J. H. Hodson, *Administration of Archives*, p. 90; National Fire Protection Association, *Fire Protection for Archives*, pp. 18–19.

64. National Fire Protection Association, *Fire Protection for Archives*, pp. 19–20.

65. *Ibid.*, pp. 20–21; E. I. du Pont, *Du Pont Halon 1301*, pp. 3–5.

66. C. E. Welch, "Protection from Fires in Libraries," pp. 881–882; E. I. du Pont, *Du Pont Halon 1301*, p. 7; and a letter of Harold Tribolet to Lester Reinke, June 15, 1971. Tests mentioned in the text were visual examinations of materials which had been subjected to prolonged exposure to Halon 1301. Du Pont has conducted physical and chemical tests upon plastics and metals exposed to Halon, but not upon papers. (See E. I. du Pont, *Du Pont Halon 1301*, pp. 9–10.)

CHAPTER 3

1. Walter Rundell, Jr., *In Pursuit of American History: Research and Training in the United States*, p. 104.

2. Ralph R. Shaw, *Literary Property in the United States*, p. 141.

3. Robert L. Zangrando, remarks made at the session entitled "Recruitment and Training of Archival Personnel," annual meeting of the Society of American Archivists, November 2, 1972.

4. O. Lawrence Burnette, Jr., *Beneath the Footnote: A Guide to the Use and Preservation of American Historical Sources*, pp. 105–116, 111–112, 116.

5. T. J. Easterwood, "The Collecting and Care of Modern Manuscripts," p. 8.

6. William H. Bond, "Manuscript Collections in the Houghton Library," p. 32.

7. Lucile M. Kane, "Manuscript Collecting," p. 43.

8. *Ibid.*, p. 44.

9. Richard D. Altick, *The Scholar Adventurers*, pp. 116–117.

10. Lucile Kane to Kenneth Duckett in comments on this chapter, November 14, 1972.

11. Justin Winsor, "Manuscript Sources of American History—The Conspicuous Collections Extant," p. 11.

12. "The Handling & Storage of Magnetic Recording Tape," p. 4.

13. Roy B. Basler, "The Modern Collector," p. 27.

14. Rundell, *In Pursuit of History*, pp. 339–400.

15. *Ibid.*

16. Andreas L. Brown, "Valuation and Appraisal," p. 23. Many dealers sell both books and manuscripts. Only a handful scattered on the two coasts deal exclusively in manuscripts, although one of their number, Kenneth Rendell, estimates that the great bulk of the manuscripts sold, perhaps as high as 90 percent, pass through the hands of specialists rather than the book sellers who handle manuscripts as a sideline. (Kenneth Rendell to Kenneth Duckett, October 4, 1972.)

17. It is stressed, however, that even the 20 percent is misleading in that dealers often act as agents for dealers in other cities, who in turn are acting as agents for private or institutional collectors. The second dealer probably makes a 10 percent profit on a transaction of this kind, which is recorded as a dealer-to-dealer sale. (Letters of Kenneth Rendell to Kenneth Duckett, October 4, 1972, and October 20, 1973.)

18. A much-needed supplement to the auction sales records will be published after 1976, according to the following news note in the *Library of Congress Information Bulletin* 32 (1973), 325: "The Index to Manuscripts of Prominent Americans 1763-1815, a definitive record of book sellers' and autograph dealers' catalogs from the earliest 19th-century activities down to the present, has been transferred from the Papers of James Madison at the University of Virginia to the American Antiquarian Society at Worcester, Massachusetts."

The index began as a serious undertaking in 1972, with support from a consortium of historical editing projects, aimed at the creation of an all-inclusive index of any historical manuscripts dated between 1763 and 1815, and offered for sale. A master index will result and publication of the information is expected after the 1976 completion date.

19. To the author's knowledge, only one man in this country, Robert Metzdorf, makes his living exclusively as an appraiser of manuscripts and rare books.

20. Andreas Brown, "Valuation and Appraisal," p. 24. Mr. Brown gives a figure of $200 per diem. The figures in the text are based upon the author's general knowledge of fees charged his institution and others prior to the inflation of the mid-1970s.

21. This is the clause in a person's will reading something similar to the following: "All the residue of my property, both real and personal, I leave to Sara Winter. . . ." (See chapter 8, footnote 54).

22. Robert F. Metzdorf, "Appraisal of Literary Properties," p. B15.

23. Roland Baughman, "The Evaluation and Insurance of Great Rarities," pp. 265–268.

24. The principle of added value for research potential would not apply to a similar series of letters offered to the dealer for sale. He will justify this by saying that, while he may be able to sell the letters as a group, more likely he will have to sell them separately. Also, he might point out that prices are dependent upon supply and demand and, while he can sell one letter at $150, it is doubtful that there is a demand for twenty.

25. Dealers arrive at figures cited in appraisals in several ways. The example used in the text is predicated upon a series of more or less uniform letters. Ordinarily, a series like this would contain letters of varying value which the appraiser would total. But occasionally he will price an average letter in the series and multiply that by the number of letters. Sometimes, as indicated in the text, he determines a per-page value and multiplies by the number of pages. In each instance above, the dealer has a knowledge of the value of the manuscript based upon past sales. But when he must appraise material without a sales record, he guesses, basing his appraisal upon values of what he feels is comparable material.

26. Ralph G. Newman, "Apprisals and 'Revenooers': Tax Problems of the Collector."

27. Seymour V. Connor, "A System of Manuscript Appraisal."

28. *Digest of Public General Bills and Resolutions, 93rd Congress, 1st Session* (Washington: Library of Congress, 1973), pp. E145, E420, A219, A25.

29. Andreas Brown, "Valuation and Appraisal," pp. 23, 24.

30. U.S. Treasury Department, Internal Revenue Service, *Valuation of Property.* (Washington: Internal Revenue Service, 1968).

31. Donald R. Briggs, "Gift Appraisal Policy in Large Research Libraries," pp. 506–507; William Matheson, "An Approach to Special Collections," p. 1153.

32. Newman, "Apprisals and 'Revenooers' "; Winston Broadfoot in a letter to Mary Benjamin which she quotes in *The Collector: A Magazine for Autograph and Historical Collectors* 85, no. 824 ([ca. 1972]): 1–2.

33. "On Taking Copies of Manuscripts," pp. 1–2.

34. *Ibid.*; "Odds and Ends," p. 2.

35. Carl L. Cannon, *American Book Collectors and Collecting from Colonial Times to the Present,* pp. 44–45.

36. Winsor, "Manuscript Sources of American History," pp. 15–16.

37. Colton Storm and Howard Peckham, *Invitation to Book Collecting: Its Pleasures and Practices; With Kindred Discussions of Manuscripts, Maps, and Prints,* p. 129.

38. Maryland, Department of General Services, *Hall of Records Report no. 36,* p. 2.

39. Morris L. Radoff, *27th Annual Report of the Maryland Hall of Records, 1963,* as quoted in *American Archivist* 27 (1964): 13.

40. *AB Bookman's Weekly* 44 (1969): 546.

41. S. C. Newton, "The Archivist as Legislator," p. 657.

42. David C. Duniway, "Conflicts in Collecting," p. 55.

43. *Ibid.,* pp. 62–63.

44. Robert S. Gordon and John E. Wickman, remarks made at the session entitled "Collecting Personal Papers: Ethics and Realities," annual meeting of the Society of American Archivists, September 28, 1973.

CHAPTER 4

1. George M. Cunha and Dorothy G. Cunha, *Conservation of Library Materials: A Manual and Bibliography on the Care, Repair and Restoration of Library Materials* (rev. ed.), p. 52.

2. Letters to Kenneth Duckett from Harold Tribolet, October 24, 1972, and Virginia Ingram, October 23, 1973.

3. The curator who is hard pressed for space may want to consider the experience of the Manuscript and Archives Division at Yale. There, manuscripts have been stored for years in cloth-covered flat boxes, which the staff recently began turning on their sides at what they estimate is a saving of one third in shelf space. Similarly, of course, Hollinger cartons can be laid down to store manuscripts flat; and, stacked two high, they take the same amount of space as two cartons shelved as they were designed to be stored.

4. Gladys T. Piez, "Archival Containers—A Search for Safer Materials," pp. 433–438.

5. Richard D. Smith, "Paper Impermanence as a Consequence of pH and Storage Conditions," p. 186; Harold W. Tribolet, "Rare Book & Paper Repair Techniques."

6. George M. Cunha and Norman P. Tucker, editors, *Library and Archives Conservation,* pp. 99–101.

7. In replies to direct questions, both Harold Tribolet, formerly manager of the Graphics Conservation Department, Lakeside Press, and Paul Banks, Conservator, the Newberry Library, recommended against any do-it-yourself fumigation. Cunha and Tucker, *Library and Archives Conservation,* pp. 137–142, list several chemicals used in pest control, and Cunha and Cunha, *Conservation of Library Materials,* pp. 108–109, discuss how to build a homemade fumigation chamber. The North Carolina Department of Archives and History uses a Union Carbide, Linde Division, product called Carboxide (ethylene oxide and carbon dioxide) for fumigation, but it is both toxic and inflammable. (H. G. Jones to Kenneth Duckett, May 2, 1973.)

8. Harold Tribolet to Kenneth Duckett, October 24, 1972.

9. D. B. Wardle, *Document repair,* p. 15; Tribolet to Duckett, October 24, 1972.

10. See Charles G. Weber, Merle B. Shaw, and E. A. Back, "Effects of Fumigants on Paper," p. 271.

11. See photographs of the cleaning tables and the compressed-air jets in use at the National Archives in Lucile M. Kane, *A Guide to the Care and Administration of Manuscripts,* p. 12.

12. Donald C. Anthony, "Caring for Your Collections: Manuscripts & Related Materials"; Carolyn Horton, *Cleaning and Preserving Bindings and Related Materials,* pp. 5, 7. Miss Horton recommends a piece of screen or cheesecloth over the opening in the vacuum cleaner brush to avoid bits of loose paper being sucked into the bag.

13. Horton, *Cleaning and Preserving,* p. 32.

14. *Ibid.,* pp. 7, 32–33. The conservator of prints and drawings at the Museum of Modern Art admits that bleaching stains "is one of the most controversial areas of paper conservation," but for the curator who has the temerity to try the process, she offers some explicit instructions to get him started in his experimentation. (See Antoinette King, "Conservation of Drawings and Prints," pp. 116–119.)

15. Ellen S. Brinton, "Inexpensive Devices to Aid the Archivist," p. 285.

16. George M. Cunha, *Conservation of Library Materials,* pp. 165–174. Mr. Cunha, formerly conservator at the Boston Athenaeum, offers an alternative in these pages, that is, a series of regional cooperative conservation centers. His proposal includes a preamble, articles of association, and a table of organization and staffing of a nonprofit center which renders conservation services to members. In the spring of 1973, under the direction of Mr. Cunha, the New England Document Conservation Center was formed, and currently similar units are in the formative stage in Maine, Hawaii, California, Oregon, and Canada. (See Dianne S. O'Neal, "1973 Meeting of American Institute for Conservation," pp. 1, 4.)

17. *All the King's Horses,* pp. 8–13.

18. Interview with Paul Banks, May 22, 1972.

19. Workshop on "Paper Conservation and Restoration Techniques,'" annual meeting of the Society of American Archivists, November 2, 1972. A participant at the meeting noted that the preservation office of the Library of Congress might have an operative training program in eighteen months. Also mentioned at this workshop was a limited training program at the Rochester Institute of Technology, an informal internship (without pay) at the National Archives, and the training given to purchasers of laminating equipment by the Barrow Laboratory in Richmond.

20. Wardle, *Document Repair,* pp. 10–14, 75–78.

21. "NYSHA Seminar on American Culture," p. 263. This contains the report of a seminar taught by Harold Tribolet and Carolyn Horton on "Conservation of Rare Books, Manuscripts and Related Materials." (See also Horton, *Cleaning and Preserving,* pp. 14,

26-27.) To use the tape on weak or flimsy paper, Miss Horton recommends serrating the edge of the tape with pinking shears. This helps to eliminate the wrinkling of the paper and takes the hard edge off the tape, making it less likely for the paper, under stress, to tear. Since Miss Horton's book was revised in 1969, Dennison has stopped manufacturing its adhesive paper in rolls of tape. It must now be purchased in sheets. This illustrates one great difficulty in conservation: that is, firms are continually dropping products or changing their ingredients. One restorer thinks changes over the years in the glue formula may have caused the few cases he has encountered of irreversible stains on papers mended with Dennison tape. These have been a few very old repairs, and he admits that exterior influences on the tape may have caused the discoloration, but he advises against a blanket approval of the tape. (Letter of Colton Storm to Kenneth Duckett, November 4, 1973.)

22. Nancy Storm to Kenneth Duckett, August 10, 1972. Conservators suggest dating PVA when it is received. After being opened, it should be replaced with fresh adhesive every six months; unopened, it has only a one-year shelf life. (See appendix for recommended brands of polyvinyl acetate.)

23. Horton, *Cleaning and Preserving*, pp. 22, 28; Wardle, *Document Repair*, p. 35. Experiments are being conducted to find a way to freeze-dry paste. Since paste must be made sometimes as often as once a week to keep it from souring, this technique, if perfected, will be a great time-saver. (see O'Neal, "1973 Meeting of American Instutute for Conservation," p. 5.)

24. Denis Blunn, "A Method of Dry Repair," pp. 521-522.

25. Y. P. Kathpalia, "Hand Lamination with Cellulose Acetate," pp. 271-272; Wardle, *Document Repair*, pp. 58-59.

26. Margaret Scriven, *Preservation and Restoration of Library Materials*, pp. 6-7.

27. See Virginia N. Lawrence, "The Case Against Plastic Tape," p. 233, and Wacky Packages Ⓣ, Registered trademark, Topps Chewing Gum, Inc.

28. Horton, *Cleaning and Preserving*, pp. 14, 27.

29. Interview with Thomas Etherington, April 2, 1973, and a letter from Virginia Ingram to Kenneth Duckett, October 23, 1973.

30. "Tapes for Paper Repair," pp. 1-2.

31. *Barrow Method of Restoring Documents*, pp. 3-13; Richard Smith, "Paper Deacidification: A Preliminary Report," pp. 273-277.

32. Wardle, *Document Repair*, pp. 56-61; J. H. Hodson, *The Administration of Archives*, p. 137; W. R. Privett, Ademco Ltd., to Kenneth Duckett, May 11, 1973.

33. D. G. Vaisey, "The New Manuscript Repair Room," p. 2.

34. See Richard Smith, "New Approaches to Preservation," p. 149.

35. Richard Smith, "The Nonaqueous Deacidification of Paper and Books," pp. 186, 191; Richard Smith, "New Approaches to Preservation," pp. 149-164; Richard Smith, *Patents nos.* 3,676,055 and 3,676,182. Harold Tribolet, formerly manager of the Graphics Conservation Department, Lakeside Press, says the solution was used on the copy of the Declaration of Independence discovered in Leary's Book Store, Philadelphia, in 1969; on an important Washington letter recently reproduced in facsimile by Donnelley's; "and [on] many other significant pieces of paper." Mr. Tribolet further states: "We are convinced his deacidification process is good, otherwise we wouldn't have used it on the pieces mentioned above, however, many of the conservators are now in the process of trying it, and all their comments have not been received by Smith." (Harold Tribolet to Kenneth Duckett, July 26, 1972.)

36. Paul McCarthy, "Vapor Phase Deacidification: A New Preservation Method,"
pp. 333–342; W. H. Langwell, "Vapour-phase De-acidification: A Recent Development,"
pp. 597–598.

37. Wardle, *Document Repair*, pp. 16–17; W. H. Langwell, "Methods of Deacidifying
Paper," pp. 491–494; Richard Smith, "Restoration of Records," p. 27.

38. Letter from Robert Goldsmith to Ralph McCoy, November 5, 1973, containing
a mimeographed statement, "Morpholine Vapor Deacidification Process," dated September 19, 1973, and letters from Forestier Walker to Kenneth Duckett, December 12,
1974, and January 2, 1975.

39. Ademco, *Heat Sealing*, and an undated press release, "Lamatec, Archivists'
Laminating Tissue."

40. Letters to Kenneth Duckett from Mrs. W. J. Barrow, April 21, 1972, including
Cost Estimates for Restoration of Documents; from Joseph Boak III, Arbee Co., October
19, 1972; and from W. J. Privett, Ademco, May 11, 1973.

41. Workshop on "Paper Conservation Techniques," annual meeting of the Society
of American Archivists, November 3, 1972; Frazer G. Poole, "Preservation Costs and
Standards," pp. 617–618.

42. O'Neal, "1973 Meeting of American Institute for Conservation," pp. 4–5.

43. *Ibid.*; interview with Walter Ristow, April 4, 1973.

44. N. S. Baer, N. Indictor, and A. Joel, "The Aging Behavior of Impregnating
Agent-paper Systems as Used in Paper Conservation," pp. 5–23.

45. Letter from Mrs. W. J. Barrow to Kenneth Duckett, August 18, 1972; and interview
with Virginia Ingram, April 8, 1973.

46. Vaisey, "New Manuscript Repair Room," p. 2.

47. Horton, *Cleaning and Preserving*, p. 2.

48. Wardle, *Document Repair*, pp. 10–14, 75–78; J. H. Hodson, *The Administration
of Archives*, pp. 156–158.

49. American Library Association, *Protecting the Library and Its Resources: A Guide
to Physical Protection and Insurance*, pp. 248–258.

50. After the fire at the Military Records Building, National Personnel Records Center,
St. Louis, in July 1973, the center was sprayed with a 3 percent solution of thymol
dissolved in trichloroethane. Mold, which was expected to form within thirty-six hours,
was still not much in evidence after three weeks. (Peter Waters, untitled speech, annual
meeting of the Society of American Archivists, September 27, 1973.)

51. Peter Waters, *Emergency Procedures for Salvaging Flood or Water-Damaged
Library Materials*, p. 4. The remainder of this section on flood- and water-damaged
salvage is based upon this fine pamphlet, a copy of which should be in every curator's
possession. Requests for copies far exceeded the initial printing, but the pamphlet, after
being revised, was scheduled to be issued as a regular Library of Congress publication
late in 1973. (Undated letter from Frazer Poole to Kenneth Duckett, ca. October 15, 1973.)

52. The St. Louis records center fire involved the federal government in a monumental
restoration program embodying an estimated 450,000 drawers of wet records. During
the fire, a million gallons of water per floor were poured into the building. Records
on the bottom shelves, which were under water, were almost completely salvaged.
Immediately after the fire, the McDonnell Douglas Corporation offered its space simulation chamber for use in a variation of the freeze-dry technique. Classified files from
the center were packed in large plastic boxes (designed to carry four half-gallon milk
cartons), two thousand of which could be fitted into the sealed fourteen-foot chamber.

There, in a four-to-six-hour cycle, they were first heated to 140° and then frozen gradually while the air pressure was lowered to almost a vacuum. Then the warm air was reintroduced and the cycle repeated until the records were completely dry, which took about five days. Although thirty thousand documents could be salvaged each five days, the space chamber could accommodate but a fraction of the damaged records. Other records were placed in hog pens to dry under thirty army tents which had been set up in the center's parking lot. (*McDonnell Douglas Spirit,* September 1973, pp. 1-2; Peter Waters, untitled speech, annual meeting of the Society of American Archivists, September 27, 1973.)

53. Waters, *Emergency Procedures,* pp. [18-19]. The appendix of Mr. Waters's pamphlet contains lists of the names of persons known to have advised or supervised salvage operations of flood-damaged materials and gives sources of supplies and equipment.

CHAPTER 5

1. Archivists who have shied away from the use of the term *bibliographic* because of its library connotations need to go to the root of the matter as their revered mentor Ernst Posner did in his recent book, *Archives in the Ancient World.* Describing record-keeping as it was developed by the Romans in the Egypt of the Ptolemys, Posner wrote: "A *biblion,* it should be remembered, signifies a roll of papyrus regardless of the content of the writing that appears on it; hence a *bibliothéké* is a container for papyrus rolls and, in a wider sense, an institution or agency that preserves such rolls, whether of literary or business character. Thus a *bibliothéké* may be a repository for books, that is a library, or a repository for records. In our context it is the latter: a record office or archival agency." (See Posner, p. 141.)

2. Elfrieda Lang, "Arrangement and Cataloging of Manuscripts in the Lilly Library, Indiana University, Bloomington, Indiana," p. 5.

3. Theodore R. Schellenberg, *The Management of Archives,* p. 90; Oliver W. Holmes, "History and Theory of Archival Practice," p. 4.

4. Thomas H. Johnson, "Establishing a Text: The Emily Dickinson Papers," pp. 146-154.

5. Another method of keeping a multi-paged letter together is to enclose it in a folder or half folder of bond or thin, acid-free paper.

6. Usually, envelopes are placed in the institution's philatelic collection, or sold to a dealer specializing in stamps and manuscripts. No curator would leave currency in a collection, and stamps are almost as attractive to the light-fingered.

7. If the curator arranges the correspondence by chronology, he should sort the letters and replies by their own dates. If the two are attached, the researcher would have to cite both to find the reply.

8. Very little has been written about the technique of sampling—a simple form of which is described in the text—but it can be especially useful in processing voluminous files of business records. One authority suggests "sampling based upon high and low points of the business," or upon "uniform periods (such as 10-year intervals or selected points in the business cycle)." This same source suggests that the first and last volume of a series ought to be retained, and detailed records should be kept of what is destroyed. (Robert W. Lovett, "The Appraisal of Older Business Records," pp. 233-234. See also Harold T. Pinkett, "Selective Preservation of General Correspondence," pp. 33-43, and Paul Lewinson, "Archival Sampling," pp. 291-312.)

9. Ruth B. Bordin, "Cataloging Manuscripts—A Simple Scheme," p. 82.

10. For the three paragraphs above outlining special concerns of the curator who arranges the very large organization or company collections, the author is indebted to Lucile Kane.

11. Letters to Kenneth Duckett from Lee Scamehorn, February 23, 1973, and Virginia Fowler, Archival Associates, February 15 and March 10, 1973. See appendix and Directory.

12. Ruth B. Bordin and Robert M. Warner, *The Modern Manuscript Library*, pp. 47–48, 123–129.

13. Lucile M. Kane, *A Guide to the Care and Administration of Manuscripts*, pp. 53–54.

14. Lester J. Cappon, "The Historian as Editor," p. 181.

15. Society of American Archivists, Committee on Techniques for the Control and Description of Archives and Manuscripts, received sample registers and inventories from more than a hundred institutions from which the committee drew up a "Draft Standards for the Preparation of Registers and Inventories." This draft, which attempts to codify present practices, has been submitted to the SAA Council for action. (Letter to Kenneth Duckett from Frank Burke, November 14, 1973.)

16. Edward C. Papenfuse, "Retreat from Standardization: A Comment on the Recent History of Finding Aids," pp. 540–541.

17. U.S. Library of Congress, *Subject Headings Used in Library of Congress*.

18. U.S. Library of Congress, *National Union Catalog of Manuscript Collections*, Information Circular no. 5; American Library Association, *Anglo-American Cataloging Rules*.

19. American Library Association, *Anglo-American Cataloging Rules*, pp. 344, 266–268.

20. Kane, *Guide to Care of Manuscripts*, p. 60.

21. American Library Association, *Anglo-American Cataloging Rules*, pp. 192, 259–264.

22. Bordin and Warner, *Modern Manuscript Library*, pp. 62–63.

23. American Library Association, *ALA Rules for Filing*.

24. The system described in the text, with very minor variations, is used at the University of Virginia, which in the 1972–1973 fiscal year added 10,718 cards to the main catalog and 597 cards to the chronological catalog. Researchers have been very complimentary of the combination card catalog and guide-inventory system, and the curator says that it would take "a really earth-shaking decision" to force the university to abandon it. (Letter from Edmund Berkeley, Jr., to Kenneth Duckett, October 10, 1974.)

25. Amy W. Nyholm, "Modern Manuscripts: A Functional Approach," p. 327.

26. William H. Bond, "Manuscript Collections in the Houghton Library," p. 35.

27. Evert Volkersz, "Neither Book nor Manuscript: Some Special Collections," p. 494.

28. Lang, "Arrangement and Cataloging of Manuscripts," p. 9. Knowledge of the subject-heading file at the Oregon Historical Society and the other systems described in this portion of the text is not based upon the literature but upon personal visits to these institutions in 1972–1973.

29. Richard C. Berner, "Manuscript Catalogs and Other Finding Aids," pp. 367–372.

30. Mattie Russell, "The Manuscript Department in the Duke University Library," pp. 441–442.

31. Richard C. Berner and M. Gary Bettis, "Description of Manuscript Collections: A Single Network System," pp. 411–413, 416.

32. Carolyn A. Wallace, "The Southern Historical Collection," p. 433.

33. See, for example, Laurence G. Avery, compiler, *A Catalogue of the Maxwell Anderson Collection at the University of Texas*; Walter Timms, compiler, *Edmund B.*

Chaffee: An Inventory of His Papers in Syracuse University Library; and *Inventory of the Erasmus Gest Papers, 1834-1885.*

34. Wisconsin State Historical Society, *Descriptive List of the Manuscript Collections of the State Historical Society of Wisconsin; Together with Reports on Other Collections of Manuscript Materials for American History in Adjacent States;* Grace L. Nute and Gertrude W. Ackermann, compilers, *Guide to the Personal Papers in the Manuscript Collections of the Minnesota Historical Society;* Alice E. Smith, editor, *Guide to the Manuscripts of the Wisconsin Historical Society;* Josephine L. Harper and Sharon C. Smith, editors, *Guide to the Manuscripts of the State Historical Society of Wisconsin, Supplement Number One;* and Lucile M. Kane and Kathryn A. Johnson, compilers, *Manuscript Collections of the Minnesota Historical Society.*

35. Martin Schmitt, compiler, *Catalogue of Manuscripts in the University of Oregon Library;* Kermit J. Pike, *A Guide to the Manuscripts and Archives of the Western Reserve Historical Society;* and Andrea D. Lentz, editor, *A Guide to Manuscripts at the Ohio Historical Society.*

36. *The First One Hundred: A Catalog of Manuscripts and Special Collections.*

37. U.S. Smithsonian Institution, *A Preliminary Guide to the Smithsonian Institution Archives: 125 Anniversary of the Smithsonian Institution.*

38. University of Illinois at Chicago Circle, *Guide to Manuscript Collections.*

39. U.S. Library of Congress, *National Union Catalog of Manuscript Collections, 1971,* p. iii.

40. *Ibid., National Union Catalog of Manuscript Collections, Report, July-December, 1971,* p. 2.

41. John D. Cowley, *Bibliographical Description and Cataloging,* p. 147.

CHAPTER 6

1. Artel Ricks, "Can a Computer Help the Archivist and Librarian," p. 5.

2. Fred Shelley, "The Presidential Papers Program at the Library of Congress," pp. 429-433; Frank G. Burke, "The Application of Automated Techniques in the Management and Control of Source Materials," pp. 259-260.

3. Rita R. Campbell, "Machine Retrieval in the Herbert Hoover Archives," pp. 298-302.

4. Jay Atherton, "Mechanization of the Manuscript Catalogue at the Public Archives of Canada," pp. 303-309.

5. Frank B. Evans, "Automation and Archives," p. 12.

6. Burke, "Application of Automated Techniques," pp. 264-268; Evans, "Automation and Archives," pp. 8-9.

7. Evans, "Automation and Archives," pp. 9-10; Burke, "Application of Automated Techniques," pp. 260-278; U.S. National Archives and Records Service, a draft of "History of the Project," and "User's Introduction to the System," chapters 1 and 2 of the final report on SPINDEX II to be submitted by NARS to the Council on Library Resources, p. 5 (hereafter cited as NARS, CLR "Report").

8. U.S. Library of Congress, *Manuscripts: A MARC Format,* p. 1.

9. *Ibid.,* p. 37; U.S. Library of Congress, *National Union Catalog of Manuscript Collections, Report, 1971,* p. 2.

10. NARS, CLR "Report," pp. 5-7.

11. *Ibid.,* pp. 7-8.

12. *Ibid.,* p. 9; Evans, "Automation and Archives," p. 11.

13. NARS, CLR "Report," pp. 9–10; Cornell University, "Processing; SPINDEX II"; and a letter from Douglas Bakken to Kenneth Duckett, November 16, 1972.

14. Evans, "Automation and Archives," pp. 10–12.

15. NARS, CLR "Report," p. 12; U.S. National Archives and Records Service, "SPINDEX Users Conference," p. 1.

16. Jessica Hellwig, *Introduction to Computers and Programing*, p. 121.

17. U.S. National Archives and Records Service, "SPINDEX Users Conference," p. 2.

18. *Ibid.*, pp. 1–3.

19. *Ibid.*, pp. 4–5, 7.

20. Interviews with Richard Lytle and Alan Bain, April 4, 1973.

21. Letters of Richard Staar to Lucile Kane, November 2, 1972, Franz Lassner to Kenneth Duckett, October 26, 1973, and an interview with Charles Palm, January 22, 1973.

22. South Carolina Department of Archives and History, "SPINDEX Adaptation Project," p. 1; interview with Charles Lee, September 11, 1973.

23. Interview with Charles Lee, September 11, 1973.

24. *Ibid.*; South Carolina Department of Archives and History, "SPINDEX Adaptation Project," pp. 1–2; Charles Lee, remarks at the session, "The Finding Aid in Perspective," annual meeting of the Society of American Archivists, September 26, 1973.

25. Phyllis Platnick, "Proposal for Automating a Manuscript Repository," p. 440.

26. John C. Allen, "Item Indexing for Information Coordination in the Archival Depository," pp. 95, 98.

27. Tour of the records center, September 27, 1973.

28. Ricks, "Can a Computer Help," pp. 2, 9.

29. Campbell, "Machine Retrieval," p. 299; letter from Franz Lassner to Kenneth Duckett, October 26, 1973.

30. Lucile Kane to Kenneth Duckett, notes on this chapter, n.d.; U.S. National Archives and Records Service, "SPINDEX Users Conference," p. 7.

31. U.S. National Archives and Records Service, "SPINDEX Users Conference," p. 7; Lucile Kane to Kenneth Duckett, notes on this chapter, n.d.; interview with Charles Lee, September 11, 1973; and Charles Lee, comments on this chapter [January 15, 1974].

32. Michael E. Carroll, remarks at a workshop in "Machine Readable Records and Data Archives," annual meeting of the Society of American Archivists, November 3, 1972.

33. Evans, "Automation and Archives," pp. 13–16.

34. University of Illinois, University Archives, *Ninth Annual Report*, pp. 2, 5.

35. Campbell, "Machine Retrieval," p. 299; Frank G. Burke, "Automation and Historical Research," p. 83.

36. Ricks, "Can a Computer Help," p. 12.

37. George H. Harmon, "The Computer-Microfilm Relationship," p. 280.

38. *Ibid.*, p. 281; Susan Artandi, *An Introduction to Computers in Information Science*, p. 104.

39. Harmon, "Computer-Microfilm Relationship," pp. 281–282.

40. Roger Meetham, *Information Retrieval: The Essential Technology*, p. 43; Don M. Avedon, *Computer Output Microfilm*, pp. 1–6; Basil Doudnikoff, *Information Retrieval*, pp. 42–50. The sources disagree as to whether it was 1955 or 1957 in which COM was developed.

41. *Ibid.*, p. 49.

42. U.S. National Archives and Records Service, *Managing Information Retrieval, Microform Retrieval Equipment Guide,* pp. 4–6, 58–61.

43. *Ibid.,* pp. 8–9.

44. *Ibid.,* pp. 60–61.

45. *Ibid.,* pp. 8–9. If the curator is to rely upon microfilm equipment manufacturers, he may have difficulty purchasing an automatic counter. A series of letters written to equipment manufacturers by the author in 1972 did not locate any for sale. One company, Regiscope, offered a solution, however: "Documents can be stamped with a simple mechanical numbering device that stamps consecutive numbers." (Letter of William Chmiel to Kenneth Duckett, September 29, 1973.) It is hoped that Mr. Chmiel is not acting as advisor to any microfilming projects for NHPC or NEH! Other salesmen, who are anxious to sell expensive retrieval systems, are not likely to tell the curator that many electronic supply houses sell automatic image counters (electrically activated pulse counters) suitable to his needs for as little as $25 to $50.

46. Dolores C. Renze, "The Archivist's Responsibility for Integrity and Protection of the Record," p. 81; Albert H. Leisinger, Jr., *Microphotography for Archives,* p. 10.

47. Frederic Luther, "The Language of Lilliput: A Thesaurus for Users of Microfilm," pp. 3743–3746.

48. Hubbard W. Ballou, editor, *1970 Supplement to the Guide to Microreproduction Equipment.*

49. *Ibid.,* pp. 11, 15.

50. U.S. National Archives and Records Service, *Managing Information Retrieval: Microform Guide,* p. 2.

51. *Ibid.,* pp. 1–2; Eastman Kodak Co., *Recordak AHU Microfilm.*

52. Luther, "Language of Lilliput," pp. 931–932, 3745.

53. Frank B. Evans, *The Selection and Preparation of Records for Publication on Microfilm,* pp. 6–7.

54. Allen B. Veaner, *Evaluation of Micropublications: A Handbook for Librarians,* pp. 38–39; Frances G. Spigai, *The Invisible Medium: The State of the Art of Microform and a Guide to the Literature,* p. 7; and *Introduction to Micrographics,* p. 7.

55. Stephen R. Salmon, *Specifications for Library of Congress Microfilming,* pp. 3–7; Evans, *Selection of Records for Microfilm,* pp. 8–13.

56. One authority recommends using black paper which will not show fingerprints or smudges (see Allen Veaner to Kenneth Duckett, April 4, 1974), but the curator should experiment to see if he needs to adjust his normal light meter readings to compensate for this much exposed dark surface.

57. Leisinger, *Microphotography for Archives,* pp. 25–26; Evans, *Selection of Records for Microfilm,* pp. 8–13; and Veaner, *Evaluation of Micropublications,* pp. 41–42.

58. Veaner, *Evaluation of Micropublications,* pp. 41–42; Leisinger, *Microphotography for Archives,* pp. 25–26; Evans, *Selection of Records for Microfilm,* pp. 8–13.

59. Black paper probably will not work as well as white on letterpress copies, but it is more effective on manuscripts written on both sides where the reverse image of the verso is visible on the recto. (See Veaner, *Evaluation of Micropublications,* p. 35; D. B. Wardle, *Document Repair,* p. 36; and Evans, *Selection of Records for Microfilm,* p. 6, for suggestions on filming letterpress copies.)

60. Luther, "Language of Lilliput," p. 3239; Evans, *Selection of Records for Microfilm,* pp. 13–14; and Salmon, *Specifications for Microfilming,* pp. 14–15.

61. Estimates given to the author in the spring of 1972, in interviews with Elsie Frievogel, Archives of American Art, and David Maslyn, Manuscripts and Archives, Yale University.

62. Avedon, *Computer Output Microfilm,* pp. 34-76.

CHAPTER 7

1. Richard C. Berner and M. Gary Bettis, "Disposition of Nonmanuscript Items Found Among Manuscripts," pp. 275-281.

2. Lucile M. Kane, *A Guide to the Care and Administration of Manuscripts,* p. 37.

3. Walter S. Dunn, Jr., "Cataloging Ephemera: A Procedure for Small Libraries"; Evert Volkersz, "Neither Book nor Manuscript: Some Special Collections," pp. 497-499.

4. O. Lawrence Burnette, Jr., *Beneath the Footnote: A Guide to the Use and Preservation of American Historical Sources,* p. 335. See also Richard C. Berner, "On Ephemera: Their Collection and Use," pp. 335-339, for the theory and the system of collecting this material at the University of Washington.

5. A. M. Ferrar, "The Management of Map Collections and Libraries in University Geography Departments," p. 163; Lloyd A. Brown, "The Problem of Maps," pp. 224-225.

6. J. Douglas Hill, "Map and Atlas Cases," p. 483.

7. *Ibid.,* pp. 482, 485.

8. Burnette, *Beneath the Footnote,* p. 327.

9. Arch C. Gerlach, "Geography and Map Cataloging and Classification in Libraries," p. 250.

10. Walter W. Ristow, "The Emergence of Maps in Libraries," p. 407; John B. White, "Further Comments on Map Cataloging," p. 78.

11. Gerlach, "Geography and Map Cataloging," p. 250.

12. U.S. Library of Congress, *Classification: Class G;* Walter W. Ristow and David K. Carrington, "Machine-Readable Map Cataloging in the Library of Congress," pp. 344-345.

13. At Yale University, as in some other institutions, subjects are part of the map classification system. Commonly used subjects include outline maps, pictorial maps, relief maps, road maps, linguistic maps, aeromagnetic maps, and navigation charts. (Yale University, Map Collection, "Notes on Procedures," pp. 4-5.)

14. If the curator wants to build the collection actively, he should see Richard W. Stephenson, "Published Sources of Information About Maps and Atlases," pp. 87-98, 110-112. This very useful article lists journals of geography, journals reviewing maps, selective accession lists, bibliographies, dealers of out-of-print maps, and map publishers and sellers.

15. Marie T. Capps, "Preservation and Maintenance of Maps," p. 461.

16. Ansel Adams, *The Print: Contact Printing and Enlarging,* pp. 83-89; and a movie, *Wet Mounting,* produced by the University of Indiana, Bloomington. One authority describes a method of wet mounting on a wallboard utilizing techniques somewhat like applying wallpaper—"a deceptively simple, revolutionary idea." (See J. H. Hodson, *The Administration of Archives,* pp. 151-153.)

17. Newberry Library, *Hermon Dunlap Smith Center, Dedication Proceedings;* untitled publicity release from the dedication; and a letter from David Woodward to Kenneth

Duckett, February 27, 1973. The three libraries noted in the text as having well-cared-for map collections were recommended by Mr. Woodward, who is program director of the Hermon Dunlap Smith Center for the History of Cartography.

18. John Flory, "Doomsday for Film: The Crisis in Motion-Picture Archives," p. 410.

19. Glenn E. Matthews and Raife G. Tarkington, "Early History of Amateur Motion-Picture Film," pp. 106, 110, 114, 115.

20. Eugene Ostroff, "Preservation of Photographs," p. 310. Ostroff states that partially decomposed nitrate film might ignite at temperatures as low as 120° F. (See also Allen L. Cobb, "Burning Characteristics of Safety vs. Nitrate Film," pp. 66–68.)

21. Eastman Kodak, *Storage of Motion-Picture Film*, pp. 67–68.

22. Eastman Kodak, *Storage and Preservation of Motion-Picture Film*, pp. 14–16; John M. Calhoun, "The Preservation of Motion-Picture Film," p. 520. The Kodak pamphlet describes the five stages of decomposition of nitrate film, and Calhoun suggests that film in the soft, frothy, or powdery stages be immersed in water and the local fire department called.

23. Calhoun, "Preservation of Motion-Picture Film," p. 521.

24. Letters to Kenneth Duckett from Edward Rinker, DeLuxe General, June 14, 1973, and Donnie Moore, Eastman Kodak, August 22, 1972.

25. Eastman Kodak, *Storage of Motion-Picture Film*, pp. 59–62; Allen B. Veaner, *The Evaluation of Micropublications: A Handbook for Librarians*, p. 10.

26. John Wall, "Overcoming the Problem of Permanency in Colour Archives," pp. 141–143.

27. *Ibid*. See also section in this chapter on preservation of color transparencies.

28. Deane R. White et al., "Polyester Photographic Film Base," pp. 674, 678; Calhoun, "Preservation of Motion-Picture Film," p. 522.

29. Commercial firms charge approximately $12 per hour to splice and repair films and approximately $25 to clean a film. Do-it-yourself cleaning is not recommended, because the curator will probably scratch the film to a certain extent in the process. Even the cleaning done by a commercial firm scratches a film slightly, but the experiment of an Ohio State University student, John Schleffendorf, with the solvent n-Butyl chloride and ultra-sonic agitation, holds great promise of a much-improved cleaning method for film. His results indicate that the sonic vibrations did not loosen the emulsion, but took off hardened adhesive tape, dirt, and grease. It cleaned the dirt out of scratches so that the film *appeared* to be less scratched. (Robert W. Wagner, "Preservation and Restoration of Photographic Materials Through Nuclear and Ultra-Sonic Methods," pp. 14–15.)

30. Letter of William Murphy to Kenneth Duckett, August 29, 1973.

31. Patrick H. Griffin, editor, "The National Archives and the Historian's Use of Film: William Murphy in an Interview with *The History Teacher*," p. 123. The last paragraphs of this section of the text draw heavily upon pp. 119–134 of Griffin's interview of Mr. Murphy, film archivist, NARS. Murphy notes that films are covered under statutory copyright and that they can be registered for twenty-eight years with the provision for an additional twenty-eight years' renewal. (See Griffin, "National Archives and Historian's Use of Film," p. 128.)

32. One authority estimates that amateur photographers alone make four billion photographs a year. (Wagner, "Preservation through Ultra-Sonic Methods," p. 10.) Unfortunately, many of these are color or polaroid prints which are not of archival quality, and if the curator is to preserve their record, they must be copied.

33. J. H. Croucher, "The Description of the Process," *Daguerreotypist and Photographer's Companion*, 1855, as reprinted in *The New Daguerreian Journal* 1, no. 2

(1971): 4–5, 8. This journal, produced by a nonprofit organization in Columbus, Ohio, is devoted to the preservation of the daguerreotype process.

34. Robert Taft, *Photography and the American Scene: A Social History, 1839–1889*, pp. 7, 78; Harvey Zucker, "Old-Time Processes: How to Identify and Date Them," p. 101.

35. Ostroff, "Preservation of Photographs," p. 309; Taft, *Photography and the American Scene*, p. 120.

36. Taft, *Photography and the American Scene*, pp. 123–124.

37. *Ibid.*, pp. 153, 163.

38. *Ibid.*, pp. 139, 150–152.

39. *Ibid.*, pp. 171–178.

40. *Ibid.*, pp. 323–324.

41. Zucker, "Old-Time Processes," p. 101.

42. George T. Eaton, "Preservation, Deterioration, Restoration of Photographic Images," p. 85.

43. Letter from Vernon Nelson to Kenneth Duckett, June 20, 1973, enclosing a tentative data sheet on SO–015 (estar thick base) black-and-white direct duplicating film. The film is available in 4 by 5-, 5 by 7-, and 8 by 10-inch sizes at a cost of approximately twenty to sixty-five cents a sheet, depending on size.

44. Nancy E. Malan, "A Review of the Photographic Holdings of the National Anthropological Archives," p. 4.

45. Eaton, "Preservation of Photographic Images," pp. 85–98; Ostroff, "Preservation of Photographs," pp. 310–312.

46. *Procedures for Processing and Storing Black and White Photographs for Maximum Possible Permanence*, pp. 1–33.

47. Ostroff, "Preservation of Photographs," pp. 310–312.

48. As a result of World War II experiences of the British Museum, when steel shelves buckled during the blitz and damaged rare books and manuscripts, wood shelves were recommended by some to house rare materials because they afforded "better protection and lower insurance rates." (See "NYSHA Seminar on American Culture," p. 260.)

49. Ostroff, "Preservation of Photographs," p. 309; Eaton, "Preservation of Photographic Images," pp. 85–98; *Procedures for Processing Photographs*, pp. 18–19.

50. *Procedures for Processing Photographs*, p. 31; Ostroff, "Preservation of Photographs," pp. 311–312. Acetate jackets have one very positive advantage over the acid-free paper jackets in that they allow the curator or the patron to look at the negatives without getting fingerprints on the emulsion.

51. Taft, *Photography and the American Scene*, pp. 99, 451–452; Illinois State Historical Library and Society, "Old Photographs," pp. 1–2. The curator is urged to exercise great caution in using either of the two cleaning methods mentioned in the above sources and to develop his technique on expendable material.

52. Illinois State Historical Library and Society, "Old Photographs," p. 2.

53. See Antoinette King, "Conservation of Drawings and Prints," p. 119, for instructions.

54. Paul Vanderbilt, "Filing Your Photographs: Some Basic Procedures." In a decade or so, the resin in the shellac—the ingredient in the dry-mount tissue which melts and forms the bond—loses its solvency in ethanol, but recent experiments show that methoxyethanol can be used to dismount old dry-mounted photographs. (See A. D. Baynes-Cope, "The Dismounting of 'Dry Mounted' Photographic Prints," pp. 1–3.)

55. Wagner, "Preservation through Ultra-Sonic Methods," p. 13.

56. The East Street Gallery, one of the laboratories, states that the residual hypo level in their reprocessed prints will be less than .001 milligrams per square inch. (*Procedures for Processing Photographs*, p. [35].)

57. Renata V. Shaw, "Picture Organization: Practices and Procedures," pp. 448–453.

58. *Ibid.*, pp. 502, 504–505.

59. *Ibid.*, pp. 502, 505.

60. Vanderbilt, "Filing Your Photographs."

61. George Bowditch, "Cataloging Photographs: A Procedure for Small Museums."

62. Jane Howe, "Cataloguing A Photograph Collection," pp. 8–12; letter of Jack Haley to Kenneth Duckett, June 26, 1972.

63. See Malan, "Review of Photographic Holdings," p. 10.

64. Harry S. Truman Library, "Audio-Visual Cataloging System"; letter to Kenneth Duckett from Philip Lagerquest, August 23, 1972.

65. Letter of J. Patrick Wildenberg to Kenneth Duckett, January 16, 1973.

66. Renata V. Shaw, "Picture Searching: Techniques," p. 23, and Helen Faye, "May We Use This Picture?—Rights and Permissions," pp. 23–26.

67. See Renata Shaw, "Picture Searching," p. 526.

68. Renata Shaw, "Picture Organization," p. 454.

69. One authority notes that the early wax cylinders, many of which were white, ivory, or light to dark brown, manufactured by the National, Columbia, and Edison phonograph companies from 1898 to about 1912, and the Edison Diamond Disc records—all should be stored in an "absolutely dry atmosphere" of 10 percent or less humidity. (Walter L. Welch, "Preservation and Restoration of Authenticity in Sound Recordings," pp. 90–91.)

70. For example, to store cylinders, the Rogers and Hammerstein Archives at Lincoln Center uses modular-unit polystyrene wine racks, which lend themselves to easy access by numbering individual storage compartments in an alphanumeric grid system of filing. (See David Hall, "Phonorecord Preservation: Notes of a Pragmatist," p. 358.)

71. A. G. Pickett and M. M. Lemcoe, *Preservation and Storage of Sound Recordings*, pp. 15, 24, 26, 41–42, 46–48.

72. *Ibid.*, p. 48.

73. Walter Welch, "Preserving Authenticity in Sound," pp. 93–94.

74. Pickett and Lemcoe, *Preservation of Sound Recordings*, pp. 54, 58–59. Apparently, the dangers of accidental erasure of recording tape by magnetic fields had been greatly exaggerated. One manufacturer notes that the average bulk degausser, which is the device designed to erase tapes on their reels, developed a field of 1500 oersteds. Laboratory tests have shown that exposing tape to fields of 50 oersteds or less "caused no descernible erasure," and since most motors, generators, transformers, etc., to which tapes would be exposed are designed to contain their magnetic fields to do their job, there is relatively little danger. Distance from the magnetic field is important, too: "If the tape is kept as little as 3 inches away from even a strong magnetic source, this spacing should be sufficient to offer adequate protection." At 2.7 inches from the degausser developing 1500 oersteds, the tape will be subjected to only a 50-oersted field. This same manufacturer exposed a tape for six seconds at a distance of thirty-six inches from an x-ray machine operating with 200 MA at 110 KV and found "no signal loss or degradation." (See "The Handling & Storage of Magnetic Recording Tape," pp. 2, 4, 7.)

75. "Handling of Magnetic Recording Tape," p. 3; Pickett and Lemcoe, *Preservation of Sound Recordings*, pp. 61–62; and Hall, "Phonorecord Preservation," p. 358.

76. "Handling of Magnetic Recording Tape," p. 5.

77. Charles W. Conaway, "Lyman Copeland Draper, 'Father of American Oral History,' " pp. 234–241. Some practitioners of oral history, who say historians miss the point in calling Draper an oral historian, miss the point themselves. Even the most casual examination of the Draper Manuscripts will indicate that he was systematically collecting oral history interviews for the use of scholars.

78. Gary L. Shumway, *Oral History in the United States: A Directory*, p. 3, *passim*.

79. Donald C. Swain, "Problems for Practitioners of Oral History," p. 65.

80. Interview with Elizabeth Mason, June 4, 1973, and discussion at the session, "A Critical Look at Oral History," annual meeting of the Society of American Archivists, September 26, 1973. One authority estimates an average of six to twelve hours for a rough transcript. (See Willa K. Baum, *Oral History for the Local Historical Society*, p. 52.)

81. Gould P. Colman, "Oral History at Cornell," p. 626.

82. Interview with Elizabeth Mason, June 4, 1973.

83. Steven Lowe in a letter to Kenneth Duckett, June 8, 1972.

84. Baum, *Oral History*, pp. 17, 19. In several sections of the country, small oral history projects have banded together in consortiums to share personnel and equipment costs.

85. *Ibid.*, pp. 21–22.

86. Saul Benison, "Reflections on Oral History," p. 76; Helen McCann White, "Thoughts on Oral History," pp. 27–28; Gould P. Colman, "Oral History—An Appeal for More Systematic Procedures," p. 82; and Elizabeth Rumics, "Oral History: Defining the Term," p. 605. Each of these writers presents slightly differing views about preserving the tapes, but the present consensus seems to be that they are rarely used by researchers. It is perhaps ironic that Columbia, the founder and acknowledged leader of the oral history movement, has what tapes it has retained since 1960 in a jumble of rough cardboard boxes in an airless storeroom.

87. David Rosenblatt, "The Cost of Oral History" (paper read at the annual meeting of the Society of American Archivists, September 26, 1973), pp. 2, 3. The quotation which Mr. Rosenblatt used in his paper is from "What Price Oral History," a paper submitted by Nancy Marshall to the seminar in Archives and Manuscript Administration, the Library School, University of Wisconsin, Madison, 1972.

88. See, for example, Lewis A. Dexter, *Elite and Specialized Interviewing*, especially the chapter, "Suggestions for Getting, Conducting, and Recording the Interview," pp. 23–80.

89. Amelia R. Fry, "The Nine Commandments of Oral History," pp. 63–66.

90. Colman, "Oral History at Cornell," p. 625.

91. Baum, *Oral History*, pp. 23, 26, 47–48.

92. One authority says the interviewer must demonstrate his own competence, but avoid sounding either officious or obsequious (See Swain, "Problems of Oral History," p. 67). William G. Tyrrell, "Tape-Recording Local History," offers several pages of practical advice, but ultimately, as the assistant project director at Columbia says, interviewing is learned by doing with critical self and staff review. (Interview with Elizabeth Mason, June 4, 1973.)

93. Interview with James Mink, January 23, 1973. Mink also made reference at the session, "A Critical Look at Oral History," annual meeting of the Society of American Archivists, September 26, 1973, to the fact that UCLA had received a very generous gift to its general endowment fund from a recent interviewee. Mink says that this is an example of the often intangible rewards of an oral history program that should be

taken into account in assessing costs. (See also Chester V. Kielman, "The Texas Oil Industry Project," p. 618; Benison, "Reflections on Oral History," p. 72; and Manfred J. Waserman, "Manuscripts and Oral History: Common Interests and Problems in the History of Medicine," pp. 173-176.

94. Lawrence Hackman, remarks made at the session entitled "A Critical Look at Oral History," annual meeting of the Society of American Archivists, September 26, 1973.

95. Rumics, "Defining Oral History," p. 603.

96. Herbert Hoover Presidential Library, *Historical Materials in the Herbert Hoover Presidential Library*, pp. 13-26; letter from Carole Sue Warmbodt DeLaite to Kenneth Duckett, September 1, 1972.

97. Tyrrell, "Tape-Recording Local History"; Ohio Historical Society, ["Index to the Oral Interview of Mrs. R. R. Litehiser."]

98. Elizabeth I. Dixon, compiler, *The Oral History Program at UCLA: A Bibliography*. The bibliography contains paragraph-length descriptions of 103 interviews, a great many of which were still "in progress" when the guide was compiled.

99. Undated form memorandum from the Bancroft Library to the director of the manuscript repository being solicited, offering copies of the California Wine Industry oral interviews, May 1973. The Berkeley campus receives copies of all interviews done at UCLA also.

100. Louis M. Starr, *Oral History: 25th Anniversary Report*, pp. 10-11.

101. U.S. Library of Congress, *National Union Catalog of Manuscript Collections, Information Circular no. 7*, p. 1; Lawrence Hackman, remarks made at the session entitled "A Critical Look at Oral History," annual meeting of the Society of American Archivists, September 26, 1973. Twenty years after its origin, oral history was officially recognized by the cataloging division of the Library of Congress, which, in its *Subject Heading Supplements, 1966-1971* (Berkeley: University of California, 1972), established the following subject heading for published works on the subject:

Oral history
     Here are entered works on recording the oral recollections of persons concerning
     their knowledge of historical events. The content of their recollections is entered
     under the appropriate subject, e.g., U.S.—Civilization—1918-1945.
xx History—Methodology

102. Lawrence Hackman, remarks made at the session entitled "A Critical Look at Oral History," annual meeting of the Society of American Archivists, September 26, 1973; Rumics, "Defining Oral History," p. 605; and E. Douglas Hamilton, "Oral History and Law of Libel," pp. 52-53.

103. Hamilton, "Oral History and the Law of Libel," pp. 41-56. This excellent article is broader than the title implies. It spells out violations of libel, privacy violation, and copyright, and gives defenses for each. (See also the chapter in this volume, "Use of Collections," for a discussion of some of these legal questions.)

104. Baum, *Oral History*, pp. 47-48.

105. John Jellicorse, remarks made at the session entitled "The Effective Use of Audiovisual Records as Primary Sources," annual meeting of the Society of American Archivists, October 31, 1972.

106. Robert M. Diamond, "A Retrieval System for 35 mm Slides Utilized in Art and Humanities Instruction," pp. 346-359; Wendell Simon, "Development of a Universal Classification System for Two-by-Two Slide Collections," pp. 360-373.

107. See discussion earlier in this chapter on two methods of preserving colored film. See also the appendix for the names of two firms which can prepare color separation negatives. A color process called Cilchrome apparently is the most promising for producing prints which seem to be relatively permanent. (See Vanderbilt, "Filing Your Photographs.")

108. Arthur Poulos, "Audio and Video Cassettes: Friend or Foe of the Librarian," pp. 222-224.

109. Hall, "Phonorecord Preservation," p. 358; Valerie Noble, "Business Information Audio Cassettes: Their Care and Feeding," p. 421.

110. "Handling & Storage of Magnetic Recording Tape," p. 2.

111. Gould P. Colman, "Making Library History," pp. 133-134.

112. Poulos, "Audio and Video Cassettes," p. 225; Mediatech, *Price List: Video Tape to Film Transfers* (Park Ridge, Ill.: Mediatech, n.d.).

113. Poulos, "Audio and Video Cassettes," pp. 224-226.

114. *St. Louis Post-Dispatch,* December 23, 1973, p. 18A.

115. Albert H. Leisinger, Jr., *Microphotography for Archives,* pp. 29-30; Don M. Avedon, "Standards: Microfilm Permanence and Archival Quality," pp. 93-94.

116. C. S. McCamy, *Inspection of Processed Photographic Record Films for Aging Blemishes,* p. 1; Leisinger, *Microphotography for Archives,* p. 18.

117. Gerald R. Shields, "From the Editor," p. 1; "Comments and News," *Microform Review* 2(1973): 255-259.

118. Felix Reichmann and Josephine M. Tharpe, *Bibliographic Control of Microforms,* pp. 12-13, 168-230.

119. Walter Rundell, Jr., *In Pursuit of American History: Research and Training in the United States,* p. 217.

120. See Leisinger, *Microphotography for Archives,* pp. 25-26, for guidelines used by the National Archives in describing microfilm. For samples of guides to microfilm, see those prepared by the Ohio and Minnesota historical societies: Ohio Historical Society, *Microfilm Sales List* and Minnesota Historical Society, *Catalog of Microfilm.*

121. Clark A. Elliot, remarks made at the session entitled "Archival Potentials of ADP Media," annual meeting of the Society of American Archivists, September 28, 1973.

122. Roger Meetham, *Information Retrieval: The Essential Technology,* pp. 42-45; "Disk Pack Initialization," p. 1.

123. Meetham, *Information Retrieval,* p. 43; Monty Morris, "Magnetic Tape Life," p. 18.

124. Meetham, *Information Retrieval,* pp. 35-36, 43; Bruce Shapley, "The Care and Storage of Magnetic Tape," p. 80.

125. Hall, "Phonorecord Preservation," p. 357; Shapley, "Care and Storage of Magnetic Tape," p. 81; and George Cole, "Computer Tapes and Their Care," p. 14.

126. "The Handling & Storage of Magnetic Recording Tape," p. 3; and Jerome Clubb, remarks at the session, "Archival Potential of ADP Media," annual meeting of the Society of American Archivists, September 28, 1973. It will be noted that this book advises that acoustic tape be stored on edge and that computer tape be stored flat. Tape has not been in use long enough for either method of storage to have been proven superior, and most of the recommendations to house tape on edge are not based upon conservation practices but rather practicalities of space and ease of access.

127. Shapley, "Care and Storage of Magnetic Tape," p. 81; Max A. Butterfield, "Care and Preservation of the New Media: Equipment Needs," pp. 61, 62.

128. "Magnetic Tape Erasure—How Serious is the Threat?," p. 2.

129. *Ibid.,* pp. 3-5.

130. Cole, "Computer Tapes," p. 11; "Handling & Storage of Computer Tape," p. 6.

131. W. Howard Gammon, "Software as it Relates to Documentation," p. 15; Clark A. Elliot, remarks made at the session, "Archival Potential of ADP Media," annual meeting of the Society of American Archivists, September 28, 1973; and Meyer H. Fishbein to Kenneth Duckett, February 11, 1974.

132. Society of American Archivists, Committee on Data Archives and Machine-Readable Records, *Report: Fiscal Year, 1973*; Meyer H. Fishbein, "Appraising Information in Machine Language Form," p. 42.

133. Charles M. Dollar, "Documentation of Machine Readable Records and Research: A Historian's View," pp. 30-31.

CHAPTER 8

1. Jean Preston, "Problems in the Use of Manuscripts," p. 379.

2. See the several statements of manuscript repositories in the Society of American Archivists, College & University Archives Committee, *Forms Manual*, pp. 127-144.

3. See Preston, "Problems in Use of Manuscripts," p. 368.

4. According to law, the papers held by the presidential libraries are "subject to such restrictions . . . agreeable to the Administrators as to their use" or "as may be stated by the donors or depositors." (Presidential Libraries Act, 1955, 69 *Stat.*, pp. 695-697, as quoted in Philip C. Brooks, *Research in Archives: The Use of Unpublished Primary Sources*, pp. 60-61.) Brooks states that the instruments of gift vary, "but in general provide for the closing of broad categories of papers, rather than individual documents. . . . These categories include items which might be used to embarrass, harass, or damage any living individual or that might jeopardize the conduct of current foreign relations; those that relate to family business or personal affairs; and of course those that are security-classified. In applying these stipulations, the library officials must have all the papers reviewed and must bear in mind general principles of privacy and property." The policy itself has recently come under review by NARS. In the spring of 1972, the Archivist of the United States announced that 58,000,000 pages of classified documents would be opened by the end of the year. (See the *Kansas City Star*, May 14, 1972.)

5. *AB Bookman's Weekly* 49 (1972), 752.

6. One archivist has noted that many young graduate students, and reputable scholars as well, do not know "the first thing about archives," and the purpose of the interview is to "assuage the researcher's fears with soothing counsel to the effect that he is not supposed to know anything about archives." (See Frank G. Burke, "The Impact of the Specialist on Archives," p. 313.) Substantiating this is the statement of a scholar writing on the use of archives in historical research to the effect that he had completed his degree without having "spent a day in the archives (as distinct from easier-to-use manuscript collections.)" Unfortunately, the author does not elaborate on this statement. (See Oscar E. Anderson, "The Use of Archives in Historical Research," p. 45.)

7. Perhaps the strongest public statement of what he feels is the curator's responsibility has been made by the Harvard University archivist. "Sometimes the scholarship of the would-be user is inadequate. . . . I do not think that any archivist is appointed just to be a vending machine, handing out whatever is indicated by the user. He has, I think, been appointed to exercise his discretion and to make use of his knowledge as an archivist. It is not an easy thing to make these unpleasant decisions against

applicants, but such a policy of discrimination is absolutely essential." (Clifford K. Shipton, "The Reference Use of Archives," pp. 74-75.)

8. Brooks, *Research in Archives,* p. 48.

9. Herbert Finch, "The Problem of Confidentiality in a College Archives," p. 240.

10. See Preston, "Problems in Use of Manuscripts," p. 373.

11. *Ibid.,* p. 376.

12. Brooks, *Research in Archives,* pp. 59-61. It should be remembered that the presidential libraries were a new problem for NARS. The libraries collected not only official papers or archives but also personal papers or manuscripts. (See also H. G. Jones, *The Records of a Nation: Their Management, Preservation, and Use,* pp. 144-171.)

13. *Congressional Record,* February 28, 1972. See also Herman Kahn, "Some Comments on the Archival Vocation," p. 11.

14. Preston, "Problems in Use of Manuscripts," pp. 371-372.

15. National Fire Protection Association, *Manual for Fire Protection for Archives and Records Centers,* p. 13.

16. *Ibid.,* p. 8.

17. *Ibid.,* p. 7.

18. *Ibid.,* p. 9. Experts who viewed the results of the fire in the federal personnel records center, St. Louis, July 12, 1973, said that temperature at the center of the "fireball" was in excess of a thousand degrees F. (Peter Waters, untitled speech, annual meeting of the Society of American Archivists, September 27, 1973.)

19. Kenneth Spencer Research Library, "Manual of Operations."

20. Walter Rundell, Jr., "Relations between Historical Researchers and Custodians of Source Materials," pp. 475, 469.

21. *AB Bookman's Weekly* 51 (1973), 1184; *Manuscripts* 25, no. 4 (1973), 292; and *Southern Illinoisan,* September 14, 1973.

22. *Manuscripts* 25, no. 4 (1973), 283.

23. *New York Times,* January 7, 1964, p. 23, col. 3; and January 8, 1964, p. 34, col. 6; letter of Philip Mason to Kenneth Duckett, October 23, 1972.

24. O. Lawrence Burnette, Jr., *Beneath the Footnote: A Guide to the Use and Preservation of American Historical Sources,* p. 138; Fred Shelley, "Manuscripts in the Library of Congress: 1800-1900," pp. 11-12. Prior to the reorganization noted in the text, the only training some employees had had was in politics. McElhone, for example, had been President McKinley's private secretary in Congress before coming to the Library of Congress.

25. Undated press release [ca. August 1973] and stolen property forms from the Antiquarian Booksellers' Association; *AB Bookman's Weekly* 51 (1973), 1184.

26. H. Richard Archer in a letter to Kenneth Duckett, May 30, 1973.

27. James B. Rhoads, "Alienation and Thievery: Archival Problems," p. 203.

28. Cecil K. Byrd, "Quarters For Special Collections in University Libraries," p. 227.

29. "Practically Speaking," *History News* 28 (1973), 88.

30. Russell M. Smith, "Stamping Manuscripts," pp. 24-27.

31. Letter of P. William Filby to Kenneth Duckett, May 24, 1973.

32. In his comments on this chapter December 3, 1973, H. Bart Cox advised that detaining a researcher for a short time in order to examine his briefcase, if it is done discreetly, is not likely to be interpreted as false arrest. He cites Notes 1958, 11 *Oklahoma Law Review* 102, and 1965, 25 *Louisiana Law Review* 956 as references.

33. American Library Association, *Protecting the Library and Its Resources: A Guide to Physical Protection and Insurance,* pp. 148-151, and in the same volume, Roland

Baughman, "The Evaluation and Insurance of Great Rarities," pp. 265-268; Charles W. Mixer, "New Insurance for Library Collections," pp. 1539-1543.

34. Brooks, *Research in Archives*, p. 47.

35. Louis R. Wilson and Jack Dalton, "Restriction on the Use of Research Materials," p. 547. This article quotes the *Ad Hoc* Committee on Manuscripts Set Up by the American Historical Association in December 1948, as saying that "the worst offender is apt to be a well-meaning staff member who cannot resist talking at length with readers, sometimes ostensibly to provide help."

36. Richard W. Leopold, "A Crisis of Confidence: Foreign Policy Research and the Federal Government," pp. 149-152; Joint AHA-OAH Committee to Investigate Charges Against Roosevelt Library, *Final Report*, pp. 423, 424.

37. S. C. Newton, "The Archivist and Dutton v Bognor Regis," pp. 596-597.

38. Rundell, "Relations between Researchers and Custodians," p. 466. The curator's understanding of the scholar's point of view regarding the use of manuscripts comes almost exclusively from historians, of whom in this area Professor Rundell is most knowledgeable. His findings, based on extensive interviews with history graduate students, are most useful but limited, in that curators must serve more than this one academic discipline.

39. Rundell, *In Pursuit of American History*, p. 21.

40. *Ibid.*, p. 22.

41. *Ibid.*, p. 77; Rundell, "Relations between Researchers and Custodians," p. 469.

42. Martha C. Slotten, "The Fruits of Two Hundred Years of Collecting Manuscripts: Their Use in the Teaching of Undergraduates at Dickinson College," pp. 155-161.

43. Kermit J. Pike, "Private Sources of Special Funds for Archives and Manuscript Repositories," p. 16.

44. Society of American Archivists, College and University Archives Committee, *Forms Manual*, pp. 225-234. One observer has commented that many librarians are unfamiliar with manuscript research. "They can," he said, "easily count the number of books checked out, and these statistics appear far more impressive than the number of researchers who might use manuscripts during any given period." The author, a historian, says historians understand "that mere numbers have little relationship to the importance of research in manuscripts." (See Rundell, *In Pursuit of American History*, p. 77.)

45. One of the few institutions that has attempted to analyze its reference requests is the Buffalo and Erie County Historical Society. In the period from May to August 1972, they answered twenty-six letters at an average of sixteen minutes per letter and seventeen telephone requests at five minutes per call.

46. It is perhaps unfortunate that archivists and curators seem to insist upon using the phrase *legal title*, which is defined variously as (1) "full and absolute title," (2) "complete and perfect title," (3) "title created by written deeds as provided by statute." All of these are fulsome and somewhat inaccurate descriptions of the informal transfer of property which characterizes most gifts of manuscripts. If he feels he must use the phrase, the curator should keep in mind the defintion of title as outlined in U.S. *v* Grossler. " 'Title' to real property is not a thing with physical attributes, but a conglomerate of jurisdiction and substantive legal rights fused with the residue of equitable remedies all developed historically out of feudal notions and medieval conditions." (*Words and Phrases: All Judicial Constructions and Definitions of Words and Phrases by State and Federal Courts* . . . [St. Paul: West Publishing Co., 1965]), pp. 491, 492, 493, 374.

47. One of the further ironies of the law may not become evident to the curator until after THS has allowed its Scribbler manuscripts to be published in the collected works. If at some future date THS wishes to publish one of its own Scribbler letters in an exhibit catalog or in its scholarly journal, the society must have the publisher's permission, and it may have to pay a substantial fee to get it.

48. Unquestionably the best articles available on common-law literary copyright as it applies to the curator are by H. Bartholomew Cox, "Private Letters and the Public Domain," pp. 381-388, and "The Impact of the Proposed Copyright Law Upon Scholars and Custodians," pp. 217-227. In the latter, however, Mr. Cox made two statements, which, depending on how they are interpreted, might confuse the curator. He notes "that common-law literary property right in unpublished manuscripts is a protection against the invasion of privacy" (p. 219), and lower on the page, "An heir of historic manuscript letters has an undisputed right to privacy regarding manuscripts within his immediate ownership and control. . . ." It is true that heirs have used their common-law literary rights as a means of protection against what they termed an invasion of their privacy, but invasion of privacy and infringement of common-law copyright (a property right) are two separate and distinct actions before the bar. Unauthorized publication of a person's own letters would constitute an invasion of his privacy, but it is very much a matter of dispute whether heirs have such rights in the letters of an ancestor or benefactor.

49. Lyman Ray Patterson, *Copyright in Historical Perspective*, p. 3.

50. *Ibid.*, pp. 19, 223.

51. Philip Wittenberg, *The Protection of Literary Property*, p. 11.

52. *Ibid.*, pp. 11-13; Patterson, *Copyright in Historical Perspective*, p. 4.

53. Wittenberg, *Protection of Literary Property*, pp. 29-31; Patterson, *Copyright in Historical Perspective*, pp. 168-179; Herbert A. Howell, *The Copyright Law; An Analysis of the Law of the United States Governing Registration and Protection of Copyright Works . . .* , p. 101.

54. Brooks, *Research in Archives*, pp. 70-72. It is unfortunate that the one book written to guide young scholars in the use of archives should contain misinformation about copyright. (See Ralph R. Shaw, *Literary Property in the United States*, pp. 27, 32; Patterson, *Copyright in Historical Perspective*, p. 227; and Wittenberg, *Protection of Literary Property*, pp. 42-43, for the opposite view to Brooks.)

55. *Corpus Juris Secundum . . .* (Brooklyn: American Law Book Co., 1952) p. 308-311.

56. Wittenberg, *Protection of Literary Property*, p. 52; Ralph Shaw, *Literary Property in the United States*, p. 18.

57. *AB Bookman's Weekly* 34 (1964), 363.

58. *Congressional Record*, 90 Congress, 1 Session (1967), pp. 8585-8595, 9021-9022, 9208.

59. *Congressional Record*, 91 Congress, 1 Session (1969), pp. 1382, 1404; *Congressional Quarterly Weekly Report* 13 (August 4, 1973), p. 2150; *Senate Joint Resolution* 247, October 11, 1973; *S. 644: A Bill for the General Revision of Copyright*, 92 Congress, 1 Session, pp. 40-41; *Publishers' Weekly* 204, no. 2 (1973), 35 and 204, no. 7 (1973), 32-33; *American Libraries* 4 (1973), 557.

60. Philip P. Mason, "The Archivist and the Law," speech delivered at the Midwest Archives Conference, September 29, 1972. In this speech, Mr. Mason stated that placing manuscripts in a library, which was open to the public, constituted "general publication." He was so advised, he said later, by the Dean of the University of Michigan Law School at the time that a number of oral history transcripts were placed in the Wayne State

University Archives. (Letter of Mason to Kenneth Duckett, October 23, 1972) One authority on literary property rights has theorized along these lines, but there are no legal precedents to substantiate the theory. (See Ralph Shaw, *Literary Property in the United States,* pp. 136-142.)

61. See [H. Bartholomew Cox], "An Analysis of S. 543 for Sections Relevant to Documentary Publication and Reproduction of Archival Materials, and Sections Relating to the *Federal Register,*" pp. 6-7.

62. E. Douglas Hamilton, "Oral History and the Law of Libel," p. 41.

63. Wayne State University, "Oral History Transcript Use Contract" and "Archives Handling of Oral History Transcripts."

CHAPTER 9

1. Frances J. Brewer, "Friends of the Library and Other Benefactors and Donors," p. 457.

2. Albert H. Leisinger, Jr., "The Exhibit of Documents," p. 78.

3. P. William Filby, "Techniques of Exhibitions," pp. 8, 10.

4. John Kobler, "Trailing the Book Crooks," p. 19; Dorothy Bowen, "Techniques of Book and Manuscript Display," p. 15. Miss Bowen notes that under the terms of the deed of trust at the Huntington Library no items of the collection can leave the premises. The library does not lend manuscripts for exhibit and borrows them only on rare occasions.

5. Filby, "Techniques of Exhibitions," p. 9; H. Richard Archer, "Display and Exhibit Cases," p. 479-480.

6. See Archer, "Display and Exhibit Cases," p. 479.

7. Paul Banks to Kenneth Duckett, August 10, 1972.

8. *Ibid.*

9. Harold W. Tribolet, "Conservation," p. 64; "NYSHA Seminar on American Culture," p. 263; Leisinger, "Exhibit of Documents," pp. 80-86; Bowen, "Techniques of Manuscript Display," p. 14.

10. Tribolet, "Conservation," p. 64.

11. Two books to assist the curator as amateur exhibits preparator, which have been called by one expert "simplistic but very practical," are: Kate Coplan, *Effective Library Exhibits: How to Prepare and Promote Good Display;* and Mona Garvey, *Library Displays: Their Purpose, Construction and Use.*

12. Jean Tuckerman, "Techniques of Exhibitions," p. 18.

13. Filby, "Techniques of Exhibitions," p. 9.

14. Clifford L. Lord and Carl Ubbeldohde, *Clio's Servant: The State Historical Society of Wisconsin, 1846-1954,* p. 321; Walter Rundell, Jr., *In Pursuit of American History: Research and Training in the United States,* p. 227. Rundell is incorrect in implying that the Draper Papers were filmed in 1948 and that the Library of Congress produced the first major microfilm publication with the filming of the Thomas Jefferson Papers in 1943. Filming on the Draper Papers was begun in January 1940, with the society's camera, but went slowly. It was halted with the advent of World War II and the attendant shortage of film. At that time, work had been completed on three series, the Kentucky, King's Mountain, and Tennessee Papers, positive copies of which were sold to Vanderbilt University. Work was resumed in December 1944, on better equipment at the University

of Chicago, and the entire collection was completed by the spring of 1949. (See letter to Kenneth Duckett from Josephine Harper, October 16, 1972.)

15. U.S. National Archives and Records Service, National Historical Publications Commission, *A Report to the President Containing a Proposal by the National Historical Publications Commission to Meet Existing and Anticipated Needs Over the Next Ten Years Under a National Program for the Collection, Preservation, and Publication, or Dissemination by Other Means, of the Documentary Sources of American History,* pp. 18, 29.

16. *Ibid.,* p. 9; letter from James O'Neill to Kenneth Duckett, October 26, 1973; H. G. Jones, *The Records of a Nation: Their Management, Preservation, and Use,* p. 126.

17. H. G. Jones, *The Records of a Nation,* pp. 117, 127.

18. Rundell, *In Pursuit of American History,* pp. 220–233.

19. A. N. L. Munby, *The Cult of the Autograph Letter in England,* p. 29.

20. Lawrence S. Thompson, "Facsimiles and the Antiquarian Trade," pp. 440–441; H. Bartholomew Cox, "Publication of Manuscripts; Devaluation or Enhancement?," pp. 26, 31.

21. Rundell, *In Pursuit of American History,* pp. 206–209.

22. Some institutions have moved to correct the imbalance by grouping or consolidating entries for the small collections under headings like *Reminiscences, Stock Certificates, Land Grants, Marriage Licenses,* etc.

23. For examples of collection guides and published inventories, see chapter 5.

24. *Manuscripts for Research.*

25. See, for example, Thomas Powers, *Balita mula Maynila;* John M. T. Chavis and William McNitt, *A Brief History of the Detroit Urban League, and Description of the League's Papers in the Michigan Historical Collections;* Dennis Anderson, *James Kerr Pollock: His Life and Letters; The Michigan Historical Collection of the University of Michigan;* Elizabeth I. Dixon, compiler, *The Oral History Program at UCLA: A Bibliography;* Princeton University Library, *A Descriptive Catalogue of the Dulles Oral History Collection.*

26. Kenneth Spencer Research Library, *Guide for Readers 11: Department of Special Collections;* Henry E. Huntington Library and Art Gallery, *Readers' Guide to the Huntington Library.*

27. North Carolina, State Department of Archives and History, *Archives Information Circular,* nos. 1–4; Idem., *Genealogical Research in the North Carolina Department of Archives and History.*

28. Hannah D. French, "Access, Service, and Publications," p. 104. A variation on the journal or periodical article reprint is the reprint of speeches at seminars, workshops, and similar sessions. See, for example, Lawrence W. Towner, *Every Silver Lining Has a Cloud: The Recent Shaping of the Newberry Library's Collections.*

29. French, "Access, Service, and Publications," pp. 105, 107; Henry E. Huntington Library and Art Gallery, *Annual Report, July 1, 1971–June 30, 1972;* Western Reserve Historical Society, *Annual Report for the Year 1971;* University of Toronto, Library, Rare Books Department, *Selected Acquisitions, July 1971–January 1972.*

30. French, "Access, Service, and Publications," p. 104. Most institutions publishing Friends periodicals offer them on subscription. One of the most recent to become available, *ICarbS,* which began publication late in 1973 at Southern Illinois University, Carbondale, is listed at $5 per year.

31. Walter S. Achtert, "Scholarly Journals in the Seventies," pp. 5–6.

32. For common page sizes that can be cut without waste from regular sheets of bond (17 by 22 inches) or book (25 by 38 inches) papers to fit regular envelopes, see Edmund C. Arnold, *Ink on Paper 2: A Handbook of the Graphic Arts*, pp. 237, 323, 326.

33. Marshall Lee, *Bookmaking: The Illustrated Guide to Design & Production*, p. 33.

34. Brewer, "Friends of the Library," pp. 453–465.

35. Ruth B. Bordin and Robert M. Warner, *The Modern Manuscript Library*, pp. 115–116.

36. *Ibid.*, p. 117.

37. *Ibid.*, p. 112.

A Glossary of
Selected Terms

Most of the terms in the following glossary have been excerpted from a larger work, "A Glossary of Basic Terms for Archivists, Manuscript Curators, and Records Managers," compiled by Frank B. Evans, Donald F. Harrison, and Edwin A. Thompson, and edited by William L. Rofes. This fine compilation, sponsored by the Committee on Terminology of the Society of American Archivists, should prove a unifying force in the profession. The excerpted terms, used here in an effort to promote their acceptance, are reprinted from the *American Archivist*, vol. 37, no. 3 (July 1974), by permission of the Society of American Archivists. A handful of terms have been altered, the better to reflect good manuscript practices, but any changes have been enclosed in brackets. In a few instances, the primary and secondary definitions have been reversed in order to emphasize that portion of the term which relates to manuscript usage. The few terms supplied by the author and the few taken from other sources have been identified at the end of those definitions.

ACCESSION. 1. The act and procedures involved in taking records or papers into physical and legal custody of an archival agency or manuscript repository. 2. The materials involved in such a transfer of custody. [K.W.D.]

ALIENATION. The act of transferring or losing custody or ownership of records to an agency or person not officially related to the institution or organization whose records are involved. *See also* ESTRAY

APPRAISAL. 1. The monetary evaluation of gifts of manuscripts. 2. The process of determining the value and thus the disposition of records based upon their current administrative, legal, and fiscal use; their evidential and informational or research value; their arrangement; and their relationship to other records. Sometimes referred to as *Selective retention.*

ARCHIVES. 1. The noncurrent records of an organization or institution preserved because of their continuing value; also referred to, in this sense, as archival materials or archival holdings.   2. The agency responsible for selecting, preserving, and making available archival materials; also referred to as an archival agency.   3. The building or part of a building where such materials are located; also referred to as an archival repository (or, in U.S. Govt., archival depository). In American usage, the term "archives" is generally a plural or collective noun, although the form *archive* has been applied to a number of special collections.

ARRANGEMENT.   The process and results of organizing archives, records, and manuscripts in accordance with accepted archival principles, particularly provenance, at as many as necessary of the following levels: repository, record group or comparable control unit, subgroup(s), series, file unit, and document. The process usually includes packing, labelling, and shelving of archives, records, and manuscripts and is intended to achieve physical or administrative control and basic identification of the holdings. *See also* PROCESSING; [SORTING]

AUTOGRAPH.   1. Traditionally, a signature.   2. A manuscript, signed or unsigned, in the hand of the author.   3. A typescript signed by the author. *See also* HOLOGRAPH

BIBLIOGRAPHIC CONTROL.   As used in this volume, a general term encompassing the combined routines of arrangement/processing and description. *See also* the first note to the chapter on Establishing Bibliographic Control. [K.W.D.]

BUSINESS RECORDS/PAPERS.   Records normally growing out of a commercial or industrial enterprise. There may be included (among others) such items as accounts stated, annual reports, annual statements, articles of association/incorporation, audits, balance sheets, bank letters, bank notes, bank statements, bankbooks, bills, bills of exchange, bills of lading, bills of sale, billbooks, blotters, bonds, business cards, canceled checks, cash accounts, cashbooks, cash-disbursement journals, certificates of incorporation, checks, checkbooks, corporation records, daybooks, deeds, deed polls, disbursement books, drafts, drawing accounts, estate papers/records, estimates, evaluations, expense accounts, expense books, freight bills, household account books/records, indentures, invoices, invoice books, journals, justifications, land scrip, land warrants, leases, ledgers, letters of credit, licenses, manifests, market letters, memorandum books, mortgages, mortgage bonds, mortgage deeds, mortgage loans, mortgage notes, organization charts, partnership records, patents, payrolls, payroll profit-and-loss statements, promissory notes, purchase journals, purchase ledgers, purchase orders, purchase records, receipts, receipt books, records, regulations, rent rolls, reports, requisitions, sales journals, sales ledgers, sales notes, sales records, schedules, scrip, specifications, statements, stocks, stock certificates, stock ledgers, stores ledgers, tables, tallies, tally sheets/cards, tax certificates, time books, time sheets, trial balances, vouchers, voucher checks, warehouse receipts, waste books, and waybills. [Edwin A. Thompson, *A Glossary of American Historical and Literary Manuscript Terms* (Washington: Privately printed, 1965)].

COLLECTION.   1. A body of manuscripts or papers, including associated printed or near-print materials having a common source. If formed by or around an individual or family, such materials are more properly termed *personal papers* or *records*.   2. An artificial accumulation of manuscripts or documents devoted to a single theme, person, event, or type of record. If the cumulation is that of a corporate entity, it is more properly termed *records*.   3. In singular or plural form, the total holdings—accessions and deposits—of a repository. *See also* MANUSCRIPTS; PAPERS; RECORD GROUP; RECORDS

CORRESPONDENCE.   Letters, postcards, memoranda, notes, telecommunications, and any other form of addressed, written communications sent and received.

DEPOSIT.   Manuscripts or archives placed in the physical custody of a repository without transfer of ownership. [K.W.D.]

DEPOSITORY.   *See* REPOSITORY.

DESCRIPTION.   The process of establishing intellectual control over holdings through the preparation of finding aids. *See also* PROCESSING

DESCRIPTIVE INVENTORY.   *See* INVENTORY.

DOCUMENT.   1. A single record or manuscript item. When abbreviated, *D.* or *Doc.*, it designates any manuscript that is not a letter.   2. Recorded information regardless of medium or characteristics. Frequently used interchangeably with *record*. *See also* ITEM; RECORD

ESTRAY.   The legal term applied to a record or document not in the custody of the original records creator or its legal successor. [Many historical manuscripts are estrays.] *See also* ALIENATION

EVALUATION.   *See* APPRAISAL.

FINDING AIDS.   The descriptive media, published and unpublished, created by an originating office, an archival agency, or manuscript repository, to establish physical or administrative and intellectual control over records and other holdings. Basic finding aids include guides (general or repository and subject or topical), inventories or registers, location registers, card catalogs, special lists, shelf and box lists, indexes, calendars, and, for machine-readable records, software documentation.

GUIDE.   At the repository level, a finding aid that briefly describes and indicates the relationships between holdings, with record groups, papers, collections, or comparable bodies of material as the units of entry. Guides may also be limited to the description of the holdings of one or more repositories relating to particular subjects, periods, or geographical areas.

HOLOGRAPH.   A handwritten document. Synonymous in most contexts with *autograph*. [K.W.D.]

INVENTORY.   The basic archival finding aid. An inventory generally includes a brief history of the organization and functions of the agency whose records are being described; a descriptive list of each record series giving as a minimum such data as title, inclusive dates, quantity, arrangement, relationships to other series, and description of significant subject content; and, if appropriate, appendices which provide such supplementary information as a glossary of abbreviations and special terms, lists of folder headings on special subjects, or selective indexes. *See also* REGISTER

ITEM.   The smallest unit of record material which accumulates to form file units and record series, e.g., a letter, memorandum, report, leaflet, photograph, or reel of film or tape. [In establishing quantities, a letter, whatever the number of pages, a letter and attachments, and a covering letter and the document it covers, all are counted as single items.] *See also* DOCUMENT; PIECE; RECORD

LEGAL DOCUMENTS.   Documents of or pertaining to the law, arising out of or by virtue of the law, or included in, based upon, or governed by the law, [including]: abstract of title, act, administrative bond, affidavit, agreement, appeal, appraisal, articles of association, authorization, award, bequest, brief, bylaw, case, case file, casebook, certificate, certificate of incorporation, certified copy, charge book/sheet, charter, citation, citizenship papers/records, claim, codicil, complaint, constitution, contract, corporation records, court-martial order, court-martial record, court order, court records, decision, decree, dedication, deed, deed of partition, deed of manumission, deed poll, deposition, digest, docket, engrossed bill, enrolled bill, exhibit, guardianship papers, homestead and preemption certificate, indenture, injunction, judgment, judgment book, land scrip, land warrant, lease, lease and release, legal file, letters close, letters missive, letters of administration, letters of marque, letters patent, letters rogatory, letters testamentary, license, literary property rights, memorial, mortgage, mortgage bond, mortgage deed, mortgage loan, mortgage note, muniments, naturalization papers/records, nuncupative will, opinion, order, order of the day, partnership records, passport, patent, petition, plea, power of attorney, quitclaim, release, resolution, roll, schedule, seal, sentence, ship's papers, testimony, title, transfer, treaty, warrants, will, writ, and writ of certiorari. [Edwin A. Thompson, *A Glossary of American Historical and Literary Manuscript Terms* (Washington: Privately printed, 1965)].

LEGAL SIZE.   1. A standard paper size 8½ by 14 inches (U.S. Govt. 8 by 12½ inches).   2. Capable of holding legal-size papers or documents. *See also* LETTER SIZE

LETTER SIZE.   1. A standard paper size 8½ by 11 inches (U.S. Govt. 8 by 10½ inches).   2. Capable of holding letter-size papers or documents. *See also* LEGAL SIZE

LINEAR FEET.   1. A measurement for descriptive and control purposes of shelf space occupied by archives, records, or manuscripts. For vertical files (records filed on edge) the total length of drawers, shelves, or other equipment occupied is calculated; in the case of material filed horizontally (flat or piled up), the total vertical thickness is used. Linear feet, except for card indexes, may be equated with cubic feet on a one-to-one basis for description of textual records.   2. A measurement for descriptive and control purposes of the length of film, tape, or microfilm. (Usually expressed as *feet*.)

MANUSCRIPT.   A handwritten or typed document, including a letterpress or carbon copy. A mechanically produced form completed in handwriting or typescript is also considered a manuscript.

MANUSCRIPTS (BY TYPE).   The most familiar types of manuscripts are: diaries; correspondence (incoming letters and outgoing letters, the latter appearing as carbon, letterpress, and looseleaf copies, or in copybooks and in drafts); telegrams and cablegrams; memoranda of telephone conversations; daybooks; ledgers; journals; cashbooks; trial balances; accounts receivable and bills payable; profit and loss statements; auditors' or examiners' reports; annual statements; invoices; bills of lading; warehouse receipts; waybills; cancelled checks; checkbook stubs; receipts; drafts; bankbooks; vouchers; time checks; time books; payrolls; personal accounts (household accounts and individual expense accounts); inventories (personal property, real estate, merchandise); bills of sale; agenda; minutes of meetings; proceedings; reports; organization charts; bonds; stock records and certificates; articles of incorporation or association; bylaws; constitutions; contracts; agreements; indentures; deeds; abstracts; mortgages; plats; tract books; homestead and preemption certificates; land patents; land warrants and scrip; tax records; field notes; map and tracings; birth, baptismal, marriage, and death certificates; certificates of membership, election, and award; licenses; commissions; legal or court records (testimony, briefs, etc.); enlistment and discharge papers of military service; citizenship or naturalization papers; manumission papers; passports; lists (membership, committee, and subscription); school essays, copybooks, report cards, and diplomas; drafts and copies of bills; memorials, resolutions, proclamations, and treaties; patents, with sketches and other supporting papers; notebooks and research notes; registers; cemetery inscriptions; petitions; case files (doctors', lawyers', and social workers'); memoranda; manuscripts of literary works; friendship books; recipes; lectures; speeches; sermons; reminiscences; autobiographies; biographies; genealogies; family histories; interviews (notes and transcripts); questionnaires; and obituaries. [Lucile Kane, *A Guide to the Care and Administration of Manuscripts* (Nashville: American Association for State and Local History, 1966)].

MANUSCRIPT COLLECTION.   *See* COLLECTION.

MANUSCRIPTS.   Documents of manuscript character generally having historical or literary value or significance. All manuscript records may thus be regarded as manuscripts, but generally the term is used to distinguish nonarchival from archival material. Included in the term are bodies or groups of personal papers with organic unity, artificial collections of documents acquired from various sources usually according to a plan but without regard to provenance, and individual documents acquired by a manuscript repository because of their special importance. See also COLLECTION; PAPERS

ORGANIZING.   *See* PROCESSING; SORTING.

PAPERS.   1. A natural accumulation of personal and family materials, as distinct from records.   2. A general term used to designate more than one type of manuscript material. *See also* COLLECTION; MANUSCRIPTS; PERSONAL PAPERS

PERMANENT/DURABLE PAPER.   A term generally applied to pH neutral papers.

PERSONAL PAPERS.   The private documents accumulated by an individual, belonging to him or her and subject to his or her disposition. *See also* PAPERS

PIECE.   1. A discrete object or individual member of a class or group, as a letter [in a correspondence file.] In this sense, piece is synonymous with item or document.   2. A fragment or part separated from the whole in any manner—for example, by cutting or detaching, as a separated leaf of a multipage document.

PRELIMINARY INVENTORY.   *See* INVENTORY.

PROCESSING.   The operations performed to facilitate the use of manuscript collections generally comparable to arrangement and description of archival material. Used in this volume as generally synonymous with *sorting* and, to a lesser extent, *arrangement*. [K.W.D.]

PROVENANCE.   1. Information of successive transfers of ownership and custody of a particular manuscript.   2. In general archival and manuscript usage, the "office of origin" of records, i.e., that office or administrative entity that created or received and accumulated the records in the conduct of its business. Also the person, family, firm, or other source of personal papers and manuscript collections.   3. In archival theory, the principle that archives of a given records creator must not be intermingled with those of other records creators. The principle is frequently referred to by the French expression, *respect des fonds*. A corollary, frequently designated as a separate principle, is the Principle of Sanctity of the Original Order (or *respect pour l'ordre primitif, Registratur Prinzip,* or Registry Principle).

RECORD.   1. Recorded information regardless of media or characteristics.   2. In machine-readable records/archives, two or more data fields in predetermined order and treated as a unit. *See also* DOCUMENT; ITEM

RECORD GROUP.   A body of organizationally related records established on the basis of provenance with particular regard for the administrative history, the complexity, and the volume of the records and archives of the institution or organization involved. Collective and general record groups represent modification of this basic concept for convenience in arrangement, description, and reference service. *See also* COLLECTION; SUBGROUP

RECORDS.   All recorded information, regardless of media or characteristics, made or received and maintained by an organization or institution in pursuance of its legal obligations or in the transaction of its business.

RECORDS CENTER.   A facility, sometimes especially designed and constructed, for the low-cost and efficient storage and furnishing of reference service on semicurrent records pending their ultimate disposition.

RECORDS MANAGEMENT.   That area of general administrative management concerned with achieving economy and efficiency in the creation, use and maintenance, and disposition of records.

REGISTER.   1. (U.S. Govt.) A term applied to the finding aid developed in the Manuscript Division of the Library of Congress to describe groups of papers, collections, and records by giving their provenance and conditions of administration; scope and general content including span and bulk dates; a biographical note about the person, family group, or organization whose material it is; its arrangement; a container list which is essentially a folder listing; and, on occasion, selective document indexes.   2. The list of events, letters sent and received, actions taken etc., usually in simple sequence, as by date or number, and often serving as a finding aid to the records, such as a register of letters sent or a register of visitors. *See also* INVENTORY

REGISTRY PRINCIPLE.   The basic archival principle, sometimes referred to as the Principle of Sanctity of the Original Order, or *respect pour l'ordre primitif,* or *Registratur Prinzip,* which maintains that archives should be retained in their original organizational pattern or structure and in their original filing arrangement in order to preserve all relationships. *See also* PROVENANCE

REPOSITORY.   A place where manuscripts, whether gifts, deposits, or purchases, are stored and serviced. Used throughout this volume as synonymous with *depository.* [K.W.D.]

RESPECT DES FONDS.   *See* PROVENANCE

SERIES.   File units or documents arranged in accordance with a filing system or maintained as a unit because they relate to a particular subject or function, result from the same activity, have a particular form, or because of some other relationship arising out of their creation, receipt, or use. Sometimes known as a *record series.*

SORTING.   The process by which manuscripts are physically divided into appropriate alphabetical, chronological, numerical, subject, or other groups. Less frequently used with archives, except when restoring them to their original or intended order. [K.W.D.]

SUBGROUP.   A body of related records within a record group, usually consisting of the records of a primary subordinate administrative unit. Subgroups may also be established for related bodies of records within a record group that can best be delimited in terms of functional, geographical, or chronological relationships. Subgroups, in turn, are divided into as many levels as are necessary to reflect the successive organizational units that constitute the hierarchy of the subordinate administrative unit, or that will assist in grouping series entries in terms of their relationships. *See also* RECORD GROUP

SUBSERIES.   An aggregate of file units within a record series readily separable in terms of physical class, type, form, subject, or filing arrangement.

TEXTUAL RECORDS.   The term usually applied to manuscript or typescript, as distinct from cartographic, audiovisual, and machine-readable records and archives.

WORKING PAPERS.   Documents such as rough notes, calculations, or drafts assembled or created and used in the preparation or analysis of other documents.

Bibliography

Achtert, Walter S. "Scholarly Journals in the Seventies." *Scholarly Publishing: A Journal of Authors & Publishers* 5 (1973):3–11.

Adams, Ansel. *The Print: Contact Printing and Enlarging.* Vol. 3. The Basic Photo. New York: Morgan & Morgan, 1968.

Adams, Herbert B. *The Life and Writings of Jared Sparks Comprising Selections from His Journals and Correspondence.* 2 vols. 1893. Reprint. Freeport, N.Y.: Books for Libraries Press, 1970.

Ademco. *Heat Sealing.* High Wycombe, Buckinghamshire, England: Ademco, [ca. 1973].

Alderson, William T., Jr. "Securing Grant Support: Effective Planning and Preparation." American Association for State and Local History, Technical Leaflet 62. *History News* 27, no. 12 (1972).

All the King's Horses. Chicago: Lakeside Press, R. R. Donnelley & Sons Co., [1954].

Allen, John C. "Item Indexing for Information Coordination in the Archival Depository." American Society for Information Scientists, *Conference Proceedings, 1968,* pp. 95–99.

Altick, Richard D. *The Scholar Adventurers.* New York: Macmillan Co., 1950.

American Academy of Arts and Letters and the National Institute of Arts and Letters. "On the Use of Private Papers." *Proceedings.* 2d ser., no. 21, pp. 43–60. New York: Spiral Press, 1971.

American Book-Prices Current, 1966: A Record of Literary Properties Sold at Auction in the United States and in London, England, From September 1965 through August 1966. Vol. 72. New York: Columbia University Press, 1969.

American Library Association. *ALA Rules for Filing Catalog Cards.* 2nd. ed. Chicago: American Library Association, 1968.

———. *Protecting the Library and Its Resources: A Guide to Physical Protection and Insurance.* Library Technology Project Publications, no. 7. Chicago: American Library Association, 1963.

Amtmann, Bernard, compiler. *Montreal Book Auction Records, 1967–1971.* Montreal: Bernard Amtmann, Inc., 1972.

Anderson, Dennis. *James Kerr Pollock: His Life and Letters.* Bulletin no. 21. Ann Arbor: Michigan Historical Collections, 1972.

Anderson, Oscar E. "The Use of Archives in Historical Research." In *Research Methods in Librarianship: Historical and Bibliographical Methods in Library Research,* edited by Rolland E. Stevens, pp. 42–50. Urbana: University of Illinois, Graduate School of Library Science, 1971.

Andrews, Charles M., and Frances G. Davenport. *Guide to the Manuscript Materials for the History of the United States to 1783, in the British Museum, in Minor London Archives, and in the Libraries of Oxford and Cambridge.* Washington: Carnegie Institution of Washington, 1908.

Angle, Paul M. "The University Library and Its Manuscript Collection: An Excursion into Other People's Business." *Library Quarterly* 15 (1945): 123–130.

Anglo-American Cataloging Rules. Prepared by the American Library Association, the Library of Congress, the Library Association, and the Canadian Library Association. Chicago: American Library Association, 1970.

Anthony, Donald C. "Caring for Your Collections: Manuscripts & Related Materials." American Association for State and Local History, Technical Leaflet 8. *History News* 18, no. 6 (1963).

Archer, H. Richard. "Display and Exhibit Cases." *Library Trends* 13 (1965): 474–480.

–––. "Special Collections." *Library Trends* 18 (1970):354–362.

–––, editor. *Rare Book Collections: Some Theoretical and Practical Suggestions for Use by Librarians and Students.* Association of College and Research Libraries Monograph, no. 27. Chicago: American Library Association, 1965.

Arnold, Edmund C. *Ink on Paper 2: A Handbook of the Graphic Arts.* New York: Harper & Row, 1972.

Artandi, Susan. *An Introduction to Computers in Information Science.* 2nd ed. Metuchen, N.J.: Scarecrow Press, 1972.

Atherton, Jay. "Automation and the Dignity of the Archivist." *Canadian Archivist* 2 (1970):56–58.

–––. "Mechanization of the Manuscript Catalogue at the Public Archives of Canada." *American Archivist* 30 (1967):303–309.

Atherton, Lewis E. "Western Historical Manuscripts Collection—A Case Study of a Collecting Program." *American Archivist* 26 (1963):41–49.

Avedon, Don M. *Computer Output Microfilm.* National Microfilm Association Monograph, no. 4. Annapolis: National Microfilm Association, 1969.

–––. "Standards: Microfilm Permanence and Archival Quality." *Journal of Micrographics* 6 (1972):93–94.

Avery, Laurence G., compiler. *A Catalogue of the Maxwell Anderson Collection at the University of Texas.* Towner Bibliographical Series, no. 6. Austin: University of Texas at Austin, Humanities Research Center, 1968.

Baer, N. S.; N. Indicator; and A. Joel. "The Aging Behavior of Impregnating Agent-paper Systems as Used in Paper Conservation." *Restaurator* 2, no. 1 (1972):5–21.

Ballou, Hubbard W., editor. *Guide to Microreproduction Equipment.* 5th ed. Annapolis: National Microfilm Association, 1971.

———, editor. *1973 Supplement to the Guide to Microreproduction Equipment.* Silver Spring, Md.: National Microfilm Association, 1973.

Banks, Paul. "Lamination." *Paper Conservation News* 1, no. 1 (1973):1–3.

Barnes, Christopher. "Classification and Cataloging of Spoken Records in Academic Libraries." *College & Research Libraries* 28 (1967):49–52.

Barrow, William J. *Manuscripts and Documents: Their Deterioration and Restoration.* 2d ed. Charlottesville: University of Virginia Press, 1972.

Barrow, William J., and Ann M. Carlton. "Durability of Three Current Laminating Tissues." *American Archivist* 30 (1967):526–529.

The Barrow Method of Restoring Deteriorated Documents. Richmond: W. J. Barrow Restoration Shop, 1970.

Basler, Roy B. "The Modern Collector." In *The American Collector,* edited by Donald R. McNeil, pp. 24–35. Madison: State Historical Society of Wisconsin, 1955.

Baughman, Roland. "The Evaluation and Insurance of Great Rarities." In American Library Association. *Protecting the Library and its Resources: Guide to Physical Protection and Insurance,* pp. 265–268. Library Technology Project Publication, no. 7. Chicago: American Library Association, 1963.

Baum, Willa K. *Oral History for the Local Historical Society.* Nashville: American Association for State and Local History, 1971.

Baynes-Cope, A. D. "The Dismounting of 'Dry Mounted' Photographic Prints." *Restaurator* 2, no. 1 (1972):1–3.

Beasley, Kenneth E. "Library Administration: An Overview." In *Administration and Change: Continuing Education in Library Administration,* edited by the Graduate School of Library Service, pp. 9–20. New Brunswick: Rutgers University Press, 1969.

Bell, Lionell. "The Professional Training of Archivists." *Unesco Bulletin for Libraries* 25 (1971):191–197.

Bellomy, Fred L. "Management Planning for Library Systems Development." *Journal of Library Automation* 2 (1969):187–217.

Benison, Saul. "Reflections on Oral History." *American Archivist* 28 (1965):71–77.

Benjamin, Mary A. *Autographs: A Key to Collecting.* 2d ed., rev. New York: Walter R. Benjamin Autographs, 1963.

———. "Columbia Wakes Up!" *Columbia Library Columns* 3, no. 1 (1953):5–15.

Bennis, Warren. "The University Leader." *Saturday Review of Education,* January 1973, pp. 42–50.

Berner, Richard C. "Archivists, Librarians, and the *National Union Catalog of Manuscript Collections.*" *American Archivist* 27 (1964):401–409.

———. "Manuscript Catalogs and Other Finding Aids: What Are Their Relationships?" *American Archivist* 34 (1971):367–372.

———. "On Ephemera: Their Collection and Use." *Library Resources & Technical Services* 7 (1963):335–339.

Berner, Richard C., and M. Gary Bettis. "Description of Manuscript Collections; A Single Network System." *College & Research Libraries* 30 (1969):405–416.

——— and ———. "Disposition of Nonmanuscript Items Found Among Manuscripts." *American Archivist* 33 (1970):275–281.

Bibliotheca Americana; A Catalogue of A Valuable Collection of Books and Pamphlets Relating to History and Geography . . . Together with Many Valuable Miscellaneous Works, Autographs etc. etc. For Sale by Charles B. Norton. New York: n.p., 1857.

Blunn, Denis. "A Method of Dry Repair." *Journal of the Society of Archivists* 4 (1972):521–522.

Bond, William H. "Manuscript Collections in the Houghton Library." *Manuscripts* 4, no. 3 (1952):32–39.

Book-Auction Records: A Priced and Annotated Annual Record of International Book-Auctions. Vol. 69. London: Dawsons of Pall Mall, 1973.

Bordin, Ruth B. "Cataloging Manuscripts—A Simple Scheme." *American Archivist* 27 (1964):81–86.

Bordin, Ruth B., and Robert M. Warner. *The Modern Manuscript Library.* New York: Scarecrow Press, 1966.

Bornet, Vaughn D. "Oral History Can Be Worthwhile." *American Archivist* 18 (1955):241–253.

Boston. Public Library. *Manuscripts of the American Revolution in the Boston Public Library: A Descriptive Catalog.* Boston: G. K. Hall & Co., 1968.

Bowden, Ann. "Training for Rare Book Librarianship." *Journal of Education for Librarianship* 12 (1972):223–231.

Bowditch, George. "Cataloging Photographs: A Procedure For Small Museums." American Association for State and Local History, Technical Leaflet 57. *History News* 26, no. 11 (1971).

Bowen, Dorothy. "Techniques of Book and Manuscript Display." *1968 AB Bookman's Yearbook*, pt. 2, pp. 11–15.

Bowers, Fredson. "Textual Criticism." In *The Aims and Methods of Scholarship in Modern Languages and Literatures*, 2d ed., edited by James Thorpe, pp. 29–54. New York: Modern Language Association, 1970.

Brewer, Frances J. "Friends of the Library and Other Benefactors and Donors." *Library Trends* 9 (1961):453–465.

Brichford, Maynard, editor. *Descriptive Inventory of Resources for Ecology of Mental Health and Work with the Disadvantaged.* Champaign-Urbana: University of Illinois, 1967.

Briggs, Donald R. "Gift Appraisal Policy in Large Research Libraries." *College & Research Libraries* 29 (1968):505–507.

Brigham, Clarence S. "History of Book Auctions in America." *Bulletin of the New York Public Library* 39 (1935):55–90.

Brinton, Ellen S. "Inexpensive Devices to Aid the Archivist." *American Archivist* 13 (1950):285–286.

Brooks, Philip C. *Research in Archives: The Use of Unpublished Primary Sources*. Chicago: University of Chicago Press, 1969.

Brown, Andreas L. "Valuation and Appraisal." *1968 AB Bookman's Yearbook*, pt. 2, pp. 22–24.

Brown, Lloyd A. "The Problem of Maps." *Library Trends* 13 (1964):215–225.

Brubaker, Robert L. "Archive and Manuscript Collections." In *Advances in Librarianship*, 3 vols., edited by Melvin J. Voigt, 3:245–278. New York: Seminar Press, 1970–1972.

———. "Archival Principles and the Curator of Manuscripts." *American Archivist* 29 (1966):505–514.

———. "Manuscript Collections." *Library Trends* 13 (1964):226–253.

Burnett, A. D. "Considerations on the support of Antiquarian and other Special Collections in University Libraries." *Journal of Librarianship* 5 (1973):203–213.

Burnette, O. Lawrence, Jr. *Beneath the Footnote: A Guide to the Use and Preservation of American Historical Sources*. Madison: State Historical Society of Wisconsin, 1969.

Burke, Frank G. "The Application of Automated Techniques in the Management and Control of Source Materials." *American Archivist* 30 (1967):255–278.

———. "Automation and Historical Research." *Libri* 19 (1969):81–91.

———. "Automation in Bibliographical Control of Archives and Manuscript Collections." In *Bibliography and the Historian*, edited by Dagmar H. Perman, pp. 96–102. Santa Barbara: Clio, 1968.

———. "The Impact of the Specialist on Archives." *College & Research Libraries* 33 (1972):312–317.

———. "Manuscripts and Archives." *Library Trends* 15 (1967):430–445.

Butterfield, Lyman H. "Draper's Predecessors." In *The American Collector*, edited by Donald R. McNeil, pp. 1–23. Madison: State Historical Society of Wisconsin, 1955.

Butterfield, Lyman H., and Julian P. Boyd. "Historical Editing in the United States." *Proceedings of the American Antiquarian Society* 72 (1963):281–328.

Butterfield, Max A. "Care and Preservation of the New Media: Equipment Needs." In *Pioneer Presentation of a National Symposium on the Impact of Automation on Documentation*, pp. 60–64. Denver: [University of Denver], 1968.

Byrd, Cecil K. "Quarters For Special Collections in University Libraries." *Library Trends* 18 (1969):223–234.

Calhoun, John M. "The Preservation of Motion-Picture Film." *American Archivist* 30 (1967):517–525.

Campbell, Rita R. "Machine Retrieval in the Herbert Hoover Archives." *American Archivist* 29 (1966):298–302.

Cannon, Carl L. *American Book Collectors and Collecting from Colonial Times to the Present*. New York: H. W. Wilson Co., 1941.

Cappon, Lester J. "The Historian as Editor." In *In Support of Clio: Essays in Memory of Herbert A. Kellar,* edited by William B. Hesseltine and Donald R. McNeil, pp. 173–193. Madison: State Historical Society of Wisconsin, 1958.

———. "Walter R. Benjamin and the Autograph Trade at the Turn of the Century." *Proceedings of the Massachusetts Historical Society* 78 (1966):20–37.

Capps, Marie T. "Preservation and Maintenance of Maps." *Special Libraries* 63 (1972):457–462.

Catalogue of Manuscripts of Books Printed Upon Vellum of Editiones Principes et Aldinae . . . by Payne and Foss. London: n.p., 1830.

A Catalogue of a Valuable Collection of Books on Sale by Payne and Foss . . . Among Which Will Be Found Interesting Manuscripts. London: n.p., 1841.

Catalogue of a Valuable Collection of Manuscripts Recently Imported from the Continent by Payne and Foss. London: n.p., 1825.

Center for Editions of American Authors. *Recovering and Preserving the Author's Intention.* Columbia, S.C.: Center for Editions of American Authors, 1972.

Chavis, John M. T., and William McNitt. *A Brief History of the Detroit Urban League, and Description of the League's Papers in the Michigan Historical Collections.* Bulletin no. 20. Ann Arbor: Michigan Historical Collections, 1971.

Cobb, Allen L. "Burning Characteristics of Safety vs. Nitrate Film." *Journal of the Society of Motion Picture and Television Engineers* 66 (1957):66–68.

Cole, George. "Computer Tapes and Their Care." *Data Processing* 2, no. 10 (1960):11–16.

Colman, Gould P. "Making Library History." *Journal of Library History* 7 (1972):130–140.

———. "Oral History—An Appeal for More Systematic Procedures." *American Archivist* 28 (1965):79–83.

———. "Oral History at Cornell." *Wilson Library Bulletin* 40 (1966):624–628.

Conat, Mabel L. "History of the Friends of the Library." In *Friends of the Library: Organization and Activities,* edited by Sarah L. Wallace, pp. 1–11. Chicago: American Library Association, 1962.

Conaway, Charles W. "Lyman Copeland Draper, 'Father of American Oral History.'" *Journal of Library History* 1 (1966):234–241.

Coney, Donald. "Management in College and University Libraries." *Library Trends* 1 (1952):83–94.

Conference in the Study of Twentieth-Century Literature. "Approaches to the Study of Twentieth-Century Literature." *Proceedings,* 3d Session. East Lansing: Michigan State University, 1963.

Connor, Seymour V. "A System of Manuscript Appraisal." American Association for State and Local History, Technical Leaflet 41. *History News* 22, no. 5 (1967).

Coplan, Kate. *Effective Library Exhibits: How to Prepare and Promote Good Display.* New York: Oceana Publishers, 1958.

"Copyright Bill Awaits Senate Action." *American Libraries* 4 (1973):189.

"Copyright: Educators Dig in Their Heels." *Publishers Weekly* 204 (1973):32–33.

"Copyright Hearings in Senate." *American Libraries* 4 (1973):557.

Copyright Law Revision: Hearings Before the Subcommittee on Patents, Trademarks, and Copyrights of the Committee on the Judiciary, United States Senate, Ninety-Third Congress, First Session, Pursuant to S. Res. 56 on S. 1361, July 31 and August 1, 1973. Washington: U.S. Government Printing Office, 1973.

Cornell University. Collection of Regional History and University Archives. "Processing, SPINDEX II and Cornell." Mimeographed. Ithaca: Cornell University, [ca. 1970].

Cost Estimates for Restoration of Documents. Richmond: W. J. Barrow Restoration Shop, 1971.

Council on Library Resources, Inc. *Sixteenth Annual Report for the Year Ending June 30, 1972.* Washington: Council on Library Resources, Inc., 1972.

Cowley, J. D. *Bibliographical Description and Cataloguing.* 1949. Reprint. New York: Burt Franklin, 1970.

[Cox, H. Bartholomew.] "An Analysis of S.543 for Sections Relevant to Documentary Publication and Reproduction of Archival Materials, and Sections Relating to the *Federal Register.*" Mimeographed. [Washington: National Archives and Records Service, 1970].

———. "The Impact of the Proposed Copyright Law Upon Scholars and Custodians." *American Archivist* 29 (1966):217–227.

———. "Private Letters and the Public Domain." *American Archivist* 28 (1965):381–388.

———. "Publication of Manuscripts: Devaluation or Enhancement?" *American Archivist* 32 (1969):25–32.

Cunha, George M. *Conservation of Library Materials: A Manual and Bibliography on the Care, Repair and Restoration of Library Materials.* Metuchen, N.J.: Scarecrow Press, 1967.

Cunha, George M., and Dorothy G. Cunha. *Conservation of Library Materials: A Manual and Bibliography on the Care, Repair and Restoration of Library Materials.* 2 vols. 2d ed., rev. Metuchen, N.J.: Scarecrow Press, 1971–1972.

Cunha, George M., and Norman P. Tucker, editors. *Library and Archives Conservation.* Boston: Library of the Boston Athenaeum, 1972.

Dexter, Lewis A. *Elite and Specialized Interviewing.* Evanston: Northwestern University Press, 1970.

Diamond, Robert M. "A Retrieval System for 35 mm. Slides Utilized in Art and Humanities Instruction." In *Bibliographical Control of Nonprint Media*, edited by Pearce S. Grove and Evelyn G. Clement, pp. 346–359. Chicago: American Library Association, 1972.

Dionne, R. Dennis. "Approach to Computer Output Microfilm Implementation." *Records Management Journal* 9, no. 1 (1971):11–16.

"Disk Pack Initialization." *Computer Talk* 2, no. 1 (1969):1–3.

Dixon, Elizabeth I., compiler. *The Oral History Program at UCLA: A Bibliography.* Los Angeles: University of California Library, 1966.

Dollar, Charles M. "Documentation of Machine Readable Records and Research: A Historian's View." *Prologue* 3 (1971):27–31.

Dollar, Charles M., and Richard J. Jensen. *Historian's Guide to Statistics;
Quantitative Analysis and Historical Research.* New York: Holt, Rinehart,
and Winston, 1971.

Doudnikoff, Basil. *Information Retrieval.* Philadelphia: Auerbach Publishers,
1973.

Draper, Lyman C. *An Essay on the Autographic Collections of the Signers
of the Declaration of Independence and of the Constitution.* New York:
Burns & Sons, 1889.

Driscoll, Emily. "Great Collector: Andre De Coppet, 1891–1953." *Manuscripts*
8, no. 2 (1956):81–84.

Duniway, David C. "Conflicts in Collecting." *American Archivist* 24
(1961):55–63.

Duke, Angier Biddle. "Public Life, Private Papers, and the Right to Know."
Duke University Library Notes, no. 44 (1973):5–21.

Dunn, Walter S., Jr. "Cataloging Ephemera: A Procedure for Small Libraries."
American Association for State and Local History, Technical Leaflet 58.
History News 27, no. 1 (1972).

Eastman Kodak Co. *Recordak AHU Microfilm.* Sales Brochure. Rochester:
Eastman Kodak Co., [1972].

———. *Storage and Preservation of Motion-Picture Film.* Rochester: Eastman
Kodak Co., [1957].

Easterwood, T. J. "The Collecting and Care of Modern Manuscripts." *Call
Number* 24, no. 1 (1964):4–17.

Eaton, Andrew J. "Fund Raising for University Libraries." *College & Research
Libraries* 32 (1971):351–361.

Eaton, George T. "Preservation, Deterioration, Restoration of Photographic
Images." *Library Quarterly* 40 (1970):85–98.

Edel, Leon. *The Age of the Archive.* Center for Advanced Studies, Monday
Evening Papers, no. 7. Middletown, Conn.: Wesleyan University, 1966.

Edwards, Edward. *Lives of the Founders of the British Museum; With Notices
of its Chief Augmentors and Other Benefactors, 1570–1870.* 1870. Reprint.
New York: Burt Franklin, 1969.

E. I. du Pont Nemours & Co. *Du Pont Halon 1301 Fire Extinguishant.* Wilmington, Del.: E. I. du Pont Nemours & Co., 1972.

Elton, Geoffrey R. *Political History: Principles and Practices.* New York: Basic
Books, 1970.

Erney, Richard A., and F. Gerald Ham. "Wisconsin's Area Research Centers."
American Libraries 3 (1972):135–140.

Evans, Frank B. *The Administration of Modern Archives: A Select Biblio-graphic Guide.* Washington: National Archives and Records Service, 1970.

———. "Automation and Archives." Mimeographed. Washington: National Archives and Records Service, 1973.

———. "Modern Methods of Arrangement of Archives in the United States." *American Archivist* 29 (1966):241–263.

———. *The Selection and Preparation of Records for Publication on Microfilm.* Staff Information Paper 19. Washington: National Archives and Records Service, 1970.

Fassett, D. W.; F. J. Kolb, Jr.; and E. M. Weigel. "Practical Film Cleaning for Safety and Effectiveness." *Journal of the Society of Motion Picture and Television Engineers* 67 (1958):572–589.

Faye, Helen. "May We Use This Picture?–Rights and Permissions." *Special Libraries* 56 (1965):23–26.

Ferrar, A. M. "The Management of Map Collections and Libraries in University Geography Departments." *Library Association Record* 64 (1962):161–165.

Fielding, Raymond. "Archives of the Motion Picture: A General View." *American Archivist* 30 (1967):493–500.

Filby, P. William. "Techniques of Exhibitions." *1968 AB Bookman's Yearbook,* pt. 2, pp. 8–10.

Finch, Herbert. "Administrative Relationships in a Large Manuscript Repository." *American Archivist* 34 (1971):21–25.

———. "The Problem of Confidentiality in a College Archives." *American Archivist* 31 (1968):239–241.

Finch, Jean L. "Some Fundamentals in Arranging Archives and Manuscript Collections." *Library Resources & Technical Services* 8 (1964):26–34.

The First One Hundred: A Catalog of Manuscripts & Special Collections. Pensacola: University of West Florida, 1972.

Fishbein, Meyer H. "Appraising Information in Machine Language Form." *American Archivist* 35 (1972):35–43.

Fletcher, William Y. *English Book Collectors.* 1902. Reprint. New York: Burt Franklin, 1969.

Flory, John. "Doomsday for Film: The Crisis in Motion-Picture Archives." *Journal of the Society of Motion Picture and Television Engineers* 72 (1963):410–412.

Ford, Robert N. *Motivation Through the Work Itself.* [New York]: American Management Association, Inc., 1969.

French, Hannah D. "Access, Service, and Publications." In *Rare Book Collections: Some Theoretical and Practical Suggestions for Use by Librarians and Students,* edited by H. Richard Archer, pp. 92–107. Association of College and Research Libraries Monograph, no. 27. Chicago: American Library Association, 1965.

Friedman, Hannah B., and Wayne Eley, compilers. *Conservation of Library Materials: A Suggested Reading List.* New York: New York Public Library, 1973.

Fry, Amelia R. "The Nine Commandments of Oral History." *Journal of Library History* 3 (1968):63–73.

Gammon, W. Howard. "Software as it Relates to Documentation." In *Pioneer Presentation of a National Symposium on the Impact of Automation on Documentation*, pp. 14–22. Denver: [University of Denver], 1968.

———. "Remotes and Displays." *Ibid.*, p. 119.

Garvey, Mona. *Library Displays: Their Purpose, Construction and Use*. New York: H. W. Wilson, 1969.

Gerlach, Arch C. "Geography and Map Cataloging and Classification in Libraries." *Special Libraries* 52 (1961):248–251.

Gilchrist, Alan. "Work Study in Libraries." *Journal of Librarianship* 2 (1970):126–138.

Gondos, Victor, Jr. "Archival Buildings—Programing and Planning." *American Archivist* 27 (1964):467–483.

———, editor. *Reader for Archives and Records Center Buildings*. [Washington]: Committee on Archives Buildings and Equipment, Society of American Archivists, 1970.

Griffin, Patrick H., editor. "The National Archives and the Historian's Use of Film: William Murphy in an Interview with *The History Teacher*." *History Teacher* 6 (1972):119–134.

Haber, Francis C. "Robert Gilmor, Jr.—Pioneer American Autograph Collector." *Manuscripts* 7, no. 1 (1954):13–17.

Hale, Richard W., Jr., editor. *Guide to Photocopied Historical Materials in the United States and Canada*. Ithaca, N. Y.: American Historical Association, 1961.

Hall, David. "Phonorecord Preservation: Notes of a Pragmatist." *Special Libraries* 62 (1971):357–362.

Halsband, Robert. "Editing the Letters of Letter-Writers." In *Art and Error: Modern Textual Editing*, edited by Ronald Gottesman and Scott Bennett, pp. 124–139. Bloomington: Indiana University Press, 1970.

Hamer, Philip M., editor. *A Guide to Archives and Manuscripts in the United States*. New Haven: Yale University Press, 1961.

Hamilton, E. Douglas. "Oral History and the Law of Libel." In *The Second National Colloquium on Oral History*, edited by Louis M. Starr, pp. 41–56. New York: Oral History Association, 1968.

"The Handling & Storage of Computer Tape." *Computer Talk* 1, no. 1 (1968):1–7.

"The Handling & Storage of Magnetic Recording Tape." *Sound Talk* 3, no. 1 (1970):1–7.

Harmon, George H. "The Computer-Microfilm Relationship." *Special Libraries* 62 (1971):279–282.

Harper, Josephine L., and Sharon C. Smith, editors. *Guide to the Manuscripts of the State Historical Society of Wisconsin, Supplement Number One*. Madison: State Historical Society of Wisconsin, 1957.

Harry S. Truman Library. "Audio-Visual Cataloging System." Mimeographed. Independence, Kansas: Harry S. Truman Library, 1962.

Hearing before a Subcommittee of the Committee on Government Operations, House of Representatives, Ninety-second Congress, Second Session on H.R. 15763 . . . August 8, 1972. Washington: U.S. Government Printing Office, 1972. [Testimony of Dr. James B. Rhoads, Archivist of the United States, concerning the National Historical Publications Commission.]

Heinritz, Fred J. "Quantitative Management in Libraries." *College & Research Libraries* 31 (1970):232-238.

Hellwig, Jessica. *Introduction to Computers and Programing.* New York: Columbia University Press, 1969.

Henry E. Huntington Library and Art Gallery. Annual Report, July 1, 1971-June 30, 1972. San Marino: Henry E. Huntington Library and Art Galley, 1972.

———. *Readers' Guide to the Huntington Library.* San Marino: Huntington Library and Art Gallery, 1972.

Herbert Hoover Presidential Library. *Historical Materials in the Herbert Hoover Presidential Library.* West Branch, Iowa: Herbert Hoover Presidential Library, 1971.

Hesseltine, William B., and Donald R. McNeil, editors. *In Support of Clio: Essays in Memory of Herbert A. Kellar.* Madison: State Historical Society of Wisconsin, 1958.

Hill, J. Douglas. "Map and Atlas Cases." *Library Trends* 13 (1965):481-487.

Historical Manuscripts Commission: "Appendix 1, Additional Items Respecting Historical Manuscripts." *Annual Report of the American Historical Association for the Year 1900.* 2 vols. Washington: Government Printing Office, 1901:1:595-607.

Hockett, Homer C. *The Critical Method in Historical Research and Writing.* New York: Macmillan Co., 1955.

Hodson, J. H. *The Administration of Archives.* Oxford: Pergamon Press, 1972.

Hoffman, Alice M. "Oral History in the United States." *Journal of Library History* 7 (1972):277-285.

Holmes, Oliver W. "History and Theory of Archival Practice." In *University Archives,* Allerton Park Institute no. 11, edited by Rolland E. Stevens, pp. 1-21. Champaign: University of Illinois, 1965.

Horton, Carolyn. *Cleaning and Preserving Bindings and Related Materials.* Library Technology Program Publications, no. 16. 2d ed., rev. Chicago: American Library Association, 1969.

Howe, Jane. "Cataloguing A Photograph Collection." *Oklahoma Librarian* 13 (1963):8-12.

Howell, Herbert A. *The Copyright Law; An Analysis of the Law of the United States Governing Registration and Protection of Copyright Works . . .* 3d ed. Washington: Bureau of National Affairs, 1952.

Illinois State Historical Library and Society. "Old Photographs." Mimeographed. Springfield: Illinois State Historical Library and Society, [ca. 1972].

Illinois, University of. University Archives. *Ninth Annual Report, July 1, 1971, to June 30, 1972.* Urbana-Champaign: University of Illinois, 1972.

Illinois, University of, at Chicago Circle. The Library. *Guide to the Manuscript Collections.* Chicago: University of Illinois at Chicago Circle, [1967].

Introduction to Micrographics. Silver Spring, Md.: National Microfilm Association, 1973.

Inventory of the Erasmus Gest Papers, 1834-1885. Inventory and Calendar Series, no. 4. Columbus: Ohio Historical Society, 1962.

Jasenas, Michael. "Cataloging Small Manuscript Collections." *Library Resources & Technical Services* 7 (1963):264-273.

Jenkins, Harold. "Volunteers in the Future of the Library." *Library Journal* 97 (1972):1399-1403.

Johnson, Thomas H. "Establishing a Text: The Emily Dickinson Papers." In *Art and Error: Modern Textual Editing,* edited by Ronald Gottesman and Scott Bennett, pp. 140-154. Bloomington: Indiana University Press, 1970.

Joint AHA-OHA Ad Hoc Committee to Investigate the Charges Against the Franklin D. Roosevelt Library and Related Matters. *Final Report.* [Baltimore: Port City Press], 1970.

Jones, H. G. *The Records of a Nation: Their Management, Preservation, and Use.* New York: Atheneum, 1969.

Jones, Howard Mumford. *One Great Society: Humane Learning in the United States.* New York: Harcourt, Brace & Co., 1959.

Kahn, Herman. "Some Comments on the Archival Vocation." *American Archivist* 34 (1971):3-12.

Kane, Lucile M. *A Guide to the Care and Administration of Manuscripts.* 2d ed., rev. Nashville: American Association for State and Local History, 1966.

———. "Manuscript Collecting." In *In Support of Clio: Essays in Memory of Herbert A. Kellar,* edited by William B. Hesseltine and Donald R. McNeil, pp. 29-48. Madison: State Historical Society of Wisconsin, 1958.

Kane, Lucile M., and Kathryn A. Johnson, compilers. *Manuscript Collections of the Minnesota Historical Society.* St. Paul: Minnesota Historical Society, 1955.

Kathpalia, Y. P. "Hand Lamination with Cellulose Acetate." *American Archivist* 21 (1958):271-276.

Kellermann, J. O. "Observations on Archives Depositories in Overseas Countries." In *Reader for Archives and Records Center Buildings,* edited by Victor Gondos, Jr., pp. 49-68. [Washington]: Committee on Archives Buildings and Equipment, Society of American Archivists, 1970.

Kenneth Spencer Research Library. *Guide for Readers 11: Department of Special Collections.* Lawrence: University of Kansas Libraries, [ca. 1969].

———. ["Manual of Operations."] Typewritten. Lawrence: University of Kansas, 1970.

Kielman, Chester V. "The Texas Oil Industry Project." *Wilson Library Bulletin* 40 (1966):616-618.

King, Antoinette. "Conservation of Drawings and Prints." *Special Libraries* 63 (1972):116-120.

Knightbridge, A. A. H. "Sulphur Dioxide Test Papers." *Journal of the Society of Archivists* 4 (1970):64-65.

Kobler, John. "Trailing the Book Crooks." *Saturday Evening Post,* March 13, 1943, pp. 18-19.

Kraus, Michael. *A History of American History.* New York: Farrar & Rinehart, 1937.

Kujoth, Jean S., editor. *Readings in Nonbook Librarianship.* Metuchen, N.J.: Scarecrow Press, 1968.

Lang, Elfrieda. "Arrangement and Cataloging of Manuscripts in the Lilly Library, Indiana University, Bloomington, Indiana." *Serif* 10, no. 1 (1973):3-12.

Langwell, W. H. "Methods of Deacidifying Paper." *Journal of the Society of Archivists* 3 (1969):491-494.

———. "Vapour-Phase De-Acidification: A Recent Development." *Journal of the Society of Archivists* 4 (1973):597-598.

———. "The Vapour Phase Deacidification of Books and Documents." *Journal of the Society of Archivists* 3 (1966):137-138.

Lawler, John. *Book Auctions in England in the Seventeenth Century (1676-1700).* 1898. Reprint. Detroit: Gale Research Co., 1968.

Lawrence, Virginia N. "The Case Against Plastic Tape." *Manuscripts* 8, no. 4 (1956):233-234.

Laying, Theodore H. "Problems in the Map Room." *Canadian Library* 18 (1961):63-66. Reprint. In *Readings in Nonbook Librarianship,* edited by Jean S. Kujoth, pp. 280-285. Metuchen, N.J.: Scarecrow Press, 1968.

Layton, Edwin T., Jr., editor. *A Regional Union Catalog of Manuscripts Relating to the History of Science and Technology Located in Indiana, Michigan, and Ohio.* Cleveland: Case Western Reserve University, 1971.

Lee, Marshall. *Bookmaking: The Illustrated Guide to Design & Production.* New York: R. R. Bowker Co., 1965.

Le Gear, Clara E. *Maps: Their Care, Repair and Preservation.* Washington: Library of Congress, 1949.

Leisinger, Albert H., Jr. "The Exhibit of Documents." *American Archivist* 26 (1963):75-86.

———. *Microphotography for Archives.* Washington: International Council on Archives, 1968.

Lentz, Andrea D., editor. *A Guide to Manuscripts at the Ohio Historical Society.* Columbus: Ohio Historical Society, 1972.

Leopold, Richard W. "A Crisis of Confidence: Foreign Policy Research and the Federal Government." *American Archivist* 34 (1971):139-155.

Lewinson, Paul. "Archival Sampling." *American Archivist* 20 (1957):291-312.

Lingelbach, William E. "An Early American Historian." In *Bookmen's Holiday:*

Notes and Studies Written and Gathered in Tribute to Harry Miller Lydenberg, edited by Deoch Fulton, pp. 355–361. New York: New York Public Library, 1943.

Logsdon, Richard H. "Time and Motion Studies in Libraries." *Library Trends* 2 (1954):401–409.

Lord, Clifford L., editor. *Keepers of the Past*. Durham: University of North Carolina Press, 1965.

Lord, Clifford L., and Carl Ubbelohde. *Clio's Servant: The State Historical Society of Wisconsin, 1846–1954*. Madison: State Historical Society of Wisconsin, 1967.

Lovett, Robert W. "The Appraisal of Older Business Records." *American Archivist* 15 (1952):231–239.

–––. "Of Manuscripts and Archives." *Special Libraries* 64 (1973):415–418.

Luther, Frederic. "The Language of Lilliput: A Thesaurus for Users of Microfilm." 7 pts. *Library Journal* 86 (1961):929–931, 931–932, 2425–2430, 3238–3241, 3743–3746; 87 (1962):48–54, 920–931.

Lyle, Guy R. *The Administration of the College Library*. 3d ed., rev. New York: H. W. Wilson Co., 1961.

"MDC Salvaging Burned Veterans' Records." *McDonnell Douglas Spirit*, Eastern ed. 3, no. 9 (1973):1–2.

McCamy, C. S. *Inspection of Processed Photographic Record Films for Aging Blemishes*. National Bureau of Standards Handbook 96. Washington: U.S. Department of Commerce, 1964.

McCarthy, Paul. "Vapor Phase Deacidification: A New Preservation Method." *American Archivist* 32 (1969):333–342.

McCosker, M. J. *The Historical Collection of Insurance Company of North America*. Philadelphia: Insurance Company of North America, 1967.

McDiarmid, Errett W. "Role of the Friends in the Library Organization." In *Friends of the Library: Organization and Activities*, edited by Sarah L. Wallace, pp. 12–19. Chicago: American Library Association, 1962.

McDonald, Jerry. "The Case Against Microfilming." *American Archivist* 20 (1957):345–356.

The McGraw-Hill Author's Book. New York: McGraw-Hill Book Co., 1955.

McGregor, Douglas. *The Human Side of Enterprise*. New York: McGraw-Hill Book Co., 1960.

McKay, George L. "American Book Auction Catalogues, 1713–1934; A Union List Compiled by George L. McKay." *Bulletin of the New York Public Library* 39 (1935): 141–166, 389–410, 461–478, 561–576, 638–663, 724–744, 815–828, 891–914, 955–980; 40 (1936):56–78, 139–165, 375–390, 535–557, 671–703, 775–800, 859–877, 955–984, 1065–1098.

McNeil, Donald R., editor. *The American Collector*. Madison: State Historical Society of Wisconsin, 1955.

Madigan, Thomas F. *Word Shadows of the Great: The Lure of Autograph Collecting*. New York: Frederick A. Stokes Co., 1930.

Magnetic Tape Erasure—How Serious is the Threat? St. Paul: Minnesota Mining and Manufacturing Co., 1972.

Malan, Nancy E. "A Review of the Photographic Holdings of the National Anthropological Archives." Mimeographed. Washington: National Archives and Records Service, Audiovisual Archives Division, 1973.

A Manual of Style ... Together with Specimens of Type. 11th ed., rev. Chicago: University of Chicago, 1949.

Manuscripts for Research. Syracuse: Five Associated University Libraries, 1969.

Martell, Charles. "Administration: Which Way—Traditional Practice or Modern Theory?" *College & Research Libraries* 33 (1972):104–112.

Maryland. Department of General Services. *Hall of Records Commission, Activities Report no. 36; Fiscal Year 1971.* Annapolis: Department of General Services, 1971.

Mason, Elizabeth B., and Louis M. Starr, editors. *The Oral History Collection of Columbia University.* New York: Oral History Research Office, 1973.

Matheson, William. "An Approach to Special Collections." *American Libraries* 2 (1971):1151–1156.

Matthews, Glenn E., and Raife G. Tarkington. "Early History of Amateur Motion-Picture Film." *Journal of the Society of Motion Picture and Television Engineers* 64 (1955):105–116.

Mauck, Virginia L. "Selection and Purchase of Archival Equipment and Supplies." *Illinois Libraries* 53 (1971):18–21.

Mearns, David C. "Nineteenth-Century Comments on Autographs and Collectors." *Manuscripts* 4, no. 2 (1952):49–50.

Meetham, Roger. *Information Retrieval: The Essential Technology.* Garden City, N.Y.: Doubleday & Co., 1970.

Mersel, Jules. "Storing Software in an Archive." In *Pioneer Presentation of a National Symposium on the Impact of Automation on Documentation,* pp. 11–12. Denver: [University of Denver], 1968.

Metcalf, Keyes D. *Planning Academic and Research Library Buildings.* New York: McGraw-Hill Book Co., 1965.

Metzdorf, Robert F. "Appraisal of Literary Properties." *1965 AB Bookman's Yearbook,* pt. 2, pp. B15–B16.

The Michigan Historical Collection of the University of Michigan. [Bulletin no. 13.] Ann Arbor: Michigan Historical Collections, [1963].

Minnesota Historical Society. *Catalog of Microfilms for Sale by the Minnesota Historical Society.* St. Paul: Minnesota Historical Society, 1970.

———. "The Nature of Manuscripts and the Special Occupation Descriptions for Employees of a Manuscripts Center." Mimeographed. St. Paul: Minnesota Historical Society, [1971].

———. "Functions of the Manuscripts Division." Mimeographed. St. Paul: Minnesota Historical Society, [ca. 1972].

Mixer, Charles W. "New Insurance for Library Collections." *Library Journal* 79 (1954):1539–1543.

Modern Library Association of America. American Literature Group. *American Literary Manuscripts: a Checklist of Holdings in Academic, Historical and Public Libraries in the United States.* Austin: University of Texas, 1960.

Morris, Monty. "Magnetic Tape Life." *Data Management* 10, no. 2 (1972):17–19.

Morrissey, Charles T. "Truman and the Presidency—Records and Oral Recollections." *American Archivist* 28 (1965):53–61.

Mott, Lawrence V. "Activities of the Friends of the Library." In *Friends of the Library: Organization and Activities,* edited by Sarah L. Wallace, pp. 30–34. Chicago: American Library Association, 1962.

Munby, A. N. L. *The Cult of the Autograph Letter in England.* London: Athlone Press, 1962.

"NYSHA Seminar on American Culture." *AB Bookman's Weekly* 32 (1963):259–266.

National Endowment for the Humanities. *Sixth Annual Report.* Washington: National Endowment for the Humanities, 1971.

———. *Seventh Annual Report.* Washington: National Endowment for the Humanities, 1972.

National Fire Protection Association. *Manual for Fire Protection for Archives and Records Centers.* Boston: National Fire Protection Association, 1972.

———. *Recommended Practice for Protection of Library Collections from Fire.* Boston: National Fire Protection Association, 1970.

Newberry Library. *The Hermon Dunlap Smith Center for the History of Cartography at the Newberry Library.* Chicago: Newberry Library, 1973.

———. *The Hermon Dunlap Smith Center for the History of Cartography at the Newberry Library, Dedication Proceedings, November 1st, 1972.* Chicago: Newberry Library, 1973.

Newman, Ralph G. "Appraisals and 'Revenooers': Tax Problems of the Collector." American Association for State and Local History, Technical Leaflet 31. *History News* 20, no. 10 (1965).

Newton, S. C. "The Archivist and Dutton v Bognor Regis." *Journal of the Society of Archivists* 4 (1973):596–597.

———. "The Archivist as Legislator." *Journal of the Society of Archivists* 4 (1973):654–659.

Noble, Valerie. "Business Information Audio Cassettes: Their Care and Feeding." *Special Libraries* 64 (1973):419–422.

North Carolina. State Department of Archives and History. *Archives Information Circular, no. 1.* Raleigh: State Department of Archives and History, 1966.

———. *Archives Information Circular, no. 2.* Raleigh: State Department of Archives and History, 1967.

———. *Archives Information Circular, no. 3.* Raleigh: State Department of Archives and History, 1968.

———. *Archives Information Circular, no. 4.* Raleigh: State Department of Archives and History, 1969.

———. *Genealogical Research in the North Carolina Department of Archives and History.* 4th ed., rev. Raleigh: State Department of Archives and History, 1969.

Nute, Grace L., and Gertrude W. Ackermann, compilers. *Guide to the Personal Papers in the Manuscript Collections of the Minnesota Historical Society.* St. Paul: Minnesota Historical Society, 1935.

Nyholm, Amy W. "Modern Manuscripts: A Functional Approach." *Library Resources & Technical Services* 14 (1970):325–340.

"Odds and Ends." *The Collector: A Magazine for Autograph and Historical Collectors* 85, no. 824 ([1972]):1–2.

Ohio Historical Society. ["Index to the Oral History Interview of Mrs. R. R. Litehiser."] Mimeographed. Columbus: Ohio Historical Society, [1973].

———. *Microfilm Sales List.* Columbus: Ohio Historical Society, 1973.

O'Neal, Dianne S. "The 1973 Meeting of the American Institute for Conservation." *Paper Conservation News* 1, no. 2 (1973):1, 4–5.

"On Taking Copies of Manuscripts." *The Collector: A Magazine for Autograph and Historical Collectors* 85, no. 823 ([1972]):1–3.

Ostroff, Eugene. "Preservation of Photographs." *Photographic Journal* 107 (1967):309–314. Also reprinted in *Picturescope* 18 (1970):76–84.

Paltsits, Victor H. "An Historical Resume of the Public Archives Commission from 1899 to 1921." *Annual Report of the American Historical Association for the Year 1922.* 2 vols. Washington: Government Printing Office, 1926:1:152–163.

———. "Scope of the Manuscriptophile as a Collector of Writing." *Manuscripts* 2, no. 2 (1950):27–29.

Papenfuse, Edward C. "The Retreat from Standardization: A Comment on the Recent History of Finding Aids." *American Archivist* 36 (1973):537–542.

Patterson, Lyman Ray. *Copyright in Historical Perspective.* Nashville: Vanderbilt University Press, 1968.

Peckham, Howard H. "Acquisition of Rare Materials." In *Rare Book Collections: Some Theoretical and Practical Suggestions for Use by Librarians and Students,* edited by H. Richard Archer, pp. 26–34. Association of College and Research Libraries Monographs, no. 27. Chicago: American Library Association, 1965.

Pickett, A. G., and M. M. Lemcoe. *Preservation and Storage of Sound Recordings.* Washington: Library of Congress, 1959.

Piez, Gladys T. "Archival Containers—A Search for Safer Materials." *American Archivist* 27 (1964):433–438.

Pike, Kermit J. *A Guide to the Manuscripts and Archives of The Western Reserve Historical Society.* Cleveland: Western Reserve Historical Society, 1972.

———. "Private Sources of Special Funds for Archives and Manuscript Repositories." Paper read at the annual meeting of the Society of American Archivists, September 30, 1970. Typewritten.

Pinkett, Harold T. "Selective Preservation of General Correspondence." *American Archivist* 30 (1967):33–43.

Pioneer Presentation of a National Symposium on the Impact of Automation on Documentation. Denver: [University of Denver], 1968.

Plant, Marjorie. *The English Book Trade: An Economic History of the Making and Sale of Books.* 2d ed., rev. London: George Allen & Unwin, 1965.

Platnick, Phyllis. "Proposal for Automating a Manuscript Repository." American Documentation Institute, *Proceedings, 1966,* pp. 437–442.

Pocket Pal: A Graphic Arts Digest for Printers and Advertising Production Managers. 10th ed. New York: International Paper Co., 1970.

Poole, Frazer G. "Preservation Costs and Standards." *Special Libraries* 59 (1968):614–619.

Posner, Ernst. *Archives in the Ancient World.* Cambridge: Harvard University Press, 1972.

Poulos, Arthur. "Audio and Video Cassettes: Friend or Foe of the Librarian." *Special Libraries* 63 (1972):222–226.

Powell, Benjamin E. "Sources of Support for Libraries in American Universities." In *The Library in the University: The University of Tennessee Library Lectures, 1949–1966,* pp. 171–194. Hamden, Conn.: Shoe String Press, 1967.

Powers, Thomas. *Balita mula Maynila.* Bulletin no. 19. Ann Arbor: Michigan Historical Collections, 1971.

"Practical Problems." *Paper Conservation News* 1, no. 3 (1973):1–4.

Preston, Jean. "Problems in the Use of Manuscripts." *American Archivist* 28 (1965):367–379.

Prince, Thomas. *The Chronological History of New England . . .* Boston: Kneeland & Green, 1786, as it appears in the *American Cultural Series.* Ser. 122, reel no. 11. Ann Arbor: University Microfilms, 1941.

Princeton University Library. *A Descriptive Catalogue of the Dulles Oral History Collection.* Princeton: Princeton University Library, 1967.

Procedures for Processing and Storing Black and White Photographs for Maximum Possible Permanence. Grinnell, Iowa: East Street Gallery, 1970.

"Propose New U.S. Copyright Law." *AB Bookman's Weekly* 34 (1964):363.

"Publishers May Face A 'Real Rumble' on Copyright." *Publishers Weekly* 204 (1973):34–35.

Reichmann, Felix, and Josephine M. Tharpe. *Bibliographic Control of Microforms.* Westport, Conn.: Greenwood Press, 1972.

Reingold, Nathan. "Subject Analysis and Description of Manuscript Collections." *Isis* 53 (1962):106–112.

Rendell, Dianna J., and Kenneth W. Rendell. *Fundamentals of Autograph Collecting.* Somerville, Mass.: Kenneth W. Rendell, Inc., 1972.

Renze, Dolores C. "The Archivist's Responsibility for Integrity and Protection of the Record." In *Pioneer Presentation of a National Symposium on the Impact of Automation on Documentation,* pp. 77–87. Denver: [University of Denver], 1968.

Rhoads, James B. "Archival Values in the New World of Automation." In *Pioneer Presentation of A National Symposium on the Impact of Automation on Documentation*, pp. 3-8. Denver: [University of Denver], 1968.

———. "Alienation and Thievery: Archival Problems." *American Archivist* 29 (1966):197-208.

Ricci, Seymour de. *English Collectors of Books & Manuscripts (1530-1930) and Their Marks of Ownership*. New York: Macmillan Co., 1930.

Ricks, Artel. "Can a Computer Help the Archivist and Librarian." *Records Management Journal* 9, no. 2 (1971):2-17.

Ristow, Walter W. "The Emergence of Maps in Libraries." *Special Libraries* 58 (1967):400-419.

———. "Map Librarianship." *Library Journal* 92 (1967):3610-3614.

———, and David K. Carrington. "Machine-Readable Map Cataloging in The Library of Congress." *Special Libraries* 62 (1971):343-352.

Roberts, R. J. "Rare Book Collecting—A View from Mid-Atlantic." *Long Room*, no. 6 (1972):7-16. [*Long Room* is the publication of the Friends of the Library, Trinity College, Dublin.]

Rothenberg, Leslie B., Judith Lucianovic, David A. Kronick, and Alan M. Rees. "A Job-Task Index for Evaluating Professional Utilization in Libraries." *Library Quarterly* 41 (1971):320-328.

Rothwell, R. H. "Access to Records on Magnetic Tape and Punched Cards in Archives: A Summary." Library Association of Australia, 15th Biennial Conference, *Proceedings 1969*, pp. 422-423.

Rumics, Elizabeth. "Oral History: Defining the Term." *Wilson Library Bulletin* 40 (1966):602-605.

Rundell, Walter, Jr. *In Pursuit of American History: Research and Training in the United States*. Norman: University of Oklahoma Press, 1970.

———. "The Recent American Past v. H.R. 4347: Historians' Dilemma." *American Archivist* 29 (1966):209-215.

———. "Relations between Historical Researchers and Custodians of Source Materials." *College & Research Libraries* 29 (1968):466-476.

Russell, Mattie. "The Manuscript Department in the Duke University Library." *American Archivist* 28 (1965):437-444.

Salmon, Stephen R. *Specifications for Library of Congress Microfilming*. Washington: Library of Congress, 1964.

Schellenberg, Theodore R. *The Management of Archives*. New York: Columbia University Press, 1965.

———. *Modern Archives: Principles and Techniques*. Chicago: University of Chicago Press, 1956.

Schmitt, Martin, compiler. *Catalogue of Manuscripts in the University of Oregon Library*. Eugene: University of Oregon, 1971.

Scott, Robert W. "Governor's Records: Public Records." *American Archivist* 33 (1970):5-10.

Scriven, Margaret. *Preservation and Restoration of Library Materials.* 3d ed., rev. 1956. Reprint from *Special Libraries.* [Chicago: Chicago Historical Society], 1967.

Sellers, David Y. "Basic Planning and Budgeting Concepts for Special Libraries." *Special Libraries* 64 (1973):70–75.

Shafer, Boyd C., Michel Francois, Wolfgang J. Mommsen, and A. Taylor Milne. *Historical Study in the West.* New York: Appleton-Century-Crofts, 1968.

Shapley, Bruce. "The Care and Storage of Magnetic Tape." *Data Processing Magazine* 10, no. 4 (1968):80–81.

Shaw, Ralph R. *Literary Property in the United States.* [Washington]: Scarecrow Press, 1950.

Shaw, Renata V. "Picture Organization: Practices and Procedures." *Special Libraries* 63 (1972):448–456; 502–506.

———. "Picture Searching: Techniques." *Special Libraries* 62 (1971):524–528.

———. "Picture Searching: Tools." *Special Libraries* 63 (1972):13–24.

Shelley, Fred. "Manuscripts in the Library of Congress: 1800–1900." *American Archivist* 11 (1948):3–19.

———. "The Presidential Papers Program at the Library of Congress." *American Archivist* 25 (1962):429–433.

Shelley, Henry C. *The British Museum: Its History and Treasures.* Boston: L. C. Page & Co., 1911.

Shields, Gerald R. "From the Editor." *American Libraries* 4 (1973):407.

Shipton, Clifford K. "The Reference Use of Archives." In *University Archives,* Allerton Park Institute no. 11, edited by Rolland E. Stevens, pp. 68–81. Champaign: University of Illinois, 1965.

Shumway, Gary L. *Oral History in the United States: A Directory.* New York Oral History Association, 1971.

Simon, Wendell. "Development of a Universal Classification System for Two-by-Two Slide Collections." In *Bibliographical Control of Nonprint Media,* edited by Pearce S. Grove and Evelyn G. Clement, pp. 360–373. Chicago: American Library Association, 1972.

Skillin, Marjorie E., and Robert M. Gay, compilers. *Words into Type: A Guide in the Preparation of Manuscripts; For Writers, Editors, Proofreaders and Printers.* New York: Appleton-Century-Crofts, 1964.

Slotten, Martha C. "The Fruits of Two Hundred Years of Collecting Manuscripts: Their Use in the Teaching of Undergraduates at Dickinson College." *Manuscripts* 25, no. 3 (1973):155–161.

Smith, Alice E. "The Draper Manuscripts." In *The American Collector,* edited by Donald R. McNeil, pp. 45–61. Madison: State Historical Society of Wisconsin, 1955.

———, editor. *Guide to the Manuscripts of the Wisconsin Historical Society.* Madison: Wisconsin State Historical Society, 1944.

Smith, G. C. K., and J. L. Schofield. "Administrative Effectiveness: Times and Costs of Library Operations." *Journal of Librarianship* 3 (1971): 245-266.

Smith, Richard D. "Maps, Their Deterioration and Preservation." *Special Libraries* 63 (1972):59–68.

———. "New Approaches to Preservation." *Library Quarterly* 40 (1970):139–171.

———. "The Nonaqueous Deacidification of Paper and Books." Ph.D. dissertation, University of Chicago, 1970.

———. "Paper Deacidification: A Preliminary Report." *Library Quarterly* 36 (1966):273–292.

———. "Paper Impermanence as a Consequence of pH and Storage Conditions." *Library Quarterly* 39 (1969):153–195.

[———]. Patent no. 3,676,182. *Treatment of Cellulosic Materials.* July 11, 1972. Washington: U.S. Patent Office, 1972.

[———]. Patent no. 3,676,055. *Preserving Cellulosic Materials Through Treatment with Alkylene Oxides.* July 11, 1972. Washington: U.S. Patent Office, 1972.

———. "Restoration of Records." *Records Management Quarterly* 5 (1971): 27.

Smith, Russell M. "Stamping Manuscripts." *Manuscripts* 14, no. 3 (1962): 24–27.

Society of American Archivists. *Archival Education Directory.* Ann Arbor: Society of American Archivists, 1971.

———. College and University Archives Committee. *Forms Manual.* Madison: University of Wisconsin-Madison, 1973.

———. Committee on Data Archives and Machine-Readable Records. *Report: Fiscal Year, 1973.* [Washington: Society of American Archivists, 1973].

———. Committee on Techniques for the Control and Description of Archives and Manuscripts. "Draft Standards for the Preparation of Registers and Inventories." Mimeographed. [Washington: Society of American Archivists, 1973].

South Carolina. Department of Archives and History. "SPINDEX Adaptation Project." Mimeographed. Columbia: Department of Archives and History, [1973].

Spigai, Frances G. *The Invisible Medium: The State of the Art of Microform and a Guide to the Literature.* Washington: American Society for Information Science, 1973.

Starr, Louis M. *Oral History: 25th Anniversary Report.* New York: Columbia University, 1973.

"Static Electricity and its Effects." *Computer Talk* 1, no. 2 (1968):1–2.

Stephenson, Richard W. "Published Sources of Information about Maps and Atlases." *Special Libraries* 61 (1970): 87–98, 110–112.

Storm, Colton, and Howard Peckham. *Invitation to Book Collecting: Its Pleasures and Practices; With Kindred Discussions of Manuscripts, Maps, and Prints.* New York: R. R. Bowker Co., 1947.

Strassberg, Richard, compiler. *Cornell University Libraries Manual of Manuscript Processing Procedures.* Ithaca: Cornell University Libraries, 1973.

Strauss, William S. "Protection of Unpublished Works." In *Studies in Copyright,* edited by the Copyright Society of the United States, pp. 189–227. South Hackensack, N.J.: Fred B. Rothman Co., 1963.

Suter, Eugenie M., Elinor N. Brink, and Dorothea O. Christian. "How to Organize a Friends of the Library." In *Friends of the Library: Organization and Activities,* edited by Sarah L. Wallace, pp. 20–29. Chicago: American Library Association, 1962.

Swain, Donald C. "Problems for Practitioners of Oral History." *American Archivist* 28 (1965):63–69.

Taft, Robert. *Photography and the American Scene: A Social History, 1839–1889.* New York: Macmillan Co., 1938.

"Tapes for Paper Repairs." *Paper Conservation News* 1, no. 3 (1973):1–2.

Thompson, Lawrence S. "Facsimiles and the Antiquarian Trade." *Library Trends* 9 (1961):437–445.

Timms, Walter, compiler. *Edmund B. Chaffee: An Inventory of His Papers in Syracuse University Library.* Manuscript Inventory Series no. 11. Syracuse: Syracuse University Library, Manuscript Collections, 1968.

Toronto, University of. Library. Rare Books Department. *Selected Acquisitions, July 1971–January 1972.* Toronto: University of Toronto, 1972.

Towner, Lawrence W. *Every Silver Lining Has a Cloud: The Recent Shaping of the Newberry Library's Collections.* 1970. Reprint. A. N. L. Munby and Lawrence W. Towner. *The Flow of Books and Manuscripts: Papers Read at a Clark Library Seminar, March 30, 1968.* Los Angeles: University of California, 1969.

Tribolet, Harold W. "Conservation." In *University Archives,* Allerton Park Institute no. 11, edited by Rolland E. Stevens, pp. 62–67. Champaign: University of Illinois, 1965.

———. "Rare Book & Paper Repair Techniques." American Association for State and Local History, Technical Leaflet 13. Rev. ed. *History News* 25, no. 3 (1970).

Tuckerman, Jean. "Techniques of Exhibitions." *1968 AB Bookman's Yearbook,* pt. 2, pp. 16–21.

Turner, Robert W. S. "To Repair or Despair?" *American Archivist* 20 (1957):319–334.

Tutor, Dean. "The Special Library Budget." *Special Libraries* 63 (1972):517–527.

Tyrrell, William G. "Tape-Recording Local History." American Association for State and Local History, Technical Leaflet 35. *History News* 21, no. 5 (1966).

U.S. Library of Congress. *Manuscripts: A MARC Format; Specifications for Magnetic Tapes Containing Catalog Records for Single Manuscripts or Manuscript Collections.* Washington: Library of Congress, 1973.

———. *National Union Catalog of Manuscript Collections, Information Circular no. 5.* Washington: Library of Congress, 1966.

———. *National Union Catalog of Manuscript Collections, Information Circular no. 7.* Washington: Library of Congress, 1971.

———. *The National Union Catalog of Manuscript Collections, 1971: Index, 1970–1971.* Washington: Library of Congress, 1973.

———. *National Union Catalog of Manuscript Collections, Report, 1971.* Washington: Library of Congress, [1972].

———. Subject Cataloging Division. *Subject Headings Used in the Dictionary Catalogs of the Library of Congress.* Edited by Marguerite V. Quattlebaum. 7th ed., rev. Washington: Library of Congress, 1966.

———. Subject Cataloging Division. *Classification: Class G.; Geography, Anthropology, Folklore, Manners and Customs, Recreation.* 3d ed., rev. Washington: Library of Congress, 1954.

U.S. National Archives and Records Service. A draft of "History of the Project," and "User's Introduction to the System," chapters 1 and 2 of the final report on SPINDEX II to be submitted by NARS to the Council on Library Resources. Washington: National Archives and Records Service, [1973].

———. "SPINDEX Users Conference, Summary of the Meeting, June 11–12, 1973." Mimeographed. Washington: National Archives and Records Service, 1973.

———. National Historical Publications Commission. *A Report to the President Containing a Proposal by the National Historical Publications Commission to Meet Existing and Anticipated Needs Over the Next Ten Years Under a National Program for the Collection, Preservation, and Publication, or Dissemination by Other Means, of the Documentary Sources of American History.* Washington: National Archives and Records Service, 1963.

———. Office of Records Management. *Managing Information Retrieval: Information Retrieval.* Records Management Handbook. Washington: National Archives and Records Service, 1972.

———. Office of Records Management. *Managing Information Retrieval: Microform Retrieval Equipment Guide.* Records Management Handbook. Washington: National Archives and Records Service, 1970.

U.S. Smithsonian Institution. *Preliminary Guide to the Smithsonian Institution Archives: 125 Anniversary of the Smithsonian Institution.* Archives and Special Collections of the Smithsonian Institution, no. 1. Washington: Smithsonian Institution Press, 1971.

Vaisey, D. G. "The New Manuscript Repair Room." *Bodleian Library Record* 9, no. 1 (1973):2–3.

Vanderbilt, Paul. "Filing Your Photographs: Some Basic Procedures." American Association for State and Local History, Technical Leaflet 36. *History News* 21, no. 6 (1966).

Van Tassel, David D. "John Franklin Jameson." In *Keepers of the Past,* edited by Clifford L. Lord, pp. 81–96. Durham: University of North Carolina Press, 1965.

———. and James A. Tinsley. "Historical Organizations as Aids to History." In *In Support of Clio: Essays in Memory of Herbert A. Kellar,* edited by William B. Hesseltine and Donald R. McNeil, pp. 127–152. Madison: State Historical Society of Wisconsin, 1958.

Veaner, Allen B. *The Evaluation of Micropublications: A Handbook for Li-*

brarians. Library Technology Program Publications, no. 17. Chicago: American Library Association, 1971.

Volkersz, Evert. "Neither Book nor Manuscript: Some Special Collections." *Library Resources & Technical Services* 13 (1969):493–501.

Wagner, Robert W. "Preservation and Restoration of Photographic Materials Through Nuclear and Ultra-Sonic Methods." *Illinois Libraries* 53 (1971):10–17.

Wall, John. "Overcoming the Problem of Permanency in Colour Archives." *Photographic Journal* 107 (1967):141–145.

Wallace, Carolyn A. "The Southern Historical Collection." *American Archivist* 28 (1965):427–436.

Wallace, Sarah L., editor. *Friends of the Library: Organization and Activities.* Chicago: American Library Association, 1962.

Wardle, D. B. *Document Repair.* London: Society of Archivists, 1971.

Warner, Alice S. "Voluntarism and Librarianship." *Library Journal* 97 (1972):1241–1245.

Warner, Robert M. "Secretary's Notes." *36th Annual Meeting, Society of American Archivists,* pp. 34–36. Columbus, Ohio: Society of American Archivists, 1972.

Waserman, Manfred J. "Manuscripts and Oral History: Common Interests and Problems in the History of Medicine." *Bulletin of the Medical Libraries Association* 58 (1970):173–176.

Waters, Peter. *Emergency Procedures for Salvaging Flood- or Water-Damaged Library Materials.* Washington: Library of Congress, 1972.

Wayne State University. Archives of Labor History and Urban Affairs. "Archives Handling of Oral History Transcripts." Mimeographed. Detroit: Wayne State University, [ca. 1970].

———. "Oral History Transcript Use Contract." Mimeographed. Detroit: Wayne State University, [ca. 1970].

Weber, Charles G., Merle B. Shaw, and E. A. Back. "Effects of Fumigants on Paper." *Journal of Research of the National Bureau of Standards* 15 (1935):271–275.

Weihs, Jean R., Shirley Lewis, and Janet Macdonald. *Nonbook Materials: The Organization of Integrated Collections.* Ottawa: Canadian Library Association, 1973.

Welch, Claude E. "Protection from Fire in Libraries." *New England Journal of Medicine* 287 (1972):881–882.

Welch, Walter L. "Preservation and Restoration of Authenticity in Sound Recordings." *Library Trends* 21 (1972):83–100.

Western Reserve Historical Society. *Annual Report for the Year 1971.* Cleveland: Western Reserve Historical Society, 1972.

White, Deane R., Charles J. Gass, Emery Meschter, and Wilton R. Holm. "Polyester Photographic Film Base." *Journal of the Society of Motion Picture and Television Engineers* 64 (1955):674–678.

White, Helen McCann. "Thoughts on Oral History." *American Archivist* 20 (1957):19–30.

White, John B. "Further Comments on Map Cataloging." *Library Resources & Technical Services* 6 (1962):78.

Whitehill, Walter Muir. *Independent Historical Societies: An Enquiry into Their Research and Publication Functions and Their Financial Future.* Boston: Boston Athenaeum, 1962.

Wilson, Louis R., and Jack Dalton. "Restriction on the Use of Research Materials." *Library Trends* 2 (1954):545–553.

Wilson, Louis R., and Maurice F. Tauber. *The University Library: The Organization, Administration, and Functions of Academic Libraries.* 2d ed., rev. New York: Columbia University Press, 1956.

Winsor, Justin. "Manuscript Sources of American History—The Conspicuous Collections Extant." *Papers of the American Historical Association* 3, no. 1. New York: G. P. Putnam's Sons, 1888.

Wisconsin. State Historical Society. *Descriptive List of the Manuscript Collections of the State Historical Society of Wisconsin; Together with Reports on Other Collections of Manuscript Materials for American History in Adjacent States.* Edited by Reuben G. Thwaites. Madison: Wisconsin State Historical Society, 1906.

Wittenberg, Philip. *The Protection of Literary Property.* Boston: Writer, Inc., 1968.

Wolter, John A. "Source Materials for the History of American Cartography." Special Libraries Association. Geography and Map Division. *Bulletin,* no. 88 (1972):2–16.

Yale University Library. Map Collection. "Notes on Procedures." Mimeographed. New Haven: Yale University, 1964.

Zucker, Harvey. "Old-Time Processes—How to Identify and Date Them." *Popular Photography,* December 1972, pp. 99–101, 170, 216.

Index